For Carol Norris, asking
many blessings.

William J. Leonard, S.J.

The Letter Carrier

William J. Leonard, S.J.

Sheed & Ward

Sheed & Ward™ is a service of The National Catholic Reporter Publishing Company.

_____

Library of Congress Cataloguing in Publication Data

Leonard, William J.
    The letter carrier / William J. Leonard.
        p.   cm.
    ISBN   1-55612-651-4   (hard cover : alk. paper). --
    ISBN   1-55612-671-9   (pbk. : alk. paper)
    1. Leonard, William J.   2. Catholic Church--United States--Clergy--
Biography.   3. Jesuits--United States--Biography.   I. Title.
    BX4705.L5435A3   1993
    271'.5302--dc20   93-18887
    [B]   _____   CIP

Published by: Sheed & Ward
               115 E. Armour Blvd.
               P.O. Box 419492
               Kansas City, MO 64141-6492

To order, call: (800) 333-7373

Photos courtesy of the author and University Archives, John J. Burns Library, Boston College, Chestnut Hill, MA 02167.

Contents

To the Society of Jesus
in gratitude and affection
after almost seventy years

"Quam bonum et jucundum . . ."

Preface

During high school summers I carried mail over a long, long route in and out of the Blue Hill Parkway in Milton. So when we graduated, and the class "prophecies" appeared in the yearbook, my classmates predicted that I would be a letter carrier—a white collar job, they called it. As things turned out, they spoke more truly than they knew. It would be my vocation, no less in old age then in my prime, to carry mail. St. Paul writes to the Corinthians, "Clearly you are a letter of Christ which I have delivered, a letter written not with ink but by the Spirit of the loving God, not on tablets of stone (or on perishable paper) but on tablets of flesh in the heart" (2 Cor 3:3). This was the kind of mail that had to "go through," first-class mail. And the letter carrier, who couldn't think of retirement until his last breath, would indeed have a white collar job. But the collar would be a clerical one.

It was Mary Lou and Jack Bowler, six years ago, who suggested perseveringly that I write this memoir, and then, as it came to them in spasmodic chapters, made perceptive, helpful comments on it. I am much indebted to them and to my Rector, Father Joseph Appleyard, S.J., and Father John P. Foley, S.J., of the Jesuit Community at Boston College, who generously read the bulky manuscript and offered encouragement. Sister Frances Krumpelman, S.C., using her keen editorial eye, made many practical suggestions, and, in particular, saved me from possible infamy by reminding me, again and again, to use "inclusive language." I wish to acknowledge the generous assistance of Mr. Dane Baird and Mr. Vincent Stanton in the publication of this book. I am grateful to Ms. Dorothy McLaughlin and Ms. Susan Rainville, secretaries and to John Atteberry, Senior Reference Librarian, in the Burns Library at Boston College, for substantial and repeated kindnesses, and I should like to acknowledge with profound thanks the assistance of Ms. Catherine Madigan and Ms. Carole Meskil in organizing my "Liturgy and Life Collection" in the same Library. For Dr. Robert O'Neill, the Burns librarian, there are no adequate thanks. This book would simply not have appeared without his energetic prompting and resourcefulness.

CHAPTER 1

The Way It Was With Us

I WAS OUT IN CALIFORNIA RECENTLY, AND NOTICED THAT WHEN I was introduced to people their first question invariably was, "Where do you come from, Father?" Because, perhaps, one gets to thinking long thoughts as the anniversaries mount up, I began to ponder the question myself. Where do I come from? Or better, since localities don't matter nearly so much as people, from whom do I come?

In the first instance, of course, I come from my mother and father. And I have often wondered whether it was for me a greater grace and privilege to witness my father's fifty-year love affair with my mother or to be its fruit and beneficiary.

In a larger sense I come from World War I and the early Twenties. Only recently have I realized how long ago those days are now—the days of Teapot Dome, the Ku Klux Klan, Sacco and Vanzetti, Horatio Alger and Tom Swift and the Rover Boys, the flapper and the cake-eater, Rudolph Valentino and Irving Berlin. In those days radio was just coming in; we clamped the ear-phones to our heads and strained to hear erratic broadcasts on our crystal sets. Television was not dreamed of. Telephones were still a luxury, and at night we lighted the gas jet or the kerosene lamp. In winter the snow lay knee-deep on the streets until horse-drawn wagons or "pungs" (heavy sleighs that delivered coal or ice and were great for "hopping a ride") created somewhat navigable ruts. The affluent few who owned a "flivver" (a Model T Ford) or a Hupmobile cranked them—by hand—for the last time in November and put them in storage until April.

In Boston, as elsewhere across the country, we sang "K-K-K-Katy" and "There's a Long, Long Trail a-Winding" and "Keep the Home Fires Burning Till the Boys Come Home" during World War I, and "Barney Google," "Bye-bye Blackbird," "Limehouse Blues," and Al Jolson's "Mammy" as the Twenties came roaring in. At the

Magnet Theater we graduated from "The Perils of Pauline" to Tom Mix, William S. Hart, Harold Lloyd, and Theda Bara, while the piano accompanist followed the action on the silent screen with thumping crescendos if the chase was hot and melting melodies as the reunited lovers walked blissfully into the sunset. We cheered Jack Dempsey in the ring and Clarence Demar in the marathon. We read about the Four Horsemen and the Galloping Ghost from Illinois, but we attended the Boston College-Holy Cross game and shouted for Chuck Darling and Jimmy Fitzpatrick. We exulted when the Red Sox won the World Series in 1918, and mourned when Harry Frazee sold Babe Ruth to the hated Yankees and the Sox slipped to the cellar, never to rise again.

I come, too, from the Irish-American transition, when the immigrant was not yet altogether domesticated—the world so well described by Ed O'Connor in "The Edge of Sadness." Ancestral voices said pungent, memorable things in a soft, lilting brogue; they spoke now not so much of the Sassenach and his iron grip on the land but of how difficult it was to win stability and recognition in a country dominated by the Yankee mill-owner, the Yankee banker. One's elders were policemen, letter-carriers, street-car conductors, small shop owners, elementary school teachers, parish priests, clerks—not yet university professors, executives in corporations—not even, as yet, doctors or lawyers in any large numbers. It was a rather small and isolated world. Names like those of James Michael Curley and Martin Lomasney were household words. Very occasionally someone like David I. Walsh would to our wonder rise to national prominence in the governor's chair or the Senate. By and large, we seldom heard the Boston Symphony or went to the Art Museum; we rarely patronized the legitimate theater. I can't recall even attending a solemn high Mass more than once or twice before I went to the novitiate.

The Faith, though, was stalwart and piety was genuine. I did inherit and was nourished by the substance of the two-thousand-year-old Christian tradition, and for this I must profess myself forever indebted and grateful. I see now that as the tradition reached me it had been filtered through the Counter-Reformation. As a result it was triumphalist, ultramontane, autocratic, intransigent, legalistic, given to peripheral and sometimes weakly sentimental devotions rather than to biblically oriented prayer, definitely low church in its staple parish ritual, heavily reliant on an *ex opere operato* theology of the sacraments. It had been seriously damaged, as well, by Jansenism, imported from France by way of Ireland, and certainly not mellowed by being domesticated among the Boston Puritans. (Sunday baseball, even of the sandlot variety, was still frowned on in my boyhood.) Personal and family morality was strong, but there was a general expectation that public servants would not become poorer during their term of office, and sometimes one even sensed an amused admiration for their peculations or their dubious strategies at election time. Culturally, great store was set by conformity to the community mores (even in the novitiate, how often we were told not to be "singular") and on respectability. We thought a great deal about sin, death, judgment, hell. Authority had been canonized and pronounced infallible—or at least irreversible. Due process was something known only to civil lawyers. Patriotism was enthusiastic and unquestioning; I doubt if most people would have espoused in theory the "my country right or wrong" doctrine, but they *were* the same people who in the next twenty years would listen eagerly to Father Coughlin and Joe McCarthy. The sobering and chastening lessons of Vietnam and Watergate were still far in the future.

Well, I come from all that. But I come also—I think and hope—at least partially from the great-hearted and large-minded people whom our generous Lord has sent my way, and whose names are for me a litany of gratitude and benediction. It would be impossible to list them all; some of them I never met except through their writings. But I think of them as personal friends who tumbled down walls that had blocked my vision and my growth—people like Gerry Ellard, Tom Carroll, Cardinal Suhard, Columba Marmion, Harding Fisher, Martin Luther King, Ed Skillin and the editors of *Commonweal,* Mike Walsh and Bill Guindon, John XXIII, Karl Rahner and Henri de Lubac, Richard Cushing, Bill McGarry, Frank Sheed and Maisie Ward, Joseph Jungmann, and the human authors who, under the inspiration of the Holy Spirit, put together the documents of the Second Vatican Council.

I come, too, from an immense throng of people who patiently listened to me, and to whom I tried hard to listen. Such a multitude—in classrooms, churches, auditoria, living rooms, offices, tents . . . They listened, argued or agreed with me, corrected and matured my ideas. Especially am I grateful to the students of almost forty years. Quite simply, I loved them and enjoyed them, and Alumni Night is for me the happiest night of the year. If our teaching be a long Advent, a travail until Christ be born again, then Alumni Night is a bit of Christmas. When Evelyn Waugh (not one of my favorite personalities) visited our campus he asked me, "Do you think there is any point in teaching scholastic philosophy to future tradesmen and dentists?" My answer was energetic: "Before these men are tradesmen and dentists they are men; they are husbands, fathers, citizens, Christians. Yes, I think there is a great point in it." And with each Alumni reunion I am more profoundly convinced that what we have done on our campuses is worthwhile, for this world and the next.

So, as the poet says, I am a part of all that I have met. For one who used to lie in his narrow cot at Weston, listening to the Montreal train whistling at Cherry Brook and yearning to be aboard it, yearning for faraway places, it is consoling to recall now that one has prayed in the loveliest shrine of our Lady, the cathedral at Chartres, and also in the Church of the Holy Wisdom in Constantinople, which Justinian dedicated on St. Stephen's Day in 542, exclaiming, "Glory to God for finding me worthy to do such a work. Solomon, I have beaten you!" It is nice to have walked on a quiet afternoon through the Roman Forum, saying delightedly with old Horace, "*Ibam forte via sacra.*" Who could forget the steaming, teeming Chowringee Road in Calcutta, or the shimmering Taj Mahal, or Fatehpur Sikri, where Rudolf Aquaviva wrestled for an emperor's soul before his own martyrdom? I remember the Fishermen's Bastion in Budapest, and the Old Town Square in Prague, bloodied like Belfast by scandalous wars between Christians, and Checkpoint Charlie in Berlin, and the crematory at Dachau, and the Isles of Greece. I remember the shattered, tottering buildings along Escolta Street in Manila after we recaptured the city in '44, with clouds of flies rising from the dead bodies in the tropical sun, and the endless, silent cemeteries at Normandy, Anzio, Maastricht, Cambridge, Chateau-Thierry—and that especially frightening one in Leningrad where, acre after endless acre, the starved or broken victims of the Nine Hundred Days lie in mass graves unmarked except for the year of their deaths.

Most vividly of all I remember that pathetic first cemetery we established at Binalonan on Luzon, just inland from the beachhead, where I myself buried 3500 young Americans. It was the war, I guess, that either shaped or hardened most of my outlook. In answer to the question, "Where do you come from?" I'd have to answer, "From World War II." There is nothing, you see, so silent and yet so accusing as the body wrapped in its blanket, awaiting burial. There is no one so soft-spoken, so courteous and gentle as the GI's assigned to supervise the cemetery. A great pity for the young dead—perhaps a kind of shock at what one has done, a sense of corporate guilt, of having shared somehow in the fratricide of Cain—mutes all voices and blunts all passion. It's motherly, tender, eager to forgive, but it is also anxious to be forgiven.

The first day I went to the cemetery with the Protestant chaplain, they gave us a list of names and the numbers of the graves, and we divided them according to faith. But they didn't know the faiths of a lot of boys, and there were some unknowns, and the graves, when we got to them, were too fresh to have been adequately marked, so all I could do was walk back and forth and sprinkle a little holy water here and there. And even though St. Paul speaks of primary interest for those of the household of the Faith, and the Church directs (or used to direct—it seems irrelevant now) that only Catholic graves be blessed, I was unable to do anything but pray for them all, swindled of their bright youth. How empty, how irreconcilable with the Gospel seemed the Just War theory then! I became gradually through reflection on all this a quite uncompromising pacifist. What did Paul VI say at the United Nations? *"Jamais encore!"* There simply has to be another way.

In New Guinea, shortly after I landed at Oro Bay and was awaiting transportation to my new outfit at Finschhafen, I fell one day into conversation with an Australian sergeant who was in charge of a detail of natives cutting logs in the hills. I asked him what the "fuzzy-wuzzies," as the G.I.'s called them, thought of the war. "Oaow," he answered, "They don't mind. The Jap wanted to tyke the country, and we're stoppin' 'im." Was it as simple as that? What about the cost of "stoppin' 'im"—the brutalization, the disgusting and degrading filth, the indescribable suffering of mind and body, the blinding and the mutilation and the drowning in burning oil and the pathetic, vain scramble to take cover from strafing planes? When the war was over we came home, all the khaki-clad army—back through the Golden Gate we had dreamed of to God's Country, back to L.A. and Sioux City and Fall River. We shucked our khaki and tried to pick up where we had left off. But on all our memories were etched unforgettable, incommunicable things. I think of our first morning in Lingayen Gulf, for instance, with the shell cases of the Navy bombardment floating black in the calm water, and the sheared-off palm trees on the beach, and the low hills beyond, full of enemies, and us going down the scramble-nets to the landing craft. Would this be it? For many of us it was.

I don't remember that I thought of the war, while we were fighting it, as just another episode in the history of salvation. The convulsion it brought into all our lives was too gigantic. And if we had known the demonic things associated now with names like Dachau and Auschwitz, Katyn Forest and Bataan and Lubyanka Prison, it would have seemed such a sickening concentration of misery that we could not have endured it, much less seen it in perspective against the panorama of cosmic human history. It was not a pretty time to be alive. We had known the stagnations and seen the breadlines of the Depression, and as the Thirties drew to a close we heard Mussolini ranting in the Piazza Venezia and saw the appalling Stormtroopers goose-stepping into Prague and Vienna. The lights went out, then, all over the world; it was the scorched earth of the Ukraine and the Nine Hundred Days of Leningrad, it was disaster at Dunkirk and death raining from the skies over London, it was, finally, Pearl Harbor and the Murmansk Run, Monte Cassino and the Kokada Trail, Omaha Beach and Hiroshima. The convulsion, they said, was the birth-pangs of a new order, the kind of thing that happens about every five hundred years. But this was too cataclysmic; no new order could be worth that much wretchedness. One clasps his hand to his mouth and falls silent in the presence of an evil so hideous, so enormous.

But it's bad form, or poor rhetoric, to get so far ahead of one's story. Let's backtrack a little. On that bright July morning in 1925 there were eight of us on the Boston-to-Pittsfield train. We were just out of high school; others in our class, a little older, would join us in August and September. We had little of this world's goods and no great endowment for the struggle to acquire more. What we were leaving behind was the world we had grown up in—our very modest homes, the familiar neighborhood, a carefree boyhood, and, chiefly, our parents. They *let* us go, in an act of faith that far surpassed our own, and went back to the daily round, where there was now only an empty place at the table, and—to be grimly practical about it—an absence of one who might have begun to supplement the meager family income.

Strange, when you think about it seventy years after. We were leaving in compliance with an insistent pull, an attraction that had given us no peace until we yielded to it. ("Are you sure?" my father said. "How long have you been thinking of it?") We thought we knew what we were leaving. For one thing, we liked very much the sound our pockets made when they jingled. Again, there were some very pretty girls around, and we had eyes to see. We liked, moreover, to do things our way, at our pace and for our ends. We suspected that that could not continue altogether, though we did not foresee the all-embracing regimentation we would march to for the next fourteen years. But there was nonetheless that curious pull, not, at least in my case, clearly identified or personalized. We had caught a glimpse, we had sensed an invitation. It was big. It was mysteriously, irresistibly alluring.

In St. Mark's Gospel (1:16-20) we read that the Lord Jesus, walking along the beach one day at the beginning of his public life, came on Simon Peter and Andrew, who were fishing. Without any sort of preliminaries (though there must have been some in earlier encounters), he said to them, "Follow me and I will make you fishers of men." And "immediately they left their nets and went after him."

The "nets" we left behind are, in hindsight, scarcely impressive. They were, none the less, all we had. And by abandoning them we were imitating the merchant in the parable, who sold all his lesser treasures to buy the one really valuable pearl. We "went after" it, realizing only later that we were going after him, not it.

Culturally, Boston College High School had given us a great deal. We were drilled extensively in Latin, Greek, and English grammar, and went on to read Cicero and Virgil and Xenophon and Homer. We discussed Dickens and George Eliot and Thackeray, and memorized the whole of "The Lady of the Lake" and "The Ancient Mariner," with great gobs of Shakespeare and the Golden Treasury. We imitated in our weekend "compositions" the styles of Carlyle and Newman, the rolling periods of Burke and Pitt and Robert Emmett. We learned (most of us did; I myself came a cropper) algebra and geometry and trigonometry. But there was no science, none whatever, in spite of a resplendent Jesuit history—Ricci, Clavius, Kircher and Boscovich and Secchi—in that field. Nor, though our school motto read "For religion and the fine arts," was there any music, or painting, or sculpture, or architecture. We studied ancient history and "civics," and we had a choice—our only "elective"—of French, Spanish, or German. Strong encouragement was given to extra-curricular activities, and very many participated in them to their profit: dramatics, debating, the school paper, the literary magazine. Parents and relatives thronged the school hall for the "elocution contest," the prize debates, and plays like "Seven Keys to Baldpate" and "It Pays to Advertise"—adapted by the faculty for all-male roles, since there were no girls in the school, nor was thought ever given to importing any. Tickets for the professional theater were usually too high-priced for us, though one of our teachers took a group of us to see David Warfield play Shylock in "The Merchant of Venice" and I myself pinched pennies somehow and saw from the second balcony several of George M. Cohan's and Jerome Kern's tuneful musicals. But it never occurred to us to frequent Symphony Hall, or the museums, or events like the glorious Flower Show that came in February to the old Horticultural Hall and tantalized shivering Bostonians weeks before flowers could be looked for anywhere outdoors.

It would have been impossible, of course, for us to leave behind our religious heritage and formation. We had grown up in what amounted to a sheltered Irish Catholic enclave, centered upon our parish church, and had gone on then to a Jesuit high school, large (1500 boys), serious of purpose, staffed almost exclusively by priests and young religious in training for the priesthood. Our parents had taught us our prayers and the rudiments of our faith almost from infancy. Then some of us went to parochial school, taught by the nuns. There was at that time no parochial school in my parish, which had only recently been established, but the teachers in the public school were almost all Catholics, and once a week we went to Sunday School, taught by young ladies of the parish not much older than ourselves, who "heard" us recite the "lessons" we had memorized in the Baltimore Catechism. During four years of high school we memorized and recited the whole of DeHarbe's catechism, which was more detailed and sophisticated. I wonder now about that pedagogical device. Much of what we memorized stayed, no doubt, somewhere in the subconscious, but I remember being able to reel off the "types" or foreshadowings of Christ in the Old Testament (the burning bush, the brazen serpent, etc.) without the remotest idea of what they were or how they related to the Gospel. Our acquaintance with the Bible was limited to the snippets of the Gospel that were read to us at Mass once a week—after the priest had read them in Latin.

Everyone in the parish, of course, "went to Mass" on Sunday. It would have caused scandalized whispering, if not outright ostracization, if you didn't go, but I don't honestly believe that was the motive for attendance. People went because they felt they should; the Mass, they were convinced, was the supreme event of their religious life. They might not have been able to articulate its theology, but they knew that the Mass was indispensable. And, to reinforce that conviction, there was the serious obligation, binding under sin, to attend.

So we attended, in all weathers and often at the expense of great inconvenience. Our church at that time was only a basement. The pastor scrimped and saved all during my boyhood, and eventually built a handsome superstructure, but the first Mass celebrated in it, alas, was his requiem. The basement was dark, and was, moreover, paneled in dark wood. If your pew was near the door you shivered in winter. We entered, bobbed in genuflection, rose when the priest entered, and knelt for the rest of the hour except when the Gospel was read and the sermon delivered. We called it the sermon rather than the homily because very often it had little to do with the Scripture but was a catechetical instruction—on the sacraments, on the commandments—or a moral discourse on the evils of the times.

Pope Pius, ten years before, had urged everyone to receive Holy Communion frequently, even daily, but the old Jansenism was still in the air, and many could not overcome their early rigid upbringing. My grandfather, in his last years, bent almost double with arthritis, took his cane, to which he had affixed a sharp steel point (he had been a blacksmith), and went out into the winter dark every morning to the seven o'clock Mass, jabbing his stick into the ice on the sidewalks to prevent falling. But he received Communion only at Christmas and Easter, and then only after Advent and Lenten penance and a meticulous confession. When we went to Marshfield in the summer my father learned that the nearest church was in Scituate, and that the shortest route was down the railroad tracks. So we walked the unshaded tracks, five miles to the church and five miles home, under the blazing summer sun. There were three railroad trestles over the river, and my poor mother, who could not look down at the rushing, foaming water between the ties, took my father's arm, closed her eyes, and stepped bravely into space. But we went to Mass.

Of course there was no active participation on our part until Mass itself was over and we joined in the prayers—in English— prescribed by Pope Leo XIII, invoking the protection of our Lady and St. Michael the Archangel, and ending—to the relief of us children, at any rate—with the climactic "Blessed be God in his angels and in his saints." Otherwise people knelt in reverent silence, privileged to witness what their priest was doing at the remote altar. Some prayed the rosary; others read prayers from books of devotion. The children's choir sang at the children's Mass, the senior choir later in the morning. The hymns chosen were largely irrelevant to the action of the Mass and were either sentimental or, if they had robust content and a good musical setting, were rendered so often that they lost their attraction.

I don't think it unfair to say that our faith was fed on subsistence rations. Our people, as I have said, knew almost nothing of the Bible as such. Their role in the formal worship of the Church was that of spectators. The sacramental rites, conducted in Latin, left them feeling that the right thing had been done even if they were not always clear what it was. They knew little of the Church's history. Even the lives of the great saints, who might have inspired them, suffered from an admixture of legend and were written in such an adulatory style that ordinary people could not hope to find in them models for imitation. Aside from Christmas and Lent-Holy Week, the liturgical year did not touch them intimately.

They turned—and were mightily encouraged to do so—to devotions. They recited the rosary—in their families at home, during Mass, at the "wakes" of their dead, and privately. They dropped regularly into church to "visit" the Blessed Sacrament. They prayed with tender insistence to the Mother of Jesus. May for them was not the Ascension or Pentecost, but the month of Mary, climaxed in the "May Procession" and the crowning with flowers of Mary's statue. Benediction was popular on Sunday evening. (Vespers had disappeared except at the cathedral and a few parishes, where it was sung in unintelligible Latin.) Novenas in honor of one or another of the saints brought out thousands of earnest petitioners, especially at the churches staffed by the religious orders. Hymns were enthusiastically sung by the entire congregation (odd how the same voices that rang out at novenas were never raised at Mass), prayers were said in concert, a panegyric, with very explicit references to contemporary moral problems, was preached, and the assembly was blessed with a relic of the saint. No Scripture was read. Downtown churches conducted such "services" repeatedly, even hourly, during the business day to accomodate the throngs that came. Magazines related to the various devotions enjoyed large circulation; Clare Booth Luce was astounded, after she came into the Church, at their number, and said that if the Transfiguration were to occur again Peter would exclaim, "Lord, it is good for us to be here. Let us now start three Catholic magazines, one for Moses, one for Elijah, and one for you."

"Missions," however, were something else. People attended novenas because they wanted to; they "made the mission" because they virtually had to. Antecedent pressure from the pulpit was intense; exhortations by one's wife were unwearying; even the children were sometimes urged to cajole reluctant parents into attending. In the larger parishes a full week would be given to each of four groups: married women, unmarried women, married men, and unmarried men. The schedule called for Mass, with a short doctrinal instruction, at five or six every morning; there were prayers and a forty-five minute, fire-and-brimstone exhortation in the evening. My father used to tell how his mother, on the Friday or Saturday of the mission week, would rouse him from sleep, and, when he would groan and try to roll over, would say, "Come, now. As you gave the candle, give the inch."

It was a grim week; the missionary, invited usually from one of the religious orders and for his oratorical powers, addressed such topics as the creation of our race and its utter dependence on God, the malice of sin, the distinct possibility of eternal punishment, the frightful cost of the atonement, the magnanimity of God's mercy. The chief purpose of the mission was to bring everyone to "a good confession," and if fear were not the sole motive it was usually a predominant one. Lurid descriptions of sudden, unprovided death and of the undying fires of hell linger in one's memory, naturally—I had heard many of them before I read the one in James Joyce's *Portrait of the Artist*—along with the denunciations of "immorality," understood always by both preacher and audience as sexual immorality. I remember how fiercely condemned were "those magazines that reek of hell!" Compared with what one sees on the newstands today, they seem to have been fairly innocuous. The holiness of faithful marriage was extolled, and indeed there were no divorces in our neighborhood, no birth control. Children were to be seen, not heard, but they were cherished.

All in all, the "mission" was a grim experience; we felt when it was over that we had had spiritual surgery. Now we left the hospital, a little weak and dizzy, relieved that the operation was safely over, yet confident that the past was forgiven and we could with hope begin a life more consistent with Christian values.

The pastor was introduced at public gatherings as "our beloved pastor." He was scarcely loved, since we saw him seldom, or only in the distant sanctuary, but he was respected as an administrator, and of course his word was law. The three curates, as they were known then, being younger, were more approachable, but still politely remote. The Irish had a maxim that must have come over in the immigrations, "With the priest be civil and strange," and it was observed among us. The priests seemed to follow the same precept in reverse. They were dedicated men, however; they visited every home in the parish four times a year, and they walked to their sick calls; curates were not permitted to own cars. Both my parents came down with pneumonia in 1917, and we children were farmed out to relatives. In those days there were no antibiotics, and only the well-to-do went to the hospital, so the long battle was fought at home. We did not realize then how nearly we had become orphans; if it had not been for heroic exertions by the family doctor and the district nurse we would have been. But one of the parish priests was in the house every day for three months, prayed with my parents, cheered them and bolstered their courage. May Christ the Priest, who "went about doing good," and whom they imitated, have given them long since a lavish reward.

Sometimes I linger now after a funeral in Calvary Cemetery or St. Joseph's, and look out at the acres of gravestones that commemorate the good people of those days, including my own parents and grandparents. Inevitably the Eucharistic Prayer comes to mind: "From age to age you gather a people to yourself, so that from east to west a perfect offering may be made to the glory of your name." I am convinced that I shall see those dear faces again, and be taken into an eternal, utterly compensating embrace. Theirs was a sturdy piety, even a grim one; "saving my soul" was for them the only real purpose in life, and ideas like "sacrifice" and "discipline" governed their choices. They must have wondered sometimes at the inequities of life as they scrimped to pay the rent, gave up some personal perquisite to finance an education, hid their heartache over a wayward son, endured the endless round of hard work in a very circumscribed existence. But their faith was vivid and strong, and out of it they looked mutely up to God for consolation and support. And they spared no effort to transmit that faith to us.

I lived with my maternal grandmother for three months while my parents were ill, and my grandfather, her husband, spent his last years in our home, but I never heard either of them speak about Ireland, though they had grown up there, or about the relatives who had stayed behind when they came over, and whom they never saw again. Had their situation—poverty, political oppression, absence of any foreseeable improvement—been so dismal that they preferred to forget it altogether? Years later I stood with Hamilton Delargy, the renowned Irish folklorist, on the top of Slievenamon, "the Hill of Fair Women," looking off into the smiling Tipperary valley below, and Delargy sighed and said, "No wonder they fought for it." But they had lost the fight to decidedly unneighborly neighbors from across the narrow sea, and saw no prospect of ever winning the valley back. So they left, in their thousands, and did their best, apparently, to expunge memories. A friend of mine tells me that her great-grandparents, who had given up hope of any future in the political and economic turmoil of 19th-century Germany and come to America, never spoke of their native land. It would be interesting to know whether Polish, Italian, Russian, or other expatriates so resolutely shut the door on their origins.

About my father's people we knew even less; his parents had died before we were born, and he never mentioned them. His mother, we somehow learned, had married a second time after his father's death, and very unhappily; perhaps that explained his silence. The Smiths, my mother's family, had (it was said) taken their name from the forge they had operated time out of mind in Lisronagh, near Clonmel in Tipperary, but when I went to Lismore, in Waterford, whence the Leonards were supposed to have come, I found no evidence that anyone we could claim had ever lived there. I remembered then the day that I met Helen Landreth, the curator of our Irish Collection at Boston College, as she came out of the library.

"Father," she cried, "You must see this lovely book!"

Indeed the book was handsome, bound in leather and beautifully printed. It was a dictionary of Irish family names, and of course I had to look up the Leonards. The learned author gave such details as the variant spellings of the name, the several places (chiefly the County Waterford) where the clan had lived, and so on. But his last sentence read, "No one of this name has ever distinguished himself in either the civil or the ecclesiastical life of Ireland." I snapped the book shut and gave it back to Miss Landreth.

"Take your old book," I said, "And throw it in the dumpster."

Some time later a friend in California sent me a newspaper clipping that was a bit more comforting. According to the genealogist cited in the paper,

"Leonard" may be either English or Irish. The English Leonards are traced to a Saxon warrior called Leon-Hard, meaning "brave as a lion." Early family records list William Leonard of Huntingdonshire, 1273. The English Leonard coat-of-arms has three silver fleurs-de-lis on a blue stripe across the center of a gold shield. Irish Leonards anglicized their name from O'Leannan, an ancient Gaelic cognomen for "sons of the man who wore a cloak." The primary American ancestor was Henry Leonard, who obtained a large land grant near Boston in 1626 following his arrival. Irish Leonards were represented by James Leonard of Fermanagh, who settled in Westmoreland County, Pennsylvania, in the mid-1700's.

Maybe there was some distinction in wearing a cloak. I myself had worn one for a time about the campus; it was warm in January, and it was convenient. But when we discarded cassocks after Vatican II I began to think of it as an affectation, and gave it to our dramatic society for use in any swashbuckling melodrama they might produce. At least I now knew that I was related to the Linnanes, the Lannons, the Linehans, and any others who thought of the ancestral O'Leannan as their patriarch. I definitely did not like the name I had been accorded at baptism. My mother had wanted me to be "Charles," but she was not well enough to go with me to the church, and when I returned I was "William." My father wanted a junior. But "William" turned out to be too formal, and it was used only by the primary school teachers, whom I disliked. "Willie" was intolerable, obviously; it rhymed with "lily" and my peers used it when they wanted to tease me. Then there was "Bill," but in every novel I read "Bill" was the villain: Bill Sykes, Three-fingered Bill, Bill the Cut-throat Cabdriver, and so on. Why, I asked my poor mother, couldn't I have been called something inconspicuous but classy like Algernon, or Demetrius, or Cadwallader? I found greater consolation in the motto inscribed on the Leonard coat-of-arms: "*In hoc signo vinces.*" Against all the seductions of the world, the flesh, and the devil—and their name was legion—I might confidently hope, in the grace and power of the Cross, to overcome.

William Cowper, a pretty much forgotten poet of the 18th century, had a sad life. Bullied as a schoolboy, he suffered from depression and periods of insanity as an adult. In his latter days someone gave him a picture of his mother, painted before her early death, and he wrote these pathetic lines:

On the Receipt of My Mother's Picture

Oh, that those lips had language! Life has passed
With me but roughly since I heard thee last.
Those lips are thine—thine own sweet smile I see,
The same that oft in childhood solaced me;
Voice only fails, else how distinct they say,
'Grieve not, my child; chase all thy fears away!'
The meek intelligence of those dear eyes
(blest be the Art that can immortalize,
The art that baffles Time's tyrannic claim
To quench it) here shines on me, still the same.

I have not been asked to endure suffering like that of poor old Cowper, but I have stood not seldom before my mother's picture, seeing as he did sweetness and intelligence and limitless devotion to myself, and wishing indeed that "those lips had language." The only surviving girl in her own large family, she was the peacemaker to a troop of belligerent brothers, combining authority—she could be firm!—with an unmistakable and impartial love for them all. The quality of her love, in fact, was extraordinary; it was tender, provident, patient, forgiving, faithful. I wince now when I remember how she scrubbed her youth away over the old "set tubs" in our kitchen (no electric washers and dryers in those days—no electricity, even), how she waited for me to come home from school to turn the wringer because she wasn't well enough to do it herself. When I was born she sustained injuries that were not surgically corrected for twenty-seven years, during which there were four more births and at least two miscarriages. She developed a prolapsed uterus and a permanent curvature of the spine, so that she could not stand or sit upright except by wearing a heavy leather jacket ribbed with steel, cumbersome at any time, insufferable in hot weather. I went to see her after her surgery; she was in the last bed in a ward with some twenty other patients, and when she saw me her smile was like a sunburst in that long, dark room. "It's a good thing I went to church when I was young," she used to say wistfully, and I would tease her about relying on "cold storage piety." Her voice was not strong, but it was sweet and true, and as

she cooked or ironed or mended or crocheted she would sing the
hymns she had learned as a girl. I remember now only one of
them, Father Faber's hymn for our Lady:

> I think of thee and what thou art,
> Thy majesty, thy state,
> And I keep singing in my heart,
> Immaculate, Immaculate!

One day in the spring of my last year in high school I came
home to find her ironing. "There's a letter for you," she said. It
was from the Jesuit who had been our teacher for three years; he
was then studying theology at Woodstock in Maryland in preparation for the priesthood, but he kept in touch with many of us. I
opened it, read it, and passed it to her. "That's a nice letter," she
said as she handed it back. "Yes," I said. "I think I'll be off to
join him next year." She dropped the iron with a clatter. *"What
did you say?"* I repeated what I had said; she stared at me for a
long moment and then began to cry. I was mystified, as I suppose
imperceptive males always are when their women weep. Had my
way of telling her been that abrupt, that clumsy? Was she crying
because she foresaw separation from her first-born, the first break
in the family circle? Or had she been silently praying for a long
time that I might come to her some day with just such an announcement? I put my arms around her but couldn't think of anything more to say, and at last she dried her tears. "You will have
to tell your father," she said. I quailed. "Won't you tell him?"
"Oh, no," she said decisively. "That's for you to do."

My father's was a complex personality. In many ways he was
more talented than any of his children. He never, for example, had
a piano lesson in his life, and he could not read music, but on Sunday evenings we listened to his playing—and sang delightedly
along with him, for he had a mellow baritone voice—as we never
did when someone who had studied was at the piano. One Christmas morning he gave my brother Fran a violin, and by noontime,
though he had never touched the instrument before, he was coaxing
a tune out of it. His father died when he was in fifth grade, and
he had to go to work at whatever jobs a small boy could find to
help support himself and his mother. But he read insatiably; he
had an old red rocker, placed under the gas lamp in our kitchen,
and he would read into the small hours before kneeling at the chair
to say his night prayers. Many a night, coming from my bedroom,
I would see him there, fallen asleep on his knees—an enlightening

and exemplary experience for a boy to have. He could write with grace and vigor, as I found out when for seven years—four when I was at Shadowbrook and three while I was in the Army—he wrote me a letter every day—every day, I said. They were not "newsy" letters. My mother was better at keeping me aware of everyday life at home. Instead, he would mention some event or celebrity on the national scene, or some personal memory of his own, and then ruminate about it like an essayist, turning it urbanely this way and that to bring out its full meaning. As a young man he had taken the civil service examination for employment as a postal clerk, a prized appointment not to be aspired to by the generally unlettered sons of immigrants in South Boston, and when he qualified and was appointed he was regarded with considerable awe in the neighborhood. On the strength of that appointment he gave my mother her ring and they set the date for the wedding. A year later, disregarding some waspish comments about their social climbing, they moved to what was then a quite rustic Dorchester, where woods, fields, and ponds stretched out toward Milton and we could climb trees and skate and play sandlot baseball.

My memories of those very early years in my life are scanty now. But some things are unforgettable. Once, when I was trying to comfort my father, I asked him if he remembered that as a small boy I had a heavy cold and fever. I would fall asleep, have a terrifying nightmare, and wake up moaning in fear. "This went on again and again all night," I said, "and every time I woke up you were there, sitting by the bed and saying, "There, there. It's all right." "I don't remember that," he said. "Well," I said, "I do. And I think God does, too."

What did St. Paul say? "You have had many teachers, but not many fathers" (I Cor 4:15).

Money was vastly different in those days, but even allowing for that I wonder how with five children they managed on $26 a week. We had a car, an elderly but dignified ark, a 1917 "Paige." We went to the beach in Marshfield for two months in the summer. We had lavish Christmases. Years later I asked my father where he had found the money to pay my tuition bill at B.C. High, a hundred dollars a year. "Loan sharks," he said. He would borrow the needed sum and, in small amounts, pay it back at extortionate rates of interest until the next bill arrived and he had to start the process again.

As we moved into the twenties and what the papers called "the High Cost of Living" began to be felt, a psychic wear and tear became evident in his personality. Postal salaries could not be raised except by an act of Congress, and when, finally, a bill was enacted, Mr. Coolidge, with Vermont parsimony, vetoed it. My father was in his middle years by this time; he did not know or declined to learn the political strategies all but obligatory for obtaining promotion in the civil service, so he was still what he had been twenty-five years before—a clerk, with no prospect of advancement and no prospect of an increase in salary to match his increased liabilities. Two characteristics had always distinguished him: a quite rigid propriety in dress, speech, and manner, and the "Black Irish" disposition to melancholy. He was gentle and companionable, but not jovial, never the life of the party. He would warn us children when we were merry: "Too much laughing comes to crying." He sang the sad songs favored by the Irish about exile and enforced separation from the beloved. And he liked, increasingly as the years went on, to sit alone in the living room, smoke his pipe, and stare out the window.

All of which might have prepared us children, had we known anything about the disease, for the discovery that he was an alcoholic. Of course no one in those days thought of it as a disease. Drunkenness was a moral fault, a sin, a grave offense against one's personal integrity and a source of scandal to others. The alcoholic was told that he could perfectly well stop drinking if he would. If he didn't he was convicted *ipso facto* of bad will. He might try pathetically to hide his affliction—the more so if the proprieties were dear to him—but eventually the neighbors would know. He would have to deal with a baffling mystery at the center of his being—an insane, frightening compulsion to do what gave him no joy and only compounded his problems. And he would be increasingly alone, his family distressed but uncomprehending, God (as he saw it) offended and threatening.

My father fought the disease, I see now, valiantly. For ten years, when we were very young, he touched nothing. But as he grew older and his difficulties multiplied the struggle became intense. When Lent began we could predict almost certainly that he would not make it to Easter; the dreary New England winter hung on interminably, and the Lenten season, especially in the grim way that we observed it then, induced in a man of his temperament only introspection and guilt. He was hospitalized more than twenty times, and always emerged with the assurance that "things will be better from now on." He relied, unfortunately, too much on his own strength. When we urged him to go to A.A. meetings he would refuse with pathetic dignity: "I don't need that. I am *not* an alcoholic."

My mother was his good angel. No matter how often he slipped and fell—and in those ugly days of the Depression and the War it was sometimes three or four times a year, for periods of six weeks or more—she ministered to him tenderly, reminded us of how good he had been to us, talked to him seriously but never in anger or reproach. Friends suggested that if she left him for a time the shock might help him to recover, but that was a proposal she refused to consider. I cried the day I brought him home from the hospital for the umpteenth time and saw them in each other's arms.

All that pain is over and done with now, and they are sleeping together in St. Joseph's Cemetery, at rest "until the dawn break and the shadows flee away." When I drive through Lagrange Street I can see the stone that marks their place. I wave and tell them "it won't be long now."

Well, there we were on the train to the Berkshires and what we sensed would be the high adventure. That gray little man, Harding Fisher, the "Master of Novices," looked us over appraisingly when we arrived, smiled, and said, "Postulants are very precious." How he saw us as potential "fishers of men" is hard to understand now. But he took in faith what the Lord had brought to him. Some of the "nets" still clinging to us he gently loosed, or, better, taught us how we ourselves might get out of their tangle. Some he left untouched, but showed us how we could use them and still be free. Best of all, by word and example he stripped the film from our eyes. We saw distinctly the Person who had been calling us, and, captivated, enthralled, we "went after" him.

CHAPTER 2

As It Was in the Beginning

A CURIOUS INCIDENT TOOK PLACE WHEN I WAS ABOUT TEN YEARS old, though I did not hear of it until I had been a Jesuit for a long time and was about to be ordained. My parents, who had been afraid that it might put some undue pressure on me, told me finally what happened. My uncle's father-in-law, a man I rarely saw and scarcely knew, was dying. But for a brief moment he emerged from coma and said to his daughter, my uncle's wife, "Did you know that Bill Leonard's oldest boy is going to be a priest?" Then he relapsed into coma and died within the hour.

There had never been any "vocations," male or female, in our family, nor, though nephews and nieces, grand-nephews and grand-nieces have come on the scene in generous numbers, have there been any since, except my own. Our parish priests, as I have said, were remote figures, encountered personally only when someone was ill or when the routine visitations took place. There were at that time in the parish no organized activities, no social groups or clubs where young people might meet a priest on an informal basis. There was as yet no parish school where one might come under the influence of religious women.

If we thought about it at all, our idea of a "vocation" was that few, very few, had one. The word was used exclusively in reference to the priesthood or the religious life. "Ordinary" Christians were not considered to have a call from God. They were the also-rans who would probably marry, and if they did there was a second chance: they might have a son or a daughter on whom God would confer the privileged grace of a vocation.

And yet the idea, a truly stupendous idea, that all Christians are called individually, personally, to receive the grace of baptism and to be incorporated into God's people, is clear and compelling in Scripture and the teaching of the Church. The prophets of the Old Dispensation reproached the people of Israel, who had been called to be God's holy people, with their failure to respond to that vocation, and predicted that a new people would be called who would respond generously. The Lord Jesus condemned the leaders of the chosen people of his time for the same reason. As the Second Vatican Council put it (Dogmatic Constitution on the Church, #9), "Christ instituted the new covenant in his blood by calling together a people made up of Jew and Gentile . . . the new People of God, 'a chosen race, a royal priesthood, a holy nation, a purchased people of God' (I Peter 2:9-10)." St. Paul put the idea before his converts as the most inspiring, challenging motivation he could offer them:

"Blessed be God the Father of Our Lord Jesus Christ, who has blessed us with all the spiritual blessings of heaven in Christ. Before the world was made, he chose us, chose us in Christ, to be holy and spotless, and to live through love in his presence, determining that we should become his adopted children, through Jesus Christ, for his own kind purposes, to make us praise the glory of his grace, his free gift to us in the Beloved, in whom, through his blood, we gain our freedom, the forgiveness of our sins." (Eph 1:3-14)

Were we, in those years before the Council, the impressionable years of our youth, made aware of this common vocation? Well, we all memorized (and most of us can still recite it) the answer to the Catechism's question, "Why did God make you?" which was, "God made me to know him, to love him, and to serve him in this life, and to be happy with him forever in the next." That would be as explicit a statement of our vocation, and of the love that prompted God to issue it, as one could ask for. Again, many of us made retreats that were developed along the lines of St. Ignatius' *Spiritual Exercises*, or listened to mission sermons, Sunday homilies, or other instructions from people who had made such retreats, and we heard, over and over, some version of the "Principle and Foundation" with which the *Exercises* begin: "Human beings are created to praise, reverence, and serve God our Lord, and by this means to save their souls." Here, too, was as clear and comprehensive a statement as one could wish.

But such reflections can be presented with very different emphases. For instance, what could be stressed is God's incalculable generosity in creating us—the infinite genius and energy expended. This presentation would naturally lead to appreciation of God's love and an answering love on our part. It would evoke admiration, enthusiasm, optimism. But the emphasis could fall instead on the creature's responsibilities and obligations in view of his utter dependence on the Creator. And then there would be the warning finger, the atmosphere of threat, the motivation of fear. "As a creature you are suspended by a thread over an abyss of nothingness. If God should ever let go of that thread . . ."

Of course it's true, as the old scholastic axiom has it, that "whatever is received is received according to the capacity of the receiver." There is, I believe, a temperamental disposition, individual or racial, to see the dark, the cheerless side of things, to prefer and indeed to take a perverse pleasure in melancholy. And, accordingly, it will be the dismal or at least the somber messages that register and are remembered. What it comes to is that God's call will be heard by some as a supremely gracious invitation and by others as a subpoena.

Another factor to be considered might be this: many immigrants and children of immigrants suffered from what would now be called an inferiority complex, or a poor self-concept. For "foreigners," especially if they were poor and uneducated, this was natural enough, and it was aggravated when the newcomers did not speak English well, as in the case of the Italians, the Germans, the French, the Poles. The Irish spoke the language, albeit with their own lilt, but any confidence one of them might have drawn from that was undermined by the others' determination not to let him develop exaggerated ideas of his own importance. The Irish had (still have?) a talent for mockery and a quiver of shafts that could puncture any developing self-confidence. Parents' gentlest admonition to their children was "Don't let that go to your head," or "Don't get too big for your boots." In such a climate a sense of personal worth could scarcely grow, while the idea that God would ever choose *me* was ridiculous.

But wasn't baptism regarded as a choice by God of individuals, of this individual? Let's see whether it was presented in that light to us. The old (1917) Code of Canon Law speaks (#737) of baptism as "the door and the foundation" of the other sacraments, and says (#87) "By baptism a human being is established in the Church of Christ as a person, with all the rights and duties of Christians." Nothing explicit about God's choice there. The *Baltimore Catechism*, from which most people learned their Christian doctrine, offered this definition: "Baptism is a sacrament which cleanses us from original sin, makes us Christians, children of God, and heirs of heaven." Subjects then discussed were the meaning of "catechumen," the meaning of "heir," the remission of actual sins and their eternal and temporal punishment, the necessity of baptism for salvation, what happens to the unbaptized, the ordinary and extraordinary minister of the sacrament, the manner of baptizing, the obligation not to defer an infant's baptism, baptism of water, desire, and blood, the meaning of the accompanying ceremonies, the renunciation of the devil and "all his works and pomps," the selection of a saint's name for the child, the sponsors and their relationship and obligations to the child, the ceremony of "churching." Again, a quite comprehensive summary, yet, curiously, not a syllable about the sovereign, munificent, humanly inexplicable but, for the creature, momentous option exercised in his regard.

All in all, the preconciliar awareness of God's love was scanty, and the prevailing spirituality was, largely, bleak. God's overtures (described too often in coldly rational terms) for many good people were only a reminder that life is fragile and brief, and a strict accounting of it would be demanded. They thought of God as did the Puritan poet Milton, who spoke of "living ever in my great Taskmaster's eye." Perhaps the only thing that saved some of them was the Irish sense of humor ("the situation is desperate but not really serious, or if serious not wholly desperate'), but for too many others there was only anxiety, legalism, scrupulosity.

Trying to summon up recollections of a boyhood seventy-plus years ago is a chancy business. And trying to pinpoint events that gave shape in those far-off days to one's personality and outlook is an effort even less likely to succeed. Memories are few by this time, and deceptive; I wonder if some things really happened to me or whether I read about them in a novel and was so struck by them that gradually I slipped them into my personal experience.

I have been thinking in particular of late about the religious influences that gave me my faith, especially the impact of formal religious practice. What was the effect on an impressionable boy of Mass on Sunday after Sunday in the parish church, of First Communion and Confirmation, of the celebration of holydays? I don't doubt that these events had their cumulative strength. What puzzles me is that my memories of them are so meager, so seemingly disproportionate to the result. Shouldn't I have more vivid and more substantive memories?

For example, my only recollection of Christmas Mass is of walking over the hill to a neighboring parish where they had Midnight Mass—something our pastor did not approve of—and reveling in the beauty of the new-fallen snow, the good companionship of two inseparable friends, and, no doubt, the excitement of being abroad at so late an hour. Of Holy Thursday the only surviving memory is of "making" the Seven Churches. We could do that by walking straight in Dorchester Avenue and stopping to visit the repositories in six parishes along the way until we ended our pilgrimage at the Polish church in Andrew Square. On Good Friday we had to stay indoors and be quiet from noon until three o'clock. Holy Saturday meant interminable and largely uncomprehended rituals at the break of dawn; in the afternoon every family brought a bottle to the sacristy for "Easter water," which my mother would scatter through the house when we had a thunderstorm. All I can remember of First Communion is the new blue serge suit, the fragrant carnation in my button-hole, and the good lady who told me, "This is the happiest day of your life"—a remark which perplexed and dismayed me a little, since I was not in fact feeling especially blissful that day, and hated to think there were no better things in my future. And of Confirmation, alas, I recall only a certain lovely face, framed in dark hair, which was over on the girls' side, and of which I had recently become very much aware.

One of these days I must sit down with an expert in the new science of developmental psychology and find out why only these few pathetic memories remain, or how it is that attitudes and convictions can be fixed for a lifetime without the subject's being conscious of the process. But in the meantime I ask myself two questions: first, if it were all to be done again, what I should like to be taught by the Christian celebrations of my boyhood, and second, how these celebrations could be enlivened so that precious and inspiring memories of them might linger in the adult mind.

As to the first question, here is a summary tabulation:

Advent: a sense of the history of salvation, of God's merciful interventions in human affairs, of Christ's promised, climactic second coming to the world, and of how all this touches me personally.

Christmas: a perception of love enveloping me and soliciting my love in response.

Lent: an understanding of this annual retreat of the Church as an opportunity to know the Lord more intimately, love him more ardently, follow him more closely, so that at Easter I might renew my covenant with him.

Holy Week: a perception of love enveloping me and soliciting my love in response.

Easter: an appreciation of Christ's victory over evil and death, and mine in him; the *noblesse oblige* of living as he did, since I am risen in him.

Pentecost (and *Confirmation*); an awareness of the presence in me and governance of me by the Holy Spirit.

First Communion: the lesson of full incorporation, by eating the body of the Lord, into that body of his which is the Church.

Sunday Mass: what it means to be a worshiper in spirit and in truth; how my prayer is enhanced by being merged with the prayer of other Christians and united with the prayer of the one Mediator; what my vocation to live and worship in a community asks of me; how God's commitment to me invites a growing surrender of myself to him; how, as a disciple of Christ, I am to advance steadily in imitation of him as I grow older.

As to the second question, one might reply, aye, there's the rub. Still, there is great value in determining what we want to teach before settling on ways of presenting it. And any instructor (i.e., any "president of the assembly") who can call on such elemental and vivid teaching aids as bread and wine, water, oil, fire, incense, candles, time and place, light and darkness, song, gesture and vesture, color and space, should be able to create memories enough to last a lifetime.

But what about the "vocation within a vocation," the call to a specific way of life and service? I'm quite sure that I had no idea whatever of the priesthood or the religious life until late in my junior year in high school. Then, in a fleeting, romantic moment, I wondered how it would be to go off like St. Francis Xavier to the pagan peoples of the East. I even saw myself, as in the idealized pictures of the saint, lifting the crucifix, baptizing thousands. But I spent a good bit of time on the beaches that summer, and any such notion evaporated in the hot sun. On the first day of class in my senior year, however, I turned into James Street, saw the dingy red brick of the old Boston College High School, and the whole thing came flooding in on me. No romance this time, though. I hated the idea. I fought to expel it from my mind. But there was no truce in the battle. The idea distracted me as I read the *Iliad* and the *Aeneid*. Like an importunate beggar whom I sought vainly to brush off it matched strides with me as I walked downtown after school to sort mail in the South Postal Station. One November day a couple of the young Jesuits who were our teachers showed us snapshots they had taken on a weekend visit to Shadowbrook, the novitiate. There, looking brave and very contented in their cassocks, were two novices from last year's senior class, whom I had known and admired when we worked on the school magazine and shouted at each other in the debating society: John Peter Sullivan and John McCarthy. And I remember vividly how, going home on the rumbling, swaying train of the old Boston Elevated, I clung to the strap over my head, saying desperately to myself, "Well, maybe it wouldn't be too bad."

My desperation grew as Christmas approached. I didn't want to talk about the idea with anyone, fearing, I suppose, that I might be influenced by arguments for which I could think of no adequate answer. At last I went to the shrine of our Lady in the basement of our church, knelt, and said something like this: "They tell me that you're good at finding out what God wants of young people. I've tried and tried and I can't decide what he wants of me. So I'm putting the whole thing in your hands. Let me know."

Now I shiver as I think, "Suppose she never answered. Or suppose she brought word that, after all, I was mistaken: I was not being called." But the answer did come—not, to be sure, by way of any direct revelation, not even by a blinding flash of sudden clarity, but by a slowly gathering conviction and a growing peace with it. It was calming, heartening, inspiring; exactly the kind of response one would look for from a mother. And it gives me joy now to acknowledge it, to assert firmly my belief that Mary was the mother of my vocation.

I had no idea of how my father would react when I told him. I knew his faith was deep and all-prevailing; there would be no obstacles there. And he had never discussed his financial situation with us, never visited his worries on us, so it didn't occur to me— an innocent or imperceptive seventeen-year-old—that he might well have been looking forward to my contribution, after I graduated, to the family income. But he never alluded in any way to that issue; it came home to me only later, after I had grown up a little. His concern was fatherly, for me rather than for himself. "Are you sure you want to do this?" he said. "How long have you been thinking of it?"

He pondered it and prayed over it, I'm sure, and discussed it with my mother, and finally gave his consent. There was only one condition: "Don't come back." The Irish aversion for the "spoiled priest" or the "spoiled nun"—people who went off to the seminary or novitiate and then decided that the life was not for them—was strong in him. It was a completely unreasonable view; it gave no credit to a candidate who was willing at least to make a gallant try. And, after all, the whole purpose of a novitiate is to discover whether, in fact, the candidate's "call" is genuine or imagined. But in my case the injunction was, perhaps, a salutary grace. There would be days during my novitiate when, as someone put it, I had "one foot outside the door and the other on a banana peel." On those days I would remember his "don't come back" and set my jaw again.

One of the stories we used to tell in later years, to the accompaniment, I noticed, of a kind of rueful laughter, was of the day when three of us were out for a walk. Three of us, because that was the rule ("never two, always three"). We were to avoid "particular friendships;" our charity was supposed to be universal. And to make sure of it, the membership of the walking "band" was not a matter of our choice, but was assigned by the "manuductor," a senior novice appointed to supervise the novitiate and to be our liaison with "Father Master." In any case, as we three walked the country road, an open "convertible," with the top down, flashed by. In the front seat were a boy and a girl about our own age, and in the "rumble seat" another young couple. They waved and shouted something we couldn't catch, but which sounded like good-natured mockery. There was silence for a moment and then one of the band, a very young and painfully pious novice, sighed and said, "But they're not happy."

Which brings up the interesting question of whether *we* were supposed to be happy. We were learning a great deal about ourselves—how, for instance, it was possible to be contented—"at peace," we were taught to call it—on a profound level and still be disturbed by some passing annoyance. The ocean's surface, after all, can be tossed by the winds while its depths remain tranquil. But were we expected to maintain that precarious balance consistently? The novitiate was supposed to be a place and time of testing, wasn't it? We were to learn, by actually living it, whether we wanted or were suited to religious life, and our superiors were to determine whether we were acceptable candidates. As we became acquainted with ourselves and with the very high and exacting ideals proposed to us, it was inevitable that we should be torn. If we were not, it would have to be because we hadn't yet awakened to the warring between flesh and spirit.

So we were being tested. And what were the tests, or trials, as we called them? There was, first of all, the "Long Retreat," a thirty-day period spent in silence and solitary prayer, following— and performing—the *Spiritual Exercises* of St. Ignatius. Four times a day we assembled for a presentation by the Master of "points" for our meditation: the fact that we were created by God, for instance, and what this told us about the meaning of life. Or it might be some event in the life of Christ. These topics were not chosen at random; they had been marshaled by Ignatius with shrewd psychological insight in such a way as to help us know the will of God and inspire us to follow wherever it led. The rest of the day was given over to both community and private prayer, to "spiritual reading" and "examination of conscience," to solitary strolling outdoors. In order to relieve the strain that inevitably builds up in such a program, we had three "break days," during which we went for long walks in "bands" of three and talked and laughed until the tensions relaxed. The night before the first such day we prayed that it wouldn't rain, and it didn't; it snowed, a good six inches though the date was early October, and we got some intimation of what winter in the Berkshires would be like. But we went walking nonetheless; we needed to, especially we seventeen-year-olds, for whom life had taken on a very new seriousness. Some wise man has observed that "goodness has the longest awkward age," and our first efforts to live in intimate union with God were bumbling indeed.

Two of the "trials" usually imposed, the "pilgrimage," in which the novice walks to some fairly distant shrine, begging his food and lodging along the way, and the month spent as orderly in some hospital, were suspended in my time; we would have welcomed either or both, since the most trying of our "trials" was the monotony. We lived in the outskirts of a country town, without neighbors. We were permitted visitors only two or three times a year. We had no newspapers, no radios, and only a couple of rather treacly religious magazines. (Lindberg flew the Atlantic in 1927, but I learned about it in 1929.) Our "library" was a pathetic assemblage of dreary treatises on asceticism and historically questionable biographies of saints, neither of which we had much opportunity to read because of the way our day was broken up. Our incoming mail was censored and newspaper clippings confiscated.

Since we were expected to become "detached" from our previous way of life, we had to get permission to write to anyone outside the family.

In the house (and we were in the house most of the time) the rule called for silence except on necessary matters, and then the conversation was to be in Latin. Here was a new hurdle. Most of us had had at least four years of Latin, but had never spoken it. Wasn't it a dead language? No, we were told, it would be indispensable when we came to study philosophy and theology, and in our religious order it was a *lingua franca*, enabling us to converse with our brethren wherever in the world we might meet them. Actually, it did work out to my personal advantage in Rome, during the Second Vatican Council, when I had a delightful two-hour conversation in Latin with Father Karl Rahner, whose English was about on a par with my German. And I remember meeting, after World War II, two Polish priests on a train from Genoa to Marseilles. They had no English, I had no Polish, so we tried Latin, and I learned that both had been imprisoned by the Nazis for five years at Dachau. Every prisoner, they told me, had to learn some skill and work at it; they became masons and were assigned to a construction job whose purpose they could not figure out. Only after the work was finished did they discover that they had built ovens for the incineration of executed prisoners. They had been unwitting collaborators in the grisly "final solution."

As time went on we acquired a decent fluency in Latin, but in the beginning it was a matter of patching English words together with such Latin phrases as we could remember. My boss in the scullery gave me directions: "*Noli* put the dirt here," he said; "put it over there if you want to, but *noli* here." The regulation certainly dampened any temptation to indulge in small talk inside the house.

Lack of privacy was a hardship. No one in the group was temperamentally a "loner," but—especially at a period in our experience when we were encountering brand-new challenges, or wrestling, perhaps, with the temptation to throw it all up and go home to a normal, rational way of life—it would have been helpful to "go apart," to have a door we could close behind us. Alas, there was no place to hide. We slept in a long, barn-like dormitory, on cots about three feet apart. Except when we were in the chapel or engaged in housekeeping, we spent the day in the "ascetory" or study-hall, at tiny desks that must at one time have served the sixth grade somewhere. There were three such ascetories, and we would be moved periodically from one to another so as to cultivate "indifference" to our location, but only when we were sick did we have a room to ourselves in the infirmary. The strain was subtle but intense.

However, as I have said, the most difficult feature of our life was its monotony. We knew when we got up in the morning exactly what we would be doing at any moment of the day. Very occasionally, if the ice on the lake was good, and if the Master, who kept a vigilant and perceptive eye on us, sensed that tensions were reaching a boiling-point, a surprise skating holiday would be declared, or we would be turned loose on the grounds to swing an axe or push a lawnmower. But such diversions were rare. For the most part we followed "regular order," and that ran as follows:

5:00   Rise (with a cold shower in the basement three floors below)

5:25   "Morning visit" in the chapel

5:30   Meditation in the ascetory

6:25   Mass in the chapel

7:15   Thanksgiving in the chapel

7:30   Breakfast and "free time" (I learned how to shave, and did so every third day. My beard was light and almost invisible then.)

8:30   "Manualia" (light housekeeping)

9:00   Conference by the Master on some aspect of our Constitutions

9:45   Free time (a chance to begin the weekly letter home)

10:00   Study of Latin or Greek grammar (so we wouldn't forget)

11:00   Class in Latin or Greek grammar (no reading of the literature, which we would study after the novitiate was over, but which might distract us now)

12:00   Free time

12:15   Examination of conscience

12:30   Dinner (some would be assigned to serve table or help in the kitchen or the scullery; one would be assigned to read to the community during the meal from a book chosen by the "prefect of reading" who would call out corrections in pronunciation). Dinner and supper were formal meals; we filed in silently, took napkins from boxes with our names on them, responded to the "grace" led by "Father Minister," and sat down, reminding ourselves of St. Ignatius' "Rules for the Consumption of Food" and trying to listen to the reading, so that, as he said, "the soul also might have her food."

1:15   Recreation outdoors, in all weathers. (We walked up and down the lane in assigned "bands" of three—if it were not our turn to clean up in the scullery or the kitchen. Those who had worked during dinner went to "second table" and were read to.)

2:00   Spiritual reading, prescribed from Rodriguez' *Christian Perfection.* (A sleepy period.)

3:00   "Manualia"

3:30   Prayers in the chapel, followed by recitation of the Rosary outdoors, walking in "bands" of three up and down the lane (hence its name, "Rosary Lane")

4:00   Class in Latin or Greek grammar

4:45   Free time. (Incoming mail would be distributed now, but I would just have my father's daily letter out of its envelope when the bell ending free time would ring. This accounted partially for my life-long dislike of Kempis.)

5:00   Spiritual reading, from Thomas à Kempis' *The Imitation of Christ*

5:25   "Points," or preparation for meditation

5:30   Evening meditation in the ascetory

6:00   Supper, at "first" or "second table," depending on one's assignment

6:45   Recreation outdoors, as after dinner, except that during the "last quarter" we spoke—or tried to speak—Latin. (Conversation tended to lag somewhat during the last quarter.)

7:30   Spiritual reading, from a biography of some saint.

8:00   Free time

8:30   "Points" for tomorrow morning's meditation.

8:45   Examination of conscience

9:00   The Litany of the Saints, recited in chapel

9:30   Lights out. (Few had any difficulty falling asleep.)

Two whole years of that!

Our rule read that at the first sound of the bell we were to drop whatever we were doing and go at once to the new occupation, "leaving even the letter unfinished." We had no theoretical problem with the doctrine that when legitimate authority spoke God spoke, and that obedience was therefore a sacrifice and an act of faith very pleasing to God. This, after all, was what we had learned at home and in school. Nor did we question the breaking-up of our day into these short periods and the consequent mass movement of the entire group from one activity to the next. It was the pattern of the novitiate as we found it; no doubt, we thought, it served a good purpose, since as far as we knew it had been in place for hundreds of years. Wasn't there something like it in the Army, "basic training" or "boot camp," where the recruit had to do painful, even incomprehensible things in order to learn discipline and instant obedience? And we had a much loftier motivation; our love of God was manifested, one "spiritual father" told us, by doing "hard" things.

St. Ignatius had broken away from the life-style of the older monastic orders in many ways; he demanded of his sons mobility and creative initiatives. Jesuits were not to chant the Divine Office in common, or wear a fixed habit, or even live together if a good apostolic purpose could be served by living alone. He met, of course, a good deal of resistance before such innovations were approved, and in those troubled Reformation days, when the Church had its back to the wall and suspected any departures from tradition as concessions to heresy, he may have thought it impolitic to ask for too much. Or perhaps, given the "siege mentality" of Catholics during the centuries that followed, the growing centralization of all authority at Rome, and the rigid codification of church law affecting religious orders, there was a steady drift toward traditional monasticism on the part even of non-monastic communities.

The fact, too, that the Society's membership grew so rapidly may have had its influence. St. Ignatius began with ten companions; before he died (sixteen years later) there were a thousand. He might well have changed or adapted administrative or formative policies in the face of such an expansion; historical documents are not clear on the point.

By our time, certainly, community life in the Society—always excepting the communal celebration of the Office and the wearing of a distinctive habit—did not differ notably from that of older religious orders. There was a definite hour for rising, for Mass, for meals, for prayers, for retiring, and bells were rung to signal each "duty." We moved in silent file (the "Long Black Line," we called it) from chapel to dining room to chapel to recreation room. There was a period of special or "sacred" silence from the time we began preparations for the following morning's meditation until after breakfast. There was reading during lunch and dinner, and announcements, in stylized formulas, were published from the reader's pulpit. "Father Minister" stood at the dining room door as we entered and nodded permission for us to perform various "penances," like kneeling on the floor, arms out-stretched, during the "graces." We wore the cassock all day, except during games; later, after the novitiate, we even wore the biretta during meals. We had no chapter, as the monks did, but we had monthly "days of recollection," and twice a year there was a "triduum of renovation," with exhortations in the chapel by the "spiritual father" and reading at table from the letters of our Superiors General. At the end of the triduum "Father Minister" would solemnly ascend the pulpit and read (in Latin) the "defects" in the observance of the rule which each of us accused ourselves of, and then impose a penance to be carried out by all. The next morning, at Mass, we would "renew" our vows. This was not canonically a re-enlistment, since we had made perpetual vows at the end of the novitiate; it was a devotional exercise intended to renew the fervor of our commitment.

We always considered ourselves blessed in having had Father Fisher as our novice-master. (The man who fills that office now is called the "director," a gentler term, with overtones indicating a more suasive approach, but "master" originally meant "teacher" and it was in the best sense of that word that we thought of Father Fisher.) He was not grim, as some of his successors seemed to be; he laughed a good deal, he was ever the courteous, soft-spoken gentleman, and he strove to create a joyful community. There was real solicitude in his concern for each of us, though he could be firm. I shall never forget the day, in my second year, when he called me in and said, "If I don't see more peace in your eyes I'm going to have to send you home." He terrified me; it's true that I was confused and miserable, but the last thing I wanted was to give up. During the following months I smiled so radiantly at everyone that the muscles in my cheeks ached. I had inherited, partially (and partially been formed by), a strain of grimness and a need to achieve. As one of my classmates said of me years later, "If you want him to do something, tell him he can't do it." To such a "driven" personality type, high on the Minnesota Multiphasic Test and high as well on the Richter Scale, peace comes dropping slow.

Something should be said about Father Fisher's own spirituality and his way, as "Master," of communicating it to us. For one thing, he did not command; he challenged. A highly personal and intense love of Christ was manifest in all he said and did; for him no enterprise was too daring, no sacrifice too costly in the service of such a Lord. I shall always remember the evening, during our "Long Retreat," when he presented St. Ignatius' famous meditation, the "Two Standards." He pictured vividly for us the cosmic struggle between the demonic forces of evil, with their tireless lusting for the souls of men and women created in the image of God, and the legions led by Christ the Redeemer, which fought relentlessly to keep that image unsullied. Whose side would we be on? More to the point, since we had already made that choice in the meditation on the Kingdom of Christ, how much ardor and gallantry were we going to bring to the struggle? And how hard would we be willing to work in order to become expert in tactics, to acquire skill in the choice and use of weapons? Now we could see the fire in the gleaming eyes under the shaggy eyebrows; it challenged the manhood in each of us, and, I think, no one of us was ever the same again.

Father Fisher, naturally, was a child of his times, and he brought to his work the intellectual and spiritual formation he himself had been given. But he seemed to have surmounted any narrowness or pettiness in that tradition; in particular, I cannot recall his ever appealing to the motive of fear, which was so prominent in the spirituality of the period. He presided over the suffocating routine of the novitiate because he had to, and because nothing else was available in those days, but he never canonized it; he taught us, indeed, to rise above it. And he had that marvelous asset, an open mind; he would listen to our wildest ideas, looking for even the kernel of something valuable, letting us down to reality with wonderful gentleness but encouraging us to go on dreaming. One day, after we had passed from the novitiate to the juniorate, several of us were working on the grounds. The hill leading to the lake was very steep, and we were moving heavy, flat stones to provide a stairway that would make our passage easier and safer, especially in winter. He happened to be out walking, and stopped to ask what we had in mind, nodding with approval as we explained. Then I had a sudden inspiration. "Father," I said, "Why couldn't we plant rose bushes at each step along the path? Then in June we'd have a ladder of roses up and down the hill!" He caught the idea at once, his eyes lighted up—and he *let me see* the gleam— but then he said, "Is it easy to find the kind of stones you need for the steps? No? And after you had found them you would have to bring them here and set them firmly in place, and, let's see, you have finished only about a third of the work, haven't you? And you will be leaving the house and moving to Weston in about a month, right? M-m-m. Maybe the best thing would be to recruit some of next year's Juniors to carry on the work, and then we can think about the roses. But I do like the idea." He smiled and moved off. Someone else would have snorted, "What a silly notion!"

That he was a child of his times was further demonstrated by his use (or non-use) of the Bible. He certainly appealed to the Gospels, but rarely to any other book of the New Testament, and very seldom indeed to the Hebrew Scriptures. Of the proliferating "devotions" of the period he encouraged only three that I remember: the Sacred Heart devotion, a chivalrous and tender devotion to the Mother of God, and devotion to Jesuit saints. He was absolutely dedicated to the celebration of "his" Mass. It was carried out, except on feast days, when we would sing popular and more or less relevant hymns, in absolute silence. If anyone coughed or sneezed he would get a glare from the celebrant—the only expression of annoyance we ever saw. Some of us used missals to maintain contact with the action at the altar, but only the two servers made the responses. The supreme moment was the "Consecration," the words of institution spoken over the bread and wine, followed by the reverent genuflection and elevation. At Communion we received the body of the Lord (on our tongues, not in our hands), but never drank from the cup. After Mass we knelt for fifteen minutes to make our "thanksgiving," as if the Mass itself were not the great thanksgiving (the "Eucharist," as the first Christians called it) of the People of God. It was generally believed in those days that the Mass was not only a sublime prayer but also a masterpiece of art; some people took it for granted that our manner of celebration duplicated in every particular exactly what the Lord did at the Last Supper. Even to think of laying sacrilegious hands on such a treasure partook of blasphemy. As a beloved old Monsignor said to me years later, "Change the Office. Change even the sacramental rites, if you must. But don't change the Mass!" This was the attitude characterized by Father Jungmann in his monumental study of the Mass as "a time grown tired." We paid dearly for our ignorance of history, in other areas as well as in worship.

Without knowing why, I found the novitiate piety unattractive and unsatisfying. This worried me for a long time; my fellow-novices seemed to find it adequate, and I wondered, as the odd man out, whether I belonged in this way of life. After the novitiate we were allowed to choose our own spiritual reading; I tried Scaramelli and some other "classics" of asceticism, but couldn't respond to them. One day it occurred to me that I had never read the Bible straight through. It took me two years, half an hour a day, because I made copious notes, but it was a revelation—literally. "As with a banquet shall my soul be satisfied."

On the vexed issue of devotions, I found long afterward a comment that seemed to explain why I had vaguely sensed in them a certain inadequacy, an irrelevancy, and had drawn back from them almost in distrust:

> It would be unjust, of course, to discuss all these outward forms simply as "triumphalism." No, there was an honest effort to find subjective satisfaction through forms of devotion, especially devotion to the Hearts of Jesus and Mary. The trouble was that all these devotions lacked a real, conscious relation to that which is the source and origin, the center and summit, of Christian life, namely, the vital celebration of the Eucharist. Such a connection was not present in the theological consciousness of the baroque period; the people of the time calmly did what was in their power and what was felt in their day to be liturgically appropriate.[1]

I could never understand why Kempis had been one of St. Ignatius' favorite books, or why we were required to read it every day. "As often as one goes out into the world of men," Kempis said, "he returns less a man," and "the longer one stays in his cell the sweeter it becomes." This doctrine may possibly have been ap-

---

1. Johannes Emminghaus, *Eucharistia*, trans. Matthew O'Connell, Collegeville, MN, 1978; p. 78.

propriate for monks and hermits, though I doubt whether the great Benedict would have adopted it without qualification, but how did it square with the apostolic vocation? Here again, a comment from Emminghaus helps us to see the book in its historical context:

> *The Imitation of Christ* of Thomas à Kempis (1399-1471), one of the finest witnesses to late medieval piety, shows both the admirable impulses of meditative empathy that were at work in this piety and its sacramental weaknesses. In this book the reader is drawn to Christ in a moralizing way, and especially through emotion and subjective feeling; he is aroused to follow Christ as his model, yet at the same time he may well neglect the sacramental access to Christ. In this respect the *Imitation* was the forerunner of the pietism that stood apart from both Church and liturgy.
>
> It is easy to understand how, for people in this frame of mind, love for Mary and veneration of the saints could become extremely important; also how such piety could easily lead to an excessive preoccupation with relics and to an ideal of holiness as based on a multiplication of external works, for example, pilgrimages and processions. The late medieval altar tells us a good deal about the times: the bread and wine are still to be found there, of course, although they are to be adored rather than eaten; but above them on the beautiful devotional retables is depicted an imagined world of holiness that appeals to, expresses the inner longings of, the believer who is not really participating in the worship proper.[2]

Each month we had a gruesome practice known as "chapter," though we often referred to it as "*lapidatio*" or "stone-throwing." In alphabetical order each of us knelt on the floor in the middle of the group and the others were asked to comment on his deportment, especially on his observance of the rule and customs of the novitiate. Most of the comments were kind and harmless, but I never saw Father Fisher so uneasy as when he presided, with obvious distaste, at these sessions. There were two pairs of blood-brothers in our group, and he would never permit one brother to comment on the other. He limited criticisms strictly to external conduct, and would interrupt at once if we began to insinuate anything about a man's motives. Nonetheless, he found "chapter" a

---

2.   Id., pp. 73-4.

thoroughly unpleasant experience, and so, I believe, did most of us, not least when our turn came to take the floor. The exercise was supposed to increase the charity of the commentators and the humility of the victim. Perhaps it did, but the practice has been dropped, and I have not heard any expressions of regret.

The second-year novices used to exhort us to suppress any signs of individuality. "Don't be singular," they would say. This troubled me, too. Hadn't God made us "singular"? We hadn't come off any assembly line of creation. And wasn't it likely that we had been called to this life in view of the particular gifts God had conferred on each of us? Well, that counsel disappeared after the novitiate, and I used to laugh when people would say, "You Jesuits are all alike." "Come live with us," I would answer.

Probably Father Fisher, who had already spent thirty years in the preconciliar Society when we knew him, would have found it difficult to adapt the novitiate to the reforms of the Second Vatican Council. But I am confident that he would have welcomed them with all his soul. He would have known, of course, that very hard work had to be done, that a radical conversion had to be brought about and a foundation laid for a lifetime. But I think he would have chosen vastly different methods, dispensing, for instance, with the features that made our novitiate such a hot-house of formation, isolated and shielded protectively from the wintry winds of real life. Well, it was the piety of the times, raised to the nth degree. Our parents would not have found it essentially alien to their own spiritual outlook.

CHAPTER 3

Persuasive Speech

DOWNSTAIRS, IN THE "JUNIORATE," WE BEGAN THE SECOND PHASE of our formation. It would run through two years. We would read the classics in Latin, Greek, and English, studying meanwhile the literary principles derived from them by Aristotle, Cicero and Quintilian, Saintsbury. We were encouraged to read widely and according to our taste, and we did. I myself read in the original languages all forty-eight books of the *Iliad* and the *Odyssey,* the twelve books of the *Aeneid, Paradise Lost,* much of the Greek dramatists, Tacitus, Shakespeare, the orations in "Bristish Eloquence," the Greek Anthology. It was an immersion, the more complete because of our continued isolation from the outside world. We continued to live on that hill overlooking Lake Mahkeenac and "Stockbridge Bowl," where at that time there were large estates but few inhabitants, even in summer. Our families visited us only two or three times a year, after we had obtained permission to entertain them; visits by others were discouraged. We were permitted to listen to only one radio broadcast, a campaign speech by Governor "Al" Smith of New York. The published reason for this extraordinary breach of custom was that listening to the Governor might give us a contemporary example of the rhetorical principles we were studying at the time. Actually, I believe, our superiors thought that we should not be absolutely insulated from the excitement of American Catholics over the fact that one of their own was for the first time considered a possible, even a likely candidate, for the presidency of the United States. We still rose at five and retired at ten (no exceptions unless you were ill), we had meditation and Mass and community devotions and spiritual reading and periodic exhortations just as we had had in the novitiate; bells rang, if not with the same frequency, at least with the same insistence. Again, there were no newspapers, no magazines except for a few journals dealing with the classics. Long afterward I read Frederick

Lewis Allen's *Only Yesterday*, a history of the 1920s. I enjoyed the book very much because I remembered 1920-25, when I was growing up, very vividly, and because what happened from 1925 to 1929 was completely new to me. It sometimes seemed to me that we might have been living in ancient Rome; our hill might have been one of the Seven. Except on holidays, Latin was the language used in the house. In our intramural debates we argued hotly whether Caesar or Cicero had done more to advance the glory of Rome. "Immersion" might not be the appropriate word; "saturation" might be more like it.

Not all of us, naturally, enjoyed the experience as thoroughly as did we literary types (sometimes banteringly referred to as "them poets"). There were classmates who, later, found metaphysics or biology or canon law more congenial. But our education was determined by the values of our elders, and they held firmly to the principles of the Jesuit "Ratio Studiorum," which held firmly that no man could be considered educated unless he was familiar with the best that had been thought and said in the culture of the West. It was assumed that most of us would become teachers; our colleges and high schools were thriving, and their faculties, almost exclusively Jesuit, would be needing replacements down the line. We were not for that reason urged, however, to take a simply pragmatic approach to our studies. Now that I think of it I realize that it was a generous, expansive program that went far beyond any merely utilitarian advantage. But if it was expansive it was also expensive. We were now—having made perpetual vows—members of the Society of Jesus, and the Society would underwrite all the costs of our education (board, lodging, tuition, medical bills, etc.) for as many years as we would be going to school. It was a munificent endowment, given ungrudgingly in the hope that we would become not simply masters in some dusty classroom, not just gentlemen of culture and refinement, but thoroughly apt instruments in the hands of the Lord, equipped and ready for any service we might be able to offer for the spread of his kingdom. We were the *spes gregis,* the hope of the flock, and our superiors and professors looked on us as their principal responsibility.

If anything, we were, in that last age of the old Church, supervised and sheltered excessively, not only during those two years, but for ten years afterward. Our lives were hedged around by laws and regulations that governed every contingency, every activity. We had the Church's law as it affected religious (189 statutes in the old Code of Canon Law), the Constitutions of the Society (827 prescriptions); the "Custom Book" of our Province; rescripts, answers to queries, etc., emanating from various Roman congregations or from our own Superior General; particular directives by the Provincial, the Province prefect of studies, the local superior, the dean, the individual professors. Of course not all these rules obliged us with the same degree of seriousness, but we were trained to obey even "the least sign of the superior's will" as the will of God for us in every circumstance, so we did not discriminate. At an age when our peers at home were choosing a career, marrying, raising a family, making critical decisions, directing subordinates, handling money and property, we were without options, protected, watched over. It was a life-style, as Father John Courtney Murray later pointed out in a famous "exhortation" to the community at Woodstock, that could have prevented us from ever achieving a responsible maturity. It could also—and did in some instances—produce a cramping, legalistic mentality or even a sad scrupulosity, incapable of distinguishing between right and wrong, unable to come to a healthy decision. The Second Vatican Council, emphasizing an almost forgotten evangelical doctrine of responsible freedom for all human persons, would change much of this, but the change would not come until forty years later.

Our professors were, perhaps, adequate. Only one had a doctorate, and he was afflicted with a sort of literary myopia, believing that, because they were Catholics, such minor poets as Cardinal Newman, Francis Thompson, Coventry Patmore, Alice Meynell, and Father Faber should be studied assiduously. In holding this, and a number of other opinions, his style was not exactly conciliatory, and we learned to avoid open expression of dissent. One evening there was a debate, and the question was whether Percy Shelley or Francis Thompson was the greater poet. A vote of the audience was taken after the last speaker sat down, and the decision went overwhelmingly against Shelley. Next morning another of our faculty, before beginning his class in Euripides, glared at us and growled "Cowards!"

We came on the scene toward the end of the 400-year-old wrangling with Protestants. The Church was still in a state of siege, still in a defensive crouch. Books like *The Catholic's Ready Answer* abounded. Even up to the final examination in theology our courses had this polemical orientation, though I don't believe that we ourselves had any great interest in prolonging the old disputes; we were of Chesterton's mind:

> The North is full of tangled things,
>   and texts, and aching eyes,
> And dead is all the innocence of anger
>   and surprise;
> And Christian killeth Christian in a
>   narrow, dusty room,
> And Christian dreadeth Christ that hath
>   a newer face of doom,
> And Christian hateth Mary that God
>   kissed in Galilee,
> But Don John of Austria is riding
>   to the sea.

We would have ridden with Don John, I think. Which is not to say that we would have agreed with the Protestants, or they with us, on several critical points of doctrine, or that people on both sides did not for a long time continue to snipe at each other. Perhaps we had begun to believe that, culturally, Catholics and Protestants had settled into permanently incompatible factions, and there was no hope of ever opening lines of communication. I'm sure that at that time we did not dream of ecumenical harmony; it would require the forced juxtapositions of World War II, when we came to know one another as brethren, however separated, and the vast charity of Pope John XXII to knock down the old walls.

But back to the faculty. Generally speaking, it was not policy then to send young Jesuits to graduate school unless they were going to teach the "sacred sciences"—theology and philosophy, scripture, canon law, ecclesiastical history. For teaching other subjects the usual undergraduate preparation, supplemented by one's own inclinations and reading, was considered sufficient. American Catholics were, by and large, anti-intellectual, in part because of the Modernist crisis (of which more later), in part because they shared with other Americans a pragmatic, no-nonsense, get-it-done mentality, dedicated to achievement in brick and mortar and a quantitative evaluation of religious observance. Scholarship was not prized; our professors, though they were diligent enough in preparing and presenting their material, had published nothing and did not encourage us to go beyond a fairly superficial "appreciation" of our texts. A weakness that grew more and more serious as the years went on was the failure to provide direction. There was a great deal of raw talent in those days that should have been challenged, supervised, pointed toward this or that special interest or career. But we had no academic counselors, then or later; as a matter of fact we had no spiritual counselors, either, except for a "spiritual father," usually appointed from the ranks of the elderly retired, who dealt with us, for the most part, as a group rather than as individuals.

Happy the student who finds an approachable, sympathetic, erudite, but discerning mentor to whom he can bring his enthusiasms and, if need be, his uncertainties. It might be argued that people of that caliber are in short supply anywhere, at the best of times, yet the "acknowledgments" one finds in the preface to scholarly books speak often and gratefully of inspiration and assistance provided to the author by some such outstanding professor. The species must exist. So in the debate about the qualifications for tenure and promotion in academia—whom we should hire, a good teacher or a good researcher—some consideration should be given to the candidate's ability to inspire, and his interest in employing it.

I don't think we gave the future much thought. Even the priesthood, which we took for granted would be somewhere down the line, was so remote—ten or eleven years away at the earliest—that it did not touch us very nearly. After the long introspection of the novitiate it was exhilarating to turn one's attention from oneself and get down to a job of work—a work, be it said, undertaken consciously for the glory of God and the good of those people whom God would one day send into our lives. St. Ignatius, our founder and model, had been a "contemplative in action," and now we had the opportunity to imitate him. We had our hours of prayer daily, and from them sounded the challenge to labor, as he had put it, without counting the cost. We had that incomparable valley at our feet, and could rejoice over it as the earth turned and we saw it now magnificent in high summer, now utterly glorious in autumnal splendors, now tranquil under the moon in January, waiting for a new fall of snow. In such a setting contemplation was no effort; as St. Paul pointed out (Rom 1:20), "Since the creation of the world, invisible realities, God's eternal power and divinity, have become visible, recognized through the things he has made."

The pressures engendered by endless self-scrutiny were behind us now, but we were still living in the open, cheek by jowl in study halls and dormitories. All of us had our own quirky little preferences, our own little sins of commission and omission, and there was still no place to hide. I would realize later, when I lived in an open Army barracks or with a totally inconsiderate tent-mate in the New Guinea jungle, what efforts my classmates had made to be unselfish, and I had matter for remorse that I had done much less.

Thirty years after my class left there, Shadowbrook burned to the ground, with a loss of four lives and several permanently crippling injuries. It had been the palatial home of Andrew Carnegie—his ballroom, exquisitely panelled in golden oak, became our chapel—and it was situated on a rim of Stockbridge Bowl, looking off toward Great Barrington and the blue distance that was, they said, Connecticut. Father Fisher, whose soul responded to natural beauty and who thought that ours should, too, saw to it that we mowed the lawns and ministered tenderly to the rose garden. It was a lovely place to grow up in, and when we went back there, as we did sometimes in later years, we were struck again by its beauty. But I don't think we sentimentalized over it as some college graduates do when they return to their campuses. The experiences we had there had gone too deep, had transformed our thinking too profoundly, had involved too much effort and, yes, perplexity and pain, to admit of easy sentiment. We hoped, when the time came for us to move on, that God had supplemented our labors, or at least had taken them as earnest of our good will and done the work himself—the work of conversion and transformation we had groped for and prayed for. "We, with our unveiled faces reflecting like mirrors the brightness of the Lord, all grow brighter and brighter as we are turned into the image that we reflect" (2 Cor 3:18). Or so we devoutly hoped.

The emphasis in our first year of "Juniorate" was on poetry and belles lettres; in our second year it was a bit more practical. We were studying rhetoric now—the art of persuasion, and our thoughts naturally turned to the persuading we would be called on to do by preaching. Our models, though, were not the great Christian preachers, Chrysostom or Leo or Augustine, or even Bourdaloue or Bossuet or Newman, but Cicero and Demosthenes and the great English and Irish orators in "British Eloquence." Kleutgen's *Ars Dicendi* was a work published by a Jesuit in 1908 which I found immensely helpful. It showed you how to develop a speech by asking yourself questions about the central idea you wanted to propose, simple but suggestive questions like "who?" "what?" "where?" "by whom?" "how?" "when?" What I found most useful, however, and have employed ever since, not only for speeches and sermons but for other kinds of expository or persuasive writing, was Kleutgen's presentation of the classic oratorical model. You were to begin with an "exordium" or introduction, in the course of which you were to render your audience "benevolent, attentive, and docile." Then would follow a narrative section, introducing the subject or the occasion. This would climax with the "proposition," a precise, succinct statement of your theme or of the action you wanted your listeners to take. After indicating how you intended to develop your case (the *partitio*, or division), you would go on to the confirmation, demonstrating the truth or the advantage of your proposition. This would be the body and the longest part of your address, running usually through three or more arguments. Then, in the refutation, you would anticipate and answer the objections that might be raised against your proposal. And you would conclude with a peroration, a pungent summary of your argument with, if the occasion called for it, a ringing exhortation to do something about it. The model, as I said, has been very useful; it seems to me to be psychologically sound, and I have often wished, as I listened to endless rambling declamations or read disorganized term papers, that the orator or the author had been introduced to Kleutgen earlier in his life.

Everyone was required to write and memorize one sermon each year, and to deliver it while the community took dinner. This was a daunting experience; dinner was always a very formal meal, and in any case, as the old saying goes, it's hard to preach to your family. Not that this family was invariably attentive; we used to say that a sermon would be successful if the community stopped eating, and that never happened in my time.

I don't remember what I preached about when my turn came, but the effort went off reasonably well, and I sent a copy to my father, whom we had always teased about his critiques of sermons in the parish church, suggesting that he look at it judiciously and gauge its probable impact on a congregation. In the meantime one of the novices who had heard the sermon wrote his impressions of it in his weekly letter to his family, who were neighbors of ours at home, and of course his letter was shared with my family. Shortly thereafter my father's response arrived. I think it is important to note that my father had had to leave school after the fifth grade, when his father died and he had to bring in something to support his mother and himself. Where did he learn to write as he did?

Well, he read voraciously. He would position his old red rocker under the lamp near the kitchen stove and read till the small hours. Then he would kneel, put his head on the rocker, and pray. More than once I saw him in that posture after he had fallen asleep. Quite on his own, then, he learned the *ars dicendi*—how to write with grace and energy. He also learned a few *dicenda*—things worth saying. Which is why I have kept his letter for seventy years.

UNITED STATES POST OFFICE
BOSTON, MASSACHUSETTS

Dear Bill:

I suppose you are expecting something rather extraordinary, the supreme effort of your coldly critical father. H'm, well, your c.c. father is not gifted enough to put his impressions—at least all of his impressions—into understandable English. He can only look back over his three score and ten, and the things that stand out in his memory, the thoughts that were created, the emotions excited, the lasting influences obtained from listening to many sermons and speeches, he will try to convey to you. And if you find him repeating himself, just be charitable, and attribute it to his advancing years and approaching senility.

I read your sermon last night, read it again after talking with you, and tried to fix certain parts in my mind. But before going further, I want to say that I think it was your best effort so far. There were evidences in it of an advanced intellectuality, there was a clarity of thought, and a simplicity that was appealing. And therein, to my mind, lies success: simplicity. It is interesting—sometimes highly so—to listen while an orator pours forth a golden stream of flowery rhetoric, and one comes away exalted—temporarily. And the orator will be remembered as a wonderful speaker—but will his theme, his reasoning, remain with you? I doubt it. The earnest man who puts his thoughts into simple words—necessarily of course with enough personality and magnetism behind them—is far more apt to have a thinking audience leaving his church or hall.

The first sermon that impressed me—strangely enough by a Jesuit missionary in the old Gate of Heaven Church—was one on infidelity. I even remember his name: a Father Stanton, a big, powerful man with a big, powerful voice, but with language so simple that even I, a mere boy at the time, missed not a word of it, nor failed to understand any part of it. And when you consider that that was more than 35 years ago, you will appreciate that simplicity is oratory in its greatest form.

A little later on, and I wasn't much older, either—I may have told you this story before, but it will do no harm to repeat it—I was at a political rally one night, and the principal speaker of the evening was our late senator, Henry Cabot Lodge. He spoke for over two hours, and during that period never did he use a word or an expression that went over the heads of the veriest illiterate present. How do I know? I'm sure of it. I can even remember his subject: "The Ship Subsidy Bill." And he made it so clear to all of us that we came away marvelling at the genius of the man, but not forgetting how simple after all was it to understand what was hitherto an enigma to us.

And so it went on. I have heard sermons and speeches, and many times, I must confess, I was immensely relieved when they were concluded. I daresay everyone has had such an experience, and it is no reflection on the interest that should be taken in the subject, rather it is the speaker's inability to put his thoughts into a simple reasoning strain, to prove to you that two and two make four, and cannot possibly make five.

Now about your own work. It wouldn't be natural if I didn't read your sermon with a glow of pride, and if you can, on closing, leave me with a little misty feeling in the eyes, all the more reason for that glow of pride. You know of course that I am hardly capable of even attempting to diagnose each sentence and paragraph— my training has been somewhat neglected along those lines—but I am arrogantly conscious that I can detect flaws, and you know my penchant for argumentation.

And still I would not consider it a flaw. Rather a habit that may grow on you, and would reflect on the general excellence of the whole. I refer to your using the same word too often, as in your sermon—"eyes," "the eyes of Christ." That and that only seemed to me to be the only discordant note. What do your other critics think? The rest of it was splendid, and you do have a faculty of making a closing that many men do not possess. How often have I writhed in my seat as I listened to a preacher floundering around endeavoring to climax his appeal, and often failing most dismally.

You may say, "Oh, you are just catering to entertainment." We do not go to church to be entertained, I know that, and I do not expect to be, but what I do know is that first the interest must be aroused, and then conclusions proved, and proved in a manner that will retain the interest. For after all what are we but children, with but child-like faith, and the gift of that faith is the ever-present desire to know more about God, and blessed be he that can give us that knowledge in words that our puny intellects can grasp.

And that, as our colored janitor would say, "am de sum total" of my unimpassioned criticism of your sermon. To go further would be very likely to say less. I only hope that I may be spared for the day when I will sit in one of the benches of the church and gaze upward at you as you from the pulpit put the word of God in simple, understandable language. H'm, even then I'll probably follow you into the vestry and take issue with you on some part of your sermon. And you will have to stand for it, because, you see, unlike the good wine, I do not improve with age. You will find it more difficult to argue with me—no, not on the Almighty nor on his commandments, but on your manner of explaining them.

I wish I could find words to make you understand the thrill it gives us to receive a word of praise of you from an unexpected quarter. Your mother told you about Mrs. O'Brien's sending us Bill Burns' letter to read. Well, I want you to know that we do not think he was enlarging a particle. And I say that in the light of cool judgment of reading your effort, of picturing the preacher delivering them, and the necessary deductions which are to be made. Of your rather high-pitched voice, that is but nervousness; your voice is not naturally that way—doesn't run in the family. To overcome all that tendency to nervousness you must say to yourself, "I have a firm belief in my subject, an intelligent manner of preaching it, and God himself is behind me, so why be nervous? Not for myself, surely, but for the millions who hear the Word and do not heed it."

I find now that I have spent more of my Uncle Sam's time than he would care to have me spend—if he knew it, which he doesn't.

This, you see, is Sunday, and my work is all done, for a while at least, and I am master of all I survey on this floor. Tomorrow 'twill be different.

Sometimes, when the irritating days draw to a close, and the trials and temptations are many, and the inclination is to pour forth in vituperative words our dislike for insufferable and intolerable conditions and those who institute them, we find that on reaching the haven of home a word or two from someone who tells us that he is happy, that his health is good, and that he is about his Master's business, does more to aid tranquillity than anything else we can think of.

So do you keep that way, for we expect much of you. And God does, too.

    All well.

                    Love,
                    Father

    Sun. 4/7/29

CHAPTER 4

The Timeless Philosophy

IN JUNE OF 1929 OUR CLASS MOVED FROM THE BERKSHIRES TO Weston, a small town only fifteen miles outside of Boston, but curiously remote from the metropolis. It was affluent, Yankee, Republican, Protestant—all the things we were not. However, we had almost no contacts with our neighbors. As at Shadowbrook, we were a self-contained community. I have often wondered what the townspeople made of us. They surely saw us out on walks through their streets, dressed in hand-me-down, seedy, even bizarre clothing. St. Francis, according to the story (is it in the *Fioretti*?), once said to his followers, "Let us go and preach a sermon." So he and they, in their worn habits and sandals, walked up and down in Assisi and returned home, and his followers cried, "You said we were going to preach a sermon!" "We just did," Francis answered. Whether our rambles around the quiet Weston roads had any edifying impact is known, I suppose, only to the recording angel. We laughed a lot; we bothered no one; we had no female companions. We must have given cause for speculation, even for mystification, perhaps for some irritation. At the time we never gave it a thought.

In those years some of the old Yankee fortunes were drying up, and the new generation, unable or unwilling to pay taxes on manorial estates, was selling them off at throwaway prices. Religious communities, on the other hand, were revelling in an unprecedented prosperity, not so much of money as of candidates, so monasteries, novitiates, and seminaries began to appear where once all was gracious living. Bishops, who had to be consulted before the religious moved in, were mindful of the burdens borne by small towns, and were careful not to permit several such tax-free institutions to locate in the same area. But there was inevitably some resentment, and even—ridiculous as it now seems—some suspicion. Many of the old estates were situated on hills overlooking the local village. In Catholic hands, could they not serve as command posts or even vantage points for bombardment on the day when the Pope would invade the United States? Insinuations even more fantastic than these circulated during Al Smith's campaign for the presidency, and contributed largely to his defeat.

The wheel has come full circle now, and the religious have had to sell the estates or convert them to other uses. The seminary at Weston, which housed two hundred and fifty in our time, would, if it had not become a retreat house and an infirmary, be occupied today by no more than thirty students. The house was enormous; those studying philosophy lived in the south wing, those studying theology in the north; a connecting section was devoted to the chapel, the dining room, classrooms, the library, and rooms for the faculty.

After the warmth of the small, golden oak chapel at Shadowbrook, some found the spacious, silver-and-stone chapel at Weston less inviting. They nicknamed it "the Temple of Reason." "A chapel!" said Cardinal O'Connell when he first saw it. "Call it a basilica!" Surprisingly, for that period, there were no statues in it, no shrines, and perhaps it served, focusing as it did all attention on the altar, as a corrective for easy sentiment. On the other hand, it may have helped to develop the rigidly intellectual mentality that Jesuits were accused, in the sixties, of bringing to things spiritual.

On the day of our arrival we were met at the door by the class ahead of us and escorted about the house. John McCarthy showed me the chapel, the dining room, the classrooms, and finally a room on the third floor that had my name on it. We chatted pleasantly for a while, and then he left, and when he left he closed the door behind him. After four years in the open, I had a room of my own. I sat back, put my feet on the desk, and said to myself, "Now maybe I can figure all this out."

The grounds were extensive. There was ample space for playing fields, tennis and handball courts, and a nine-hole golf course. The golf course was constructed under the supervision of Father Joseph Hurley, our "Father Minister," whose accomplishments on our behalf, together with the unfathomable answers he would give when we asked a permission, entitle him to a biography. Jesuits from other parts of the world are struck, when they visit us, by our fondness, here in New England, for nicknames. I think the tendency was encouraged, at least, by the profusion among us of Irish surnames; we had to find a way of distinguishing the Sullivans, Sheas, O'Briens, and McCarthys one from another. Whatever the reason, many of the scholastics and most of the faculty had names which replaced, in common use, the one they had received at baptism. Fortunately, the faculty were not always aware of how they were generally known. Father Hurley, for reasons lost in history, was called (when he was not within earshot) "Happy Hurley," and this was in time shortened to "Haps." So of course any directive coming from him was seen as obliging "per Haps." As someone said, there was plenty of time at Weston to polish such bon mots.

Well, then, we became philosophers. And it was scholastic philosophy. We began with minor logic, a course in the rules for correct thinking and argumentation. It called for a lot of memorizing of definitions, a lot of learning what might be called an intellectual close-order drill. We passed then to major logic, epistemology. When, and under what conditions, can the mind apprehend reality external to itself? How trustworthy are the operations of the senses, the intellect? What are the merits of deduction as compared with induction? Is certitude obtainable? What is truth (Pilate's cynical question)? How does one know it when one sees it?

Then there was general metaphysics, or ontology, which took us on a high-altitude tour of topics like being as such, possible beings, change, substance and accident, relations, causality. The principles we derived from these investigations were useful subsequently; for instance, the principle of contradiction, "Nothing can be and not be at the same time and under the same respect," or the principle of sufficient reason, "Whatever is has a sufficient reason for its being." It was a relief, however, to come down from such rarefied elevations and go to the chemistry laboratory, where at the time we were studying tangible matter and its properties.

Second year was fascinating. We were studying ourselves, body and soul, and the universe that sheltered and fed us. The priest who usually taught biology, and who limited his course to botany and zoology, was away that year, and his replacement, who had been a dentist before studying for the priesthood, gave us the course in human anatomy he himself had followed in dental school. At the same time we were exploring psychology—rational psychology, as it was called, not "experimental"—investigating the nature of life, the function of the senses, the origin of ideas, the freedom of the will, and the spirituality of the soul as the substantial principle or "form" of the human body. Lectures and experiments in physics helped us to wonder at (if not to comprehend altogether) the munificent endowment that is ours in light, sound, heat, fluids, and electricity, and in cosmology we pondered notions like quantity, space, time, and especially the origin and ultimate purpose of the universe.

In our third year we had eye-opening courses in geology and astronomy, which showed us how much the human mind had discovered about the planet Earth and the vast reaches of interstellar space—and how much was still to be learned. And in our metaphysics we moved on to the peak of our speculations, to the *mysterium tremendum et fascinans*. What could the human mind, quite independently of revelation, learn about the prodigious genius which had devised and provided all this? It couldn't have come about as the result of some cosmic accident, could it? Was that enormous power and intelligence a person? If so, to what extent was he still interested or involved in our sublunar activities? Was he still physically concurring with us, even providentially guiding us, yet in ways that left our free choice intact? And if that were the case, how explain the presence in our world of moral and physical evil?

Another thing: we were not alone in our world. We had relationships and responsibilities to the Person who had brought us into being, to one another, and even to ourselves. So in ethics (again arguing simply from reason, not from any religious premises) we began to inquire into the purpose of human life and the morality of conduct. We studied the concepts of duty, of law, of conscience, of virtue and vice. Do we have an obligation to be religious? To take reasonable care of our health? What is justice? Who has rights, and why must they be respected? How stable should marriage be? How extensive is the authority of the state, and what are the functions of government?

Philosophy, obviously, was the *pièce de résistance* at this banquet of knowledge. For dessert, so to speak, we had some options: higher mathematics, aesthetics, Hebrew, classics, Anglo-Saxon literature, advanced chemistry and physics, the history of education, one or another modern language. It was an ample repast, and it should have been more nourishing than, in retrospect, it now seems to have been. I think the chief reason for this was our continued isolation. We were all (to keep the metaphor) eating the identical meal. There was no one, faculty or students, who came from a sharply different background, who might have given us a taste of some slightly different menu. It would have been stimulating to meet and discuss questions with lay students, or even seminarians from another religious order, like the Dominicans, whose doctrine on some knotty points differed from ours. It would have been healthy for us to be shaken up by a really challenging lecturer from outside the house.

Our isolation for so many years indicated how immobile the Church was at that time. And of course it had the effect of encouraging immobility in many of us. The world about us was changing at a furious pace, but we had no personal experience of the changes, and since our own situation was reasonably serene we assumed that things could and should go on as they always had. Our courses in church history were not very good; at least they did not demonstrate that the world to which the Church was missioned has never been static, and that therefore, if it was not to be considered quite irrelevant, the Church would have to look hard at new developments and change its style and structures and language to meet them. On this count our education, almost exclusively in the literary classics and the *philosophia perrenis*, failed us—or it did so because we were so out of touch with our contemporary world. There were those of us who could applaud a book called *The Thirteenth, Greatest of Centuries*, published at that time, and nostalgically wish that century back again.

Not only were we carefully sequestered and sheltered from contaminating influences (although by this time we were in our mid-twenties), but it was not suggested that we look appraisingly at the people who were shaping our culture. Most of their writings were on the *Index of Forbidden Books*, anyway, and could be read only with special permission. We did see some citations of Marx—but only to reject him. Darwin and Freud were not seriously proposed. The house library was locked; permission to enter it had to be obtained *"toties quoties"* from the faculty librarian. We were driven back, therefore, on our textbooks and such other manuals as were considered safe.

"Philosophy," as a result, became in large part an exercise in regurgitation. We memorized a number of "theses" or propositions, established the connection of each with those already seen, defined precisely every term involved, listed the "adversaries" of the thesis (whom we never read), and then went on to demonstrate its truth with the "iron logic" of the syllogism. Objections and contrary ar-

guments were neatly disposed of by making distinctions "in form."
Then we were ready for the next thesis.

Our isolation was again the villain of the piece—not a physical isolation this time, but an intellectual one. In 1879 Pope Leo
XIII, in the encyclical *Aeterni Patris*, recommended scholasticism
as the ideal means of uniting philosophy and theology, and so of
presenting a coherent whole of all that the human mind might learn
from reason and revelation. Since, as candidates for the priesthood, we would of course be studying theology later, we had to become acquainted with philosophy, the "handmaid" of theology.
Well, no one of us today regrets, I think, that we spent seven years
in the contemplation of that magnificent synthesis. It is a towering
achievement, one that gratifies and satisfies the mind as a good
meal does the body. But we had reservations about the way it was
presented. For one thing, it was the only system we really looked
at. Again, it was put before us in such a starched, rigid style.
And, by and large, we never guessed its fascinating history—the
personalities, the controversies that might have put flesh on its bare
bones.

In October of our first year at Weston the stock market
crashed and the Great Depression began. Now we were permitted
a daily newspaper, the old Boston *Herald*—not the tabloid that has
recently appropriated the name, but the sober Republican journal
whose news columns seemed always to reflect the interests of the
financial community. Once, years after the Depression, I checked
the *Herald* for several months and never saw a front page without
a story on money. Occasionally we might see the sedate *Transcript,* which was of course a Boston institution. Its local repute
was parodied in the familiar limerick:

> There was a young girl from Back Bay,
> In her youth was exceeding blasé.
>   While still in her teens
>   She refused to eat beans,
> And once—once—threw the *Transcript* away.

The *Transcript* did provide intelligent news coverage, at a hu-
mane noise level, and its reviews of books, music, and the arts
were, in general, excellent. The political sympathies of the *Post*
were Democratic, which made it the favorite paper of Boston's
Catholics at that time, but we did not subscribe to it. (I don't
know who made such decisions.) Nor did we read the *Globe,*
which was then a mild, family-style journal, featuring neighbor-

hood news. The *Globe* has since gone on to much loftier journalistic heights, taking over—with a high moral tone, of course, intent only on protecting the community—some of the district attorney's functions. Since Watergate, apparently, every cub reporter's ambition must be to ferret out scandals, real or imagined, and call the activity "investigative reporting."

But to get back to the Depression—to what earlier generations knew as "hard times." The 1930's were indeed that: banks failed, factories shut down, mortgages were foreclosed, marriages were postponed, even professional people sold apples in the street. The popular song, "Brother, Can You Spare a Dime?" summed up the era. But again, our curious isolation from the real world kept all that at a distance. Our superiors had financial worries, but they did not share them with us. We went to class, conned our textbooks, prayed and played just as we would have if things had been normal. Our families, on the other hand, tightened their belts and went without, but said nothing to us, lest they worry us and even, forsooth, distract us from our holy calling. My brother, for example, recently married and expecting his first child, was told on Christmas Eve that his services would not be required in the New Year. The old man who had founded the firm died, and the heirs, scenting disaster, pulled out all their money. Fran caught on for a short time with another wool company, but as soon as they felt the pinch he was on the street again. Then he delivered milk, running up and down tenement stairs; he clerked behind the counter at Schulte's cigar store; he welded steel in a boiler factory until his eyes gave out. At last before falling seriously ill, he swung a pick and shovel for the WPA, and counted himself fortunate to have even that. An uncle of mine, who owned a chain of seven restaurants, watched helplessly as, one by one, they failed. Meanwhile, Mr. Coolidge talked about a return to "normalcy" and Mr. Hoover promised prosperity "just around the corner." It was not just a hard time; it was an ugly time, because, a world away, the booted Nazis were goose-stepping into Austria and Czechoslovakia, Mussolini was grabbing at Ethiopia, and the Japanese, in China, were laying the foundations of their "Greater Asia Co-Prosperity Sphere." How painfully ironic that the only way out of our economic swamp was through Churchill's "blood, sweat, and tears"— the blood of Dunkirk, Corregidor, and St. Lô; the sweat of Burma and the Kokada Trail, the tears of Auschwitz and Lubiyanka, the Katyn Forest, Coventry, Dresden. *Kyrie eleison.*

By the time the second semester of our third year rolled around we were writing the thesis for our M.A. degree and preparing for an hour's oral examination covering the three years' work in philosophy. But we were getting very restless; we had now been in "formation" for seven years, and we were itching to put the product to work in some apostolic enterprise. We had also been in strict seclusion for seven years, and the prospect of a little liberty, a little contact with the world "out there," was exciting. What we called "regency," a two- or three-year assignment as a teacher, usually, in one of our schools, was coming up. We didn't know until the last moment where we would be sent, but it didn't matter. We were spoiling for action.

CHAPTER 5

And Gladly Teach

IN THAT SUMMER OF 1932 THE NEW ENGLAND PROVINCE OF THE
Society had only four schools: Boston College High School, Boston College, the College of the Holy Cross, and St. George's College in Jamaica. Only one of us was selected to go to St. George's; the rest of us were assigned pretty evenly to the other three schools. Our superiors tried to match the needs of the schools with our talents and inclinations, but did not always succeed. One man who had majored in chemistry for three years found himself assigned to teach poetry and belles lettres.

We went on vacation with the classes ahead of us, and one night they entertained us with a parody of Gilbert and Sullivan:

> When you were at Weston you used to drink
> All sorts of knowledge from the foaming brink
> Of Wisdom's fountain and philosophy,
> And so you all got ready for the regency.
> *Chorus*:
> And so we all got ready for the regency.
>
> You stuck to your studies like the well-known leech,
> But the studies that you studied you will never teach.
> *Chorus*:
> We stuck to our studies like the well-known leech,
> But the studies that we studied we will never teach.
>
> When you were at Weston you probably thought
> That things in general would be as they ought;
> You studied the matter with the vain idee
> That maybe you could use it in the regency.
> *Chorus*:
> That maybe we could use it in the regency.
>
> You studied your philosophy from day to day,
> But you'll soon be buying doughnuts for the school cafe.

Chorus:
We studied our philosophy from day to day,
But we'll soon be buying doughnuts for the school cafe.

When you were at Weston you had the hope
That reasoning would show you how to cope
With problems classical and tough antics
From dirty little urchins with their low-down tricks.
Chorus:
From dirty little urchins with their low-down tricks.

But you'll never stop a spitball when it comes your way
With a transcendental reference to an *ens a se*.
Now that you've left Weston you had better shun
All thought of study as a temptation;
You soon will recognize the difference
Between philosophy and common sense.
Chorus:
Between philosophy and common sense.

So put your volumes on the library shelves
And go out and show the youngsters how to bless themselves.
Chorus:
We'll put our volumes on the library shelves,
And go out and show the youngsters how to bless themselves.

Full chorus:
For we're in the regency, and truly we deserve it,
For we took our turn and served it,
And we're in the regency,
Yes, we're i-i-i-i-i-i-in the regency!

In 1932 Holy Cross was in its ninetieth year, having been founded by Bishop Fenwick of Boston, who named it for his cathedral. It was built on a steep hill, so giving rise to the hoary joke that it was built on a bluff and conducted by the Jesuits on the same principle. At one time, as we saw in ancient photographs, it was surrounded by rolling meadows, but in the 19th century the American Steel and Wire Company invaded the meadows and laid out factories, warehouses, and railroad yards. Now the little stream known as the Blackstone River wandered pathetically through the soot and sludge of the industrial revolution. In Worcester itself at that time there was little of a cultural or entertaining nature, and the students said that if you went to Holy Cross you had to find your heaven on the hill.

The enrollment at the time stood at 1094—all men, mostly from New England, New York, and New Jersey. Boarding students, as compared with the "dayhops" who commuted from Worcester and the surrounding towns, made up a majority. Many of these had attended Jesuit high schools: Boston College High School, Regis or Xavier in New York, St. Peter's in Jersey City. There was an abundance of talent on campus, but there were a goodly number of slow coaches as well, people who would normally never have been admitted, but in those straitened days (we were in the very slough of the Great Depression) the rooms had to be filled so that the doors could be kept open. But the departures at the end of freshman and even at the end of the first semester were many. Of 57 students who enrolled for the Bachelor of Science degree in 1932, only 18 took the degree four years later.

Holy Cross was (and remains) a liberal arts college, striving to impart a liberal education. Its alumni should, one thinks, feel privileged to be called "liberals," but the term has become in our day an epithet, capable even of blasting the hopes of a candidate for the national presidency. Alexander Pope's dictum on education, "The proper study of mankind is man," is famous, but Plato said it first: "The noblest of all studies is the study of what men and women are and of what life they should live." Plato elaborated on that definition in his treatise on law: "By education I mean that training in excellence from youth upwards which makes one passionately desire to be a perfect citizen, and teaches how one may rule, and obey, with justice. This is the only education which deserves the name; the other sort of training, which aims at the acquisition of wealth or bodily strength, is not worthy to be called education at all." Sir Richard Livingstone, President of Corpus Christi College at Oxford, pointed out that a free person must be more than a breadwinner; he or she must know not only how to make a living, but how to live. Liberal education has for its purpose the making of complete men and women, who have bodies, minds, characters, each of which has its proper virtues, and each of which should be developed not because they produce happiness or success, but because they are good things in themselves. And Professor Mark Van Doren insisted that a liberal education makes the person competent not merely to know or do, but also, and indeed chiefly, to be. The last sign of education one can reveal, he said, is serenity in decrepitude, a sense that there is still something to be if not to do.

At Holy Cross there was an unrelenting effort to attain these educational ends, grandiose or obsolete though they may seem to be today. Even the students majoring in science had to carry the "humanistic" courses; their choice meant, simply, that their burden was heavier. ("Gosh, Mister," said Freshman Jack Scott, a "premed," as he raced out of the lab in an effort to get to dinner before Brother McCarthy closed the doors, "You don't see daylight in this course!")

Discipline on campus was, in retrospect, mind-boggling. All resident students had to be at Mass at seven in the morning. Classes began at nine and ran till about three; attendance was scrupulously taken and someone from the Prefect of Discipline's office collected the record. Dinner was served at 5:30; then everyone had to attend evening devotions in the chapel. Attendance was taken here, too, as it had been at Mass; you could lose your weekend pass if you were delinquent. At seven o'clock the corridor prefect, usually one of the younger Fathers, checked to see that every student was in his room. If you wanted to go to the library, or to visit some other corridor, you had to have written permission. A chit signed by your prefect, with the time of your departure marked on it, had to be presented to the prefect at your destination, who would make sure that no significant time had elapsed. A similar routine had to be followed when you returned. No radios were permitted in private rooms. At ten o'clock there would be a mad scramble to the cafeteria for a snack, and at ten-thirty the prefect would patrol the corridor and see that all lights were out. Classes were held every day except Sunday; there were half-holidays on Thursday and Saturday, and on Saturday you could leave campus (if you had no "demerits" for infraction of the rules) after signing out. Freshmen had to return by 10:30; upperclassmen might stay out until midnight. All students had to make the annual retreat of three days; there were not many nonCatholics on campus, but they were required to make it, too, and they were not excused from religion classes or from attendance at chapel.

I wonder now why there was not an occasional revolt. Occasionally some blithe young spirits would slide down a drainpipe and go off to town, hoping that a confederate would be handy to open the back door when they returned, but they were usually caught and campused for the rest of the term. And after the first snowfall there would probably be a free-for-all snowball fight, summarily broken up by the Prefect of Discipline, whose appearance in long black cassock and biretta was enough to subdue the riot. Brother McCarthy was the autocrat of the dining room, and any mischief there meant that the offender was ushered out straightway. If you appealed his edict you were given the standard answer: "All Holy Cross men look alike to me, Mister." And out you went.

All this seems now to have been a kind of petty tyranny, more suited to a penitentiary than a college. But the homes from which these students came were generally not less exacting; "permissive" parents would not come on the scene for forty years yet; authority (and the college deliberately assumed the *in loco parentis* attitude) still elicited a compliant if not always cheerful obedience. The striking thing was that there was a real affection between boarders and prefects, as there was between students and professors, and that many such friendships endured for years after graduation. If a particular prefect or professor was rigid or even harsh, he was accorded an easy tolerance, on the supposition that he did what he did out of an exaggerated sense of duty. He might mellow some day, and meanwhile one could look forward to a more enlightened dispensation.

One of my extracurricular assignments was to "prefect" the students' weekday Mass. Each student had his place; if he was not in it I had to record the fact for the Discipline office. Their alarm clocks pulled them out of their warm beds as close to seven o'clock as possible and sent them scurrying across the frozen campus to the chapel, where some simply slumped down and resumed their slumbers. In not a few cases it was obvious that pants had been hurriedly pulled on over pajamas.

Ten of the Fathers heard confessions during Mass, and were kept busy. A few students had missals; the rest fingered rosaries or knelt in silence. There was no singing, not even any doodling on the organ. The Mass, of course, was in Latin—a faint murmur in the distant sanctuary. The Scripture was not read in English, or even in audible Latin. Almost everyone received Holy Communion, their only active participation.

All this vaguely bothered me, though I couldn't at the time have given a clear reason why, but an amusing incident one morning made me thoughtful. One of my freshmen, as we emerged from the chapel, was the center of a group of his laughing classmates. "Mister, come over and see this," they shouted. Bill, who had been partying the night before on Vernon Hill, had evidently jumped out of bed and raced to the chapel without washing his face, and now his face was covered with pretty little cupid's bows in unmistakable lipstick. The hoots of laughter were louder because Bill was considered and was in fact shy and bashful.

Later that day I stopped the Rector. "Father," I said, "I've been reading in *The Queen's Work* about a new way for the congregation to assist at Mass. It's called the Dialogue Mass."

"What is it?" he asked.

"Well, the congregation makes the responses usually made by the servers, and recites prayers like the *Gloria* and the *Creed* in unison with the celebrant. Could we do that here at Holy Cross?"

He was a kind and gentle man, and he pondered for a moment. Then he explained that it wouldn't be possible. "You see," he said, "The boys go to confession during Mass, and the confessors wouldn't be able to hear them if there were all that noise in the chapel."

Um. Somehow, I felt, there had to be an answer to this objection, but I didn't know what it was. I began to realize, however, in a dim sort of way, that a renewal of the liturgy would involve more sweeping changes of attitude than I had imagined.

My teacher in high school wrote to me after I had entered the Society and urged me to begin praying then for the boys whom some day I should have in class. I did, every day, and maybe that's why my years of teaching were so flawlessly happy and fulfilling. In the magazine *America* I found a prayer composed by a Father Joseph de Jouvancy, S.J., and made it my own:

> Lord Jesus Christ, you did not hesitate to endure for these boys a most bitter death, you hold them in boundless love, you bade the children be brought to you, you accept as bestowed on yourself whatever is done for the least one of these. I beg and implore you, keep them in your name. They are yours, and you have given them to me. Put your words into my mouth, and open their hearts so that they may learn to love you. Turn your face away from my sins, so that no obstacle to your loving kindness may be caused by me. Grant that I may fulfill with prudence, holiness, and courage this task you have given me of teaching these young people, to your glory, which alone I keep before me as my aim in this my duty.

It didn't take long to get acquainted. I had a little room on third Fenwick, and it was a poor night when there were not six or seven knocks on the door. Sometimes they brought a real problem, academic or other; more often they had a question that simply justified their coming in, and they stayed for sociability. Harold and Bob were both lovesick and couldn't concentrate on Newman's *Essay on Literature* or on anything else. They didn't survive the first semester. Nick and George had to leave, too, for lack of funds; George discovered that his family had been stinting themselves seriously to keep him in school. Ernie was a great raconteur. He was complaining one night in October about his sore arm, and when we asked what was wrong with it he told us in vivid detail how, as quarterback on his high school team, he ran back a punt, scored the winning touchdown, but fell against the goalpost and broke the arm. I became a little sceptical when, in January, he described how the arm was broken when he crashed into the boards after scoring the winning goal in hockey. And his mother unwittingly made any further versions of the story impossible when she explained to one of his classmates that he had broken the arm in a fall down the cellar stairs at home.

My impression of Jerry was that he was bright but very lazy; he found his niche later, however, in the Navy, and rose to the rank of captain before retiring. Bill was from the South; he was redheaded and shy, and had an engaging drawl. "At mah hagh school graduation," he said, "Ah was asked why ah didn't go up and shake hands with mah teachers. Ah said ah didn't go *in* for that sorta thing." John was a patient, careful student of science, and did well in all his classes except English. Poetry to him was simply incomprehensible. One day in class we were reading Francis Thompson's "The Hound of Heaven," and came on the line, "Evening lit her tapers round the day's dead sanctities." "What's that mean?" I asked John. In complete frustration he said, "I don't know." I turned to his neighbor, Paul, and put the same question. "Why," said Paul, "That means that the stars came out." "Right," I said. "Now do you see that, John?" John burst out: "Well, if he meant stars why didn't he say stars?" Early in Advent I urged the class to buy Christmas cards that would carry some indication of the real meaning of the feast—not reindeer or snow scenes or periwigged English noblemen smoking long pipes and quaffing pints of ale. "Whose birthday is this?" I demanded. So my Christmas mail was full of mangers and angels, with one exception. Santa Claus, pulled in his sleigh by Donder and Blitzen, and no doubt by Rudolph of the red nose, arrived in my mail box. On the card was the seemingly gruff greeting: "This isn't your kind of card, but I'm broke. Merry Christmas. John." And, for fifty-six years now, I have had a Christmas letter from John.

Tom was a madcap, just sixteen, whom I made my beadle (my liaison with the class) because I felt that someone should keep an eye on him. He came to my room Hallowe'en night, dressed in a tuxedo and, of all things, a top hat. "Where are you going?" I asked. "Over to Vernon Hill," he said. "Walking?" "Sure." "Not in that outfit," I protested. "Oh, no problem." So he went, but the top hat was too great a temptation for the townies. Someone threw a stone that knocked it off. Tom turned to give battle, but was overwhelmed. Next day he brought a black eye and several nasty gashes to class. Parenthetically, I met him ten years later in the infantry, where he was a battalion commander and a major, two ranks higher than the mere lieutenant who had been his professor.

Billy came to Holy Cross to learn Greek, which candidates for the Society had to learn in those days. At the end of the year he applied, but was turned down because of poor eyesight. I told him there had been a large number of applicants that year, and suggested that he should return to college and try again after sophomore. His doctor asserted that, while there was some deformity in the eye, it would not get worse, but he was turned down again, and came to my room in despair. Not knowing how to advise him, I knocked at Father Louis Wheeler's door; he was giving a retreat at the time on campus. "Tell the boy to go to the diocesan seminary and get the oil on his hands," Father Wheeler said; "and then, perhaps, if he's of the same mind, he can try again." So Bill went off to Montreal, was ordained in due course and invited me to be the deacon at his first Mass. When I was leaving at the end of the day I asked him if he still thought of becoming a Jesuit. "Oh, Father," he said, "That would have been for me a terrible mistake." And he was a happy and dedicated pastor thereafter until his death, forty years later.

When they graduated I was back at Weston, studying theology, and knew I would not be permitted to attend commencement. So I started in January and wrote each day a note of congratulations and good wishes, and sent them all up to Holy Cross in June. Some of the replies did not come in until a year or more later, and then I was struck by the frequency of reports like "Not much of a job yet, Father," or simply "Unemployed; please pray that I can get something soon." Jim was "smashing baggage" in Grand Central Station, and "glad to have the work." Charlie wrote: "I hope I can land something steady (he was working as a barker in an amusement park in Rhode Island), because I'd like to get married to that Regis girl in a few years and raise kids for God and Holy Cross. The happy days on the Hill are over and I shall miss them more and more as time goes on, but I have the consolation that no matter what happens to me during life no one can ever take away from me those happy memories that will be with me to my dying day, and after that, I hope."

Only a handful assemble now for reunions of the Golden Jubilarians. Pete was killed in action in Germany in 1945; Bob died somewhere in the South Pacific aboard a destroyer. Jim, ordained only six years, died in a freak accident. Tony took a degree in law, enlisted when war broke out, and came home to spend the rest of a long life in a mental hospital. Dick wrote, ten years after graduation, "Just a note to let you know that the baby died on August 14 and was buried on the feast of the Assumption. We are recovering from the shock with the knowledge that everything possible was done for the baby and it was just to be. Also that other people have had more troubles than we. We both want to thank you for all the prayers you offered for our little fellow." Now, when I celebrate Mass, memories of "my boys" crowd in on me, and then I am glad that we have the new Eucharistic Prayers:

> "From age to age you gather a people to yourself, so that from east to west a perfect offering may be made to the glory of your name." And again: "Have mercy on us all. Make us worthy to share eternal life with Mary, the apostles, and all the saints who have done your will throughout the ages."

The teacher is the one adult outside the family whose instruction and personality mold the lives of most people. We drink up the teacher's standards and principles more copiously than the information he or she proffers, and they live with us much longer. This is so true that sometimes, when people asked me what I taught, I answered, only half-jokingly, "Myself." For better or for worse, I shared my outlook, my faith, my values, myself with younger brothers and sisters. I keep my reservations about the worth of all that, but in the nature of things there is no other way. Reflections of this sort can and should make anyone in my profession tremble a bit at one's responsibilities. On the other hand, the teacher can and should be exhilarated by the shining opportunities that every classroom presents, to say nothing of those even more profitable encounters outside the classroom, which come about only because a relationship of curiosity or questing or trust has been somehow established in class. Reverberations are set up that echo in the inmost chambers of some souls, apparently, forever: an off-hand remark, a chance exchange of conflicting opinion, a happy bon mot . . . Twenty-five years later the old student says, "Father, I'll never forget what you said one day in class," and not only can you not remember saying it, you can't remember even thinking it. It's humiliating, unless one believes he is being used, and indeed offers himself to be used, prays that he may be useful. The teacher, precisely because of his or her eminence, and because he or she is "making waves" that wash up, yes, on the eternal shores, needs to ask for many virtues, and to exemplify them.

Several quite unrelated incidents in my own experience illustrate how a teacher's handling of a situation can linger in the student's memory and influence him long after he has forgotten whatever it was the teacher gave as formal instruction. The family used to take a sly delight in reminding me that as a child in kindergarten I refused to pirouette around the schoolroom, arms uplifted and gently waving. The class regarded this mutiny with consternation, and the teacher sent for my mother, who, it may be supposed, could give no reasonable explanation why her child was unwilling to share with normal children the pretty illusion of fluttering and dipping like the silky butterfly. More distinct is the memory of gouging my initials on the varnished top of a fifth-grade desk, and of another parental summons—more grim this time, since it was my father who came to discuss my criminal tendencies. I recall vividly how the teacher's hair was brushed straight back from her very white forehead, and pinned in neat little buns over her ears. I remember her long-suffering, this-hurts-me-more-than-it-does-you expression, and how the lines about my father's mouth tightened when the extensive damage was pointed out. I remember sunny afternoons after school, in bitter solitude chafing the desktop with sandpaper until the offensive scorings were smooth, and the janitor called in to apply fresh varnish.

But the most painful of my memories, one that keeps yet the ancient sting of justice overthrown, concerns a morning in the sixth grade. How clear across the years are the splotched green and yellow globe, the new words on the blackboard, and the dreary chart that was, for me, the pointless, hated multiplication table. Miss Dixon, our teacher, used to say that she knew how to handle boys.

Her classes *were* rather more interesting than those of other teachers I remember. But every spring the school board used to conduct city-wide examinations in arithmetic, called "Curtis Tests." We would be given a number of problems in addition or multiplication and a prescribed number of minutes in which to work them out. Then we would be graded as to speed and accuracy. To prepare us for these momentous events, dreaded by most of us, tests given in previous years would be administered.

I can see the classroom vividly still. Miss Dixon would distribute the printed sheets face down, and then stand at her desk with one hand raised and her eyes on her watch. "Begin!" she would cry, and we would flip over the sheets with a loud slap and start furiously to add, subtract, or whatever. After the appointed minutes had elapsed she would shout, "Stop!" and all the frantic calculating had to end.

"Now," she would say, "These are the correct answers. Compare them with your answers. We'll see who the bright pupils are. How many did you have right, Beatrice?"

"Nine, Miss Dixon."

"Nine out of ten. Very good, Beatrice. And how many did you have right, Ralph?"

"Eight, Miss Dixon."

"Good. And you, Margaret?"

"Eight, Miss Dixon."

"Good. And you, Henry?"

"Ten, Miss Dixon."

"Excellent, Henry. And you, William?"

I drew a deep breath. "None," I said.

The class was (or pretended to be) horrified. "Oooooooh," they said, and my frustration and mortification struck out at them like a cornered animal.

"Shut up," I said, and then there really was a silence. Miss Dixon waited.

"You will apologize to the class, William."

"I won't."

"You will apologize or leave the class."

"They should apologize to me!"

"Leave the class and don't come back until you are ready to apologize."

I left, and for three days managed without going near the school to leave home and return at times roughly coinciding with school hours. But something gave me away at last, and my mother demanded the story. Alas, unwell and preoccupied, she saw this as only another threat to peace.

"You will have to go back," she decided.

The injustice of it cut deep. (It still rankles.) "No!" I cried.

But she had a trump card, and played it. "I'll tell your father," she said.

I knew then that I was beaten. That afternoon I appeared in the school yard and stood in the line of boys drawn up in silence after the bell rang. They grinned in fiendish anticipation.

"You gonna 'pologize?" one whispered.

"Ah, shut up," I answered. The grins multiplied.

Class got under way normally. Miss Dixon made one or two announcements, protracting and enjoying the suspense. Then it came.

"One of our number," she announced, "has something to say to us."

I stumbled to the front of the room and faced the horde. One or two of the little girls' faces betrayed sympathy; one or two boys leered their delight; most were fixed in fascinated horror. My face, I am sure, was alternately dead white and flaming with impotent rage, but somehow I got out the most dishonest words I ever spoke.

"I'm sorry for what I said."

Miss Dixon waited till I had regained my seat. "Now," she said, "We shall resume. I think one of us has learned an expensive but profitable lesson. We shall all forget the incident and go on with our work."

What the lesson was escapes me still. Perhaps it was to mistrust teachers and to expect no quarter from one's peers. In which case I am glad that I met other teachers with more sensitivity and friends who gave support when I needed it, so that the iron did not penetrate to the depths of my soul. Miss Dixon, no doubt, went on saying that she knew how to handle boys.

Ten years later I was a seminarian, studying philosophy. A message came from home that my mother, who lived fifteen miles away, was ill with pneumonia. This was in the days before wonder drugs had been discovered, and pneumonia was a justly dreaded threat to life.

"But I don't see any need for you to go home," the Rector said. "The doctor doesn't expect the crisis for two or three days."

That evening I went the rounds of the faculty, asking the Fathers to remember my mother next morning at Mass. They were all cordial and promised their prayers, but Father Arthur Sheehan, the Dean, was particularly solicitous.

"Why aren't you at home?" he asked. I told him what the Rector had said, and he nodded. But between classes on the following morning he stopped me in the corridor.

"Now don't be alarmed; your mother isn't any worse, but I've seen the Rector and you have permission to go home. Go and get dressed and I'll see you in the dining room in fifteen minutes."

He served my lunch, gave me some money he had got for me from the Treasurer, and, at the front door, waved me off. My mother "passed the crisis" of her pneumonia on Christmas Day, the best Christmas the family had ever had, and I went back to the seminary. But when I was ordained seven years later it was Arthur Sheehan whom I asked to assist me at my first Mass and to share in the family's happiness on that day of fulfillment.

Life, the social scientists tell us, is interaction—not only being, but being with, coexistence. The stresses we exert on one another pull us out, push us in, develop protective shells that we can hide behind, or open us up so that the blossom that is our best self can burst forth and bloom in freedom. Gentleness, concern, reverence for what God has made in his own image, patience with slow growth, forgiveness, these would seem in the long run the virtues most to be cultivated in our mutual dealings.

So ended regency. It was a halcyon time, a kind of honeymoon in ministry. There were all these new friends, whose loyalty would be proven across the years. Then there was the confidence that develops as one perceives that his first responsibilities have been met and adequately handled. And there was a new maturity as one reflected on the experience and tried to assess the apostolic potential that teaching might hold in the years to come. We were given a little more liberty (not much, really), but even that was not as welcome or useful as the reentry, after seven years' vigilant sequestration, into the real world. We learned as much from our students, or from our experience with them, as they did from us, and theology, we felt, would mean more to us because of that experience.

CHAPTER 6

Sacred Science, Safely Taught

THERE WAS NO TELEVISION IN 1934, SO WE HAD TO PROVIDE our own entertainment. It lacked, to be sure, a smooth professionalism, but it was creative and had a situational pungency. One evening at Keyser Island, our "villa" in Connecticut, we listened to a parody of "My Blue Heaven," a popular song of the time:

> When Regency's done it isn't much fun
> To hurry to dear old Weston.
> They're waiting for us, a trip on the bus
> Will bring you to dear old Weston.
> You've had your bust and now you must make your adieu,
> For Suarez and St. Thomas both are calling you.
> You've taken a fall, you're nothing at all,
> You're filling a room at Weston.

Was the prospect really that bleak? Well, yes, it was. We had had a little change from the ineffable round of study and class, class and study. We had had the stimulating experience of responsibility, of doing a man's work in the world. We had been treated to some extent as grownups; now we would be treated as boys again.

"What's it like?" I asked one of the second year men when the bus deposited us at Weston. "Oh, not bad," he replied. "You're here today—and here tomorrow."

If our family lived within fifteen miles of the house, we would be permitted to visit once a year, not leaving before 9:00 in the morning and returning before 9:00 in the evening. Otherwise, except for routine visits to doctors and dentists, we were immured. Years later I came on Erving Goffman's definition, in his book called *Asylums: Essays on the Social Situation of Mental Patients and Other Inmates*:

> A total institution may be defined as a place of residence
> and work where a large number of like-situated individu-
> als, cut off from the wider society for an appreciable pe-

71

riod of time, together lead an enclosed, formally administered round of life. Prisons serve as a clear example, providing we appreciate that what is prisonlike about prisons
is found in institutions where members have broken no
laws.

"Houses of formation" (seminaries for future priests, novitiates or "motherhouses" for training religious women) were almost
invariably located in rural, out-of-the-way places. The country air
was undeniably salubrious, and the inaccessibility of the property
did, no doubt, emphasize in a subtle way the desire of those within
to do their work without distraction. But the unrelieved isolation
through many years from the affairs and concerns of the world
tended to create a kind of introversion, an immaturity amounting
almost to naiveté. We had been ten years in religious life—a respectable commitment, and arguably a permanent one. We should
have been trusted as responsible adults, not kept like thoughtless or
potentially naughty children out of harm's way.

Probably, though, this sort of incarceration was to be expected, given the history of the Church during the preceding four
hundred years. It was of a piece with the "siege mentality" that
came in after the Reformation, and was aggravated later by painful
conflict with Deism, Jansenism, Gallicanism, the Enlightenment,
the French Revolution, secular liberalism. There was a failure of
nerve, a ceaseless state of alert, a preoccupation with safety. Authority was canonized and made, even at its lowest levels, infallible, or at least unquestionable. Jesuits, of course, were the
Church's Light Brigade, according to popular classification, so
"ours not to reason why" was thought peculiarly applicable to us.
We did not have to endure the petty tyranny exercised in some
convents of religious women, but the mantle of omniscience assumed by some of our superiors on taking office was a little hard
to accept with equanimity. There was no democracy at Weston;
Father always knew best.

Because a defensive crouch had been the attitude of the
Church for so long, the military metaphor became dominant. Instead of a flock of sheep, or branches on a Vine, or members of a
body whose Head was the Lord, we were grimly purposeful soldiers. Life was a battle, a campaign, a war. Missionaries, having
learned "tactics" and "strategies," and having survived a rigorous
and lengthy boot camp, went out to "conquer" the heathen. There
was a world to be "won," but it could be taken only if the

"enemy" capitulated altogether. Unconditional surrender. No quarter. Error has no rights.

Discipline, indispensable as it is for the pursuit of any objective, was of course highly regarded and seemed often to be imposed for its own sake. We marched in silent, tight formation to and from the chapel, the dining room, the classrooms, and we had another parody to sing on picnics. It was, actually, an inheritance from Woodstock College, in Maryland, where generations of Jesuits before us, including our professors, had studied, but we adopted it because it mirrored exactly our own close-order drill. It was sung to the tune of "Put on Your Old Gray Bonnet," and it went like this:

It begins before September,
It's the last thing you remember,
When the last bell rings in June;
You can never quite escape it,
You're a link and you can't break it,
And it gets you mighty soon.

With dull tread it goes on creeping,
You could follow it while sleeping,
Though its path is sombre, black, and serpentine.
Without an inch digressing,
Oh, the lockstep's most depressing
In the Weston long black line.

Chorus:
Not a man, just a number, for four years you wonder
How you'll make your mark by keeping time
In a life so quiet that you sigh for a riot
In the Weston long black line.

Like the march of death it's steady,
Like the sad sea's endless eddy,
It may stop but never stay.
If you dodge it on the morrow,
You'll find out to your sorrow
It will wait for you next day.
Now the long black line goes winding
In and out and ever finding
Other links that go to make an endless chain.
When your place is vacated,
Why, some other victim's slated,
And the long line looks the same.

Chorus:
Just a plain man's duty, it's not a thing of beauty,

Straight ahead without a word to say.
In the refectory it's the same old story,
Face about and march away.

It's enough to set you raving,
As you see that black flag waving
When you've been two years away.
Then you get some little notion
Of what's meant by endless motion
As you tramp in line each day.
Why, the thought is most appalling
When the Judgment trumpet's calling
The long black line will still be on its way!
Then a custom will be broken,
When the word to halt is spoken,
And the long line stops to stay.

Chorus:
Up the stairs you're filing, and you don't feel much like
    smiling
As you tramp the dead march every day.
For an old scholastic, oh, the long line's drastic,
It can make your hair turn gray!

One wit among us compared the four years of theology to the action of an internal combustion engine: first year, intake; second year, compression; third year, explosion (our ordination); fourth year, exhaustion.

Discipline, however, cannot be enforced without sanctions. As the saying was in World War II, you had to "shape up or ship out," you were "on the ball or on the boat." So for infractions of the rule (breaking silence, for instance, or staying up after the ten o'clock curfew) you would be given a "culpa;" you knelt down in the dining room, after "grace" had been said, and recited a set formula in the presence of the whole community: "Dear fathers and brothers, I say to you my culpa for all my faults and negligences in the observance of our holy rule, but especially for . . ." Sometimes the wording of the "especially" clause made us grin, though one formulation was almost certainly apocryphal: "but especially for making an ass of myself by imitating superiors." Very rarely indeed there was a "public culpa;" this was an admonition solemnly read from the pulpit in the dining room by the Father Minister, indicting in one case that I remember three culprits for "visiting the home of externs without permission," and imposing a fairly stiff penance.

These were minor matters. More serious, because it was characteristic of the whole Church at the time, and because it affected our spirituality so profoundly, was a chronic recourse to the motivation of fear. We heard it in retreats; some retreat directors delighted, seemingly, in reminding us that we were God's creatures, which in their presentations was not a reason for exulting in our origin and dignity, and for responding wholeheartedly to God's prodigal generosity, but meant only that life was fragile and brief, and a strict accounting of it would be demanded on the "Day of Wrath." We heard it in our liturgies, where, if the almost ludicrous *"apologiae"* of the Middle Ages had been excised in the Missal of Pius V in 1570, there were still plentiful reminders of our guilt in the "Prayers at the Foot of the Altar," the quaking *"Dies Irae,"* the triple "Lord, I am not worthy," accompanied by remorseful striking of the breast, before Communion. We were made aware, too, though it was not held over us precisely as a threat, that if we didn't toe the mark we wouldn't be admitted to vows, or we wouldn't be ordained, or our final profession would be held up. Well, we are, God knows, frail and weak and even rebellious beings ("how little understood thy great commanded good!"), and we should tremble sometimes as we review our loveless conduct, but surely this consideration should not dominate our outlook. It's true that, as the Psalm (111:10) says, "the fear of the Lord is the beginning of wisdom." But only the beginning. 'You have a Father!'' our Lord cried.

Fear governed our study of theology, too. In 1907 Pope Pius X published two momentous documents: a decree, *Lamentabili,* listing and condemning the errors of the Modernists, and an encyclical letter, *Pascendi Dominici Gregis,* which not only refuted these errors but instituted very severe measures to prevent their spread, especially in seminaries. In the words of Monsignor John Tracy Ellis,[1]

> The encyclical's most somber paragraphs were contained
> in the concluding section where the bishops were given
> practical instructions on how to proceed in their dioceses.
> If an administrative officer or a professor in a seminary or
> a Catholic university was found "in any way" to be tainted

---

1. "The Catholic Priest in the United States, an Historical Perspective;" Collegeville, Minn., 1971, Pp. 61-62.

with "modernism" he was to be excluded "without compunction." Equal diligence "and severity" were to be used in examining and selecting candidates for the priesthood, the *imprimatur* and *nihil obstat* were to be employed on all books touching religious subjects, priest-editors of newspapers and periodicals were to be closely scrutinized for their policies, and for the future meetings or congresses of priests were not to be permitted "except on very rare occasions." . . . In each diocese a vigilance committee was to be set up for the purpose of extirpating errror, removing teachers of unsound doctrine, etc., and the bishops were told that they were to report to the Holy See every three years on all the points contained in these instructions.

Monsignor Michael V. Gannon, in an essay, "Before and After Modernism" in the same volume, has this to say:

There was never any question that the American Church would comply with the Roman directives. The encycylical was accepted quietly, obediently, and . . . with no marked trauma. For all that one could see, nothing special had happened. Seminaries continued classes as before, bishops and priests continued on their accustomed rounds, and the poor had the gospel preached to them. The face that the Church presented to the nation at large remained the same. Still, something had occurred, something unperceived at the moment, something whose long-range impact on American Catholic thinking would be hard to exaggerate. The Church of the United States was overcome by a *grande peur*. As 1908 proceeded on its course a gradually enveloping dread of heresy settled over episcopal residences, chanceries, seminaries, and Catholic institutions of higher learning. Security, safety, conservatism became national imperatives. Free intellectual inquiry in ecclesiastical circles came to a virtual standstill. The nascent intellectual movement went underground or died. Contacts with Protestant and secular thinkers were broken off. It was as though someone had pulled a switch and the lights had failed all across the American Catholic landscape. (p. 340-341)

At that time (1930) the thirteenth century was everywhere the model of orthodoxy, and worshipful Thomism was the normative science. That the scholastic method was the sole approved mode of thinking for clerics, *Pascendi* had left no doubt. . . . All across the country seminarians were indoctrinated in the science of matter and form, substance and accident, essence and existence. They were asked to memorize, in Latin, answers to questions and problems that had not been posed for hundreds of years. A combative atmosphere prevailed. Adversaries were seldom considered in their context; instead, straw men were set up for swift knocking down. Students developed the weakest of all attitudes toward adversaries, that of contempt. Thus the young priest went 'out into the world' with an unarticulated protective tariff against threatening ideas and a sufficient number of absolute first principles to allow him to bask in certainty all his days. . . . It was not Thomism, as such, which created the intellectual desert which was the American seminary system, but the manner in which Thomism was masticated, predigested, and force-fed. . . . Here everything was arranged on a philosophical base, perennially fixed theses were provided for the benefit of rote memory, and the Bible was available as a source-book for rational-historical 'proofs.' One came out of the course equipped with a consoling number of immutable certainties of faith, not to mention a strong orientation toward apologetics, which was needed, it goes without saying, to show that the intellectual world outside the Catholic system was one of bewildering confusion.[2]

Thomas Bokenkopper[3] sums up the period:

Modernism was indeed successfully stamped out, but at a tremendous price; the Catholic intelligence was inoculated against error, but the dosage was almost fatal. The liberal Catholic movement suffered another grave setback, and social Catholicism lost a decade of valuable time. Many of the Church's most brilliant thinkers were silenced or driven out of theology and into a kind of spiritual schizophrenia. Catholic seminaries remained medieval ghettos until the middle of the twentieth century, and future priests were taught a biblical fundamentalism embroidered with theories like the one that proved that Jonah could have lived inside the whale since a French scholar had found toads that lived inside stones for thousands of years.

---

2.   Pp. 351-3
3.   *A Concise History of the Catholic Church,* revised edition, New York, 1979, p. 366.

As one familiar with history knows, a crisis not resolved is a crisis postponed and destined to erupt again with greater violence. One wonders if a less hysterical and more historical approach to Modernist errors might not have proven wiser in the long run. What was of value in liberal thought might then have been sifted out in leisurely fashion and assimilated and the Church spared the trauma it now suffers with the sudden reappearance of the questions first raised by the Modernists.

On the other hand, one might justify the severity of the hierarchy by admitting that their primary responsibility was not to history but to millions of souls who knew nothing about Wellhausen and whose faith would have been gravely disturbed if the speculations of a Tyrrell or a Loisy became common currency in its pulpits. And, it must be added, some of the Modernists engaged in systematic deceit by using pseudonyms and ambiguous formulas to cloak their radical rejection of the traditional faith in order to stay in the Church and subvert it from within. But whoever deserves the most blame, the Modernist crisis was a catastrophe for the Church. It led to an intellectual sterility that still weighs heavily on its life and caused a cultural lag that was most apparent in Italy itself, where the long arm of the Curia made the repression most severe. The Italian clergy were completely isolated from the university life in their country, and even at Rome ecclesiastical standards of scholarship fell very low. Rome in the twentieth century became a byword for intellectual sterility.

We came on the scene twenty-five years after the decrees of Pius X were published. Their impact had been enormous. For example, most of us never suspected that there was any other way of "doing" theology except in the scholastic mode. All our professors assembled at the beginning of the academic year to take the oath against Modernism, and we ourselves had to take it before we were ordained. Our courses, predictably, were oriented to polemics. Great stress was laid on apologetics, since the rationalists who had denied or watered down fundamental presuppositions had to be refuted before anything else could be done. A course on the Church, however, was rescued from endless controversy with Protestants when our professor, newly returned from studies, discarded the established textbook and centered his lectures around St. Paul's doctrine of the Church as the Body of Christ. And in our third year a new textbook on Grace was introduced by the Dean. It replaced an arid outline of definitions and syllogisms, and, though it retained the usual structure of theses, proofs, and refutations, it drew on Scripture, the Fathers, and history so abundantly that our professor, an agile metaphysician, nearly threw up his hands, admitting openly that he had no idea how to handle it.

Some idea of the dry-as-dust presentation may be gained from the fact that in the lectures and the manuals there was so little one could use for prayer. Theology and devotion, it seemed, were in different worlds. It had not been so in the writing of the Fathers of the Church, where reflection on God and his attributes, or on his immensely merciful interventions in human history, took fire in gratitude and adoration. But the snippets from the Fathers that we found in our manuals were cited only as proofs, as props for orthodoxy. Nor were we encouraged to read further. Moreover, the preponderant attention paid to moral theology and canon law—duties, regulations, obligations, sanctions, meticulous refinements to confront every variation of human conduct—tended to make legalists of us, or at least to deflate our enthusiasm for the Good News.

Once more, we suffered from our isolation, intellectual isolation especially. There were no visiting lecturers, or not more than two or three in our four years. The "theologians' library" had only tattered manuals or compendia—no journals, no reference material. The "house library" was still locked, and one could effect an entrance only by obtaining a key from the Father Librarian, something he was notoriously careful not to part with very often. There was, of course, a "floating library" of novels, detective stories, odd copies of *Life* and *Time*, that passed surreptitiously from hand to hand. Not enough was asked of us in the way of papers, theses, or even class participation; we hadn't in any case the resources for such exploration.

Attendance at class was not a matter of option, although the lectures of our old professor of church history were rambling and, it seemed to us, pointless, so that one afternoon, surveying the sparsely populated benches, he protested in his heavy German accent, "I see many who are not here." Theology lectures, of course, were given in Latin, which added very little to their sparkle. We tried to console ourselves with the reflection that students in graduate and law schools everywhere were probably listening to soporific monologues of a similar kind. But were our ears the only avenue by which knowledge might reach us? One of us (a physicist, naturally) was asked after an unbroken week of class how he was feeling. "I'm punch-drunk from stopping sound waves," he replied. The hours of listening went on and on: thirty-two "conferences" in the annual retreat, six in the semiannual triduum of renovation, monthly "exhortations," an hour's reading in the dining room during lunch and dinner, four and sometimes five hours of class except on Sundays and holidays. We did finally come to think of Jesuits as the most talked-at body of men in the world.

The propositions asserted in our theses were hierarchically graded: they were to be held as defined pronouncements pertaining to the faith, or not formally defined but evident in Scripture, or certain from reasoning on the data of faith, or "more probable," or simply "probable." We grew a little impatient with some of the fine points in the last two categories, feeling that many of them could be tossed through the back window and nobody except a few moth-eaten professors would know they were gone. Is actual grace, for instance, a "non-living, flowing thing," as the 17th century Dominicans asserted, or is it an "indeliberate act elicited by a faculty only externally elevated," as the Jesuits of the same era taught? Some day, we grumbled, there would be a grand revolt against such subtleties. And it did come, but much too late for us.

William M. Halsey, in *The Survival of American Innocence,*[4] quotes a remark of George Shuster that the average diocesan seminarian of those days "studied medieval philosophy, French pietistic literature, German church history, British apologetics, and Irish poetry." Our apologetics (unless one read the triumphalist Belloc or the paradoxical Chesterton) was Roman, not British, and our pietistic literature came out of the *devotio moderna* and the Counter Reformation, but otherwise there was no great difference. Certainly there was nothing American—not after the fulminations against "Americanism" and "Modernism" that put an end to theological scholarship and speculation on our shores for sixty years.

Meanwhile the long black line went trudging on. We had, in first year, our memories of regency to sustain us, and in third year there was the prospect of ordination. Second year, though, was a tunnel, without light at either end. One night we had a movie called "The Big House," in which all the action took place in a

---

4.   Notre Dame, Indiana, 1980, p. 96.

penitentiary. There were so many parallels between our life and that of the inmates that for a long time we referred to our abode as "The Big House." Well, we said with as much stoicism as we could manage, it's the last installment of the price we had to pay for the priesthood.

An enormous privilege and grace was the company of like-minded comrades. It was something to live with these men intelligent, richly and variously talented, eager. With their vows they had sold all they owned to buy the one pearl of great price. It was a total commitment, and they would persevere in it to the end of their days, forty, fifty, sixty years later. They went without the achievement or reputation that might have been theirs in another way of life. They went without the supportive and consoling company of women. They might give ground sometimes but never surrender in their warfare against the world, the flesh, and the devil. They prayed, steadfastly, patiently. They chaffed one another constantly in that delightful masculine banter that seeks to poke fun rather than to give offense. They gave then and continued to give later a cheerful and generous service to one another, and they overlooked or forgave the frictions that inevitably occur when frail human beings live at close quarters.

I could not complain that my students at Holy Cross had forgotten me. Their letters came in such numbers that I was hard put to keep up with them, and they themselves came often to visit, although for the most part they were turned away by the vigilant Father Minister. We were permitted visitors only at intervals and during stated hours. Their attempts gave me at least the consolation of knowing that I had not devoted too much time to them when they were my students.

As we moved into third year, at the end of which we would be ordained, the prospect of becoming priests took precedence over every other consideration. American Catholics, at that stage of their ecclesiological sophistication, regarded priests as men apart, delegates from the All-high whose least word on almost any subject had for them the aura and authority of divine revelation. It was axiomatic that the priest was not to be contradicted, and never, regardless of his human failings, to be criticized. There was something very touching, a quite simple, childlike faith, in this attitude, this desire on the people's part to put the priest on a pedestal, and to show him every mark of honor and affection. But, though we had ourselves come out of the same culture, we had been educated through self-knowledge and our studies away from it, and found it, often, more than a little embarrassing. I don't in all honesty believe that the likelihood of our being exalted or venerated played any part whatever in our desire to be priests.

Since Vatican II the mission of the priest, like the mission of the Church itself, has been seen as that of a servant. He is to carry on a ministry—the word *means* "service"—to the People of God, bringing them every spiritual or material assistance he can as they—and he—journey together to the Kingdom. In this he is to resemble the Lord himself, who "emptied himself," as St. Paul says, in the service of his brethren.

But I am not sure that this concept was uppermost or even distinct in our minds in 1937. We thought of the priesthood then, I believe, as an incalculable privilege, whereby we were taken into an association, an intimacy with the Lord like that of the disciple "whom Jesus loved." We would be even more his confidantes, his companions, than we were as religious. Of course we would preach, absolve, celebrate the liturgy for the people, but as his emissaries rather than as their servants. But a priest is a bridge— something people walk on—between God and God's creatures. He is to be wide open to this sublime, two-way traffic. He must with God's help mend or remove any impediments to its flow. His own advantage or even his own sensibilities are not, in the final analysis, items for his consideration. He is, as Christ was, a servant, spending and being spent.

We stood in the early morning half-light, silent, vested, waiting for the signal for the ordination to begin. Each of us held a lighted candle, and from it a cone of light shone on each man's face. Twelve years before we had begun the journey to this day, and had come to it *per varios casus, per tot discrimina rerum*, as old Virgil put it. The procession formed; we moved into the chapel, where the bishop, in that setting of love and mutual service which is the Eucharist, laid commissioning hands on our heads. There in the front pews were our mothers and fathers, who had been *our* servants from babyhood, who had in faith let us go off into the unknown, and now were tremulous with awe and joy over what was happening to us. We laid our newly-anointed hands on their heads and begged God's richest blessings on them.

Next morning, surrounded by our families, we celebrated our first Masses. It was customary to invite a nephew or a young cousin to be our acolyte, but I had another idea. A month or so before ordination my father asked who was going to serve my first Mass. "You are," I said. "I've never served Mass in my life!" he protested. "It will be easy," I said. "Father Sheehan will make the Latin responses and prompt you to move the book and bring up the cruets if you need prompting. How about it?" He hesitated, but I could see that he was delighted. And he did serve, though the family, watching from the pews, were quietly amused to notice that his knees were visibly knocking as he genuflected. He told me years later that the day was one of his brightest memories.

And a day or so after that a group of us were talking on the porch with old Father Henry Brock when the Father Minister came out. He had had several requests from neighboring parishes for assistance with confessions and Masses on the weekend, and he asked for volunteers. We were silent for a moment. Were we ready so soon to do this? Father Brock spoke up: "Go ahead! You're sent!" "What's that, Father?" "You're sent, you're sent!" His meaning dawned on us, and we went.

In fact, we went all summer, helping especially in little seaside towns that were crowded with vacationers. We got accustomed to being called "Father," and we were touched by the faith of the people, even of people much older than ourselves, as they told us their problems and sorrows. The Depression still lay like a blight on the land, jobs were scarce and ill-paid. Our immersion in reality was sudden and chilling, but it had the good effect of making us work hard on our Sunday homilies so that we might say something sympathetic and encouraging, not trite, not platitudinous.

"Summer's lease hath all too short a date." School bells rang again, for our course in theology had another year to run. And before it was over there would be a two-hour oral examination covering the seven years' work in philosophy and theology. This year we would be concentrating on the sacraments and Scripture, and the prospect seemed attractive. In the event, though, the course on the sacraments dealt with the number of the sacraments and the formal, material, efficient, and final cause of each, while in the Scripture course, which was on the Prophecy of Jeremiah, we heard nothing about the anguish of that timid, tormented, infinitely lonely man, the prophet, nothing of the perplexing divine imperative that forced him, against all his natural inclinations, to predict disaster and ruin for his own people. We did spend two weeks discussing which of several hostile nations might be the one threatening Judah "from the north," and for a time the professor was known as "the enemy from the north."

All things end, and so did our seemingly interminable stay in "the Big House." We had of course been enriched by the experience, but, in view of the investment of time and energy, we felt even then how much richer it might have been. Alas, we had come to theology in the last days of the old Church. Pope John's window, letting in, as he said, a little fresh air, would not be opened for twenty-five years. The second stanza of the parody we sang at Keyser Island four years before had more than a little bite in it:

> When Theology's done we'll be on the run
> > To hurry from dear old Weston.
> But where'll we go? We haven't a show
> > To get very far from Weston.
> A trolley car will go as far as you can go;
> > You can't get to the places that you used to know,
> For Worcester is small, and Boston's a pall.
> > You might as well stay at Weston.

CHAPTER 7

Catholics on the Brink of War

THE REV. PETER GOMES, MINISTER IN THE MEMORIAL chapel at Harvard University, once defined the Proper Bostonian as "a person with a seat at the Symphony, a membership at the Athenaeum, a plot at Mount Auburn Cemetery, and a relative at McLean (a mental hospital)." Cleveland Amory, Edwin O'Connor, and a host of others have established a permanent and universally credited folklore about Boston and Bostonians—so much so that when in other parts of the country I have been asked where I lived, and answered that I was from Boston, I don't remember getting an indifferent acceptance. It was either a species of awe ("Oh, really?") or a knowing smile, as who should say, "Well, now I understand." And I've wondered what the name of my native city conjured up in their minds. Was it an image of bewigged patriots in knickers and tricornered hats—Paul Revere, Ben Franklin, the Adamses, John Hancock, somehow related to the Boston Tea Party, the Midnight Ride, Bunker Hill, Concord and Lexington? Was it—if their tastes were literary—a medley of names like Longfellow, Lowell, Whittier, Emerson, Thoreau, Hawthorne, Alcott, Harriet Beecher Stow, Julia Ward Howe? Perhaps it was place-names: Louisburg Square, Faneuil Hall, the Parker House, the Esplanade, Harvard Yard, Brimstone Corner, King's Chapel. In some circles, to be sure, it could have been the Red Sox, the Bruins, the Celtics, or the Marathon and "Heartbreak Hill." Or it may have been the politicians who did not own the city (the "Yankees" did) but ran it—James Michael Curley, the Fitzgeralds, the Kennedys. Very probably there rose in some minds an image of a rigid, forbidding censor of public morals. It is a fact that books and plays enjoyed an unmerited success elsewhere because they were advertised as "banned in Boston." (This practice may have been confused in some minds with the Boston Massacre.) Most non-Bostonians who cherish this impression would undoubtedly agree with the wit who said, "How much better it would have been for us all if, instead of the Pilgrims landing on Plymouth Rock, Plymouth Rock had landed on the Pilgrims." They would agree, too, with whoever said that Boston is not so much a place as a state of mind—and they would thank God piously that they do not inhabit it.

Well, the Brahmins' "standards" of decorum were, ultimately, a bit suffocating. They did, however, leave ample room for civility, for individuality, for character. The Boston streets are not laid out in a grid, but wander in an irregular, human fashion. People *live* in this city—downtown. At one time, it's true, there was a painful cleavage between two communities, the Protestant Yankees and the more recent immigrants, largely Catholic, from Ireland and Italy. My father remembered the sign, "No Irish need apply," posted outside lodging houses and employment offices. But now priests are members of the Boston Ministers Club, and an honorary degree is conferred by Harvard on the president of Boston College, while a Presbyterian chaplain at Boston University (a Methodist foundation) is invited to preach on the feast of Corpus Christi at the Catholic Cathedral of the Holy Cross.

Mistakes of other kinds are being corrected: the hideous and thunderous stanchions of the Elevated Railway have been torn down, and the equally repugnant Central Artery is being decently interred in a tunnel. The warren of wharves and warehouses along Atlantic Avenue has been razed in favor of handsome hotels and apartments. Sleazy Scollay Square is gone, replaced by the symmetrical dignity of Government Center. Local churches and neighborhood improvement associations are fighting blight and providing neat, affordable housing. The noxious Combat Zone, we are assured, will vanish shortly.

In sum, a livable city, with a usable past. As for the future, the kitchen-Latin distich of James Jeffrey Roche gives fair warning:

> *Dies erit praegelida*
> *Sinistra cum Bostonia.*

("It will be a very cold day when Boston gets left.")

I myself prefer the Latin on the Great Seal of the city: *"Sicut patribus sit Deus nobis"*—"As God dealt with our fathers so may he deal with us." At once a prayer of thanksgiving and a petition, this was not bad for a bunch of supposedly crusty old Puritans. I find myself in sympathy with the summary inscription on the base of Phillips Brooks' statue in Copley Square: "Born in Boston, died in Boston." A recipe for the good life.

There is a story about the annual parade of the Holy Name Society in Boston—thousands of men in line, led by a jaunty, straw-hatted Cardinal Cushing, on their way to a rally at Fenway Park. Two spectators, one a Protestant, the other a Catholic, are watching from the sedate windows of the Algonquin Club. The Protestant says, "I had no idea you people were so numerous." "Oh," says the Catholic, "Those are only the men who don't swear."

Certainly the American Church was prosperous in those years, so far as numbers were concerned, and not only in Boston. Across the northern tier of the country churches, colleges, primary and secondary schools, seminaries and motherhouses, hospitals, orphanages dotted the landscape. According to one estimate, there were six thousand American priests, sisters, and brothers on the foreign missions. World War I and the Great Depression had shaken the country's assurance badly.[1] Catholics, rigid in their convictions about this world as well as the next, constituted an armed camp in the midst of growing skepticism and doubt. There was only one philosophy: Thomism. There was only one theology: the Tridentine, buttressed by the definition of papal infallibility. *The Catholic's Ready Answer* provided solutions for every problem. There could be no dialogue with the hopelessly mistaken world outside the Church, so the Catholic Philosophical Association was founded, and the Catholic Historical Society, and the Catholic Hospital Association, and Catholic Charities, and the Catholic Labor Guild, and the Catholic Alumni Club, and even the Catholic Poetry Society.

Much of this defensiveness stemmed from an identity crisis. By and large, American Catholics were immigrants or the children or grandchildren of immigrants—people who had been peasants in the old country and had as best they could to make a transition from the soil to urban society. Their experience in America had been that of a minority, poor and without influence, often discriminated against and sometimes persecuted. Cardinal Cushing once observed that there was not a single bishop in the United States whose father had gone to college. Edwin O'Connor, in *The Edge of Sadness*, a novel that won the Pulitzer Prize in 1961, caught the

---

1. See *The Survival of American Innocence Catholicism in an Era of Disillusionment, 1920-1940*, by William M. Halsey, Notre Dame, Indiana, 1980, passim.

anguish of the intermediate generation, who belonged, really, on neither side of the Atlantic. They needed security, so they mistrusted new departures of any sort. A friend of mine said her moral education could be summed up in a single phrase: "Whatever you're doing, stop!" Her sister, who for social and patriotic reasons went to the USO dances for the military during World War II, always asked the faith of her partners before dating them. "Mixed marriage" was considered a disaster.

Education in the faith ended, for the most part, at the grade school level, and consisted of memorized formulae from the catechism; how well these were assimilated did not seem to matter. Halsey cites an article in the *American Mercury*, written by a priest under the pen name of Jack English:

> Before he was ten years of age, a Catholic youth was taught the basic tenets of God's existence; he was convinced that life has an eternal purpose; human acts were divided for him into the good, bad, and indifferent; he became acutely conscious that his every thought, word, or deed is a stroke upon the eternal canvas. If taken in isolation his training would force one to conclude that "there is not an uncertain moment in the young Catholic's acceptance of established creed. . . . There is not an elastic idea in the structure of his belief."[2]

If "*tene quod habes*" ("keep what you've got") might have been the motto of many Yankee commercial establishments (and of their political party), it could have served equally well for the American Church. The pastor—and *a fortiori* the bishop—ruled absolutely. No book or article, dealing with religion in any way, not even a pious story, not even a "holy card" could be published without an *imprimatur* from the chancery. If there was any doubt about who sat in the driver's seat, it could be resolved by quoting Pope Pius X: "In the hierarchy alone reside the power and the authority necessary to move and direct all the members of society to its end. As for the many, they have no other right than to let themselves be guided and so follow their pastors in docility."[3] The slogan, "Every Catholic child in a Catholic school," was repeated

---

2.   *Innocence,* Page 111 vol. 31, January 1934.
3.   Quoted by Walter Burghardt, S.J., in *Sermons that Laugh or Weep,* Mahwah, New Jersey, 1983, p. 291.

over and over; pastors in newly-founded parishes were advised to build and staff a school before thinking about a permanent church. One old priest, a professor in a Catholic college, said, "Harvard has *Veritas* on its shield, but we have *veritas* here."

There was a disposition to believe in hostile conspiracies undermining the faith on every side; no matter what the problem, it could be traced to the satanic malevolence of the "A.P.A.'s" (the American Protective Association), or the Masons, or the wealthy Jews. Cardinal Cushing, whenever he ran out of other topics, could always fall back on the threat of "atheistic Communism." "The neo-scholastic sensibility was rampant among Catholics after World War I. It divided up the world like the classified section of the morning newspaper. In neat arrangement, there were realists, naturalists, socialists, Communists, idealists, pessimists, humanists, and agnostics. Catholics achieved security and confidence because the 'enemies' were always somewhere else—all one had to do was look them up."[4] Evelyn Waugh, on a commission from *Life* magazine, came over from England to investigate American Catholicism, and had some stinging observations to make about "tribal loyalties." Any corrective value his satire might have had was lost in the understandable resentment felt by Catholics of Irish ancestry toward the rather nasty remarks of a supercilious Englishman—and he a very recent convert.

It was not a climate that encouraged creative artists. Gothic was the only truly religious architecture. Gregorian chant, though it was seldom heard, was considered the ideal music for public prayer. There were biographies, but chiefly of saints or religious leaders, and these were intertwined with legend and designed for edification rather than for historical accuracy. Eugene O'Neil distanced himself from the Church, and no other Catholic dramatist except perhaps Philip Barry appeared. A few genuinely lyric voices lifted briefly in a sonnet or a song, but then fell silent. It was from abroad that ideas and a fitting expression of them began at last to come, and largely from the publishing partnership of Frank Sheed and Maisie Ward. Eugene McCarthy, who taught at St. John's University in Minnesota, and whose later bid for the presidency was so vigorous as to induce Lyndon Johnson not to run again, listed the authors he read in the forties: Maritain, Gilson,

---

4.   Halsey, p. 134.

Yves Simon, Dawson; Chesterton and Belloc; Teilhard; Verner Moore; Abbot Butler, Rahner, Küng; Waugh, Greene, Bloy, Bernanos, Dorothy Parker, J. F. Powers, Allen Tate, Robert Lowell, Heywood Broun, Clare Booth Luce. Of these only seven were American-born, and of the seven only two had grown up Catholic. The "movements" that began to stir in those days—liturgical, biblical, Catholic Action—all had a foreign origin. It was, as someone said, an intellectual colonialism.

There were four buildings, utterly lovely ones, at Boston College when I was assigned to teach there in 1939; now there are over eighty, varying somewhat in loveliness. There were some two thousand students then; now faculty and staff alone number more than two thousand, and student enrollment stands at fourteen thousand five hundred. There were seven schools then: Arts and Sciences, Graduate, Law, Evening, Social Work, Management, Summer Session; now there are nine. Nursing and Education have been added, together with an ever-increasing number of institutes and special programs: Black Studies, the Environmental Center, the Junior Year Abroad, Language Houses, the Medieval Program, Exchange Programs, the Media Center, the Institute of Religious Education and Pastoral Ministry, the Career Center, the Weston Observatory, the Campus School, the Computer Center, the Social Welfare Research Institute, the Space Data Analysis Laboratory, the Center for Testing Evaluation and Educational Policy, the Theater Arts Center, the Language Laboratory, the Catholic School Leadership Program, etc., etc.

More importantly for the character of the University, there were no resident students in 1939; in those days if a student came from Lawrence or Braintree or Framingham he was considered an outlander, even a bit of a hero for undertaking such extensive daily wayfaring. A few of the more affluent traveled by car; the majority came rocking and jouncing around the curves of Commonwealth Avenue in the old green trolley, clutching their books in one hand and the paper bag that held their lunch in the other. Now dormitories range over two campuses and are inhabited by 8,000 young people, visible and sometimes distinctly audible, from every state in the Union. Some 3,000 commuters jockey for space in the parking areas on campus or precipitate neighborhood crises by parking in forbidden residential streets nearby. But the most unforeseen and pronounced change has come with the admission of women as undergraduates. A lady on campus in 1939 was somebody's secretary or a visitor—a very rare species, to be admired, perhaps, but strictly contained. Now women in all schools outnumber men by two thousand. And not only is the landscape enhanced, the quality of scholarship has been enriched.

My assignment was to teach English literature, largely in freshman classes, and to be the "moderator" (an eloquent term, as I discovered) or faculty adviser to the college magazine, the *Stylus*. It was for me a most congenial appointment, very like the one I had had in regency. I could again strive to open the eyes of the blind and the ears of the deaf to vision and music. Sometimes the captive audience found the process painful or tedious, as when I asked them to memorize a few shining lines or to create some of their own. Their original verses were not exactly imperishable. One madrigal began,

> Of all the girls I ever saw
> There's only one without a flaw;
> Oh, how I wish she were my squaw!

In other cases the divine *afflatus* seemed to peter out after the first inspiration:

> The sighing of birds, the hum of waves I do recall,
> Seeing many different shores from beneath snowy sails of
>   a boat.
> All has been beautiful, but the sights of the dear Lord I
>   boast most of all
> Are her silky voice and hair, lips and eyes so dear and
>   kind.
> They all strike within me a significant note.

Or again, "My Call":

> I came upon the open sea,
> The dark blue waters enchanted me.
> Upon this old and dreary boat
> It was cold even with a coat.

Or, once more, a summary of Arnold's "Strew on her roses":

> Place roses on her grave, but do not be sorrowful or
> mournful because she is happy. She gave to the world the
> gaiety it needed and she lived in its turmoil but now, like
> a retired champion of the turf, she has gone to pasture
> where she can remain in peace and quiet.

And thoughtfully chomp the Elysian grasses, no doubt.

But there were evidences that, here and there, the authentic fire had caught. The most convincing and comforting one was a Christmas greeting sent about five years later by a bored young second lieutenant somewhere in France to me, an Army chaplain half a world away in the New Guinea jungle:

> Dear Father:
>
> It little profits that, an idle king,
> By this still hearth, among these barren crags,
> Matched with an aged wife, I mete and dole
> Unequal laws unto a savage race
> That hoard, and sleep, and feed, and know not me.
>
> Remember, Father? Merry Christmas!
>
> George

I can never look at that "V-Mail" greeting without a pang. George came home safe and sound from the War, and was killed six months later in a traffic accident in Kenmore Square.

Working with the *Stylus* staff was something else. Here was an ambitious, merry (often hilarious), questing group, keen for ideas and eager to find expression for them. They read voraciously and talked endlessly. They debated their work with the moderator, who in those days held veto power—though he never had to use it—and they would cheerfully revise a manuscript they had already spent hours on. The result was some pretty lively writing, and (more important for college men who would probably not make writing their life-work) a zest for serious discussion and an increased hospitality to unfamiliar ideas.

The magazine, of course, was controversial. Dr. Halsey[5] cites a study ("Boston Priests, 1848-1910," Cambridge, Mass., 1973, p. 53) by Donna Merwick:

"The ideal at Boston College was to produce the 'benevolent man' from the ragtag body of immigrants entering its halls. It preached to the immigrant that to be an American was not the result of ancestry, but 'fitness.' It affirmed the value of culture as providing an aura of refinement and embellishment over the more

---

5.   *Innocence*, p. 53

day-to-day struggle to survive. It taught them that man's intellectual and moral faculties were in harmony with, and therefore could deduce the laws of the universe as basically outlined by Newton and, to some extent, Herbert Spencer. With his free will, man must also 'normalize' the more passionate urgings of the 'lower' regions of his nature. In sum, the immigrants were taught to imitate the college president, Robert Fulton, S.J., as an example of the true Christian gentleman: 'a genius, an infatuated lover of the classics, a witty and brilliant conversationalist and yet an energetic and powerful administrator.'"

A glance at earlier volumes of the *Stylus* reveals this aspiration toward gentility. One reads a graceful translation of one of Horace's odes, or an essay in praise of fine wines, or a short story involving star-crossed lovers who, happily, are wedded at last before the high altar of a medieval cathedral. No controversy here. But when Leo Murphy wrote of the veterans who were gassed and blinded in France in World War I (little thinking that he himself would be killed in Normandy in World War II), or Joe Dever wrote about getting drunk on Saturday night because he was broke and losing his girl to a rich rival, the old Fathers in St. Mary's Hall sat up straight in their wooden rockers. "Mass tomorrow, hell tonight!" said Joe. "But B.C. boys don't act like that!" cried the Fathers.

Joe Nolan wrote:

Awake, ye slaves of Bethlehem,
    Of Ford and Standard Oil,
Arise from grim assembly lines
    And subdivided toil!

Sam Lombard wrote:

O you can have your maids of Greece,
    With tresses blown 'neath Olympian thunder;
I'll take Peggy in gay cerise
    Riding the El from Park Street
        Under.

O you can take whoever you will,
I do not know nor do I care,
For I take Peggy hating fish
    With her usual Friday stare.

This was not literature, I was told—not what the textbook prescribed, "true grounds for a noble emotion." But then Joe Dever wrote a drinking song,

> Buy pails and pails of ales and ales,
> And drown your might-have-been,

and went on to compound heresy and blasphemy in some verses we called, for safety's sake, "Less Probable Opinion":

> I'd rather be in Hell, sir,
> Than left afloat in Limbo,
> Without a wing or anything,
> My arms and legs akimbo.
> To shower with derision
> The Beatific Vision
> Is most blaspheemous blasphemy,
> I readily agree.
> But all the hellish angels
> Make Limbo souls estrangels;
> Has not the blackest devil seen
> The only Thing to see?
> To see the one that saw the One,
> The only One to see,
> Is better far than Limbos are,
> Is better far to me. . . .

This brought out the Fathers Torquemada in full cry; one of them devoted most of a philosophy class to denouncing the poem, the author, the magazine, and, by guilty implication, the moderator. You simply could not, even in playful verses, voice a preference of that sort. You could not say that, because in Hell it is possible to catch at least some glimpse, some reflection, of infinite Beauty in the face of a fallen angel who had once looked on God, you would prefer to be condemned forever, rather than to be one of those who were never to catch a glimpse, perhaps even never be aware of the divine Majesty's existence—which, according to common doctrine at the time, was the lot of the person who died unbaptized.

Father Provincial, a ponderous man who, we noticed, knew almost everything, came for his annual "visitation" of the community.

"What's this trouble you're having with the *Stylus*, Father?"

"I'm not having any trouble with it," I said mildly. "But the Dean is having a great deal."

"There seems to be considerable levity in the magazine."

"Yes, Father. Young men are not always wholly serious."

"But a drinking song, Father!"

"Yes, Father. The students have been reading Belloc and Chesterton, who have written drinking songs, and they like to imitate them." (This was a low blow, since Belloc and Chesterton were accepted as champions of the Catholic Way of Life.)

"That's different, Father."

He didn't explain how it was different, and at last I said, "Well, Father, maybe you should appoint a new moderator."

"Think I will, Father."

And he did.

Dr. Halsey has described, with more scholarly detail than I can muster, the brimming enthusiasm for the faith that characterized this period.[6] Our students—at least the more literate among them—were reading not only Belloc and Chesterton but Maritain and Bloy and Bernanos and Greene and Dawson. They were talking earnestly about Peter Maurin, Dorothy Day, and *The Catholic Worker,* reading *Commonweal* and *Integrity,* and arguing fiercely about Eric Gill's "functionalism" that Dr. Lee Bowen was teaching in his history classes. They were confident that the "Catholic culture," based squarely on St. Thomas and proclaimed in the art and architecture of the Christian centuries, would prevail, and that the Christian Commonwealth would find a home at last in our green and pleasant land.

Off campus, too, the same mood was evident. A group of somewhat older people, disturbed by the absence of any Catholic bookstore in Boston that offered more than devotions and pious fiction, started—on a shoestring—their own shop, and staffed it themselves. They called it the "Pius XI Cooperative Book and Art Center," but everyone knew it as "the Pixi Coop." Father Carroll launched a guild of Catholic artists—sculptors, painters, stained glass workers, silversmiths. Another zealous group opened the St. Thomas More Bookshop in Cambridge. And I became, unofficially, chaplain and lecturer to the "Alumni Council of Catholic Action" (ACCA) and the "Federation of Newman Club Alumni"—though the Rector expressed some misgiving about my devoting attention to people who as undergraduates had chosen to attend non-Catholic schools. It was a heady time, even though France had fallen and England was in a death-struggle, and the shadow of war was reaching out across the Atlantic.

---

6.   *The Survival of American Innocence,* passim.

Stirring things were going on elsewhere in the country. "Labor priests" were not only explaining the social doctrines of Leo XIII and Pius XI but actually going to the waterfront and the factories, helping to organize boycotts and support strikes. Bishop Sheil of Chicago launched the "Catholic Youth Organization," condemned anti-Semitism and segregation of blacks, worked for slum clearance, and fought for the laboring man. Thomas Merton wrote *The Seven Story Mountain* and then, in a move sure to provoke perplexity and, later, enthusiasm among the young, went off to "bury" himself in, of all places, a Trappist monastery. The Baroness Catherine de Hueck opened "Friendship Houses" in black ghettos to combat racism; Dr. van Kersbergen brought over from Holland her ladies of The Grail, dedicated especially to the social apostolate. Father Daniel Lord, editor of *The Queen's Work,* promoter of the Sodality of Mary, pamphleteer and pianist, entertained and fired great crowds of young people who came to his peripatetic "Summer Schools of Catholic Action." If movie-goers still felt bound by the classifications of the Legion of Decency and readers by the *Index of Forbidden Books*, if the one great crusade was still anti-communism, at least Father Coughlin's tirades were off the air and Catholics were having doubts about their whole-hearted espousal of Franco in the thirties. The new generation found hope and excitement in what was coming to birth all about them. But what would tie it all together? Labor's rights, marriage and the family, education, art and literature, social welfare, racial integration—these were things one could get excited about—maybe give one's life to. But wasn't there some relationship one to another, some inner principle that gave meaning to them all?

Virgil Michel, as far back as 1925, had been saying that there was. Lambert Beauduin, Abbot Herwegen, and others—reaching as far back as the German theologians Möhler and Scheeben in the 19th century—had been saying it before him. For them it was the Church, and the Church's self-expression in her liturgy. They were saying what Vatican II would encapsulate in a neat phrase in 1963: "The sacred liturgy does not exhaust the entire activity of the Church . . . but it is the summit toward which the activity of the Church is directed; at the same time it is the font from which all her power flows."[7]

---

7.   CSL., 9-10.

At a joyous reunion in 1983 of the American "pioneers" of the liturgical movement the question was asked, "How did you get interested?" For some it was the influence of a particular person, a professor, a friend, a mentor: Msgr. Hillenbrand in Chicago, Msgr. Hellriegel in St. Louis, Father Tom Carroll in Boston. One man had been looking for a more vital and vibrant catechesis for his parish. Another, a musician, had wanted a style of prayer that would be scriptural, rich, and singable by entire congregations— not just choirs. A third, deeply involved in social welfare work, had felt the need of a link between what he did at the altar in the morning and what he did in his office all day.

The question passed to me, and I hesitated. "Well," I said, "I wish I could say that I was attracted by considerations as edifying as yours. The fact is that I came in by the back door. It was the poetry of the liturgy that won me over. I don't mean just the ritual—the choreography of the old Solemn Mass, for instance. It was the pageantry of the liturgical year, the plaintive cries and the triumphant shouts one finds in the Psalms, the breathless expectation of Advent, the splendid cadences of the old collects and prefaces. I couldn't respond to the popular devotions, but I fell in love forever with the missal and, later, with the breviary."

But if I came in by the back door I discovered little by little what an abundance there was in the house. I read everything I could find on the Church as the Body of Christ. I chased down the *sun*-compounds in St. Paul. I subscribed to *Worship* and read the seminal books coming from Michel's Liturgical Press. And I met Gerald Ellard, in his books first, and then in his delightful person, and began a friendship that grew deeper and closer until he died—in my arms, which was a great grace for me—in 1963.

Meanwhile, though, Tom Carroll had assembled a group of priests who met monthly in his rooms at the Cenacle. We recited the day-hours of the Office and sang a high Mass together, and the religious gave us a warm welcome and a hospitable lunch, and we listened to one another's papers and discussed them. Our purpose was to review the theology we had been taught in the seminary in the light of the "new" doctrine we had learned since. We did this for three years, until war came and disrupted everything (war is so enormously wasteful!). But it was a most enlightening and companionable experience, and I myself discovered the quality of the diocesan priests I would be privileged to work with in the ensuing years, at home and across the country.

We were pioneers, none the less, and, as someone said, twisting a familiar quotation, "the lot of the pioneer don't get no better." "Liturgy," for most bishops and priests, meant rubrics—a punctilious code of etiquette that had grown out of all proportion to its purpose or value. To the laity, by and large, the word meant little—another of those ecclesiastical "in words" that have small relevance to real life. When we began to urge that liturgical theory is a necessity for theology and spirituality, or to advocate changes which would promote community celebration, we were at first smiled at indulgently; "let's be sure," one pastor said, "that our people are living up to the precepts of *Casti Connubii* (Pius XI's encyclical on marriage), and then we can give them the frills." But as we persisted, and more people took us seriously, amusement turned to irritation. We became "liturgical nuts," "litniks," even "liturjerks." We had no respect for the "simple faithful."

"Liturgists?" said one archbishop. "They're just the idiots who don't like benediction." One moral theologian said he had nothing against the liturgy; he "just prescinded from it." Another hinted darkly that "the whole movement is shot through with Jansenism."

In 1943 Pius XII wrote an encyclical letter, "On the Mystical Body of Christ," which was an eloquent and beautiful statement. Unhappily for us, however, he took occasion to correct excesses in the books of some spiritual writers in Europe. They confused, he said, the physical and social bodies of Christ, or ("quietism" back in a new dress) they denied any need for human collaboration with divine grace, or they so emphasized public prayer as to minimize the value of private prayer. Of 109 paragraphs in the letter, only five were given to these topics, but of course they were seized upon and made into a condemnation of everything the "liturgists" were advocating.

We were confident enough about our orthodoxy, however, to keep a sense of humor. And some things were amusing. The members of ACCA, for instance, gathered monthly for a "dialogue Mass," an innovation at the time, under grave suspicion in local chanceries. We were allowed to use the chapel of Mount St. Joseph Academy, but the Sister Superior, a valiant woman or she would not have given permission in the first place, counseled prudence, so we slipped like conspirators through a back door, kept our voices down during the "celebration," and quietly slipped away as we had come. A little later the *Stylus* staff thought we could risk a "dialogue Mass" in St. Mary's Chapel at Boston College. But would the chaplain, a good-hearted but somewhat unpredictable elderly priest, disapprove—perhaps even halt the Mass before it was well started? Things went smoothly until Mass was over; then the chaplain bore down upon us. "A wonderful experience!" he boomed. "Reminded me of my ordination!" Sighs of relief on all sides: we would not be delated for heresy.

One Sunday in December I went for a walk through the woods around Hammond Pond, and came back to hear the shocking news: the Japs had bombed Pearl Harbor. This was it, all right. Next day, we listened to the declaration of war after the President had asked for it in a brief speech to a joint meeting of Congress. The cheers for his address seemed to me sadly ironic; I remembered the cheers, the delirious relief of Armistice Day, 1918—we kids banging on tin pans as we paraded to burn the Kaiser in effigy in Roberts Square. Only it wasn't Roberts Square then, because Tom Roberts, ten or so years older than ourselves, had been killed in France that very morning, only hours, perhaps minutes, before the guns went silent at noon. I remembered how we small fry used to hold up Tom on his way home from his job as street-car conductor, and ask him for pennies. I remembered that his sister went out of her mind for a while when they brought his body home two years later.

The country went into high gear. Mobilization, first of volunteers and then of draftees, was swift. Day after day, when I called the roll in class, someone would say, "*He's* gone, Father." (Student enrollment, at its nadir, fell to 200.) I drove to Gloucester to visit Father Carroll, who was sick, stayed too long, and had to drive some miles in the coastal blackout without lights until I reached the turnpike. I held the door open and steered by the white line down the middle of the road. Luckily, I met no oncoming traffic. Father Dick Lawlor, then a scholastic, invited me to join a corps of Jesuit air-raid wardens, who prowled about the campus making sure that every light was blacked out. "What do we do if we get a warning of a raid?" I asked. "We peer," he said. "And suppose we spot a plane coming over?" "I run to make a report." "And what do I do?" "You continue to peer."

Meanwhile, from USO clubs, from ships at sea, from barracks or tent-cities in faraway places, letters were pouring in, most of them steady if not perfectly serene, a bit homesick around the edges, hinting a question or two about the sudden end of bright youth and the American dream. And these were only from ex-Boston College students. What about those thousands of others, uprooted from home while still painfully immature, made suddenly to think of death as a distinct possibility? Who would be on hand to offer them support? 1 asked twice if I might apply for a chaplaincy, but was turned down—the second time so emphatically that I went out and bought the new black suit I needed if I were to continue in civilian life. But poetry and belles lettres suddenly seemed to be very irrelevant. Everything on campus was, except math, the physical sciences, and modern languages. Nothing mattered but the prosecution of the war.

In April a number of the Class of '43 whose courses had been accelerated so that they might graduate before being called up came together for a last Mass on campus, and asked me to preside and preach. It was a painful task. I talked first about the mystery of faith which was the Mass they were celebrating, and then about the other mystery which was their summons to war, and which they would also have to confront in faith. And then I tried to say the unsayable—what parents and teachers were feeling as they watched their sons and students march away:

> You must not think that Alma Mater looks impassively on your going. Rather she is like Rachel, bewailing her sons and refusing to be comforted, because they are not. We who have taught you and given you our best and come to love you, we shall miss your bright faces, your boyish honesty, your unspoiled goodness. We shall look for the happy day when you will come back to us for the years of peace. Meanwhile we shall think of you in the Canon of the Mass, when we shall daily say, "Remember, Lord, your servants—remember Jim and George, remember Tom and Joe and Ed, whose faith and devotion are known to you, for whom we offer this sacrifice of praise to obtain the redemption of their souls, and in hope of their safety and security." My God, protect them as the apple of your eye. Keep them in the shadow of your wings.

CHAPTER 8

Liturgy on Active Duty

I WOULD FIND IT DIFFICULT TO IMAGINE A MORE DECISIVE interruption of my usual way of life than the one that came my way in 1943. I had offered myself twice for a military chaplaincy, but my Provincial twice declined the offer—and then suddenly accepted it when college enrollment fell off sharply and teachers could be spared.

I felt no attraction to the military life. And though I detested the Nazis and the outrages they had already perpetrated, I was not persuaded altogether that Americans should intervene once more in a European quarrel. Pearl Harbor and the atrocities of the Bataan death march, on the other hand, seemed to justify, even to demand some kind of reprisal. Obviously I had done little thinking until then about the morality of war. In any case, I was enlisting as a chaplain. I would carry no weapons, use none. My function would be that of a parish priest. If my parish had as its sole purpose to bring the enemy to his knees, and if that meant pouring death and destruction on his head—well, he was not innocent, and would have to be pursued, defeated, punished like any common criminal. A priest would be on hand not to collaborate actively in that mission but to provide the same services parishioners would require at home. He would lead his men in worship, absolve penitents, cheer the dispirited, comfort the dying, bury the dead.

There was very little talk in those days about the morality of war. When the country's leaders made their decision and Congress ratified it, almost all of us assumed that it was our patriotic duty to support the "war effort" in whatever way we could. Questioning began later, after we had seen the newsreels and the casualty lists. And it grew in volume after Korea and Vietnam, after Granada and Panama, and especially after Iraq. My own motivation for enlisting derived largely from my affection for the students I had come to know. They were so very young, so pathetically eager to

101

achieve the goals they dreamed about, so untouched by meanness. And there would be thousands like them, from every corner of the country. Who would go with them into boot camp, into overseas exile, into combat? Who would listen to them, remind them of their values, steady them in danger? Well, I would. At least I would try.

Chaplain School at Harvard ran for six weeks. The content of the lectures on Army organization, on military customs and courtesies, on counseling was thin. But the experience was worthwhile in that we learned something of close-order drill, marched in formation over half of Cambridge, picked up the more common Army jargon, and in general became less self-conscious in our khaki, so that when we joined the units we were posted to we were not as ignorant or clumsy as we might have been.

I had never in all my life talked to a Protestant minister. Now one was my roommate, several counted cadence with me in the same section, I sat with thirty or more in class. Four hundred years of bitter alienation lay behind us; I think both sides genuinely wanted them behind us, but we were timid and awkward in our efforts to close the breach. That would take time and patience, growing out of an ardent desire for unity in the Kingdom of our common Lord. Meanwhile, courtesy was imperative. Esteem and affection would follow. Some day . . .

The great adventure really began when, in a roaring March blizzard, I shook hands with my father—who would not let the storm deter him from seeing me off—and boarded the train for New York, Washington, St. Louis, and Alexandria in Louisiana. My recurring dream, during the long seminary years, of visiting faraway places was about to be fulfilled, though I had no notion then of how remote some of those places would be. The exhilaration I would normally feel in setting out on such a journey was tempered not only by the weather, not only by the parting from my father, but by an air of serious purpose I sensed in the other passengers. Many were in uniform, but the civilians, too, gave the impression that they were bent on business, not on any carefree holiday. This was wartime, and the war was not going all that well: we had been given a rough reception in Africa, we had not yet ventured to attack Hitler's "Fortress Europe," we were thousands of weary sea-miles from Manila and Tokyo. Husbands and sons, and some daughters, too, were off in places no one had ever heard of—Attu, or Oran, or Biak—and only God knew whether or when they might come home. It was a grim time, a time for sobriety and prayer.

My education continued at Camp Livingston. I was assigned to the 342nd Regiment, in the 86th Infantry Division. The Division was not expected to go overseas, although it finally did go to Europe when the Germans broke out in the Bulge. After that it was turned around and sent to the Philippines. Its function now was to train enlisted men and junior officers who would be sent as replacements to combat units. At the time, thinking that my assignment would be more or less permanent, I did not realize that this was exactly what was envisioned for myself. Part of my education would be to learn that in the Army nothing is permanent.

One comforting memory of my years in the service is of the support I was given as a chaplain. Officers of all ranks, even those who professed no faith, and who thought of the chaplain as simply a morale booster, were respectful and cooperative. Enlisted men, especially the all-powerful sergeants, gave me a spontaneous loyalty and affection that was manifest in touching little kindnesses and almost pathetic confidences about themselves. Of course the possession of officer-grade rank (all chaplains, on appointment, were made first lieutenants) helped a great deal; chaplains in other armies, the British, for instance, had no rank. And Army Regulations set it down firmly that the chaplain's work was to be spiritual. He was not to be made a censor of mail, for example, or a recreation officer, as chaplains in our Navy often were. If a commander made such appointments, or in any way impeded the chaplain's activities, the chaplain had only to note it in his monthly report, which had to be endorsed by the commander and sent on "through channels" to Washington—whence, if it were verified, would come a stern rebuke and an order to rescind the appointment. In the stateside installations the Army erected chapels (there were thirteen of them at Camp Livingston) of a uniform architectural design that preserved a careful neutrality in matters of faith. Overseas, in areas where it was foreseen that we would not be staying long, more casual arrangements were provided—structures under canvas or thatch—and, except in fluid, dangerous frontline situations, some sheltered space was always made available. And time for worship was set aside, too. I remember that when a lone Seventh Day Adventist in one of my companies appealed to his commander he was relieved of work on Saturdays and given an assignment on Sundays. In short, the Army acted as if it really believed that we are "one nation under God."

My parishioners were the entire regiment, irrespective of faith, although, since there were two Protestant chaplains in the regiment, my dealings were for the most part with the Catholics. The men were young, of course; their ages ranged from the late teens to the middle or late twenties. One group, however, was older; they were transfers from the Air Corps, assigned to the infantry when it was seen that footsoldiers in large numbers would be required for the forthcoming invasions. They had been holding quite cushy jobs in very safe and comfortable situations; now they went on twenty-mile hikes under full packs, and crawled on their bellies under machine gun fire on the "infiltration course." Their griping was loud and constant, but the chaplain, powerless in these cases, could only listen with such sympathy as he could muster. He was not in his first youth, either. And his muscles, he was discovering, were just as slack.

Attendance at Mass on Sundays was fair, considering that perhaps a third of the parishioners might be out in the swamps on a "field problem." But it was a very passive attendance. Only the acolyte made the responses. In the background there was a sort of mood music on the wheezing portable organ. Singing—when there was any—was desultory and dispirited. The Mass, in other word, was anything but a celebration. Of course the entire rite was in Latin, an insuperable obstacle, as I came to realize later, to active, intelligent participation. St. Paul had asked the Corinthians a perfectly sensible question (1 Cor 14:16): "If your praise of God is solely with the spirit, how will the one who does not comprehend be able to say 'Amen' to your thanksgiving? He will not know what you are saying. You will be uttering praise very well indeed, but the other man will not be helped."

I gathered a cadre of former altar boys who would lead the congregation in the Latin responses, and for a brief space I was hopeful. But Frank Gale, my assistant, wrote after I was transferred to say that the new chaplain was not interested in the "Dialogue Mass" and had suspended it. By that time I was beginning to have my own doubts about its value. All that effort to master unpronounceable words that conveyed so little meaning? What was the point of it? Later, in Manila, I tried a different tack. I asked one of the men to lead the congregation in English as I spoke the Latin. So when I greeted the assembly with "Dominus vobiscum" he would shout "The Lord be with you!" and they would respond, "And also with you." But it was a clumsy arrangement; they were getting my greeting secondhand, and it must have seemed to them that it was his greeting, not mine as the president of the assembly. The only rational course would have been to do what the Vatican Council did twenty years later: translate the entire rite into the language of the people. But we priests who were urging liturgical renewal were obedient; we did not jump the gun, however impatient we might have been. I hope there was some merit in our forbearance.

Largely because the liturgy had been closed to the laity for so many centuries, there was a widespread ignorance of the theology of public worship. In my homilies, therefore, in a study group that met weekly, in the pages of a bulletin I distributed on Sundays, I presented fundamental ideas: the nature of the Christian community and its vocation to glorify God, the mediating priesthood of Christ, the worth before God of the sacrificial atonement wrought by Christ, the share accorded to Christians as co-redeemers of the world, the all-embracing character of "liturgy" as formal worship in church and its overflow into all one's life and activities outside the church (Rom 12:12). I tried hard to teach these ideas graphically and with homely analogies; after all, St. Paul had made them familiar to the dockhands in Corinth, and they were common coin in the Church for a thousand years. They should not be altogether impossible of assimilation by a twentieth-century audience.

All this ended three months later. I received from Washington a full page of individual telegraphed orders, requiring to start with that I be in California by midnight of the following day. It was clear from the list of clothing authorized by the orders that I was going to the tropics, whereas I had unthinkingly taken it for granted that if I moved I would go to Europe, which I had never seen and where all my interests lay. My departure from Louisiana was frantic: a mad drive back to camp from New Orleans, where Father Bob Walton and I had spent a couple of pleasant days, another mad drive to Shreveport, a flight to Dallas and San Francisco, a bus to Marysville. I came triumphantly into Camp Beale at twenty minutes before midnight. Made it, by George. Now to learn what weighty or delicate mission these urgent orders might portend. So I sat at Beale for three weeks, traveled for three weeks by slow boat to New Guinea, and sat in a replacement depot there for five more weeks before going back to work. "Hurry up and wait" was the G.I.'s weary summary of troop movement. We could take the hurry if it didn't involve the waiting, or accept the waiting if the hurry hadn't preceded, but the invariable combination of the two seemed infuriatingly stupid.

There were thirteen of us chaplains in "Shipment RY-OO3," six Catholic, six Protestant, and one Jewish. The companionship was pleasant and supportive, especially since we had no idea of where we were going or what we might find when we got there. Our common lot helped to break down the reserve we might otherwise have maintained; laughing together was healthier than solitary griping. I found, then and later, that the fellowship of priests, especially, was a grace, a privilege, a happy comradeship. It didn't matter what part of the country we hailed from—Joe Durney was a diocesan from St. Louis, Bill Galvin another from Little Rock—or which religious order we belonged to—Bede Michel was a Benedictine, Harold Roth a Precious Blood father, Frank Regan a Dominican, I a Jesuit. What bound us together was our priesthood, which meant not only a similar education and formation, not only a certain detachment (we had no wives or children, and perhaps found ourselves more ready to form strong personal relationships with one another), but a single faith, jointly and unquestioningly held, and a conviction that we had a single glorious mission whose outcome we could be confident about because, though it solicited and even challenged our cooperative efforts, it did not depend on them for final success.

Packs on our shoulders and Mass kits in our hands, we marched up the gangplank at San Francisco and then watched the Golden Gate fade into the distance. How long before we would see it again, and what would happen in the meantime? We were aboard the *Noordam,* a transport converted from what had been a part-passenger, part-freight carrier before the war broke out. She was fast, and she needed to be, because we were sailing without convoy, and we might have to run away from Jap submarines. One day we saw a lowlying blotch on the horizon that they said was Hawaii, but otherwise it was three weeks of open sea. Our lives were ruled by the announcements and commands from the ship's loudspeaker. "Now hear this . . ." We had only a daily gallon of fresh water each to wash ourselves and our laundry in, so as we dropped deeper and deeper into the tropical South Pacific we became hotter and grimier. At that, we officers, packed six deep into staterooms intended for two, had a happier lot than the enlisted men, who were loaded into an airless and progressively less fragrant hold below decks.

Our destination, we hoped, was known to the people on the bridge. We ourselves, knowing almost nothing about the geography of this part of the world, speculated and laid bets as the *Noordam* chugged endlessly on and on. And we were all wrong. It wasn't Australia, it wasn't Fiji or New Zealand. It was New Guinea. Let's see: hadn't there been a battle here in the last year or so? (There had been, indeed, a magnificent but unpublicized achievement by the 32nd Division that pushed the invading Japs back, up and over the crest of the Owen Stanley Mountains, down into their last foothold in Buna, but that was nothing, of course, compared to the heroics of the lionhearted Marines on Guadalcanal, described lyrically by their own correspondents and featured day after day on page one of newspapers across the country.)

New Guinea was—well, primitive. The white beaches we stared at, ravenous for a glimpse of land, held only thatched huts and a few tents, obviously alien. Beyond them the matted jungle stretched away, up, up to some of the loftiest peaks on earth, country where the white man, if he went at all, still went in peril of headhunters. The grey-green mountains, seen from the sea, had a certain majesty, but I was never able to dispel, altogether, a sense they communicated of hostility, even of malignity, toward us, trespassers and profane intruders in their sanctuary. Probably the notion persisted because on the island there were in fact so many threats to our well-being: snakes, nauseating and venomous insects, scrub typhus, jungle rot, elephantiasis, hepatitis, enervating heat and weeks of unremitting rain.

We saw very little of the native people. New Guinea at the time was an Australian mandate, and the Australians kept a tight rein on the natives. Even the men who worked in labor gangs for the Army had Australian foremen, who at night returned their charges to compounds that were off-limits to us. Once, to celebrate some tribal occasion, the natives were having a "singsing," and we were allowed to watch. The men—no women took part— had woven brightly colored paper streamers, cut from the covers of magazines like *Time* or *Yank*, or labels from tomato cans, into their already luxuriant topknots, and now, hour after hour, they tramped in a circle around a fire, crouched over, pounding on the packed earth the sticks they carried, and chanting endlessly some dirge or slogan or prayer. The spectacle, I noticed, was weird enough to sober the G.I.'s. Could such things be in this sophisticated twentieth century? I laughed when they asked me about it, and reminded them of certain features of their own culture: cheerleaders' gyrations, animal mascots, snake dances at football games, New Year's Eve in Times Square, or their favorite jive and hokypoky.

The Fifth Replacement Depot had moved from Goodenough Island to Oro Bay just before the *Noordam* deposited us there, so their camp accorded pretty well with the primitive character of the country. No showers, for instance. No electric light for the long evenings. No mess halls; we stood for meals and balanced our mess kits on the fender of the nearest jeep. But my assignment came through, finally, and at last, after the standard huffing and puffing by the Transportation people, I arrived at Finschhafen, a couple of hundred miles up the coast, and joined the Ninth Ordnance Battalion.

The Army's Ordnance Department, as its name indicates, was originally set up to procure, maintain, and issue weapons—everything from the Colt 45 to the "Long Toms," the heavy artillery pieces. But with the coming of the motor age the Department was given charge, also, of vehicles: jeeps, recon cars, six-by-six trucks, ambulances (known to the G.I.'s by the unlovely name of "meat wagons"), generators, earth movers and cranes, tanks, ducks, weapons carriers, motorized field kitchens—anything on wheels powered by gasoline. Your typical Ordnance man, therefore, called himself a "grease monkey," and was that in fact. He was good with his hands, usually, and knew a lot about engines. His formal education had as a rule not gone beyond high school; I was shocked to discover a number of men who were illiterate. Everyone, of course, had had basic training, but their shops were normally far behind the front lines, so they had little or no combat experience.

Here, then, was my parish. I was attached to the Ninth, but another Ordnance battalion and a battalion of Engineers were close by, and it was understood that I would serve them, too. Total: some four thousand men, plus others who were permanently or temporarily in the area—"service of supply" troops like Quartermaster or Signal outfits. And as opportunity offered I would take care of orphaned units like the stevedores unloading Liberty ships down on the docks.

The battalion's headquarters company, of which I was a member, lived in pyramidal tents, two officers to a tent, in a palm grove fronting directly on the sea. The officers, especially Captain Paul

De Grieck, were uniformly cordial and helpful, though the commander did not personally sympathize with my mission. "In my family," he explained to me one day, "We are either religious men or engineers, and I'm an engineer." His concept of the chaplain's function was that of a morale builder, the man who goes about calling people by their first names, telling the little joke, slapping them on the back by way of encouragement. Alas, though I did my best to be pleasant to all and sundry, I was not by temperament his hail-fellow-well-met. The conversations at meals, too, were a little strained after a time. I knew nothing about engines, and less about artillery. The others were out of their depth in literature, history, philosophy, and, very particularly, theology. We got along, but haltingly.

The great problem in the South Pacific was loneliness. It was common enough in other theaters as well, but in most of those there were diversions. On a furlough in Europe, for instance, you could visit London or Paris. A classmate of mine, a chaplain in Italy, wrote that he had had an audience with the Pope. Our base in Finschhafen stretched along the beach for about fifteen miles; the jungle surrounded it on three sides and the ocean on the fourth. There were no roads beyond the base, and nothing to see, anyway, but more jungle or more ocean. Technically, men who had served in Guinea for a specified period—I think it was fifteen months— were entitled to a leave in Australia, but I never met anyone who got it. The Army provided movies, books at the PX, shows featuring well-known actors and singers from the States, but could not provide what young Americans most wanted: freedom to drive a car without a trip-ticket, freedom to take the girlfriend out on a date, freedom to throw up a job if one didn't like it and tell the boss what he could do with it.

I began at once to visit the companies separately, reminding *all* the men that I was their chaplain and would gladly serve them in any way I could, and then asking the Catholics to fill out a form which would give me a roster of my congregation, and also some idea of its spiritual health. The results, when I tabulated them, decided me to conduct an old-fashioned "mission." My little flock obviously needed some salutary admonitions, a generous infusion of God's grace, and a return to sacramental regularity. So for eight nights, Sunday to Sunday, I expounded, pleaded, demanded, exhorted, challenged. Statistically, perhaps, it was disappointing; my largest attendance was 295. But there was consolation in the faithful appearance of many, and especially in the confessions of long-term absentees. I really had no grounds for disappointment. These were young men, not yet very mature in character or outlook. There were no wives or mothers to prod and encourage their fidelity. They would turn out in large numbers when they were frightened, as when we were going in on an invasion, but then grow careless again. I was too well acquainted with my own backsliding to be impatient.

The most memorable event of my six months at Finschhafen was the building and dedication of our chapel what one of the priests used to tease me about by calling it "the Ordnance Cathedral." But it's a long story, and I have told it often (*Worship, America*). And the altar we designed and built and took with us when we moved now stands, with all its appurtenances, in the museum of the Army's Corps of Chaplains at Fort Monmouth, New Jersey, the central exhibit of the section on World War II. The chapel itself, of course, we could not take with us. Leaving it behind gave me the only pang I felt on bidding farewell to New Guinea.

By this time Leyte had been taken, at great cost, but Luzon, with Manila at its heart, was still in Japanese hands. When our transport (ominously, a hospital ship) came to the rendezvous at Manus Island, and we saw in the wide harbor there other transports, surrounded by battleships, aircraft carriers, destroyers, and submarines which would be convoy to an armada of two hundred fighting ships, we had a pretty good idea of what we were in for. Ordnance troops, normally, would not be in the early waves of an invasion, but somehow here we were. My men, I was glad to see, set their jaws and said nothing, but I noticed that attendance at my daily Mass expanded far beyond any previous participation.

A protective smokescreen enveloped the ship on the morning of January 11, but the breeze soon blew it away, and now it was imperative to get ashore before attacking planes from Formosa swooped in on us. The scramble nets hung over the ship's side, and we went down hand-over-hand to the landing craft and raced for the beach, three miles away, pushing aside in the water black cylinders, shell cases from the Navy bombardment of the coast on the previous day.

Once ashore we made a quick meal of K rations and struck out for the palm grove we had been assigned to near San Fabian. Everything looked and sounded and felt familiar and welcome: the firm ground we marched on, unlike the spongy earth of New Guinea, the long black-and-white arm over the road to warn traffic of a railroad crossing, the crowing of roosters and the cries of babies. We were out of the jungle at last. Best of all, Filipinos, men and women of all ages, lined the road, bowing, smiling, holding up two fingers in the V-sign for victory.

We moved several times in the next few days, looking for an area where we might set up our shops, and waiting for the LST's to bring in our gear. We were only a very small headquarters company, and although the Japs, anticipating our bombardment, had withdrawn into the hills, they sent out raiding parties at night to steal supplies and, of course, to eliminate any who, like ourselves, might be likely to give them an argument. We doubled the sentries around the perimeter of our tiny encampment and spent some wakeful nights.

Gradually, as a Regimental Combat Team steadily pushed the Japs back to Baguio, our area quieted down and things became more normal. But the Japanese soldier was committed to die rather than surrender, so our casualties kept coming down from the hills. Some went to the hospitals, but many went to the cemetery that we set up at Santa Barbara. Chaplain Marty Hardin and I were appointed to carry out the committal rites there.

Marty was a Presbyterian, a Princeton alumnus who became the closest friend I made among the Protestant chaplains, a thoroughly gracious and zealous gentleman. We spent many a merry hour chaffing each other—to the shocked astonishment of the other officers in the mess—about our theological and cultural differences.

At home the "American Way of Death" has had a softening effect on the survivors; the more immediately painful details of death and burial are attended to by professionals. But at Binalonan, where during four months I read the committal prayers for 3,500 men—and these were only the Catholics; Chaplain Hardin and the Jewish chaplain from the Base took care of many others—there were no such cosmetic devices. An unmistakable odor, sweetish, sickening, filled the air. These men had died some days before their bodies arrived here; now, without embalming, in a hot country, the bodies lay in the open, silent in their shrouds of blankets or shelter-halves, until the Filipino laborers could dig graves for them. There were older men among the dead, battalion and even regimental commanders, and, once or twice, general officers, but most of them were pathetically young, boys in their teens or early twenties. Was this, I asked myself, the best we could do for them? Poor Edna Millay's lines ran through my mind:

> I am not resigned to the shutting away of loving hearts in
>   the hard ground. . . .
> Down, down, down into the darkness of the grave
> Gently they go, the beautiful, the tender, the kind;
> Quietly they go, the intelligent, the witty, the brave.
> I know. But I do not approve. And I am not resigned.

Half a century and a thousand specious justifications later, I am not resigned, either. Nor ever shall be.

Elsewhere on Luzon people came back from the dead, or from something very like death. We stormed the prison gates at Cabanatuan, at Santo Tomas, at Los Banos, and released hundreds of starving, almost hopeless Americans, interned brutally for three years. Some were soldiers, survivors of the Death March on Bataan, some were civilians, men, women, *and* children. Among them I found old friends, Jesuits I had lived with at Weston or Boston College. They are all dead now; the experience broke their health.

In April I was transferred to Manila, to headquarters of the Philippine Base Section, which later became Base X. I had mixed feelings about leaving Ordnance. Friends in that outfit had been kind, and we had gone through some vicissitudes together. On the other hand, I was beginning to question my usefulness to the battalion. We had become a rear echelon unit again; life was no longer insecure, and the various attractions of civilization began to exert their gravitational pull. Attendance even at Sunday Mass fell off sharply, and on weekdays I saw almost nobody. It seemed to me that the neighboring parish priest could provide for the men's essential needs—if they chose to satisfy them—and I could look elsewhere for labors that offered more promise.

Not by any means for the first time, I wondered how I had got into the Army. It was certainly not owing to any love for life in the open, or for the pomp and circumstance of squadrons on parade. My tastes, any day, would take me to a library. But in the 1940's the most promising apostolate for a priest was with the troops, in the Army or Navy. And then, if in a particular situation hope of a rich harvest seemed to be fading, the only course was to move. The Lord himself gave that directive (Matt 10:23), and St. Paul surely followed it.

At any rate, by dint of pulling a wire here and there, I found myself in Manila, the only Catholic chaplain in Base X headquarters, and as nearly a bishop as I ever shall be. I hadn't the consecration, but I did have the headaches. Manila was newly wrested from the Japanese, and became the nerve center for future operations, especially for the climactic assault on the enemy's homeland.

The base headquarters was located in the Customs House, a large office building opposite Pier 7 on the waterfront. Hundreds of officers, enlisted men, and WACS put in long hours here, trying to receive, dispose, feed, shelter, and prepare for new moves the troops that were landing every day, as well as to reorganize the national government and economy, feed and employ the Filipino people, hospitalize and send home American prisoners of war and their dependents. Personnel (G1), Intelligence (G2), Plans and Operations (G3), and Supply (G4) all had their offices, and under them were ranged such diverse subsections as Quartermaster, Signal, Medical, Sanitary, Ordnance, Air Corps, Chemical Warfare, Finance, Engineers, Transportation, Special Services, Chaplain, and so on, not to speak of Navy liaison, Red Cross, War Shipping Administration, Military Government, and any number of related agencies set up for the multitudinous needs of a vast army and a disorganized civilian population. It was a new experience for me to be thrown into the midst of all this, and it took me some time to learn my way about and to overcome the diffidence of the new arrival.

As for the chaplaincy's part in all this, not only was there the usual ministry to units in the city and its suburbs, many of which had no assigned chaplain of their own, but fresh troops were coming from the States and were located farther out but still within the supervision of the Base. They, too, had to be cared for if chaplains were available and if transportation could be arranged. I spent hours on the telephone, calling the Base motor pool and the replacement depot at Angeles, where newly-arrived chaplains were awaiting assignment.

It was a problem to find housing for the headquarters personnel itself. If you were a field-grade officer (major and up) you were entitled to live "off the base," in a house or apartment of your own choosing; if you were company grade (captain and down), you lived wherever you were billeted. "Home" for me turned out to be a former automobile showroom a few doors away from the Customs House. There, where four or five cars had been displayed in prewar days, two hundred officers had cots. We were so close together that, as one wag said, you had to ask permission of the man next to you before you turned over in bed. There were no shelves, closets, or lockers, so our belongings were all over the floor. Above each cot was a mosquito netting which was necessary and welcome, but two hundred nettings prevented any vagrant breeze from getting around the room, so sleep was restless and unsatisfying in the humidity which by the end of April had descended on Manila like a heavy blanket. We were just across the street from the docks, and all night long the big QM trucks gunned their engines thirty feet from our heads. Every so often, too, someone came home in a merry or pugnacious mood, and the chaos that prevailed before he was quieted down and put to bed was destructive of peaceful slumber.

Most of the American Jesuits who had been imprisoned at Santo Tomas or Los Banos had been sent home for rest and recuperation, but a "token force" of generous volunteers had remained. They included Father John Hurley, the superior, and Fathers Harry Avery, John McNicholas, Austin Dowd, Leo Cullum, Henry Greer, and Anthony Keane. Since most of our houses had been destroyed in the war, the Fathers were living in four rooms in the back of "La Consolacion," a girls' school then operating at only a third of its capacity. Here they set up a "Catholic Welfare Organization" which was adopted by the hierarchy, disbursing food and other necessities of life to the civilian population, acting as liaison with the Army, providing information to the newspapers, assisting refugees, and in general getting the wheels of normal civilian life turning once more. Quite incidentally, their rooms became a haven, too, for Catholic chaplains assigned to or visiting the city, as well as for alumni of Catholic schools, especially Jesuit schools, in the States. It was a rare night when there wasn't a group reminiscing about old professors at Georgetown or Holy Cross or Campion or one of the Loyolas. And we all listened with fascination and roars of laughter to Father Hurley's stories of smuggling food and medicine during the occupation to American prisoners at Cabanatuan and to guerrillas in the hills, of his efforts (successful until six months before the end) to outwit the Japs, to keep the Ateneo from being taken over, and to remain himself at large in spite of Japanese suspicion that he was not wholly sympathetic to their aspirations.

But it hadn't been altogether a matter for humorous recollection. Father Hurley once showed me a tabulation of the debts he had incurred from December 8, 1941, to July 31, 1945. It cost him $282,354 to support for three and a half years 167 American, Filipino, and Spanish Jesuits and 110 diocesan seminarians, a figure which averaged out, he said, to about 98 cents a day for each man, "and this in the blackest of black markets." In addition, there were these debts:

> For helping to support, in the Provinces of Pampanga, Bataan, Cavite, and Laguna, small short-term camps of American officers and soldiers who had escaped from the Death March,
> For helping American prisoners in work gangs in the Manila Port Area with medicines and food,
> For helping Filipino guerrilla units in the mountains with medicine,
> For helping families of guerrillas in Manila, and wives and children of officers and men who were hiding in the city,
> For helping widows and orphans of dead Filipino soldiers,
> For helping some soldiers and two officers hiding for a time in Manila, ... $ 51,347

> For housing and feeding an average of about 70 internees (ill and therefore released from Santo Tomas Internment Camp to the Ateneo de Manila, where living conditions were better and the help of doctors was more readily obtained), from December, 1941, to April, 1943,
> For helping with food and quarters the Red Cross Hospital No. 7, established in the Ateneo de Manila with a patient list of sometimes nearly 100, ... $24,118

The total debt came to something like $350,000—enough to gray the hair of any mission superior.

What with the clamorous trucks outside and the all-too-frequent hubbub inside, I wasn't getting much sleep in my billet at the Base. I was, moreover, homesick for Jesuit community life. My visits to La Consolacion made me pine for the company of men who shared my background and ideals, who followed the same Rule and lived according to the same customs. Finally I asked Father Hurley if I might move in with the community, and he made me very welcome. I kept my bed in the billet, in case anyone should be inquisitive, but I lived happily at La Consolacion, and to this day I cherish bright memories of my days with those Jesuits, all of whom are now dead. They were weary from the war and imprisonment and suffering still from malnutrition, but they were cheerful and graciously kind; they prayed much and gave themselves selflessly to the Kingdom of God.

Sundays were on the strenuous side. A typical one was June 17: Father McNicholas and I drove some eight miles out to Grace Park to celebrate Mass with some Engineers who had just arrived from the States. I decided to give them some tips on overseas duty, and felt like a real veteran as I talked. Then we came into the Base for my second Mass at 10:30, where I had a goodly congregation of about 270 men. Father John helped me with confessions in both places, and of course we heard many more than I would have been able to hear alone. We returned to La Consolacion for dinner, and at four o'clock I had my third Mass at the Base. Afterward I rushed through supper and went to LaSalle College to open a week's "mission" for the WACS who were billeted there. I was a bit stale by this time, so the sermon wasn't very good, and I wondered whether many of the women would come back. But the number in attendance (about sixty) held up through the following week.

Weekdays were not exactly idle, either. A log of one of them might read like this:

1. It's considered *infra dig* for an officer to hitchhike, but there's nothing in Army Regulations to prevent him from standing on a corner and looking wistful. By using this technique I manage without difficulty to get a ride to the Base from some passing jeep.

2. Breakfast at the Base, with a quick look at the headlines of the *Daily Pacifican*, the equivalent in our theater of the European Theater's daily newspaper, the *Stars and Stripes*. Then to the office for a brief conference with my Protestant and Jewish colleagues.

3. A procession of petitioners: (a) a soldier who has just learned that his brother has the same APO as himself and wants to locate him. (b) A very young soldier who, on a month's acquaintance, wants to marry a Filipino girl. I discourage him eloquently. (c) Another soldier who wants a transfer to a new unit because he has been "busted" from corporal to private. He is a Quartermaster truck driver, and he says he was punished because he gave a ride to a civilian (this was against regulations). He pleads that the civilian was a poor old widow

whose only son was killed in the liberation of the city. I call his C.O. and learn that he was busted, actually, for exceeding the speed limit after having been warned three times. (d) Another soldier whose marriage has been approved by the Army. Can he go back to Australia and marry her? I call my friend Captain Geary in the Adjutant General's office and learn that, according to USASOS Memo no. 30, dated 30 March 45, he can. (e) A sailor from a Navy cargo ship at present tied up in the harbor. Can I get him a manual on automobile mechanics which he might study in preparation for his return to civilian life? (f) A Protestant chaplain, just landed with his unit from the States, wants Mass next Sunday for his Catholic men. I promise to get him a priest from the pool at Angeles. (g) Joe Doakes wants an emergency furlough, and Sam Boakes' wife at home is threatening to divorce him, while Tom Joakes has managed to get a Filipino girl pregnant and her family is demanding that he marry her. Then Father Spoakes, from one of the hospitals in the area, comes in for supplies (bread, wine, candles, literature) and Major Hoakes calls from the Area Command to say that he wants that overdue report by noon "at the latest."

4. I drive furiously to see old friends in the 759th Engineers, have supper with the officers, remonstrate gently with one when his language gets a little too picturesque, hear confessions and celebrate Mass in the mess hall, preach briefly about their opportunity to offer to God, in union with the offering of Christ in the Mass, a costly and precious gift, their personal purity.

5. I visit the nearby hospital to see one of the Engineers, who has picked up hepatitis.

6. At the office again, a merchant seaman drops in for confession, and then a priest I don't know calls to learn what happened to a box of supplies sent him from the States and signed for by my clerk. A young officer, a graduate of our Rockhurst College in Kansas City, comes in to talk over a problem. He has just been promoted, and to celebrate he gives me sixty pesos ($30) for the Jesuits in Manila. An enlisted man who has never made his First Communion comes in for instructions. Alone at last, I pray the night Office and look at the pile of neglected letters on my desk. But the mosquitoes and other insects attracted by my desk lamp are a nuisance, and the heat is intense, and I am beginning to feel more than a little super-

fluous to the war effort. It's time to wangle a ride home. And Father Heinie Greer will probably have to tip the bed over at 6:30 tomorrow morning to get me out of it.

The unspeakable nastiness, the agony that was the War came to an end in August, after six years. It ended with the coldly calculated Russian declaration against Japan, and the atomic bombing of Nagasaki and Hiroshima. Since then the bombing has been condemned as heinously immoral; it has been singled out as if somehow it could be considered apart from all the weary horrors which preceded it and which might conceivably be justified. To me Hiroshima was only the awful climax toward which we moved through atrocities like those at Warsaw, Coventry, London, Munich and Dresden, Auschwitz, Leningrad, Bataan. None of it was justifiable by standards of reason or decency, and certainly not by Christian standards. Humanity seemed to have got itself on a garbage chute, and went down from one level of filthiness to the next. *Facilis descensus averni.*

As the song said, "the lights went on again, all over the world," and the boys would come home again, all over the world, but though I made it the topic of six sermons, three on the holyday and three the following Sunday, I still couldn't grasp it. It might have been easier if there had been some change in our status and routine, but we went on doing the same things, and felt we might continue to do them for a long time yet. Still I tried to thank God, for myself but most of all for the men who would not have to storm any more beaches or languish in prisons, for the women who would not have to cringe under bombs or weep for the beloved they would never see again. The problems we faced in the postwar world were gigantic, but we could not even begin to solve them until we had the peace.

If I needed any evidence for the reality of original sin, I think I could find it in the madness that overtakes reasonable beings and makes them kill one another, when on every count it would be desirable that they get along peacefully together. One can never surrender the hope that some day the human race will emerge from childhood and be mature enough to settle its differences by arbitration, but a reading of history gives no grounds for optimism that it will occur soon. As Pope Pius XI exclaimed in sorrow, "This old world, that has shed so much blood and dug so many graves!"

With the coming of the peace I began to be restless. Manila had been interesting—the only assignment I had in the Army that I really enjoyed—but now the interest was fading. And the unrelenting heat was draining my energies seriously. I remember sitting in a breeze from the bay so strong that I had to put paperweights on every paper on my desk, and at the same time watching my khaki shirt turn dark with sweat. The sameness of the tropical islands was wearing, and I pined for four seasons, with all their infinite shadings and variations. Frost and October haze, and chill November rains on sidewalks under streetlamps; a June evening under the fragrant lindens along the Bapst Library walk; whitecaps off Cohasset in July; even the crunch of snow underfoot on cold days, with invigorating breaths of really fresh air. "New England," I said to myself, "I have much maligned thee in the past; take me back and I'll sing thy praises."

I applied for transfer to Japan, but there was no opening in any of the bases that were being established there, and I didn't really want to go with a small unit. I could see myself moving in, building another chapel, then settling down to a quiet parochial life. It would have been small beer after Base X and I had no stomach for it. And then the miracle happened. My Provincial wrote, ordering me to request relief from active duty in order to return to teaching. The men of the armed forces were coming home and back to college, he said, and my services would be needed in the classroom. I was dazed. The Provincial must be out of his mind, I thought. But would he have told me to ask for inactive status unless he had some assurance that I would get it? An immense hope dawned. Possibly, just possibly . .

Five days later the document was in my hands. A lovely document, it read: "By command of General MacArthur, Ch (Capt) William J. Leonard, 0544318, is relieved present assignment and attached 21st Replacement Depot. He will proceed by water transportation to Separation Center, Fort Devens, Mass., for return to inactive status." I read it over, and over, *and over*. Surely one of the greatest pieces of English literature ever written.

CHAPTER 9

Picking up the Pieces

WE WERE HOME AGAIN—HOME FROM BURMA AND "THE Hump," from Normandy and Anzio, from the Coral Sea and Murmansk and Agra and Okinawa and Leyte and all points between. One day, lecturing on *Romeo and Juliet*, I spent some time describing the town of Verona, where the action of the play takes place. Next day one of the class showed me snapshots he had taken from the nose of a bomber. "This is Verona," he said. "It was a big railroad center, and we had to put it out of business."

Settling down wasn't easy for any of us, faculty or students. The star-crossed love of Romeo and Juliet, the principles of introductory economics or physics, the rules for syllogistic argument seemed pretty small potatoes. It had been more fun, of an evening, to down a beer or two with the boys in the shadow of the Pantheon or even among the nodding palm trees on some Pacific beach than it was to sit alone over a term paper on the Carolingian dynasty. "Stick it out till Christmas," I used to say, to myself and to them. "You'll hit your stride then."

The "G.I. Bill" was the benefaction of a grateful country that brought thousands of veterans to college in 1946—2700 of them to Boston College. Even with its assistance many of them, married and with children, found the going hard. One of my students, father of three, owned a bowling alley that supplemented the family income but required his supervision every night until the small hours. When class began in September he looked fresh and eager; three weeks later he was drooping with exhaustion. But he managed, somehow, to survive, and, finally, to graduate.

Of course these were not the adolescent, sometimes giddy freshmen of prewar days. These men had grown up; further, they had lost time, and knew it, and though not solemn they were serious. I had a hundred and sixty in several classes that semester, and only six were not veterans. These were boys just out of high school who felt their youth in the midst of all this maturity and kept pretty much to themselves. The story went round of a philosophy lecture during which several of them, clustered in the back of the room, kept talking and laughing. The professor was visibly distracted and annoyed, and at last a former top sergeant stood up in the front row.

"Excuse me, Father. If you blank pups don't shut your blank mouths I'll break your blank-blank necks. Got it? Okay, Father, go ahead."

Administrators seemed to sense a need to pick up the prewar pieces and move on, but to be uncertain which of the pieces still retained value or relevance. "Get the chaplains back in the classrooms" was the watchword. "They know what's needed." So all of us (eighteen of the faculty had enlisted as chaplains) found ourselves back in black cassocks and birettas, rummaging in the attic for our notes, and being consulted to a degree we had never before experienced. Not that we ourselves had precise ideas of the direction or methods that should be adopted. We knew only that some things had to change.

People in education elsewhere were aware of this need. Charles Cole, president of Amherst, had this to say:

"We are striving to prepare men—to prepare you—to live in the world of 1950 and 1960 and 1970. It is a difficult task, because no one can guess the shape of that world of tomorrow. It is an exciting challenge because it must be done. That we are attempting it is an act of faith—faith that in any world there are some things which will bring success and happiness and peace to men and nations."

The president of the University of Illinois, George Stoddard, said:

> We cannot afford to overlook the universal, non-vocational demands of life today. In a democracy, much is demanded of every citizen, regardless of his IQ. It is easy to dig a trench, and hard to understand your family; easy to run a truck, and hard to pick a wife, a political candidate, or a place to live.

And Paul Elbin, president of West Liberty State College in West Virginia, had sound advice for returning veterans and indeed for anyone matriculating in college:

> In my judgment, the biggest problem facing the college student this year (the academic year 1946-47) is how to

obtain that balance of sociability and solitude which is indispensable for genuine educational development. The obtaining of this balanced life in college has always been difficult; this year it will be nearly impossible. But the attempt must be made by all students who are determined to get on with their education here and now. Note the two essentials: sociability and solitude. Either by itself is an extreme, an escape from the other. But without both, education is a mockery. The college years are years of transition from one kind of life to another; from life as it is to life as you want it to be. Whatever your goal, you must know people—that requires sociability; but you must also be worth knowing—that requires solitude for peace of mind, reflection, and inner renewal. . . . I repeat, you are not educated until you are equally at ease in society and in solitude.

Of course we had to reckon with the capacities of our audiences. From the English teacher's perspective, it was clear that the G.I.-turned-student had never learned or in the press of battle had forgotten some of the niceties of written self-expression. To relieve the drudgery of reading freshman papers I used to set aside occasional gems for later contemplation. Thus:

"Poetry prepares the student for life in that it teaches him to interrupt others as well as to express himself." (He means "interpret.")

"The poem ("Ulysses") was based on King Arthur and was written after his death by Tennyson."

"Mostly everyone couldn't denie that."

"We have always been told not to fool in the street. Today one of my father's friends had his oldest boy pushed through a store window which needed ten stitches to sew up."

"How many martas there have been!"

"The object of poetry is to arouse a nobaly motion."

"Wars were wagered all through history."

"My pregidous mind."

"Heart-rendering cries."

"My opinion of this poem is all for it."

Spelling tended to be phonetic rather than orthodox:

pome (poem)
rearly (really)
seames (seems, Madam, I know not seames!)

chrowds (of people)
seight (a lovely one)
a lovely seen, too
metroperless (e.g., Boston)
skyscrappers
probley (such economy!)
not even a riple
defineately!

Peter Ochiogrosso, in *Once a Catholic*[1] quotes Robert Stone: "We used to joke when I was in high school that the perfect Christian life was to graduate from that place and go on to St. John's or Fordham and become an insurance actuary and be buried in Calvary Cemetery." This was caricature, of course, but close enough to the pre-war ideal to make one squirm. When I was asked to preach at the Mass of the Holy Spirit that opened the academic year I thought I should try to push aspiration a notch higher:

> There seems no reason for elaborating the point that we stand at the beginning of a new era. Some of our contemporaries persist still in referring to World War I, World War II, and the menacing World War III as if these were isolated, unrelated conflicts, and not spasms in a convulsion that will—did I say "will"?—that is already swallowing the world we knew and disgorging a strange one. We may not like it, we may not even admit it, but it is a fact that the culture and the civilization our fathers knew are fading forever, and whether the stream of time, doubling back upon itself, will bring us to some earlier pattern of life, or whether we are being irresistibly swept toward an altogether new and frightening one, we are still to learn. . . . This is the task to which we must dedicate ourselves this mid-century morning. In the school year that lies before us, as well as in all the years that we may have, we must be the architects and builders of the Christian Commonwealth. By this I mean a society that is inspired by Christ, modeled on Christ's principles, peopled by men and women who have frankly taken Christ as their exemplar of the good life, and who are sustained in their imitation by the grace of Christ. I mean a society in which people will be free with the freedom wherewith Christ has set us free, whose heroes and heroines will be the saints

---

1.   Boston, 1987.

who have striven to be Christ-like, whose ideal will be to carry one another's burdens in imitation of Christ, who came not to be served but to serve. In that society, as in that eternal one which revelation promises us, the Lamb shall be the Lamp. . . . But the society we shall erect must be in very truth a commonwealth. Away then with any caste system, any upper or lower or middle classes, fabricated on wealth, education, or other privilege. We shall be members of a social body, in which every member shall have respect for the contribution he makes to the well-being of the whole, in which the weak shall be shielded and assisted, not ground down and exploited. With the same justice and generosity that God makes the means of supernatural life available to us in the sacraments of Reconciliation and the Eucharist, we shall make available to all men and women the means of natural life with which the earth has been replenished. No slums, then, in our Commonwealth! No ghettos where some citizens are segregated because their color or creed differs from that of the majority. No dehumanizing drudgery, in which some lose self-respect and are degraded to the level of machines for production, that others may grow rich. No pagan adoration of wealth, but rather that Christlike charity which, in the spirit of the Good Samaritan, uses its possessions for the care of the less fortunate. Of such a Christian Commonwealth we must be the architects and the builders. . . . The love of Christ, then, urges us to plan and to build a society where he may be spoken, understood, received. In all your studies here, keep the Commonwealth before you. Draw the blueprint for it as completely as you can. Write its constitutions and plan how they may be implemented. People will call you mad. Well, we want a few mad people now; see where the sane ones have landed us. People will laugh at you and your dream. But it is better and holier to have dreamed in vain for the good of one's fellow-man than never to have dreamed at all. And what if the dream, or any substantial part of it, come true! We, your teachers, shall not regret your folly in so high a cause; we shall praise and point to you as an inspiration. We have only one fear, that in this critical hour, when the one thing needful has been laid before you, you will not be equal to the quest. You will turn from it in cynicism or in selfishness. You will quail, like Hamlet, before the holy task: "The time is out of joint: O cursed spite, that ever I was born to set it right."

Indeed the time is sadly out of joint, but *we* were born to
set it right, and, God helping us, we will. . . . Such a
potential good is here assembled! So many hearts to love
God and neighbor heroically! So many good minds to
ponder the problems of our sick world, and so many hands
to minister to it! What could we not do for the building
up of the Body of Christ, for the Christian Commonwealth! The Spirit of God broods over these waters of
our souls. Come, Holy Spirit! Let there be light! Let our
darkness comprehend it!

The tone of that sermon seems to me now to be a bit perfer-
vid, but I haven't changed my mind about our aspirations at that
time; I don't think they were lofty enough. Prosperity came in
with the Eisenhower years. We put up one building after another
(some of them, mercifully temporary, we called "Visigothic" in
contrast to the Gothic towers already there). Our enrollment
swelled year by year. One good Jesuit defended his practice of
urging his students to "go out and make a million dollars," and a
surprising number of them did exactly that as Catholics across the
country moved up in the social scale. The theology we taught, in
retreats and sermons as well as in class, was still highly individualistic ("the all-important purpose of life is to save your soul!"). It
was still defensive, echoing the strictures of Trent against Protes-
tantism, setting up and demolishing the Rationalists, thundering
anathemas against Communism, pornography, birth control. "What
are we *for?*" asked one student in a small voice—anticipating the
question Pope John asked twenty years later. All students had to
take sixteen credits in this theology, and twenty-four in scholastic
philosophy, which offered substance, indeed, but in a style little
calculated to inspire.

Resident students, who came aboard in growing numbers,
were required to attend Mass daily. Their spiritual experience
could have been only an interior one, since the only active participation allowed them was kneeling, sitting, and standing—all in
total silence. The rite was carried out, of course, in Latin, a language familiar only to classics majors, and very few of these could
follow when it was spoken rapidly. It was curious how the directives of Pope Pius X with regard to Modernism and frequent Communion were obeyed so exactly, yet his prescription for instilling
the "true Christian spirit" fell on utterly deaf ears. He had said
long before, in 1903:

We are filled with a burning desire to see the true Christian spirit flourish in every respect and be preserved by all the people. We therefore are of the opinion that before everything else it is necessary to provide for the sanctity and dignity of the temple where the faithful assemble for no other purpose than that of acquiring this spirit from its primary and indispensable fount, that is, active participation in the most sacred mysteries and in the public and solemn prayer of the Church.

There were stirrings, however, if not at the universities where, as someone said, the Church was supposed to do its thinking. Locally, an immense step forward was taken in 1948, when the then-Archbishop Cushing invited the national Liturgical Conference to hold its annual "Liturgical Week" in Boston. The publicity and other preparations by the local committee (Father Carroll's pre-war study group, largely) were circumspect and thorough, and some 1500 persons assembled for opening night. Unhappily, the Archbishop's welcoming address had been written for him by a priest who was unfriendly to the Conference. It was full of dire warnings about excessive enthusiasm, preoccupation with external features of the liturgy, disdain for popular piety, failure to consider the limitations of "the simple faithful," etc. But during the Week a delegation of the Conference's officers—respected monsignori like Hellriegel of St. Louis and Hillenbrand of Chicago—impatient with the warning finger that had been shaken at them so often by prelates, asked for and obtained an audience. They must have been quite persuasive, because at the closing session the Archbishop, with characteristic blunt honesty, began *ex abrupto*: "I understand that you didn't like my talk the other night. Well, I've changed my mind. I'm throwing open the Archdiocese to your work. I'll celebrate a pontifical high Mass for you once a month, and you can have the cathedral after Mass for your educational programs." This was manna from heaven. We didn't especially want the pontifical high Mass, but we did want him. And he was as good as his word; he came for Mass faithfully for the next two years, though I could never persuade him to stay for the educational programs.

These programs took the form of lectures on such topics as the Mass, the sacraments, the liturgical year, etc. While I was discussing them in the pulpit, a simultaneous pantomine was being presented in the sanctuary by students I recruited from Boston College, Regis College, and Newton College of the Sacred Heart. The formula worked well; attendance ran as high as 1200 (a full house in the cathedral), and gave ample evidence of the people's desire to understand and participate in the Church's prayer. After two years we decided to put the show on the road, so to speak, and took it to any parish where the pastor would have us. It was fruitful education that helped to prepare minds for the reforms inaugurated by the Second Vatican Council fifteen years later. We gave it up, finally, because in most places there was no follow-through, no effort to introduce even such improvements as were then countenanced. The parish priests did not attend the presentations—not even, in some cases, the pastor who had sanctioned them. We were creating an appetite for which there was no gratification.

Nevertheless, the Archbishop's endorsement opened the way to further developments. The study group organized as the (unofficial) Sacramental Apostolate, and began publishing a journal called "Mediator," which was edited by Father Sheehan and Sister Francille, and which was circulated in several dioceses elsewhere in the country. At Boston College a "Social Worship Program" was started in the summer of 1948. Although it had an excellent faculty (Father Ellard, Father C.J. McNaspy), the graduate school refused to grant credit for its courses, so enrollments were few. Even the Sisters, who because they read seriously and attended conferences were in their thinking far ahead of the priests (who too often did neither)—even the Sisters regretfully stayed away.

One evening in 1951, I visited the novitiate of the Maryknoll Brothers for a reunion with Father Bob Sheridan and Father Tom Nolan, both of whom had become my fast friends when I was in the Army.

"What are you going to this summer?" Bob asked.

"I'm going to Dubuque for the Liturgical Week," I said.

"Take my car," said Bob.

"Not on your life!" I protested.

"Listen: I'm going to stay here all summer. I'll have no use for it. I want you to take it."

"Bob," I said, "Thanks, but that would put more than two thousand miles on your car. Nothing doing."

He insisted, and I resisted. But when I got home he called up to renew the offer. And the next day he sent me a telegram to the same effect. I concluded finally that he really meant it. And then I began to have ideas. I could do personal barnstorming along the way for the Social Worship Program of 1952, and I could finance the trip by directing week-end retreats. So I drove from Boston to Milwaukee, conducted a retreat there, went to the Liturgical Week in Dubuque, drove to St. Louis for another retreat, then to Minneapolis for a third, and finally drove back to Boston. But along the way I visited motherhouses of religious women—86 of them. Some were located off the beaten path, but there were clusters of them in and around cities like Chicago, St. Paul, Pittsburgh, and I visited more than twenty by driving up one bank of the Hudson and down the other. The superiors I saw—mothers general and provincial—were uniformly cordial and interested, but I could see their hesitation when I had to say that no credit would be available for our courses. The Sisters, laboriously working toward degrees by following courses offered during the summers, or in late afternoon classes or on Saturday mornings during the year—while carrying at the same time a full load of teaching—could not afford the luxury of a sabbatical summer. When 1952 rolled around I could count only four disciples from all my recruiting—four Franciscans from Toledo. I blessed them and did all I could to make their summer profitable, but when classes ended the rector said the program was not attracting enough students and would have to be terminated.

There were some memorable incidents along the pilgrim's way. I was crossing Wisconsin after the last retreat; it was hot, I was weary, and the road was very long. Some pretty lakes, with comfortable motels alongside, were tempting, but I pressed on, came in late afternoon to the motherhouse of the Sisters of St. Joseph in Stevens Point, and asked to see the Mother Provincial. This gracious lady came down, took one look at my bedraggled self, turned to her assistant and said, "Father will stay for dinner, and for the night, too." She never had a more willing and grateful guest. At dinner the resident chaplain learned that I was interested in liturgy and eagerly began a discussion of Father de la Taille's doctrine on the Eucharist. He was not a little dashed, poor man, when I drowsily finished dessert and made off for ten hours' rejuvenating slumber.

Outside Cleveland I noticed that the car, irreproachable in its performance until then, was, like myself, beginning to show signs of fatigue. I had to shift down to first speed to get over the hills, and even then it was a near thing whether I would make it or not. At John Carroll University, where I stayed with the Jesuit community, I asked the Father Minister to recommend a garage. "The Brother is a pretty good mechanic," he said. The Brother examined the patient and diagnosed the trouble: one of my cylinders was not firing. But the garage was closed for the long week-end, and my time was getting short. What to do?

"Want a suggestion?" Brother asked.

"Be glad of one," I said.

"Say a Hail Mary and go."

I thought a moment, then said, "That's the best idea any of us has had so far."

I prayed the Hail Mary, started the engine, waved gratefully to the Brother, and drove away. There would be a bit of trouble passing trucks that were laboring up those hills around Pittsburgh, but otherwise the working cylinders took me home. As we used to say in the novitiate, *semper Deo gratias et Mariae.*

Our Jesuit life went on pretty much as it had before the war. Bells went on ringing in St. Mary's Hall—for rising (at 5:00 a.m.), for meals, for community prayer. Administrators among us had their problems coping with an ever-growing student population, with the erection of new buildings and the maintenance of old ones. It was discovered, for instance, that Gasson Hall had been given only wooden beams to support its spires, and the wood was beginning to rot. Emergency measures had to be taken if "the Towers on the Heights" were to continue to "reach to Heaven's own blue." For most of us it was classes on campus and in the evening school downtown, with the attendant reading of papers and examinations—especially heavy for English teachers, who felt obliged not merely to put a grade on a paper but to criticize it for its content, structure, style, word-choice, spelling, and punctuation. ("Gee, Father," one freshman complained, "There was more of your red ink on my paper than the black ink I put on it in the first place.")

We served on academic committees, attended departmental meetings, and acted as faculty advisers to student activities—publications, musical clubs, sodalities, honor societies, dramatics, debating, campus radio. We were counselors, academic and spiritual. We spent hours in the instruction of converts. We celebrated liturgies in the campus chapels and in St. Ignatius Church, and assisted on week-ends in understaffed diocesan parishes. We directed retreats. We lectured all over the metropolitan area at communion breakfasts, Holy Name Society meetings, literary circles, alumni clubs. We directed discussion groups and Catholic Action councils. In short, we led busy lives. It wasn't easy, in the midst of such teeming activity, to pray, to dismiss the demands of the moment and try to focus on God. And yet everything in our vocation, our commitment, our elemental human need cried out for it. Well, what about the breviary? Here was a prayerbook expressly designed to lift the mind and heart to God at intervals all day long, and it synchronized beautifully with the rhythms of the liturgical year. Its chief component was the biblical psalms and canticles, but there was also a daily reading from the other books of the Old and New Testaments that afforded an annual review of God's merciful interventions in human history, his incredible love and solicitude for our race. And over the centuries the Church had shaped a lovely setting for this treasure by creating collects (pithy, almost laconic prayers quite unlike the effusive prayers of the devotions), passages from the Fathers and Doctors of the Church, hymns, and biographies of the saints. These last relied too much on popular legend and offended the more critical historical sense of our generation; they also glossed over human failings (the "warts") in their subjects, and thus provided impossible models for our imitation.

But here indeed was an anthology of Christian thought and feeling. Was it not what Isaiah predicted (12:3): "With joy you will draw water at the fountain of salvation?" Why then did we not think of it as a gift, as precisely what Pius X had in mind when he spoke of acquiring the true Christian spirit from its primary and indispensable source?

Alas, what might have been an exalted privilege, offering a daily, almost hourly sacrifice of praise with, in, and through Christ, our high priest, and all the members of his body throughout the world, became for many of us the *onus diei,* the burden of the day. We had had no acquaintance with the "office" as we grew up; even the practice of singing Vespers on Sunday evenings had died out in our parish churches. We did not know until we were ordained even the mechanics of recitation—where to find what came next.

More serious was our ignorance of the culture out of which the Scriptures, especially the Old Testament, had come. Our Scripture courses had concentrated on such matters as authenticity, inspiration, hermeneutics. Someone should have offered at least a seminar on Hebrew poetry, particularly the Psalms, and shown us how the spirit and ardor of that Oriental prayer had been universalized in Christian use.

Of course the office was recited, even privately, entirely in Latin, and though by the time we were ordained Latin had become a second language, it could never have the ease and immediacy of the mother tongue. But the legalism with which the prayer had become invested was its most lethal feature. The whole office had to be recited before the stroke of midnight. Its obligation was serious; our moral theologians taught that to omit deliberately even one of the "little hours" was to commit mortal sin. Moreover, there was to be no rapid scanning; each syllable had to be formed with the lips. Though it was designed to be read progressively at key hours as the day advanced, so enabling us to lift minds and hearts to God briefly but often, most of us read it in large chunks—all the "little hours" at once, for instance, or even the whole thing at one gulp. This would be done early in the day, to be sure the obligation was satisfied, or simply to get it done. Or it might be the last thing at night, when one might have to race the clock as it moved inexorably toward midnight. It was reported of one Jesuit, who was an astronomer and had to stay up at night with his instruments, that he would read today's office from eleven to twelve and tomorrow's from twelve to one. And there were many stories of the priest who, driving home at a late hour, suddenly remembered that he had not finished his office. He realized that if he kept driving he would not have time enough to finish it after he arrived, so, though it was a bitterly cold night and snow was beginning to fall, he stopped the car on a lonely road in the middle of nowhere and finished the office with the help of his headlights. As in so many other matters, the legalists led us into a swamp, and the moralists did nothing to lead us out. By making the *opus Dei* into the *onus diei*, they did everything they could to promote scrupulosity, and they surely robbed many of us of the comfort, strength, and inspiration we might have derived from the breviary.

We were busy, then, and may have deserved the reproach given to Martha in the Gospel. Jesuits in other communities sometimes said that our life-style at Boston College was impersonal, that we lived side by side without communicating very much. Well, most of us were still fairly young, we had plenty of energy, and apostolic opportunities seemed endless. Perhaps we were workaholics. It doesn't seem to me now that we suffered from the self-questioning that came in with the sixties. Nor did loneliness, which later diagnosticians considered an inescapable affliction of celibates, seem to be a common problem. There was too much we wanted to do, and in our free hours we did enjoy one another's company. On Fridays in July, for instance, we fled summer school and congregated for merry weekends at our vacation house in Cohasset. Father Bill Kenealy, then Dean of the Law School, loved to bump people off the raft into the water when they were not looking, and he had bumped Father John Ryan, whose capacity for ingenious mischief he should have respected, several times. One Sunday, when the crowd was gathered on the raft, John appeared, dressed in black clerical clothes, complete with Roman collar, and looking as if he had just returned from helping at a parish church. As he deliberately moved to the edge of the raft, Kenealy was tempted beyond his strength, and John was sent plunging into the water. He came spluttering to the surface a few seconds later, and climbed back on the raft, the clerical suit dripping. "Well, Bill," he said, "I hope you have a few dollars for the cleaners. This is your suit I'm wearing."

Our rivalry with Holy Cross was intense in those days; the climactic game of the football season involved the emotions of faculty, students, alumni, and fervent partisans of both schools. One year, when Holy Cross was favored by the sports writers to win by three touchdowns, we upset the odds and won. Ecstatic students tore down and carried away the wooden goalposts in small pieces as souvenirs, and on Monday morning the entire student body besieged St. Mary's Hall, demanded to see the President, and clamored for a holiday. They got it, and went rollicking into Boston, where, on the steps of City Hall, they solemnly elected Mike Holovak, our coach, mayor of the city. Some of us were sitting in the recreation room that morning, savoring the unlooked-for holiday, when Father Joe Connor came in, carrying one of the souvenirs of the game, and blessed us with "a relic of the true goalpost."

Father Kenealy was a strong personality whose temperament was almost diametrically opposed to that of the then President, and he was as popular in the community as the President was unpopular. There was considerable grief, then, when the President ousted him as Dean. He spent several years as professor at the Loyola University Law School in New Orleans; eventually, however, our President's term of office ended, and it was *his* turn to leave. We quietly celebrated the occasion as "Emancipation Day," and that night I sent Father Kenealy a telegram which contained just these words: "Matthew 2:20." The reference was to the verse in the Gospel which reads, "Come home, for those who sought the life of the child are dead."

The half-century drew to a close—an ugly period, marked by two ruinous world wars and the Depression. With some show of remorse for what they had done the nations came together in San Francisco and set up an organization which might keep them, they hoped, from tearing a third time at one another's throats. But the Russians kept saying "nyet," and built the Berlin Wall, and the West forged a steel ring around the Russians and built bigger and better bombs, and Joe McLellan put it pretty well with a "New Year Song" in the *Stylus:*

At last, after long years of hopeful expectation, we are about to enter upon the year MCML.

And what it will bring to us, I am sure that I, for one, cannot tell.

But I will venture to predict that it will be better than anybody expects

Because it certainly can't be any worse than MCMXLIX.

CHAPTER 10

Toward a Christian Culture

IT WAS IN 1923, I THINK, THAT I FIRST SAW THE CAMPUS AT Boston College. Our track team at Boston College High School, lacking facilities of its own, used to come out from the South End and run on a cinder track around what the present-day students refer to—inaccurately—as the Dustbowl. The wintry blasts that now cut across that open space blew in those days, too, and we wore long johns under our track suits for protection. But how could I have known then, as I pounded around the track and the Tower bells rang their sweet quarters in my boyish ears, that those bells would count off fifty years of my later life?

Historians refer to the American experience, up to World War II, as "the Age of Innocence." Dr. Halsey, as we have seen, would hold that the American Catholic Church lived through a parallel age of innocence, but that it lasted a little longer, until the Second Vatican Council. We *were* very naive. We had all the answers, for this life and the next. One might experience perplexities, but they could be quickly resolved by recalling the simple pieties of American history as it was taught then, or by reading a little book called *The Catholic's Ready Answer*. Doubts were not permitted—were even sinful. As late as 1947 a friendly but perceptive non-Catholic told his Catholic colleagues in education, "You have protected them too much."

During the forties and fifties discipline at Boston College was almost as strict as it was at St. John's Seminary across the street. Dormitory life was strictly regulated. Attendance at Mass—at seven o'clock in the morning—was required of all boarders three days a week. Every student had to make an annual retreat. Anyone who came back from summer vacation sporting a beard or a moustache had to take it off. A jacket and necktie were required for class. And if you cut class without a very serious excuse more than three times a semester you flunked the course. Given these strictures in deportment, it is not surprising that there should have been small latitude in the curriculum. As late as 1969, when I resigned the chair of the Department of Theology, sixteen credits in theology were still required, and twenty-four in philosophy. Electives in these areas had not been available before 1966.

The reason for such a concentration was the belief that some enveloping or pervading system of thought should be presented which would unify the disparate arts and sciences and afford a platform, so to speak, from which to view the world and make sense of it. And since this was a Catholic college, that world-view would naturally be the one offered by the Church. It was indeed a comprehensive system, embracing all reality up to God himself, and ordering all human activity to its final end. But the method it employed was rigidly scholastic, its content took small notice of contemporary thought, and its posture was defensive rather than open or exploratory. With the summons back to Scripture of Pius XII in 1943 and the flinging open of windows at the Second Vatican Council, the venerable but creaking old system was no longer relevant. It had to go, and go it surely did. Theology and philosophy requirements were slashed to six credits each; additional courses might be taken if the student wished, but in no particular sequence, and I would need to be convinced that the student obtained from the exposure any overarching, controlling vision of life and life's meaning.

In the academic year 1953-54 I shifted full-time out of the English Department to our Department of Theology. For several years I had had a foot in both, teaching English in the College of Arts and Sciences and Theology in the Evening College, but I was becoming more and more involved off-campus in the work of the liturgical movement, and beginning to feel that the proper apportioning of time and energies was more than I could handle. I discussed the move with Father Ellard, whose advice, delivered with how much prescience it is now difficult to say, was cryptic and forthright. "Do it. You'll never regret it." I knew I would miss the English classes; they were fun; I enjoyed them and I think the students did, too. But after the War's appalling experiences and in the face of the daunting problems posed by the nuclear age, literature did seem a luxury.

Over and beyond our cosmic perplexities, I had a few of my own. Why was it, for instance, that there were not more Catholics—and particularly Catholic college alumni—who might be called intellectuals? Or, since the great majority of our students would be laypeople, not clerics, why did we not devise and communicate a theology tailored to their specific use rather than a watered-down seminary course? And since Catholics were already moving upward socially, should that theology not have to be what Dr. Thomas O'Dea called a "spirituality of the suburbs"? What did Pius XII have in mind when he described the Church's mission as "Christian service to the world"—not conquest, not domination, not withdrawal, but service? What about those areas of modern life to which we Catholics had given small attention: mass communications, religious pluralism, the environment, urban planning, civil liberties? Was it our only function to be prophetic, counter-cultural?

In 1958 Dr. O'Dea published a temperate but searching analysis which he called *The American Catholic Dilemma: an Inquiry into the Intellectual Life.*[1] In it he summarized under six heads (p. 83) the reasons given by several Catholic historians and sociologists for "the lack of a vital intellectual tradition among American Catholics":

1. The lack of a Catholic intellectual heritage in this country related both to the lower-class origins and the present dominantly lower-and lower-middle-class composition of the American Catholic population.

2. The lack of a scholarly motivation among American Catholics related to such lower social positions and origins on the one hand, and, on the other, to the expectation that the priests will do the scholarly work while the laity concentrate on other things.

3. The inferior economic position of Catholic groups.

4. The difficulties involved in the process of assimilating millions of immigrants and the problems related to immigrant and post-immigrant status.

5. The defensive, martial, and even ghetto mentality brought about by partial alienation and the specific minority experience of American Catholics.

6. Prejudice, hostility, and discrimination.

---

1.   New York, 1958.

Lest, however, we excuse ourselves too readily, Dr. O'Dea offered two reflections (p. 91):

> We cannot blame too much of our present upon the difficulties which Catholic immigrants found in assimilating themselves to America. Experience of living among American Catholics, as well as the general level of American Catholic life as it meets the eye of the casual observer, suggests that in non-intellectual areas American Catholics have not been slow in assimilating themselves to the national milieu. The taste for automobiles, the styles of clothing and hair-dressing and the use of cosmetics, the felt necessity for radio and television, the interest in movies and sports—in short, all the other indices of superficial conformity—seem to be quite visible in the American Catholic scene. Catholics have not been slow to accept what are often called—especially by our Catholic intellectual brethren in Europe—the more materialistic aspects of American life. Catholics, laity and clergy alike, have been able to come to terms with these aspects of modern America, although it seems possible that on a deeper level some of them deserve more critical examination by the Christian conscience.

And again (p. 87):

> Intolerance is another matter, for the reality of such intolerance in the past and even its subtle persistence in some forms in the present cannot be denied. Moreover, we must not make the easy assumption that the experience of intolerance is incompatible with intellectual growth and development, for were this the case how could one possibly explain the tremendous intellectual development shown by American Jewry? Poverty has certainly been an important factor, but here comparison with the same group gives food for thought. It is doubtful if even the Irish immigrants, perhaps the poorest of the nineteenth-century arrivals to these shores, were much poorer than the eastern European and Russian Jews who came after 1890, except possibly in the worst years of the Irish potato failure of the 1840's. Yet these eastern European Jews would, upon an empirical count, be found to have contributed a larger proportion of their children and grand-children to academic and scholarly life than have Catholic immigrants as a whole.

However we define the term "intellectual," one of its components is surely wonder, the capacity to stand agape before a multiplex world, to be mesmerized by its infinite variety and lured to explore it endlessly. There is so little that is really beyond all question, so much to investigate and marvel at, beginning with the *"mysterium tremendum et fascinans"* of God and ending (if ending there can be) with the smile of a child. Chesterton found it wonderful that, given all the obstacles mechanical and human, subway trains arrived on time. Tennyson made Ulysses the voice of this wonder and aspiration:

> I am a part of all that I have met,
> Yet all experience is an arch wherethrough
> Gleams that untravelled world whose margin fades
> Forever and forever when I move.

Yes, there are some incontestable things. Otherwise we shouldn't—gratefully—recite the Creed every Sunday. But we were too eager to amplify our certainties and communicate them. The nickname some of our students gave to the Jesuit residence was "No Doubt Hall." Of course it isn't easy to be patient with adolescent opinion. 1 remember, when I was "moderator" of the student newspaper, discussing for two hours an editorial that not only attacked the Dean's policies but made some nasty insinuations about his motives and his character. I maintained that it was uninformed, unjust, defamatory. Further, it could impede some of the very good things the Dean was trying to do. The editor, a very angry young man, insisted that it should run as he had written it. At midnight, when the paper had to be "put to bed"—and I would have been glad to—he demanded, "Well, do we go with it or not?" "We don't," I replied. As if we had not discussed the question for two hours, he cried, "Why not?" My patience ran out, and I fell back on the parental cloture, "Because I said so." No doubt he has done a lot of growling ever since about clerical domineering. I've wondered how he's been faring with *his* teen-agers.

Thoughts about the intellectual life are interwoven with speculation about culture—what it is, who possesses it, how it gives shape to art, literature, conduct. And it might be frivolous, but I have pondered sometimes the students' current practice when they introduce themselves to me on campus. "Hi," they say, "I'm Joe. I'm Mary." No last names, no further identification. I feel like protesting, "Look, I know ten thousand Joes, and almost as many Marys. Can't you give me some idea of who you are, so I can remember that we met?" But I don't say that, because the horrible suspicion crosses my mind that perhaps they really don't know who they are. Their last name may be Ambrogio or Scaramelli, but do they feel any particular kinship with Dante or Michelangelo? Are they justifiably proud of Palestrina, or Rafael? If their name is O'Brien, do they identify at all with Robert Emmet or Daniel O'Connell? Would they go out of their way to see the Book of Kells? Perhaps their name is Dupuis; surely, then, they could tell you something about Francois Villon or Victor Hugo? Surely they wait eagerly for the day when they can see the Champs Élysées or the Cathedral at Chartres? All of them, perhaps, profess themselves Christians, but do they know how St. John's Gospel differs from St. Matthew's? Have they ever read Augustine, or Newman, or Sigrid Undset, or Chesterton? What to them are names like Leo the Great, or Francis Xavier, or Bernard of Clairvaux, or Catherine of Siena? In very truth, they don't know who they are; they have no idea where they came from. "I'm Joe." Poor orphan!

Christopher Dawson, the cultural historian who was the first occupant of the Stillman Chair at Harvard, believed that people could not be considered truly educated unless they had an integrated view of their religious and cultural heritage. Only this, he said, could offset the smorgasbord character of the contemporary curriculum and provide a principle of unity among the various disciplines. He advocated the establishment in some Catholic university of an institute that would study, on the graduate level, the culture of Christianity—not just the medieval contribution, as at Toronto or Notre Dame, but the whole stupendous and magnificent pageant of thought and experience in theology, philosophy, art, literature, law, and a dozen other areas, from the Hebrew Scriptures to the pastoral letters of John Paul II. There is in my files a yellowing sheaf of dreams for such an institute at Boston College. Alas, the dreams are still only dreams, although the Candlemas Lectures, intended to show how the personality and teaching of Christ have impinged on world literature during the last twenty centuries, were inaugurated here in 1947 and are still happily flourishing—a very small achievement in comparison with what might be done, but enough, maybe, to keep the dream alive and the dreamer humble. Perhaps, after one of our alumni has made his millions in cybernetics or interstellar retailing, he might think of endowing an Institute of Christian Culture at his alma mater.

But such an institute, though desirable of itself in a Catholic university, would not benefit undergraduates directly, would not send them into the world equipped with any means of growing in the Christian mind-set, the Christian tradition or culture. Is there no instrument they can use now to accomplish that? By way of reply, it might be said that no society has ever had a durable culture which has not had a cult at the heart of it. Human beings seek God by natural gravitation, not only in their private lives but socially, and strive to express what they feel inwardly about God by some outward ceremony. This is what is called worship, or liturgy, and it is the very core of culture because it involves one's deepest convictions about God and ourselves, about this life and a further life. Culture is not an abstraction floating in the air. It is something possessed by a particular group of people. Christian culture is a property of Christian people, a mélange of ideas, emotions, symbols, myths, convictions, aspirations that distinguishes them from others. They are not members of a club, or of some political entity; they are members of a body, the Body of Christ, into which they have been incorporated, made one with Christ who is the head. That is their distinctive characteristic, and what they do most naturally as a result of their incorporation, what they have the ability to do in association with him into whose body they have been incorporated, and what finally keeps them in the pulsing center of that vitality into which they have been engrafted, is their worship, their liturgy, which is the action of the whole body, head and members, and which, with its undergirding of beliefs, has molded and shaped the culture we know as Christian.

Let me see if I can substantiate that, or at least point out a few instances of it. Christ came on earth to preach the Good News, the essence of which is that the Kingdom of God is at hand. Now that proclamation is made most tellingly, most persistently, in the liturgy, where the Lord's present-day disciples assemble to hear the Christian manifesto, to be reminded of the incarnation, the passion, the resurrection, the ascension of God's Son, and to hear the assurance that he will come again. Moses, when he inaugurated the liturgy of the Old Testament, had the same purpose in mind, "lest you forget." Jesus, when he enjoined upon us the celebration of the Eucharist, said, "Do this in memory of me." There is no danger that he will be forgotten, for example, in our Archdiocese, where some four hundred parishes gather every Sunday to "do this" precisely in his memory.

Or consider this. One of the hallmarks of the Christian culture is that, without neglecting—much less scorning—our present life, it looks steadily to a life to come. And this idea is repeated in season and out by the liturgy. As the German poet Gertrud von le Fort said in one of her exquisite "Hymns to the Church," "With all your bells you ring our eternal home-coming." How this unceasing iteration shapes the outlook of a group of people it is easy to see.

Or take the Eucharist itself, where Christian men and women come together for the breaking of bread, where the gift of the Father is spread before us by the Church, and where the supreme idea proposed to those who receive it is peace. Today, because the human race is at last in a position to destroy itself, the making of peace is no longer the office of civil or ecclesiastical authorities; it is our common task. We need to know—and the Eucharist is a vivid, powerful reminder—that our God's revelation of himself to us is a will to peace. He heals, uplifts, forgives. Jesus, as St. Paul says, has made peace and is himself our peace, bringing together into a single body those who were near and those who were afar off. Blessed, then, the peacemakers—never more than at the end of this century of genocides, holocausts, and unremitting violence.

Christ, yesterday, today, the same forever, is supremely the priest, seeking tirelessly to sanctify the world. Only now he accomplishes this through the liturgy; as St. Leo said, "what was visible in Christ has passed over into the sacraments." And the liturgy sanctifies, first of all, time, which is not only the flowing substance of our lives but also the currency with which we must trade "until he comes." You have the Christian day, with its praise of God in the morning for a renewed gift of life, its prayer at mid-day for defense against the noon-day devil, its thanksgiving and contrition and surrender at nightfall. You have the Christian week, ushered in with the joyful remembrance and celebration of the risen Lord. You have the Christian year, with its feasts and its fasts, its fires and its ashes, during which, as Pius XII said, Christ "continues that journey of immense mercy which he lovingly began in his mortal life, going about doing good, with the design of bringing people to know his mysteries and to live by them." Then you have the sanctification of places and things which Christians use to serve God: churches and homes and schools and orphanages and hospitals are blessed; so are water, salt, oil, incense, bells and lights; so is the very earth in which the Christian's body is reverently laid to rest at the last. Most importantly, you have the sanctification of life itself, in baptism, confirmation, eucharist; of life regained in penance and the anointing of the sick; of life focused in marriage and holy orders.

These are some facets of the Christian culture. It is hard to say how much of it is absorbed by living for four years at a Catholic college. It is hard to say whether students discover in it a means of harmonizing everything else they learn, or whether they can in the years to come use the liturgy as an instrument to grow in that culture. If one brushes it aside, the alternative is pretty grim: rootlessness, meaninglessness. In 1940 Walter Lippman described the plight of secular man in our age: he is like the sole survivor of a shipwreck. He is adrift on a flimsy raft in mid-ocean; the sun is going down and the wind is rising. As if in answer to Lippman, one year later Pius XII issued a peremptory summons to humankind: "Back to the altars and learn!" Learn what it means to pass over (as the Israelites did, as Jesus did) from dark to light, from defeat to victory, from death to life. Learn what it means for a man or woman to be grafted on to divinity, and to live in God. Learn that reprieve, release, freedom are the real facts in any Christian's history, and that our prevailing mood is therefore one of thanksgiving, even of gaiety. Learn that, formerly thrust into exterior darkness, we are now enfranchised citizens of the City of God; once stripped, disinherited, we are now sons and daughters in our Father's house. Learn that the Lord Jesus, the first-born, is now our elder brother, and all other men and women are or could be our brethren.

The apostolic leaders who organized the Church in its infancy were surely not addressing only an élite when they exhorted their converts to follow Christ. St. Peter (1 Peter 2:4-5, 9-10) urges *all* to "come to him (the Lord), a living stone, rejected by men but approved, nonetheless, and precious in God's eyes. You too are living stones, built as an edifice of spirit into a holy priesthood, offering spiritual sacrifices acceptable to God through Jesus Christ. . . . You are a chosen race, a royal priesthood, a holy nation, a people he claims for his own to proclaim the glorious works of the One who called you from darkness into his marvelous light. Once you were no people, but now you are God's people; once there was no mercy for you, but now you have found mercy." The consequence of this is in St. Paul's exhortation (Rom 12: 1, 4-6): "And now, brothers, I beg you through the mercy of God to offer your bodies as a living sacrifice, holy and acceptable to God, your spiritual worship. . . . Just as each of us has one body with many members, and not all the members have the same function, so too we, though many, are one body in Christ, and individually members one of another. We have gifts that differ according to the favor bestowed on us."

In my early years we were not vividly aware of this diversity of gifts. There were two strata of Christian life, the clerics and the "religious" on the one hand and the laity on the other. You had a "vocation" to be a priest, a brother, a sister, or you had no "vocation" and remained "in the world"—an inferior level of membership, fraught with perils to salvation, lacking the challenges and "sacrifices" of the higher state. As Jack Ross lamented in the *Stylus*,

> Oh what a world is left within to roister
> Before we settle with the Sprite
>   Recorder:
> The nicest girls all rush off to the cloister,
> The finest fellows up and join the Order.

And inevitably, those who went into the isolation of the cloister or the order were effectively cut off from understanding or sympathizing with any notion of "lay spirituality." It's interesting that in my collection of books on preconciliar spirituality, there are volumes upon volumes devoted to the priesthood and religious life, but only a very small shelf of books about the laity.

Questions about the laity, of course, bring up the larger question of the Church's mission and function in the world. Leo XIII, in a most agreeable reversal of the attitudes and policies of Pius IX, had written encyclicals which, in their recognition of such matters as the problems of the workingman, the right of private ownership of property, and even the share in the apostolate which should be accorded to the laity, had turned the Church's gaze outward toward the human family. The popes of the twentieth century went even further, discussing, besides all manner of theological subjects, the relationship between church and state, education, equality for women, socialism, war and peace, anthropology, birth control, conscientious objection, minorities, leisure, the arts. So that amazing document, "The Church in the Modern World," produced by the Second Vatican Council, was not the bombshell that it might have been a hundred years before—even supposing that it could possibly have been proclaimed or even composed at that time. It built on and, in a way, canonized what the popes had been saying, but what was most impressive about it was its tone. It was addressed "not only to the sons and daughters of the Church and to all who invoke the name of Christ, but to the whole of humanity" (# 2). It spoke with modesty and humility, acknowledging what the Church can learn from history and the social sciences, claiming no omnicompetence for itself. It identified the Church as "a sign of that brotherhood which allows honest dialogue and gives it vigor" (# 92). The verbs used in the document are uniformly indicative of the Council's resolve to put the Church at the service of humanity: assist, collaborate, enter into conversation about, cooperate with, speak to, dialogue with, contribute to, aid, offer comments. The contrast in tone with Pius IX's "Syllabus of Errors" could not be more striking.

CHAPTER 11

A Cult for the Culture

WHEN WE WERE SCHOLASTICS—AND THAT'S AN UNFAMILIAR
term, isn't it? It refers to Jesuits, whether studying or teaching,
who have not yet been ordained priests. When we were scholastics
old Father Jimmy Kelly used to give us "points" for our morning
meditation. He had a habit of hesitating before the obvious word,
and the crowd in the front row used to prompt him with loud whis-
pers. "Tomorrow," Jimmy would say, "Let us consider the preaching of our Lord in Galilee. You remember how the Lord was
standing on the shore of the—on the shore of the—shore of
the . . ." (Loud whisper: "of the sea!") "On the shore of the sea,
and the disciples knelt down on their—they knelt down on their—
on their . . ." (Loud whisper: "on their knees!") "They knelt down
on their knees, and . . ."

Maybe it wasn't just senility that blocked old Jimmy's choice
of words. He in his time, as we in ours, had spent six to eight
years translating the Greek and Latin classics, hunting (with the
help of dictionaries and Roget's Thesaurus) for the *verbum propr-
ium*, the one word which would render the full meaning of the
original not only with accuracy but in idiomatic and felicitous English. It was slow and painful work, enlarging our vocabularies,
no doubt, and contributing to our appreciation of the masters, but
inhibiting our own spontaneous expression. I for one began then to
identify with the medieval Irish monk who wrote in the margin of
the manuscript he was copying:

I and Pangua Ban my cat,
'Tis a like task we are at:
Hunting mice is his delight,
Hunting words I sit all night.

I have often wondered what the text of the Mass would sound
like if Bishop John Carroll had got a favorable answer to his re-

quest for permission to use English instead of Latin in the liturgy. (He didn't, of course.) The translation would sound like the old Douai Bible, full of "thees" and "thous" and "shalts" and "vouchsafes"—pretty remote and alien to our modern ears. And if it were updated to suit our needs, there would surely be cries of anguish from the die-hard traditionalists.

In any case, the Bishop, who did so much to organize the Church in colonial America, did not get this permission, and we went on using an increasingly unintelligible Latin for two hundred years. "God understands Latin," we said, and it doesn't matter if we don't. That attitude prevailed generally in regard to liturgical change: we have a good thing, and this is no time for tinkering with it. Research by scholars in liturgical history had scarcely begun, and the impression was more and more firmly entrenched that the Mass had been celebrated in that language and with precisely those rubrics that had come down from apostolic times— even, perhaps, from the Cenacle itself. It was therefore unutterably sacred, inviolable.

By the late 1920's, however, a few transatlantic breezes were blowing. People went to Europe and came home with ideas that would have been startling if anyone were listening. Virgil Michel, the Collegeville Benedictine, was one. Monsignor William Busch, of St. Paul, was another. Then there were Martin Hellriegel of St. Louis and Gerald Ellard at the Jesuit seminary in Kansas. By a kind of sympathetic attraction they found one another, talked, began to work together on such projects as the magazine *Orate Fratres* (later, at Ellard's suggestion, re-named *Worship*). Each brought his own distinctive gifts to the work, but all were persuaded that the time was ripe to insist on St. Paul's teaching (see, for example, Ephesians 1:10), that our Father in heaven plans to bring everything together under Christ as head. That would seem to be pretty inclusive, not only of things obviously pertaining to the Christian life like faith, prayer, virtue, devotion, spirituality, but also of such (at first blush) secular matters as the economy, peace, education, civil rights, due process, racial justice, the arts, etc.—"in Christ, everything in the heavens and everything on earth." But, they argued with the relentless logic of the scholastic system they had been trained in, Christ is found, wants to be found, preeminently in the liturgy. Therefore all things are to be unified, evaluated, cultivated in the liturgy.

But the neat syllogism would have been improved had it been preceded in scholastic fashion by a definition of terms. Few people in those days had a clear understanding of what was meant by "liturgy." For priests it meant ritual, rubrics. For the people at large it was one of those arcane ecclesiastical words of little relevance to themselves, or perhaps it referred to the style of worship carried out by the Orthodox churches.

So a monumental work of education had to begin. Michel, besides launching *Worship*, started the Liturgical Press, which issued translations of popular primers on liturgy by Europeans. He also wrote his own books, lectured tirelessly, organized a "Liturgical Day" which expanded after his death into annual "Liturgical Weeks" around the country. Busch translated, too, but wrote books of his own and taught generations of seminarians.

Hellriegel, chaplain at a "motherhouse" of the Sisters of the Precious Blood, and later pastor in St. Louis, established a model of popular participation to which many priests came for inspiration and instruction, and his genial, charismatic presentations on lecture platforms won thousands to the cause. Ellard's books, especially *Christian Life and Worship*, became standard texts in Catholic colleges everywhere; his *The Mass of the Future* prepared minds for the changes that would be introduced by the Second Vatican Council. He, too, taught hundreds of seminarians, and lectured tirelessly across the country.

To these "pioneers" there gravitated swiftly a number of like-minded people, who in their turn became centers of influence. When Monsignor Joseph Morrison, for instance, hospitably opened the cathedral basement in Chicago to the first "Liturgical Week" in 1940, there were 1260 registered.

Michel had gone by this time to an early and lamented grave, but Godfrey Diekmann succeeded him as editor of *Worship* and for more than twenty-five years made the magazine the American voice of liturgical renewal. Subsequent "Weeks" were held in St. Paul, at St. Meinrad Abbey in Indiana, in Chicago again, in New Orleans and in New York. These took place in war-time, when transportation was difficult and the country was distracted, but the attendance increased steadily nevertheless. Monsignor Reynold Hillenbrand, rector of Mundelein Seminary in Chicago, came and brought with him the dynamic priests whom he had helped to educate and inspire when they were seminarians: John O'Connell, Daniel Cantwell, Norbert Randolph, John Egan, George Higgins,

Walter Imbiorski, William Quinn, James Kilgallon, Gerard Weber. Father Tom Carroll led a group from Boston: Shawn Sheehan, Joseph Collins, Mrs. Charles Perkins and her daughter, Mary Perkins Ryan, Ambrose Hennessey, John McEneaney. From St. Louis came Martin Hellriegel, Aloysius Wilmes, Alphonse Westhoff, Mark Ebner. The nuns who did such outstanding work with textbooks— eight for grade school, two for high school, two for college—were there: Sister Jane Marie Murray and Sister Estelle Hackett from Marygrove College in Michigan. So were the Sacred Heart nuns from the Pius X School of Liturgical Music in New York: Mother Georgia Stevens and Mother Josephine Morgan, and Mrs. Justine Ward.

A complete list of those valiant souls who came together in the early years to share their wisdom and enthusiasm would be like the "catalogue of the ships" in Homer's *Iliad*—no one reads it. Suffice it to say that they were theologians, artists, seminary faculty, musicians, pastors, publishers, educators, nuns, laypeople— even a bishop or two. They were joined soon by Scripture scholars, and then by people in various fields of social welfare. The "dogmatic" or "systematic" theologians came next, but the moralists and canonists waited until Bernard Häring had integrated their science with the liturgy. As I have written elsewhere,[1]

> The 1950's brought into the liturgical movement a sense of breathless hurry. The dawn for which the pioneers had sighed so long had broken with the publication of the two encyclicals, *Mystici Corporis* (1943) and *Mediator Dei* (1947), but then the day began to lighten so fast that they were hard put to adjust to it. Official Rome adopted what Father Ellard called "a policy of controlled concession," especially in the matter of vernacular languages. Father Jungmann's epoch-making history of the Mass, oriented sharply to make clear how the faithful had been cut off from participation in their sacrifice, appeared in Austria and was rapidly translated into other languages. Its author and other scholars were invited to four successive meetings, inspired by Rome, to make recommendations for the reform of the liturgy. Pope Pius XII himself authorized the liturgical use of a new translation of the Psalter. The

---

1. *The Liturgy of Vatican II,* vol. 2, ed. William Barauna, Chicago, 1966, p. 307.

privilege of evening Mass was rapidly extended. A reformed Easter Nightwatch rite was published in 1951, a sweeping reform of the entire Holy Week liturgy in 1955. The eucharistic fast was progressively mitigated. The calendar was simplified. An abbreviated office in the vernacular was allowed to be substituted by some religious for the canonical hours. Permissions to use vernacular rituals multiplied. (The first American ritual, energetically promoted by Archbishop Edwin O'Hara of Kansas City and composed largely by Father Gerald Ellard, was published in 1954.)

Pope Pius XII wrote the longest encyclical of his pontificate on the subject of sacred music. At Assisi in 1956, the first International Congress on Pastoral Liturgy was held; the concluding address was given by the Holy Father himself in Rome.

It was the Instruction of September, 1958, however, that gave notice of how far the day was really advanced. The startled officers of the Conference counted 1039 priests (400 more than had ever attended a Week before) at the Notre Dame Liturgical Week in 1959, all of them interested to know how the Instruction should be implemented. From that time forward, the annual Weeks attracted clergy, religious, and laity in unprecedented numbers. (Registration at Pittsburgh in 1960 was 3,676; at Oklahoma City in 1961 it was 3,381; at Seattle in 1962 it was 4,955; at Philadelphia in 1963 it was 13,944; at St. Louis in 1964 it was 10,555. The number of those who attended but did not register was much larger; thus it was estimated that the total attendance at St. Louis was 20,000.) These meetings were given columns of coverage in the Catholic and secular press. Other national Catholic congresses and conventions were usually devoted to a particular field of interest. The Liturgical Week, devoting its program to the paramount topic of Christian life and worship, and embracing in its ambit education, ecumenics, social order, the biblical awakening, spirituality, peace, interracial justice, lay activity, music, art and architecture, etc., began, like the *Katholikentag* in Germany, to take on the character of an annual witnessing and proclamation to the nation of Catholic beliefs and attitudes. This development harmonized, as we have suggested, with the declaration that would come in 1963 from the Second Vatican Council, that "the liturgy is the summit toward which the activity of the Church is directed; at the same time it is the font from which all her power flows."

It's amusing now, though it wasn't then, to remember the fortunes in those years of the Vernacular Society. The officers and directors of the Conference were almost all convinced members of the Society, but they felt that the liturgical cause, which was suspect in enough high places, would fare better if the two enterprises were not identified. Accordingly, though the Vernacular Society always held its meetings in the same place and at the same time as the Liturgical Week, there was never any announcement in the official program. A handful of hardy members, like Dr. Joseph Evans, Monsignor Robert Sherry, and Father Joseph Nolan, refused to abandon ship during some very heavy weather in the '50s and held the Society together, but its chief organizers and champions were Monsignor Joseph Morrison and the redoubtable Colonel John K. Ross-Duggan, who were perennially elected president and secretary until the Monsignor died in 1957 and the Colonel's health became impaired. The Colonel had founded and edited a magazine which promoted avidly the use of the vernacular languages in the liturgy instead of the ancient, hieratic Latin—in many minds at the time a positively sacrilegious policy. He named the magazine *Amen,* and under the name, on page one, he ran the verse from St. Paul (1 Cor 14:16): "How will the layman be able to say 'Amen' to your Eucharist when he does not know what you are saying?" In support of his convictions he did not hesitate to go to the very top, and a picture that should definitely have a place in the gallery of those years is one of the doughty Colonel terrorizing a menial who was trying to block him from seeing the empurpled head of some Roman congregation. The Liturgical Congress at Assisi was formally concluded with an address by Pope Pius XII in the Sistine Chapel in Rome, and it had been widely rumored that the Pope would announce major concessions of the vernacular. He was carried in solemnly on the *sedia gestatoria,* and spoke to us for 45 minutes, but said not a word about any changes in language. When he was being carried out the Colonel cried in a loud voice, "Take him away!" I was sitting beside him, and I said, "Sh-h-h, Colonel!" "No, no," he shouted, "He'll never do us any good. Take him away!"

The Colonel's impatience was understandable—or it is now. For the record, however, Pius had done very much to make the liturgy a living experience, and no doubt believed that "controlled concession" was the only possible course to follow. And indeed it would require the ballots of some three thousand bishops at the Vatican Council seven years later to effect the momentous change the poor old Colonel wanted.

Catholic universities and colleges were slow to incorporate the theology of the liturgy into their regular curriculum, but a great deal of educational work went on in summer schools, institutes, and the like. Courses were offered at Boston College (the Social Worship Program, 1947-52), by Dr. Clifford Bennett's peripatetic Gregorian Institute of America, by Webster College in St. Louis, Trinity College in Vermont, and Loyola University in New Orleans, among others. The most influential program was the one established at Notre Dame in 1947 by the beloved Father Michael Mathis, who assembled each summer a faculty made up chiefly of distinguished European scholars (Jungmann, Luyckx, Bouyer, Goldbrunner, Schmidt, Danielou, Hofinger, J.B. O'Connell, Grasso, et al.) and published their lectures. The school also profited by the musical talents of Father Ermin Vitry and Mr. Theodore Marier. The fact that Europeans had to be brought over in such numbers is a commentary on the poverty of American liturgical scholarship during those years.

The indispensable work of education on the popular level was carried out by other devoted workers through many media. The central office of the Conference sponsored and staffed institutes for seminary professors, diocesan liturgical commissions, architects, musicians, publishers of missals. With the cooperation of the National Council of Catholic Men, films and television programs were produced; programs for training lectors and commentators were made available to pastors. A comprehensive "Parish Worship Program" was prepared, made up of books and leaflets explaining the liturgical renewal for priests and people. By the end of 1964 more than two million of these items had been sold. Dr. and Mrs. Alfred Berger of Cincinnati originated and maintained a "Tape of the Month" service which had 35 regional distribution centers and 2600 members. It supplied recordings of lectures given at Liturgical Weeks. Contact with developments in the catechetical and educational fields were retained through Father Gerard Sloyan, then chairman of the Department of Religious Education at Catholic University, and Mrs. Mary Perkins Ryan, whose many books and articles on the liturgy should have made her nationally known even before her *Are Parochial Schools the Answer?* gave her an uneasy fame in 1964.

It might be asked at this point why such a massive effort in education was necessary. The answer would require a survey of history ranging through a thousand years, and any summary will seem inadequate. The fact is that from the end of the patristic age up to the opening of the Second Vatican Council our people were cut off from active participation in the official worship of the Church. This is not to say that they stopped praying. Rather, they went on praying, as the emergence of thousands of saints makes clear, but their prayer tended increasingly toward devotions that they found attractive—devotions that ran parallel to liturgical worship but were only sketchily related to it. And since devotions are optional, chosen freely according to the temperament of each worshiper, prayer became more and more individualistic. What was lost was any sense of the community at prayer, any awareness of a shared offering to God of what the old "Roman Canon" (now the first Eucharistic Prayer) called "faith and fidelity."

And this kind of piety was not questioned. The Mass continued to be celebrated, of course, but it was something done for the people, not with them. And the people kept coming, but to pray their private prayers or to meditate on some spiritual topic according to a "method" proposed by a "master" of the spiritual life. So, for example, the Jesuit Rodriguez, writing in the 19th century a manual that was prescribed reading in most novitiates as late as 1960, reaches back to Amalar of Metz (died 850 A.D.) for an ingenious but altogether fanciful and superficial way to identify with what was going on at the altar (see Appendix II).

One may find, in the present Roman Mass, a miniature history of the Christian ages, or of the mentalities, cultures, spiritual outlooks that have in their turn contributed something to this essentially Western act of worship. And, parenthetically, one might think that students in a Christian university would be strangely lacking in intellectual curiosity if they were not interested by this act, enshrining as it does so much of their theology, literature, and tradition, and constituting as it does the perennial expression of their Christian faith. As Edmund Bishop observed, "the history of Christian worship, in its varieties and differing forms through the centuries, is at least and lowest a subject of human interest not less worthy of attention than the ancient religions of Greece and Italy"[2] H. A. Reinhold, in his *The American Parish and the Roman Liturgy*[3] goes so far as to describe the Roman Mass as "the most perfect creation of the Christian mind" (p. 3), and if this statement seems an exaggeration to some, perhaps they can bring forward something else which will be more deserving of the tribute.

G.K. Chesterton has a poem called "The House of Christmas," the first stanza of which reads as follows:

> There fared a mother driven forth
> Out of an inn to roam;
> In the place where she was homeless
> All men are at home.
> The crazy stable close at hand,
> With shaking timber and shifting sand
> Grew a stronger thing to abide and stand
> Than the square stones of Rome.

Anyone who has visited Rome will remember the square stones of the Coliseum and the Forum, or the ruins of the aquaduct striding across the Campagna; some, perhaps, have gone down into the excavations under San Clemente and seen there, on the level of the house of St. Clement, visited by St. Peter and St. Paul, the blocks of tufa that paved the ancient street. No question, in the mind of such a visitor, about the lasting qualities of "the square stones of Rome." But Chesterton makes the point that Bethlehem, or what took place at Bethlehem, would "abide and stand" when the Roman stones were dust. And I feel that the same may be said of our Roman Mass, whose strong foundations and structure date from the epoch when the Roman stones were cut and laid in place, and whose essential characteristics remain to distinguish the Roman rite to this day from any other.

The kernel of all Mass-rites, of course, was given to us by our Lord at the Last Supper, and in the early centuries there was a great freedom and variety, suggested by the temperaments of the different Christian peoples, in the choice of the prayers and ceremonies with which this kernel was surrounded. It was in this way that the great liturgies developed, each emerging from its cultural matrix as the years went by and the need for stabilizing the forms of worship became apparent. So, in the East, there developed the two Syrian liturgies, the Egyptian, the Byzantine, the Armenian.

---

2. *Liturgica Historica*, p.x, Oxford, 1918.
3. N.Y., 1958.

And in the West there were two great families of liturgies: the Roman and African on the one hand, and on the other the Gallic, which was subdivided into the Milanese or Ambrosian, the Old Spanish or Mozarabic, the Celtic, and the Frankish or Gallican in the narrow sense. Of the beginnings of the Roman Mass in the Latin language we know almost nothing, since our oldest manuscripts go back only to the eighth and ninth centuries, and what we have been able to reconstruct with the aid of other sources is very scanty. Mass had, of course, been offered from the earliest Christian days in Rome, and we have the writings of Justin Martyr and Hippolytus to give us a tantalizingly brief but adequate description of the primitive rite. But this was in Greek, and the rite described permitted a considerable freedom to the celebrant. When we come upon the Latin Mass at last, it is to discover it already solidly constructed along the lines it has retained since. If one reads the description of the eighth-century papal Mass, in Cardinal Schuster's *Sacramentary* (1, 66-71)[4] for instance, or in Jungmann's *The Mass of the Roman Rite*[5] (1, 67-74), one senses what the letter calls "a magnificent completeness:"

> A great community exercise, heir of a thousand years' culture, had produced its final form in the church, lending to the divine service the splendor of its noble tradition. The person of the papal liturgist is surrounded by a court of many members. The ceremonial has absorbed courtly elements and has been filled out to the smallest detail. And still, through all this luxuriant growth, the bold outlines of the Christian eucharistic solemnity stand out clearly in all their essentials; the gorgeous pomp is suddenly quieted when the canon begins, and does not burst forth again until it is concluded. The old communal feeling, it is true, is no longer so strongly and immediately involved. The people apparently no longer answer the prayers, no longer take part in the singing, which has become the art-function of a small group, but the choir is not a profane intrusion into the texture of the service, but rather a connecting link joining the people to the altar. Prayer and song still sound in the language of the masses, and the people still have an

---

4. St. Louis, 1972.
5. New York, 1951.

important role in the action through their offering of gifts and their reception of Communion (Jungmann, I, 74-75).

But alas for the changeableness of mortal things! Every synthesis breaks down under the battering of time. We might lament this beautiful Mass as Wilfred Childe laments the Middle Ages:

It was too beautiful to live; the world
Ne'er rotted it with her slow-creeping hells;
Men shall not see the Vision crowned and pearled,
When Jerusalem blossomed in the noon-tide bells.

But we could not restore it if we would, and indeed we would not restore it if we could. One does not put new wine in old bottles. The liturgy of the Church is eminently pastoral; it suits itself to the needs of the faithful in every age, and every age is different. But I am getting ahead of my history . . .

In the eighth century the Roman Mass went travelling. Up in the Franco-German kingdom, north of the severing Alps, the Gallican liturgy that had evolved there showed signs of getting out of hand. It reflected, as one would expect, the temperament of the people who had developed it—a Celtic and Germanic temperament, restless, passionate, given to the dramatic and the startling. By the eighth century it began to go to extremes, to emphasize the unusual, and to vary not merely from diocese to diocese but even from church to church. At last the emperor, Pepin the Short, father of Charlemagne, decided that matters had gone far enough. He decreed that in his dominions Mass should be celebrated as it was in Rome, and sent for copies of the Roman Mass-books. And so it was done; the Roman Mass acquired a new home—a hothouse, Father Jungman says, in which it would grow and change for two hundred years.

Given the profound differences between the Roman mentality and that of the northern peoples, the changes which took place were those that might have been looked for. The Roman did not lose his natural characteristics when he became a Christian; he remained what he had been in the days of Cato and Brutus. His mind was clear, orderly, down-to-earth. His language, especially his formal language, was hammered and chiseled to a laconic conciseness. His ceremony was restrained, correct, majestic. The Gaul, by contrast, felt wild impulses and often yielded to them; his mind was no limpid pool, but a lake troubled by gusts of passion and brooded over by forests of dark self-consciousness. He expressed his joys and his sorrows (especially his sorrows!) in terms and rites that knew nothing of any classical moderation. It was inevitable that he should find the Roman Mass austere, and that he should add to it elements from his own Gallican liturgy, now superseded, or invent altogether new elements which gave more ample expression to his feelings. His predilection for the dramatic was seen, for instance, in the number of incensations he added to the Roman practice, the elaborate ceremonies he devised for the singing of the Gospel, the appearance of the poetic "sequences." He loved long prayers, and his subjectivism (as opposed to Roman objectivity) showed in the use of the singular personal pronoun instead of the Roman "we," in his folded hands at prayer instead of the outstretched arms of the "orante" of the catacombs and the earlier Roman use. It showed especially in those unlovely avowals of guilt and unworthiness ("apologiae") which he distributed with a lavish hand through the entire Mass. We find it hard to understand such a mentality, so alien from the Roman spirit, so frighteningly conscious of sin, so distant from God. Did the Gothic cathedrals, whose dark and loftly ceilings the eye cannot penetrate, draw part at least of their inspiration from this awareness of the gulf between Creator and creature? Certainly they are very different from the architecture we think of as characteristic of the Roman spirit, the so-called Romanesque, where the low arch of the ceiling hovered over the Christian assembly as if to assure it that Heaven was very close indeed.

This has been a long and perhaps not very interesting historical excursus; it does lead me to the main point I should like to make, however, that the Roman Mass, the rite that we follow by and large in this country, it basically a rational, sober, sensible rite, and that in spite of the accretions it has picked up through the centuries, its structure is solid, its mood is sober and plain even to the point of frugality. An unbeliever in a Catholic church during the celebration of Mass might not agree with this, but his difficulty would be with religious ceremony in general rather than with this or that rite. We should not take his standard as our own, even though the American tendency is to eliminate as much ceremony as possible in the interest of what we call efficiency and mass-production.

These, then, are the square stones of Rome upon which our Mass is constructed. It goes without saying that square stones are not to everyone's liking. Many people find them uncompromising, heavy, too ascetic or too plain. Certainly the northern peoples, the

Celts and the Germans, found them so. We can readily understand how a person reared from childhood in one of the gorgeous, pageant-like Eastern rites, full of color and movement and mystery, would be unable to satisfy his soul with the ancient Roman rite. We can understand, too, how a person accustomed only to the so-called "devotional" prayers and hymns encounters a strange world when he opens his Roman Missal (even the present-day Missal, the fusion of Roman and Gallican elements) for the first time. He is likely to find it, at first, all mind and no heart. "But do not misunderstand," Father Reinhold writes (p. 6).

> It is not the dry language of law-books and army orders! It is not without feeling and emotion. By no means! But it is a formed, restrained, noble, and grand sentiment, even in its alleluias; and when you meet prolixity and repetitious exuberance, superabundance and words and phrases, you may be almost sure it is a foreign body, in most cases imported from Gaul after Charlemagne. You can easily check up on this in your own Missal by comparing the blessing of the ashes with the collects and the preface of Lent. Like its Gregorian music, the restraint of the Roman liturgy is by no means poverty. Would anyone say that Renaissance is "poorer" than the Gothic, the Doric column "poorer" than the Corinthian? The Roman liturgy is rich in manly, adult, mature feeling, and that is perhaps the reason why the "counter-creations" of modern popular piety by contrast are the opposite: more feminine and talkative.

Even during the preconciliar days, the 1950's, a distinct if gradual pruning was going on—a cutting away of superfluities, of outgrowths, of repetitiousness. There was the simplification of the calendar, the reduction in the number of collects, the direction given in the new Holy Week order that the celebrant was not to read silently those parts which are sung by the deacon or subdeacon but to sit and listen. We were getting down to the square stones again.

And now, someone might ask, are we to exclude all legitimate feeling, all natural exuberance and enthusiasm? This is far from the ideal. But the genius of the Roman rite calls for dignity, acknowledgment by the community of the majesty of God, and not the private feeling of the individual, however good in itself. Individuals will differ in their approach to and appreciation of the mysteries of the Faith. But this is dangerous ground, this field of personal taste, and long treading on it can arouse scorpions. Perhaps the last word should be given to Pope Pius XI, who said in a private audience in 1935,

> The Church is very inclusive. In fact, her inclusiveness is occasionally very astonishing. She accepts all manner of prayer, for she has pity on the weakness of poor humanity. "Very well," she says, "since you cannot pray otherwise, pray as you do, so long as you really pray." But when one wishes to know what she understands by prayer, that is an entirely different matter, and it is in the liturgy that one discovers her way. It is necessary to imitate Holy Church, and not to prohibit what she consents to accept in the matter of prayer. But one should seek to elevate this prayer little by little, and to teach the faithful to pray as she prays.[6]

Occasionally one hears wistful complaints that the Mass as we celebrate it now has lost the aura of mystery that once enveloped it. Some people feel a nostalgia for the profound silence, broken only by faint tinklings of an admonitory bell or the distant murmur of an unknown language; they miss the wisps of incense, the measured, hieratic dignity of movement about the sanctuary. These things surely had their value for contemplation. They helped to capture and hold our wandering attention and to suggest something of God's majesty, something of the awe and reverence with which we should think of the All-holy. After all, one does not become chummy with God. But at Mass we are not invited to be spectators, however worshipful. We are to participate in an active, sharing way; this is our sacrifice, the gift of the entire community, and each of us is most emphatically to give it, "lest the body of Christ by short a member."[7] A certain ease of manner, a naturalness, is appropriate here, rather than an awe-struck immobility. The Lord has made us his table-companions.

The real "mystery" to be apprehended—not, to be sure, altogether comprehended—is, as Fr. Jungmann says, (I, 82), "the communion of the redeemed bound together with a glorious Christ in one Mystical Body." In the controversies of the early Church this concept is already being lost sight of. Jungmann goes on (I, 84):

---

6.   cf. text in "Documenta Pontificia ad Instaurationem Liturgicam Spectantia," ed. Bugnini, Rome, 1953.
7.   Didascalia, xiii.

Into the background recedes that interest in the symbolism of the sacrament in which Augustine laid such great—perhaps too great—stock, and which is exhibited in the prayers of the Roman Sacramentaries, particularly in the post-communions. Forgotten is the relationship between the sacramental Body—the "mystical" Body, as it was then often termed—and the Body of Christ which is the Church. The same is true for the connection between the sacrament and the death of Christ. And so, too, the conscious participation of the community in the oblation of Christ is lost sight of, and with it that approach of the community towards God to which the sacrament in its fulness is a summons or invitation. Instead, the Mass becomes all the more the mystery of God's coming to man, a mystery one must adoringly wonder at and contemplate from afar.

Attitudes developed over ten centuries will not be eradicated overnight, and reformers must strive to be patient while the currents of our time, all setting toward the concept of community, bring in a new—or rather a very old ideal of worship. The Second Vatican Council did something of a right-about-face when it pronounced that "liturgical services are not private functions, but are celebrations of the Church, which is the 'sacrament of unity,' namely, a holy people united and organized under their bishops" (SCL #26), and therefore,

The Church earnestly desires that all the faithful be led to that full, conscious, and active participation in liturgical celebrations which is demanded by the very nature of the liturgy. Such participation by the Christian people as "a chosen race, a royal priesthood, a holy nation, a purchased people" (1 Peter 2:9; cf. 2:4-5) is their right and duty by reason of their baptism. In the restoration and promotion of the sacred liturgy, this full and active participation by all the people is the aim to be considered before all else, for it is the primary and indispensable source from which the faithful are to derive the true Christian spirit. Therefore, through the needed program of instruction, pastors of souls must zealously strive to achieve it in all their pastoral work (SCL #14).

CHAPTER 12

The Liturgical Movement Begins to Move

A FRINGE BENEFIT OF BEING INVOLVED IN THE LITURGICAL MOVE-ment was that I was able to visit some highly interesting places. In 1952, for instance, Father Peter Nearing invited me to give the keynote address at the Maritime Liturgical Week in Halifax. The city itself was attractive, and the people I met gave me a very cordial welcome indeed. When the "Week" ended, therefore, and Father Nearing invited me to spend a few days at his parish in Arisaig, I was happy to accept. Arisaig was a tiny place bordering the Northumberland Straits; in the dim distance you could just make out Prince Edward Island. The coast was rugged, and the land, covered for the most part with spruce woods, broke here and there into cultivated fields, but there was no really broad sweep of open country.

When I asked Father Nearing how many of the people in his town were Catholics, he had a simple answer: "All of them." They were almost without exception Scottish; it was the country of the MacDonalds and the MacDougalls and the MacGillivrays and the MacPhersons—especially the MacDonalds. There were twenty-six priests of that name in the Diocese of Antigonish. The Cooperative Movement growing out of St. Francis Xavier University had done a great deal to promote a modest prosperity; farming and fishing and lobstering had built small but snug homes, and everyone seemed to own a car or a truck. Families were large (I had dinner one evening with a family of thirteen children), and people lived frequently into a ripe and active old age. Father Nearing's farmer was eighty-two and deaf as a post, but he took care of a wheat field, a garden, a flock of hens, and several cows. On another evening we visited a family presided over by a patriarch in his late eighties; his son and daughter, a man and woman in their forties, were quite silent (it was clear that children were to be seen, not heard), and he carried on the conversation. I asked him if there were any wildlife in the woods behind his home. "Yes," he said, "A good many deer, and last winter, when the snows were very deep, a bear tried to get into my chickens." "What did you do?" "I took my rifle and lay in the snow for six hours, but my eyes aren't as good as they used to be, and I missed him."

The trip to Assisi was very different. In 1956 the Roman Congregation of Rites raised its cautious approval of liturgical developments by a surprising notch; it sponsored a "First International Congress for Pastoral Liturgy" (there has never been a second) and located it in the city of St. Francis. There was so much contention about liturgy in those days that the location might have been chosen for symbolic reasons; Assisi still keeps the unique Franciscan spirit of love and peace.

I was blessed with permission to attend, and graced additionally with help from generous friends, one of whom made possible an Atlantic crossing at half the usual rate and two others whose companionship during the latter stages of the journey made it a delightful, even a rollicking pilgrimage. In July, then, I boarded a freighter of the American Export Lines as the only passenger. The Captain shook hands cordially and gave me the freedom of the ship—a privilege I had never enjoyed before. A tug took us out into the Hudson, and we sailed at half-speed down the harbor until, finally, we put the pilot off and headed for the open sea. On the way down we passed the *Ile de France* and the *Cape Ann*, bringing in survivors from the wreck of the *Andrea Doria*, which had gone down the night before after a collision in heavy fog. It was a bit chilling to hear from the Captain, when I asked him about it, that we had no radar equipment on our ship. But I forgot that next morning, when we were 200 miles out, and I lay in a desk chair in the warm sun, looking out on a placid blue ocean. No wonder doctors recommend a sea voyage for frayed nerves.

The Captain was Norwegian by birth; arriving in America when he was fourteen, he had learned fluent English, and come up from ordinary seaman to Master. "Do you speak Italian?" he asked. "A very little," I said. "Would you like to improve?" (He wanted to, since he expected to be given command of one of the line's passenger ships, and would have many Italians aboard.) I said I surely would, so I studied grammar in my desk chair and reviewed it with him at night in his cabin. For a while I wondered how, with so much apparent leisure, he earned his salary. Then I found out.

As we entered the Straits of Gibraltar—we had made landfall on the coast of Portugal, at Cape St. Vincent—we met dense fog. I had to abandon any ideas I might have had about sleep when the fog horn began to blow directly over my head, so I went up on the bridge. The Captain, the Chief Officer, and the mate on watch were all there, because this was ticklish. There were lots of other ships about, including small fishermen, and there was a strong current running out from the Mediterranean into the Atlantic; we could see the tide rips as we looked overside. They were about all we could see. Every now and then we would hear a fog horn close by, and the Captain would give orders: "Dead slow ahead! . . . "Stop the ship!" We inched along anxiously, and the Captain said, "I have a million dollars under me—half a million for the ship and half a million for the cargo." I can't imagine anything more eerie than trying to navigate with that swirling, gray, impenetrable blanket cutting off all vision.

In Genoa I picked up a little Fiat which I promptly nicknamed "Benzina," and set off with her up the Riviera dei Fiori, where I was severely tempted to linger indefinitely. But Provence was fascinating, and at Aix, by happy chance, I met our Father (afterward Cardinal) de Lubac, whose immensely satisfying book on the Church I had been reading on the ship. I tried to entice him to breakfast and a long conversation, but he gently parried the invitation by saying that he had an "*ouvrage urgent*" to attend to. At Aix—and later at Poitiers—I was interested to see in the floor of the cathedral sacristy a gaping hole. Here, in the early Christian centuries, adult converts, after long instruction and probation, were baptized at the Easter Nightwatch; they were led down steps into the pool, and only after they were totally immersed would the bishop, standing on the brink, pronounce the sacramental words. Then they were led up steps on the opposite side of the pool, and the symbolism was striking: just as Christ had gone down, down, down into the darkness of the grave, and then been raised by the Father to a new life of glory, so the Christian was to die totally to sin and begin to live a new life of grace. After baptism he or she would be clothed in a white robe of innocence, be confirmed, and go out into the church to share in the offering of the Mass and to receive Holy Communion for the first time.

I could not have guessed then that this Rite of Christian Initiation would be brought back to life, after a millenium and more of disuse, by the Vatican Council in 1963. The fundamental significance of baptism for the Christian life may now be understood and relished by means of a deliberate, diligent preparation of mind and heart on the part of the candidate, whose sponsor assumes the character of guide and counselor, and grows thereby in his or her own appreciation of the faith. Moreover, the participation by the community in this process educates everyone in the need for apostolic outreach, for intelligent, prayerful, even tender concern as the candidate grapples with grace, for whole-hearted gratitude to God and enthusiasm when at last a mature decision is taken and the candidate is solemnly bonded forever in the fellowship of those who are risen in Christ. Truly, as Father Robert Duggan wrote in *America,*[1]

> this "sleeper" of the liturgical reform . . . is a visionary gift of the Spirit to the Church of our time, a remarkable instrument of individual and communal conversion, a clarion call to renewed ministry on the part of all the baptized, a striking blend of ritual and catechesis, pastoral care and spiritual formation at their best.

It will be pleasant, when the European Economic Community becomes a reality, a few years hence, to pass from one nation into another as readily as we Americans now move from one of our states into another. At the Spanish border I showed my passport five times; the "douane" for the car was checked and stamped twice and the car itself inspected twice more. Having just read "The Cypresses Believe in God," I was delighted to find the cathedral in Gerona, and the Dehesa, and even to see a boy fishing in the Onar River from his living-room window, which recalled the opening scene in the novel. But no one I spoke to seemed to have read or even heard of the book.

The road to Barcelona was hot and long; I was severely tempted to swim at the deserted lovely beaches, but the undertow looked strong, too strong for a solitary bather. In the city at last, my efforts to get directions became comic. I had to begin every request with "*no hablo Español,*" so of course the very polite and kind people could not talk to me, though they did, and at last I found the Colegio San Francisco Borgia, our seminary, out in the country, and had a most cordial welcome. Two of the scholastics promptly attached themselves to me and became my companionable

---

1. 14 October 1989.

guides for three days. Their English was rudimentary but they were working at it under the tutelage of an American scholastic, who, along with other more usual pedagogical devices, taught them popular songs. Would I like to hear one? "Sure," I said, and they broke out with "She be cooming round de mountain whan she coom." They took me to Monserrat, where St. Ignatius had hung up his sword in token of his conversion, and to the cave where he made his solitary novitiate and wrote the *Spiritual Exercises*. Here, where the Society of Jesus may be said to have come to birth, I was deeply moved, even though the marble and gold which now covers the walls of the cave was a distraction; I wished the place had been left in its primitive simplicity. Equally moving was the spot, now roped off, in the church of Santa Maria del Mar near the port, where Ignatius, once the aristocratic cavalier, did violence to his pride by begging for alms. Memories of Spain's civil war were still vivid, not only in the tablets that referred to it as "the Holy Crusade," but in the badly damaged churches and the heroic statue of Christ, smashed by the Communists, on top of the hill called "Tibidabo." From the top of that hill, by the way, there is a limitless view of the entire city and the sea. Whoever gave it its name must have known his Bible and known it in Latin, so that when he looked off from the height the scene of Christ's temptation in the wilderness flashed into his mind, together with Satan's lying promise: "*Haec omnia tibi dabo si cadens adoraveris mihi*"—"I will give you all these if you fall at my feet and worship me" (Matt 4:9). I noticed, in the sacristy, that the "prescribed prayers" to be said at Mass were for the Pope, the Archbishop, and "*dux noster Franciscus*"—"*dux*" being the Latin for "*caudillo*."

The Father Minister, two of the faculty, and the scholastics who had been such delightful companions during my stay waved me off at last, and I took to the road again—a road that was excellent as far as the Pyrenees, but tortuous and scary after that as it wound through passes and snaked along the edge of unfenced abysses. Up and down through deep gorges, round and round sharp curves, and, at last, Carcassonne, the walled city, quaint and moving as are all things so old. Next morning, Mass for the even more ancient Feast of "the Falling Asleep of Our Lady" on August 15th, celebrated in the tenth-century church of Sts. Nazarius and Celsus. At Tours it was interesting, because my memories of Armistice Day were so vivid, to see stones contributed to the crypt where St. Martin is buried. One was given by "the K. of C. in

France, 1918, November 11, P.J. Hayes, *episcopus castrensis*" and another by "Foch, *Maréchal de France*." At Angers the cathedral was lovely, and more like a working church than any I had seen so far in France; people were actually praying in it. Beyond Rennes, a lovely town I should like to visit again, I was running through Brittany, enjoying the glorious morning and the countryside, full of green farms, and singing my exuberance aloud when suddenly I rounded a curve and saw Mont St. Michel, and the song died on my lips. Whew! Pictures I had seen, and descriptions I had read, but the reality was overwhelming. Alas, it was more gratifying from a distance than on close inspection. The state had taken over the place; there was no sign of monks, or indeed of anything religious anywhere. Even the abbey church was empty and bare, and the vendors of souvenirs made it seem like a cheap summer resort back home. At Avranches there was a monument with generous praise of the American Army and General Patton—not too evident anywhere else in France.

By this time a strong wind was blowing off the Atlantic, and the skies had clouded over, so that when I visited Utah Beach, and then Omaha Beach, weather conditions were pretty much what had been on June 6, 1944. Wrecked pillboxes and landing craft rusting away in the water added to the grim picture. Nearby was the American cemetery, beautifully laid out and cared for, but containing nine thousand graves. (The bodies of eleven thousand others had been exhumed and repatriated, I was told.) So though it was a lovely cemetery, it was still a cemetery. I went away sad, thinking of Leo Murphy's charming ways—Leo, one of the *Stylus'* editors, had been killed in Normandy—and of the utter waste of war. Children squabble and bicker, but when they grow up they try to find civilized methods for settling their differences. Would the human race ever get beyond its childhood?

"Benzina" refused to start the next morning, but a mechanic discovered a hole in the engine which was preventing compression (something had dropped off). He plugged it with the cork from my bottle of *eau minérale*, and I was on my way to Lisieux. There I found an absolutely huge basilica, very ornate but not as bad as I'd been led to expect, and partially justified, I suppose, by the inscription on the facade: "He who humbles himself shall be exalted." But I was repelled by the sight of Therese's arm, severed from her body and enshrined for veneration; that practice of dismemberment, however well-intentioned, always struck me as ghoulish. I was really revolted a little later, in Rouen, when I visited the site in the Vieux Marché of the burning of Joan of Arc. That was a truly horrifying barbarity, made worse because inflicted by what passed for justice at the time. Have our sensibilities been refined since then? Such an execution would be considered "cruel and inhumane" today, and outlawed. But the death penalty is still permitted among us, and defended, proving that what we are really interested in is not the rehabilitation of the criminal, or even his isolation for safety's sake, but his punishment—an eye for an eye, a tooth for a tooth. It's hard to see that we have advanced much more in this matter than in our incessant resorting to war in conflicts of interest. Still adolescents?

My companions for the next month would be Tom and Jack Bresnahan, Boston College students and sons of an alumnus who lived next door to the campus. I was by this time weary of going it alone, and welcomed their delightful company. After a day or two sight-seeing in Paris we struck out across France, through country where names were once again sadly familiar, this time from World War I—Soissons, Chateau Thierry, Verdun—and saw yet another American cemetery at Belleau Wood. I had to repress a surge of disgust as we came up to the German border; the police there, who wore peaked caps and long, gray-green overcoats, looked exactly like storm-troopers from the Nazi era. But a good dinner, obtained with many laughs from a pleasant waitress who had very little English, restored my equanimity. Cologne was crowded with people from all over Germany, even. from the East Zone, come to celebrate the annual *Katholikentag,* or Catholic Day. But we couldn't see the shrine of the Three Kings ("We three kings of Orient are," as the Christmas carol sings) because, like the massive cathedral, it was still undergoing repairs from war damage.

The toy landscape of Bavaria was utterly lovely, but Munich was still rebuilding. My most vivid memory of the city is of walking to the hotel at midnight, with Jack reading from street-signs, at the top of his powerful voice, polysyllabic German words like *versicherunsgesellschaften.* Near Oberammergau we stopped at a *bierstube* and sang and had a high time with very pleasant people; there were more smiling faces in Germany—our late enemy—than we ever saw in France. Then it was Innsbruck and Salzburg and over the Austrian Alps to Bolzano. A quick identification in Verona of Juliet's balcony ("but soft! what light through yonder window breaks?") and her "tomb" in Friar Lawrence's *convento,* and then that incredible city, Venice. We had dinner on the roof of the Hotel Danieli, overlooking the Grand Canal, and sat in the Piazza San Marco, listening to music, till the small hours. As Tom Moore said,

Memory draws from delight ere it dies
An essence that breathes of it many a year.

The Assisi Congress, which attracted some 1300 participants, had been preceded by four much smaller meetings of scholars in liturgical studies. These had been quietly inspired by the Roman Congregation of Rites, and had drawn little attention from the Church at large, but they did make some recommendations (they were meekly styled "wishes") that showed which way the wind was blowing, and had some concrete results, like the extension of the Easter Vigil reform to the whole of Holy Week in 1955. The emphasis at Assisi, as Cardinal Cicognani told us at the opening session, was to be on pastoral liturgy, whose aim, he said, "is precisely that of leading the faithful to form a closely-knit union in the Mystical Body of which Christ is the Head, and to participate '*aequo modo*', according to one's station, in the liturgical rites." The papers to be presented, he went on, would review "the magnificent work accomplished by the Holy Father" to this end, especially in the encyclicals on the Mystical Body (1943) and on the liturgy itself (1947).

The extreme caution that prelates at home had voiced so often in our Liturgical Weeks was audible in the Cardinal's address. He said the Pope was consoled by the "zeal and exuberance of the liturgical movement" but was required "to give careful attention to this 'revival' and keep the movement free from exaggeration and error." There would, accordingly, be no "debates" during the present congress, although possibly "private and unofficial discussions might well result in . . . conclusions to be submitted to the ecclesiastical authority, which in its own office will take them under examination according to their merit." In view of what happened at the Council only seven years later, it is difficult to understand the need for so much apprehension, but it is easy to understand why the Cardinal himself would be one of the "*immobilisti*" who voted consistently against reforms.

He was at pains especially to defend the use of Latin in the liturgy. He praised Latin not only as a "splendid sign of unity and universality" (he did not mention uniformity) but also as a means to form and enrich the mind, and to "clothe the sacred truths in its magnificence," while at the same time "effectively safeguarding them against the corruption of true doctrine." "It is true," he said,

> that the faithful do not attain easily to an understanding of the sacred rites in the Latin tongue. This is especially true of people in our day as compared with those in ages gone by. Still, this does not mean that the vernacular must be substituted for the Latin. . . . The faithful are not the hierarchical priesthood, a chosen class who alone offer the sacrifice in the true and proper sense and who for that reason should understand fully the sacred formulas and expressions. In their "royal priesthood" the faithful take part *aequo modo*, according to their station, in the sacrifice and the divine mysteries. Well-directed efforts should be made to lead them to such participation, and help them appreciate the meaning of the rites and of the truths which underlie them. But the value and spiritual function of the Latin language need not be lost in the process.

Forty years later, that statement seems to be as condescending, arrogant, out of touch with reality as one is likely to encounter in a day's reading. Made today, it would probably result in the hall's being emptied in protest or simple derision. In fact, no one moved. Next morning, however, the first paper was read by Father Joseph Jungmann, S.J., whose very influential history of the Mass had appeared a few years before. Without referring in any way to the Cardinal's address, he gave a beautiful description of liturgy itself: "The liturgy," he said, "is the life of the Church with her face towards God—of that Church which is the fellowship of all who in baptism have been granted membership with Christ, and who gather, Sunday after Sunday, to celebrate the memory of our Lord under the leadership of the priestly office." In describing then the evolution through the centuries of the external forms of this service, he said that the overriding concern of the authorities was always for the Church: "for the Church as comprising the sum total of the faithful, for the Church as *plebs sancta* (the holy people) who, under the guidance of her pastors, even in this earthly life should offer to God in prayer and sacrifice a worthy service and thus herself be sanctified." He recalled, without making any overt plea for language change today, that pastoral concern had dictated changes in language from the very beginning—from Aramaic and Hebrew to Greek to Latin and even, in the case of some of the Catholic peoples of the East, to the national tongues, particularly the Arabic. "The living liturgy," he said, actively participated in, was for centuries the most important form of pastoral care. This is true particularly of those centuries in which the liturgy was developed in its essentials. In the later Middle Ages, the liturgy was indeed celebrated with zeal and much splendor in numerous collegiate and monastic churches, and was also further developed in its various forms. But unfavorable circumstances brought it about that something like a fog curtain settled between and separated liturgy and people; through it the faithful could only dimly recognize what was happening at the altar. But even in those centuries we witness a certain expansion and adaptation of the liturgy—and again in the interests of pastoral care. Because the language of the liturgy had become foreign to the masses of the people, certain dramatic elements were introduced as a substitute. The Middle Ages knew only the solemn form of Mass with chant and, if possible, with sacred ministers, for the Sunday service of the people. Even this afforded considerable religious stimulation. But the solemnity was further increased. Lights and incense were now not merely carried along for the entrance procession, but the altar itself was ceremoniously censed, once, and a second time, and the censing was further extended to the choir and the people. The processional lights began to be placed on the altar. The singing of the gospel became a triumphal procession in honor of Christ. The sanctus candle was introduced to announce the nearness of the Mystery. And, finally, a striking climax was created by the elevation of the host and chalice at the consecration. Nevertheless, the fog curtain remained. The most important means of the soul's ascent to God, the word of the liturgy itself, had become inaccessible to the people. The prayers and songs by which the sacred Action is accomplished are perceived only as so many sounds in the ear. The liturgy has become a succession of mysterious words and ceremonies, which must be performed according to a fixed rule, and which one tries to follow with holy reverence—but which themselves finally harden into rigid and unchangeable forms.

Perhaps this rigidity was necessary—as a protection against heretical attacks upon the Sacrifice of the Church. It may also have been necessary to safeguard the sacred heritage for future times, for a time of greater need and of more grave decisions, such as we experience in our own day, when the faithful in an especial manner need that same guidance by the liturgy which was the privileged lot of the Christians of the first centuries. Today the rigidity is beginning to lessen. Forms which appeared petrified have come to life again. The Church feels that it no longer needs the protection of this inflexibility. Just as the Church under Pius XI, by the Lateran treaties, surrendered that external protection which, in the more crude times of the Middle Ages, had seemed so necessary to it as a world power, so now under Pius XII it has begun to loosen the protective armor which till now has encased the sacred forms of the liturgy. The interests of care of souls are again, as of old, becoming the decisive factor—those pastoral interests, in other words, from which the forms of the liturgy had taken their origin in the early days of the Church.

What was passing through the Cardinal's head as he listened to this historical survey we could not say, but there is a picture of him in the printed record of the Congress[2] in which he looks like an old bear making up his mind to charge. It was probably taken during one of those bursts of spontaneous applause with which the audience greeted Fr. Jungmann's not-too-subtle arguments for a vernacular liturgy.

There were only three American bishops—Wright, Annabring, and Dworschak—at the Congress; Archbishop O'Hara had died in Milan on his way to Assisi. And, among the English-speaking Jesuits, there were only Clifford Howell, Gerald Ellard, and myself. We were often asked why more Jesuits were not active supporters of the liturgical movement. I used to reply (dodging the question somewhat) that some of the most prominent people in the movement were Jesuits: Kramp, Hanssens, Martindale, Doncoeur, Schmidt, Howell, Danielou, Meersch, Jungmann, Hofinger, Ellard, de Lubac, Plus. And sometimes the questioner took a different tack. "How is it that you, a Jesuit, are so interested in liturgy? Shouldn't you have been a Benedictine?" Father Doncoeur, one of France's liturgical leaders, once made the classic answer to that: "I am a liturgist," he said, "not in spite of my being a Jesuit, but precisely because I am a Jesuit."

It remains true that in the period during which the movement began and grew, before the Council, most Jesuits personally held

---

2.   *The Assisi Papers*, Collegeville, MN., 1957, facing p. 45.

aloof from it. Mass in our churches and houses was celebrated invariably with scrupulous reverence and touching devotion; the sacraments were received and conferred; the office was recited faithfully. Of course the diocesan clergy used to tease us; they would say of so-and-so that "he was as awkward as a Jesuit in Holy Week." But if your chief preoccupation were teaching chemistry or philosophy, and if, suddenly asked to help out in a parish church, you found yourself cast in the role of deacon at a High Mass—a role you had not filled for many years—you might be pardoned for being a little tentative about your movements. People who took such things seriously did not know that liturgy is not synonymous with rubrics.

Father Howell tried to point out, however, that in the preconciliar days there was a lack of understanding among most Jesuits of the nature of liturgy as corporate worship, and that this was due to a circumstance inherent in our way of life. "It happens," he wrote (Letters and Notices of the English Province),

> that most of our priests celebrate Mass on most days of the year at side altars. There is no one present except a server—there is no community. This carries with it a danger that to the average Jesuit priest the Mass may seem to be just a very special sort of personal devotion—it is "his" Mass. It involves, indeed, the sacramental *ex opere operato* reenactment of the sacrifice of Calvary for the good of the whole Church, but nevertheless its form is that of an individual action of the priest. For the simple reason that there is no community behind him at "his" Mass, the Jesuit priest does not think of Mass in terms of the community. And so, on those comparatively rare occasions when he does celebrate in the presence of a community—whether of our scholastics, parishioners, or students—he does so in accordance with the habits and outlook formed in him by years of private celebration; he says Mass just as he does at the side altar, with lowered voice and no advertence to the community. He has no awareness of the dual role of a priest's office. For the priest is there not merely to consecrate and thereby offer sacrifice, but also to preside over and lead the community in corporate worship. Being intent solely on the sacerdotal function, he is not conscious of the presidential function. He neither presides nor leads, and has not the technique required for doing so, having become unfitted by disposition and outlook for something which modern pastoral methods demand with ever increasing frequency. . . . [This attitude] is formed during the years spent by our

scholastics on their way to the priesthood. Throughout the noviceship, juniorate, philosophate and theologate they attend for some three hundred and fifty days of every year a Mass which displays no sign of corporate worship. . . . Except for a few days in the year when there are High Masses they are brought up on the silent Low Mass with no external participation. The Mass is habitually presented to them under the appearance of an action in which the priest alone is to say anything or do anything. They have nothing to bring home to them the fact that the Mass is corporate worship.

"Men and women were created to praise the Lord their God." This sentence, which stands at the head of St. Ignatius' *Spiritual Exercises*, might be used to justify the interest of any Jesuit in the worship, public or private, of God. For a long time it seems to have been considered chiefly, if not exclusively, in terms of private worship, and perhaps this was owing in large measure to the fact that from 1570, or thirty years after the approbation of the Society, public worship was so carefully codified and regulated as to be virtually immutable. It would go on; Jesuits felt that objectively God was being worshiped publicly so long as the Mass was being offered, the sacraments conferred, the Divine Office recited. Their attention would be best given to private worship—meditation, examination of conscience, thanksgiving after Holy Communion, retreats—all very good exercises whose performance was always susceptible of improvement. Perhaps this attitude was formed or hardened by the emphasis on *ex opere operato* that was common in an age of anti-Protestant polemics, or perhaps it could be traced to an earlier anti-Arian reaction. It would require some honesty and humility to look about us now and appraise the quality of public worship in America—to look no further afield—and to speculate on what it might be if we had given it more of our attention.

But we must not oversimplify the historical problem or too easily indulge in the current vogue of breast-beating. If Jesuits in the past did not see the need of improving public worship, no one else did, either. The time was simply not ripe; there were dozens of vexing problems to be dealt with—Jansenism, for instance, or the Enlightenment, or Modernism. There was the enormous missionary expansion that followed on 16th-century geographical discoveries. There were the preoccupations (to put it very mildly) we associate with the names of Garibaldi, and Michael Baius, and Fénelon, and Voltaire, and Bismarck, and Taikosama, not to mention, so far as we ourselves were most intimately concerned, Pombal, de Choiseul, and Clement XIV. An epoch which saw the rise of nationalism was not likely to understand or give hospitality to the idea of the Christian community. Perhaps even the need of community was not glaringly obvious. The guns that would roar at Verdun had not been cast yet. The hobnailed legions of the Führer which would trample Czechoslovakia and Poland and the Low Countries under the Luftwaffe's murderous umbrella had not been born. Auschwitz and Dachau were pleasant little hamlets, I suspect, that never dreamed of the horror and infamy their names would one day connote. The fearful mushroom over Hiroshima, betokening an end to all human activity and to life itself, still lay in the very bottom of the witches' cauldrons. There was superb personal charity and high personal sanctity, but the institutions by which people live, the society which is the context and often the matrix of their habits, was not Christian, and in it the seed of corporate life and prayer could never thrive.

Are things so different today? Perhaps not; society seems no more Christian than before. But out of the agonies of our century, the blood baths and the terror, the gas chambers and the fall-out shelters, perhaps with no loftier motives than fear or sheer repugnance at what we have done to one another, a desperate hope has come into being, that human beings may learn to live together in peace. Every current of our time sets toward this ideal: Martin Buber talks of "I and thou;" Gabriel Marcel fights against the extinction of the human person; Viktor Frankl tells how love sustained him in a concentration camp, and Erich Fromm gives lessons in the art of loving. The United Nations, the European Economic Community, the World Council of Churches, the Ecumenical Council—are these not so many clear indications of the time-spirit? How providential was God our Lord in preparing the modern Church for this development as long as a hundred years ago, bringing back into the foreground of Catholic thought the doctrine of the Mystical Body (Moeller, Scheeben, Guéranger, Marmion). How earnestly has dogmatic and ascetical writing striven to explore its riches (Guardini, Leen, Boylan, Masure, Meersch, Bouyer, Ryan, Parsch, Jungmann, Schillebeeckx). Pius XII could say in 1958, "If it is true that there is a time for every truth, this is the hour of the Church considered as the Mystical Body of Christ."

But ideas have consequences, or, as the scholastics said, *agere sequitur esse.* The corporate Church must act corporately, and its first corporate act must be its adoring, grateful acknowledgement of him who gave it life. "We were created to praise." Nothing perfunctory, nothing shabby or second-rate will do here. The act must be limpid and lucid, so that all may understand, and it must be truly a corporate act in which all may participate. No less than private prayer, the liturgy demands that we stir up the grace that is in us, that "faith and devotion" which the old Roman Canon ascribes to the sons and daughters of God gathered about the altar. Not less but more than private prayer, the liturgy is a going into the Presence, an encounter with the living God, where we should be all tingling awareness. Anything that blocks that vision must be shorn away; anything that sharpens it must be kept.

And we are beginning to understand this need at last, I believe: that God must be worshiped in spirit and in truth, that the Father seeks such worshipers, and that the net result of all our preaching and teaching, of our universities and parishes and missions and retreat houses will be to provide them. We labor for the reintegration of modern splintered life in Christ, the Head of his body, in order that Christ may present that body to his Father holy and without stain or wrinkle in one sublime and comprehensive gesture of worship, an everlasting liturgy of which we are reminded in the liturgy for the feast of All Saints, but which is prefigured and prepared for by the sincerity and generosity of our liturgy in this world.

Well, that was Assisi. Its influence was considerable, in that it enabled the proponents of reform to cite one more authoritative document in support of their aims. Thus, for instance, Pius XII concluded the Congress in its final session in the Sistine Chapel at Rome by saying: "The liturgical movement is thus shown forth as a sign of the providential dispositions of God for the present time, of the movement of the Holy Spirit in the Church, to draw men more closely to the mysteries of the faith and the riches of grace which flow from the active participation of the faithful in the liturgical life. The Congress which has just concluded was directed to this particular object, to show the inestimable value of the liturgy in the sanctification of souls and consequently in the pastoral activity of the Church." But that this message did not reach the great masses of Catholics throughout the world became evident when Vatican II, seven years later, published its decree on the liturgy, and the changes it mandated struck bishops, priests, and laity with consternation and distress. "Why were we not prepared for this?" they demanded. The preparation had been available and abundant, in learned tracts and in popular articles, in conferences and sermons for some thirty years, but the listeners were few. In an article I wrote for *America*[3] at the time, I spoke of the immense labor that had gone into the Council's decree, but pointed out

> the larger labor still before us as we begin to assimilate the doctrine and obey the legislation. Devoted obedience will be required of us, a humble willingness to learn, a patient and persevering effort to bring about an *aggiornamento* of our own attitudes and practices. . . . But perhaps we should not dwell so much on the labor of the undertaking as on the magnificent prospects that open before us. Think, for instance, of a Sunday congregation that will hear the word of God copiously and in its mother tongue; that will sing its praises, weep for its sins and beg for its necessities consciously and together; that will know, as the Council says, how to offer the spotless Victim not only by the hands of the priest but even with him, and to offer themselves as well. Think of the priest for whom the breviary will no longer be an onerous obligation somehow to be satisfied in whatever moments can be snatched from a busy life, but an easy turning to God, at natural intervals of the day, that will give him orientation, inspiration, and comfort. Think of the missionary, the convert-maker, who will no longer be encumbered by the difficulty of explaining a way of worship utterly foreign and unnecessarily mysterious. In short, imagine a glad assembly of the redeemed, bringing to the feet of their gracious Father a tribute of thanks and praise, not because they must, but because they want to, because they enjoy it. Does it take you back to what you've read about the early Christians? That's just what it's supposed to do.

My article did not quite extend to the bottom of the page, so a piece of light verse by John Cogley was inserted as a "filler." The verse was amusing, but I never let Father Thurston Davis, the editor of the magazine, forget what he had done to enfeeble my message—he protested that it was quite inadvertent—by running it almost as a commentary on the article:

---

3.   December 21-28, 1963.

There are Jesuit progressives
To tend the Open Door,
And Jesuit conservatives
And moderates by the score.
There are Jesuits liturgical
As any O.S.B.,
And Jesuits inclined toward
Private piety.
There are Jesuits so venturesome
They can't go fast enough,
And others who are finding
Aggiornamento rough.
There are dialoguing Jesuits
And those who have their doubts;
There are Jesuits for the ins
And Jesuits for the outs.
There are Jesuits as pacifist
As any British bish,
And some who diet strictly
On the military dish.
Of welfare plans and such
Some Jesuits are leery,
While others of the brethren
Are clearly New Frontiery.
And on literary matters
The plural patterns hold:
The Jesuit *qua* reader
Fits no common mold.
There are Jesuits left and Jesuits right,
A pro and a con for most any fight,
So wherever you stand, you stand not alone:
Every little movement has a Jebbie of its own.

The Rector had made one condition when he gave me permission to go to Europe. I was to be back in time for the opening of school. But the old-style propeller plane for Boston was delayed for an hour in leaving Ciampino. Then it stopped for about 45 minutes each at Nice, Barcelona, Lisbon, and the Azores. Then Boston was blanketed in the usual autumn fog, so we flew up and down the coast until the fog lifted, two hours after our scheduled arrival. An hour later I walked into class and peered heavy-lidded at my new class of freshmen. "Gentlemen," I said, "the Holy Father was asking for you." They thought I was talking in my sleep. And I think I was.

The author's parents,
William J. and Catherine V. Leonard (ca. 1950)

Rev. Alexander J. Denomy, C.S.B., Toronto, Lecturer at First
Candlemas Lecture, February 2, 1947; Father Rector
(Keleher, S.J.), and Rev. William J. Leonard, S.J.

Rev. William J. Van Etten Casey, S.J., Evelyn Waugh and Rev.
William J. Leonard, S.J., Boston College, November 1948

L-R: Rev. F. X. Shea, S.J., Rev. Francis Sweeney, S.J., Philip McNiff, Hans Küng, the Rev. William J. Leonard, S.J.

CHAPTER 13

God's Poetry

ALL OF A SUDDEN, IT SEEMED, MY GENERATION OF JESUITS found itself in the saddle. Those we had regarded as well-nigh permanent provincials, rectors, deans, figures respected for learning and/or spirituality, passed from the scene through death or retirement. They had been such distinct personalities and had shaped our destinies for so long that they could not be forgotten—we tell anecdotes about them to this day. They had managed to govern their highly individual temperaments and put their abundant talents to work in collaboration with others who also had gifts but of a different order. The going was rough at times, as it must be whenever human beings attempt partnerships.

In those days we did not talk enough together. Decisions were handed down and were to be carried out—period. The *Rule* (read at table every month) was explicit: "No one shall curiously inquire of others the intentions of superiors in things appertaining to government, or by forming conjectures enter into conversation upon them, but each one attending to himself and to his own office must expect as from God's hand whatever shall be determined concerning himself and others." We might—after prayer and examination of our motives—"represent" our views to the superior, and he was bound to listen, but if he did not agree the case was closed. And if one did not want to seem difficult, or if the superior was known to have an autocratic turn of mind, the "subject" would usually not bring the matter up at all. He would wrestle with the ideal of obedience so emphasized in the Constitutions St. Ignatius wrote for the Society:

> It chiefly conduces to advancement and is very necessary
> that all should give themselves to perfect obedience, ac-
> knowledging the superior, whoever he be, in place of
> Christ our Lord, and yielding him inward reverence and
> love. And they must not only obey him in performing ex-

teriorly the things which he enjoins, entirely, readily, constantly and with due humility, without excuse, though the things commanded be hard and repugnant to nature, but also they must endeavor to be resigned interiorly, and to have a true abnegation of their own will and judgment, conforming their will and judgment wholly to what the superior wills and judges, in all things where there appears no sin, proposing to themselves the will and judgment of the superior as a rule of their will and judgment, that they may be the more exactly conformed to the first and chiefest rule of every good will and judgment, which is the eternal Goodness and Wisdom . . . All must especially study to observe obedience and to excel in it, and this not only in things of obligation but in others also, at the mere sign of the superior's will, though he should give no express command. And they must set before their eyes God our Creator and Lord, for whom man is obeyed, and strive to advance with the spirit of love, and not with the perturbation of fear.

In any organization there must be some leadership, some authority. It will be exercised with more or less grace, depending on the superior's talent for diplomacy, the number and gravity of the problems he has on his mind, and, sometimes, whether his breakfast agreed with him that morning. But it must be exercised, or the organization will be nothing more than a debating society. As the popular wisdom has it, "you may not like the boss, but he is still the boss." St. Ignatius wanted to lift that inescapable requirement to a higher plane, and make it a way of acquiring real virtue, by providing a loftier motivation than grudging necessity. He saw authority as descending from God to God's representatives, leaders who had been delegated to guide, inspire, and, yes, command. In his mind obedience to them was, quite simply, obedience to God.

This was easier to accept in a society that was markedly stratified, where there were nobles and serfs, gentry and peasantry, highbrows and lowbrows. It is manifestly more difficult today, when dialogue and discernment, not domination, are taken for granted, and we have been conditioned by three centuries of democracy. Decisions, accordingly, are now usually reached by consensus—a consensus that has been guided and shaped, ideally, by the leadership but to which the individual or the community has contributed. And this is seen as no less a manifestation of God's will than a decree from on high, inasmuch as good will can be presumed in both superior and subject, and divine grace is certainly not wanting to either.

Quite rarely, I think, there may occur, after prayer and candid discussion, a clear opposition of judgments as to what God's will is in a concrete situation. In such a case there seems no doubt that it is the superior's judgment that should prevail, and then the subject must in faith fall back on St. Ignatius' doctrine, however painful it may be:

> Let us direct all our powers and our intentions in the Lord to this point, that among us holy obedience be always in every detail perfect as well in execution as in will and judgment, performing with great speed, spiritual joy and perseverance whatsoever shall be enjoined us, persuading ourselves that all things are just, denying with a certain kind of blind obedience any contrary opinion or judgment of our own.

A disciple of Christ should have no problem in finding a precedent for such an attitude when he remembers a bowed, heartsick figure, alone in a garden, crying out in face of mystery, "Not my will but yours be done."

In this connection I remember most vividly the gallantry of a nun, the holiest person it has been my privilege to know. She was brilliant, the possessor of several graduate degrees, utterly dedicated to her work as dean of a small college. She was warm, loving, compassionate, but she was impatient with idlers—who, of course, made their complaints quite audible when their grades were low or when it was suggested that they choose some other way of occupying their time. And the complaints were at last effectual: she was transferred out of the dean's office, out of the college, and even out of the province to which she belonged. I visited her before she left, and found her romping gaily with some children in the neighborhood, seemingly without a care in the world. She walked me off across the campus and said, "Father, it's killing me. But if he wants to skin me alive, that's all right." I saw her only twice after that before she died; she was working as hard as ever, and never referred to what had happened.

In this as in so many other ways the nuns were magnificent. During one retreat I listened to tale after tale of petty tyranny exercised by local superiors. But on the day the retreat ended I saw the very nuns who had been suffering drive off, waving a cheerful good-bye, to resume life in the same situations they had described.

A quiet revolution has occurred since those days, symbolized perhaps by the fact that in most convents the title "superior" has disappeared, and something like "coordinator" has replaced it.

It would be impossible, of course, to record, and even more impossible to evaluate and honor adequately the achievement of religious women in American Catholic history. Very seldom indeed were they known to the public at large—even the names they were given were weird or bizarre or at least alien and hard to remember. I asked my friend Sister Francille, who accomplished so much for the liturgical and catechetical movements in Boston, where she got her name. "Oh," she said, "There were so many others called by some variation of Francis that they had to invent a completely new one." We used to tease her: she was "Sister Chinchilla" or "Sister Mary of the Seven Delicious Flavors" or even "Sister Mary of the Sweet-smelling Shavings of St. Joseph." It's pleasant to think that, by and large, the nuns have reverted to the names which might remind them of their parents' love and of their baptismal dignity as daughters of the Most High—and might prevent their being treated as little waxen figures on pedestals instead of as persons.

In the course of the recruiting I carried on for my Social Worship Program I visited eighty-six "motherhouses," huge buildings where the many novices of those days were preparing for profession. One of them was especially impressive, and I said in astonishment to the Mother General, "Mother, did you build this?" "No, Father," she replied rather grimly, "But I'm paying for it." No waxen figure there.

A degree of heroism was called for in those days from those who entered the convent and were required to conform their judgment to some of the practices and regulations they were expected to observe. At one motherhouse the chaplain, an old priest known to be something of a fuddy-duddy, came in from a walk one day and said to the Mother General, "I just saw a nun driving a car. And I hope I die before I ever see one of your Sisters at the wheel of a car." She told me the story and added, "And you know, Father, I agreed with him." I replied, with more asperity, perhaps, than delicacy, "You're right, Mother. And I hope they never use a telephone, or a refrigerator, or a vacuum cleaner, or any other of those worldly, twentieth-century inventions."

It was an age, of course, that weighed in heavily on the side of law, obligation, authority, strict observance. Some people—people who as a rule could do nothing about it—dissented privately, with a grim humor. A seminary professor who himself taught the subject defined Canon Law as "the bad side of the Good News." Another called it "the corrective supplied by the Church for the Gospels." Eugene Kennedy introduced himself at a lecture as "one who had survived the Golden Age of Canon Law."

No doubt there is a bit of legend in some of the anecdotes now recounted gleefully in our recreation rooms, but they do attest to a certain grimness in the spirituality of those preconciliar days, and it was not limited to any particular locality. It is said, for example, that in California a certain "spiritual father," giving an "exhortation" to the community, remarked, "One of the greatest sorrows we shall experience in heaven, my dear brothers, is the memory of the sins we committed during life." In Manila, after the reform of Holy Week in 1951 (previously all had been whoopee once the *Exultet* was sung on Holy Saturday morning), the Rector posted a sign which read, "Silence need not be kept today, but let a decent gloom be observed." And in my own dear Province of New England a well-known retreat director began his presentation of the Fourth Week of the *Spiritual Exercises,* which deals with our Lord's resurrection, by saying, "Joy, my dear brothers, is a difficulty that must be faced." Nor was this disposition exclusively a Jesuit property; it is related that the Rector of a diocesan seminary, having to address what he considered a notable laxity in the observance of the Rule, amended the Scripture and thundered, "Even if you do penance, you will all likewise perish." Cardinal Basil Hume of England, who preached the retreat of the American bishops in 1982, told them that as a child he was warned against taking apples from the larder; God saw him if no one else did. It was thirty years, he said, before he realized that God was the sort of person who, looking over your shoulder, would probably nudge you and say, "Take two."

And yet Catholics in the fifties manifested a real buoyancy and hopefulness. The threat of atomic devastation did not deter us from putting up buildings as if they would stand forever. Cardinal Cushing, who laid cornerstones everywhere, was said to have an "edifice complex." New techniques were devised for raising funds. "Bingo" games, doubtfully distinguished from gambling or tacitly condoned because of their good purpose, flourished in the parishes. Raffles offered spectacular prizes; one church, which placed a new automobile on its front lawn every week, was christened "Our Lady of General Motors." Building went on in other ways: previously local or inconspicuous organizations went national, like the Catholic Rural Life Conference or the Federation of Catholic College Students or the Christian Family Movement. The Knights of Columbus and the Catholic Youth Organization enrolled thousands. Bishop Fulton Sheen, who in 1940 had addressed 110,000 people at a Pontifical High Mass in the Memorial Stadium in Los Angeles, turned to radio and television and spoke to an audience estimated at thirty million. White Catholics rose steadily in the social scale, moved into the suburbs and commuted in expensive cars to executive suites downtown; their former homes were engulfed by an incoming tide of Hispanics and Blacks, who were heroically ministered to by Dorothy Day's "Houses of Hospitality" and the Baroness de Hueck's "Friendship Houses." "Labor priests" like John A. Ryan, Raymond McGowan, Francis Haas, Bernard Sheil, Charles Owen Rice, Dennis Comey not only elaborated programs of social reform but actually rubbed shoulders with the workingman in the factories and on the docks, and fought for his right to organize in labor unions.

In these and many other areas, as Jay Dolan has pointed out,[1] the Church in the United States was not only becoming more visible, it was taking on distinctly American characteristics and identifying more and more with the American culture. There was an emphasis on quantity, on statistics—so many confessions heard, so many Holy Communions, so many converts. Bishop Vincent Waters of Raleigh, a man of endless energy, told me of a pastoral visit he made to a parish high in the Carolina hills, where Father Andy Graves, a drawling, sleepy-eyed Jesuit, ministered to a scattered handful of Catholics living in a decidedly non-Catholic milieu. After dinner they sat on the porch, and Father Graves, in honor of the occasion, served coffee and cigars. Suddenly the Bishop said, "How many converts did you have last year, Andy?" Father Graves slowly blew fragrant smoke at the sunset and said, "How's that, Bishop?" The Bishop repeated, "How many converts did you have last year?" Father Graves pulled on the cigar for a long moment. "Converts, Bishop?" "Yes, Andy, converts. How many did you have?" Another long pull on the cigar, and Father Graves

---

1.   *The American Catholic Experience*, pp. 380-420, Garden City, New York, 1985.

said, "Why, Bishop, it was only last year that these people stopped calling me a son of a bitch."

Energy and optimism built and staffed 2,428 Catholic high schools educating 810,763 students; there were 175 Catholic colleges.[2] Retreat houses were thronged every week-end. Pilgrimages to shrines at home and abroad (Lourdes and Fatima and Ste. Anne de Beaupré attracted many) were popular. Novena services, especially those in honor of Mary under the title of "Our Sorrowful Mother," broke all attendance records; in Chicago, at the church of the Servite Fathers, 70,000 people attended 38 novena services every week,[3] while in Boston squads of police strove ineffectually to keep traffic flowing on Wednesday evenings outside the Redemptorist "Mission Church." Catholic publications proliferated; in 1959 there were 24,273,972 subscribers to 580 newspapers and magazines.[4] And by 1958 more than 6,000 priests, brothers, sisters, and lay people were working in overseas missions.[5]

Such a ferment of activity fed the self-confidence (edging ever closer to triumphalism) of the erstwhile immigrant American Church, linking it, as Dr. Dolan points out, with the total American experience, the "can do" mentality that was so characteristic of American troops in World War II. There was, however, a singular absence of original intellectual life; we were still reading European theology, philosophy, literary criticism, still following the European lead in art, architecture, science, psychology, social theory. Our Catholic colleges graduated thousands of bright young people who showed little inclination toward purely intellectual careers, and who—as yet—seemed to experience no difficulty in reconciling their faith and religious practice with current American attitudes. The dismay, the departures, the bedlam of the sixties were still ten years away.

Piety reached a flood tide at this time, but it was a "devotional" piety, centered on the person of Jesus, especially in his eucharistic presence, on Mary, considered as his mother but our mother, too, and on the saints, particularly in their capacity as intercessors, able as God's special friends to win "favors" for their clients right up to the miraculous. It was warm, emotional, and it slipped easily into the sen-

---

2.   Id., p. 399.
3.   Id., page 394.
4.   Id., page 394.
5.   Id., page 393.

timental. It did not displace the Bible or the liturgy but, as it were, ran parallel with them, taking from them only essential doctrine and elaborating this in its own highly individualistic fashion. Ritual was important to it, so you had, in public, such "devotions" as benediction, novenas, the crowning of Mary's statue, the veneration of relics, and in private the wearing of the scapular or medals under one's shirt, the recitation of the rosary, the use of "holy water" before retiring or in emergencies like thunderstorms. Sin and guilt were very much a part of it, so you had long lines at the confessional, sulphurous sermons on avoiding the "near occasions" of sin, long prayers of "reparation" for one's own or the world's neglect of God's commandments or failure to respond to his love.

The fact that this sort of piety is alien to many contemporary tastes does not mean that it was unorthodox or reprehensible. It certainly brought God into everyday life in a very vivid way. When someone sends me for my collection an old prayerbook, tattered and thumbed and, perhaps, smudged with tear-stains, I feel I must treat it with immense reverence: this book has prayed, more and better, probably, than I ever shall. Eugene Kennedy, in his speculations about the Catholic future,[6] is insistent that "Culture Two Catholics" whom he sees emerging today could never have come into being if they had not had the solid tradition and practice of their "Culture One" forebears. And Father Richard McBrien, in his weekly syndicated column, has an eloquent tribute:

> Much has been spoken and written about the state of the Church in the years prior to the Second Vatican Council. In some cases the discussion has been tinged with nostalgia; in others, with anger and resentment. It is the latter mood which interests me in this week's essay, for there is a prevailing and usually unchallenged assumption abroad that the preconciliar Church must have been a theological, liturgical, and spiritual disaster area.

> I am not about to defend the obvious deficiencies of the pre-Vatican II Church: its catechesis-by-rote, the unilateral exercise of authority, the undue emphasis on law and precedent, the unfavorable estimation of other churches and religions, its rigid liturgical forms, its negative spirituality, its controlled theology.

---

6.   *Tomorrow's Catholics, Today's Church: The Two Cultures of American Catholicism,* New York, 1988.

But there were, at the same time, some enormous strengths in the preconciliar Church which have, in fact, marked the Church at every age and culture: its faith in the Lordship of Jesus and in the providence of God, its respect for the mystery and sacramentality of creation, its passion for fidelity to the apostolic word, witness, and sacrifice, its hope in the power of God to give eternal life, its docility to the Word of God proclaimed by the Church, its sense of community and continuity with Christians living and dead, its realism about sin and its confidence in the grace of forgiveness.

If such strengths as these were not constitutive of the Church in the preconciliar decades, how explain the extraordinary outburst of theological, liturgical, and spiritual vitality at the council itself or in these remarkable years since the council?[7]

Meanwhile, back at the ranch . . . I had three hundred seniors in class one year, in six sections, and before I had time to grade their fourth-quarter examinations their final examinations came in. It took me eleven days, doing absolutely nothing else, to get through the six hundred "blue books," and the net result was that about twenty-five failed the course. I hated to prevent them from graduating, but their papers showed that they had done no work whatever. What was my surprise, then, on Commencement Day, to see them in cap and gown, their diplomas in their hands. In considerable fury, thinking of my eleven wasted days, I went to the Registrar and demanded an explanation. A gentleman of great integrity, he told me, reluctantly, that the Dean had raised my grades high enough to give everyone a passing mark. Theology, in the Dean's eyes, was not a really academic subject; it was enough that the students had been exposed to lectures; they were "good boys" who loved their mothers. Happily, that attitude did not survive his tenure in office.

I continued my practice of jotting down, from the "blue books," choice examples of "English as she is spoke"—or written. It helped to alleviate the drudgery every teacher knows.

---

7. *Witness*, the newspaper of the Archdiocese of Dubuque, 28 September 1978.

"Our Lord told the pharisees many times through parables the set-up of heaven."

"To prove his divinity Jesus rose from the tomb. Offhand I would say this has a slight edge on the Unitarians."

"As for sharing our clothing with everyone, I would say forget it. I think it would do more toward creating the laziest country in the world than even television."

"The Jews were had spiritually by the high priest."

"In the respect that Christ was poor doesn't mean that we must be the same although the distractions toward Hell aren't so great when we have no dough."

"The hippocracy of the Pharisees."

"We must feed the hungary and clothe the nakard."

"The ancient phroficieys."

"Separation is granted only in a case of immortality, which is a greater sin than divorce."

"It is not possible to marry another while the present pardner lives."

"Doubts as to the verititude of the book."

"He and his following ancestors."

"The Vulgate is the gate to eternal peace."

"Some of them, when asked how come the people saw him, they contribute it to hulucinations."

"There is such a thing as evolution and when Adam and Eve came a soul was put in the picture. Nothing else has souls but humans."

"The Temple of Herod was lined with gold, silver, and women of ill repute."

"Herod was an altruist, to put it mildly, if you stood in his way of gain he would have you killed."

"The mystercle number."

"I conclude that the passage is just a heretical, melladramatical creation."

"Symbols are used in Genesis because the people were simple pheasants and could not understand otherwise. E.g., the Serpent signified Satan so sly and sneekey."

"The Church has set up a Biblical Commission which interrupts the Bible."

"Actually literary form has no bearing in Holy Scripture only if you understand H.S. to mean what it says. But

when it is interpreted the meaning is one in the same like the meat inside the nut."
"The Gospel still packs a whallop today."
"Our Lord made a trip from Samarta to Galileo."
"One of Matthew's characteristics is par excellence."
"And maney, maney other examples."

During the fifties there was a growing popular awareness of liturgy—or perhaps one should say that there was a growing hunger for something more substantial than the current devotions. The Liturgical Conference attracted more and more members, the annual "Weeks" drew steadily larger audiences, and the sounds of approval from Rome, while still muffled, became more frequent. The Conference, heartened by all this, decided to establish a national office in Washington, and employed Mr. Jack Mannion as its Secretary. It was an excellent choice: Jack was personable, very eager to serve a cause he believed in, tactful and diplomatic. Under his direction the Conference prospered and became a bureau for the engagement of lecturers, a publishing business, a clearing house for inquiries and projects, a common ground where the aspirant "movements" of the time—theological, biblical, social—could meet, cross-pollinate, identify common objectives.

Across the country, "liturgists" took advantage of the new curiosity evinced by seminaries, novitiates, retreat houses, colleges, high schools, and parishes. Lecturers were in great demand. In 1953, for instance, while carrying sixteen hours of class, I gave 117 lectures or sermons off campus, many in quite remote places, for an estimated total audience of 17,500. It was, of course, exhilarating to be invited so often, but I was never tempted to think the wandering minstrel's lot superior to, or more profitable in the long run, or more downright enjoyable than the daily contact with students. For one obvious reason, you met the the students again and again throughout the academic year, whereas you reached people in a lecture or a sermon only once or twice. Then, too, the students, being young, were more open to fresh ideas than their elders. And it was fun to see how they responded. The old scholastic axiom, "whatever is received is received according to the capacity of the receiver," surely applies in the classroom. I was constantly being surprised, not so much that the substance of my lectures came back to me in examinations or in discussions outside of class, but at the new twists or combinations or realizations it took on as the different personalities absorbed it. Alas, in the great majority of cases the teacher will have to wait until eternity to discover what the total impact brought about.

Whenever the appointed reading in the breviary or the missal is from St. Paul's letter to the Ephesians I am struck anew by its beauty, and particularly by the sentence in the second chapter (v. 10): "We are God's work of art, created in Christ Jesus to live the good life as from the beginning he meant us to live it." The Greek word *poiema*, translated "work of art" by the Jerusalem Bible and "handiwork" by both the NEB and the NAB, is rendered as "workmanship" by the RSV. "Masterpiece" might be another acceptable translation. What interests me, however, is that our English word "poem" is derived from *poiema,* and so we might understand Paul as saying "We are God's poetry." And that reminds me of a lament of Cardinal Newman's that I jotted down in my commonplace book long ago (on April 12, 1932, to be precise): "Alas, what are we doing all through life, both as a necessity and as a duty, but unlearning the world's poetry and attaining to its prose?" "Poetry" here, I take it, meant for Newman aspiration, dreams; "prose" meant the struggle to realize and accomplish the ideal. In life we must reduce the hope and ambition to actuality; otherwise we are failures. It's a tedious process (hence "prosy"), but in the end our life again becomes poetry: every saint is a successful expression of a divine thought. To keep the metaphor, moreover, *poiein* means to make, to shape, to impress on raw, formless material one's own personality. The image that comes to mind is of the poet struggling to find the precise words that will express unmistakably and for the last time the concept he has in mind—crossing out, recasting, amending—the *"labor limae,"* the "drudgery of the file" that old Horace talked about. Only here it is not a human effort that is involved; Paul says that we are God's accomplishment. And that reminds me of a remark that I read somewhere—I think in C.S. Lewis: "Religion is not so much what many today consider it, a fragrant steam of incense floating upward, as, rather, strong, skilful hands reaching down to make and heal, and, sometimes, to break in order to make over." To be sure, the raw material will be stubborn, refractory, perverse. We ourselves will be the last to perceive any notable improvement in the design. Once, when I was talking in this vein, a young man said, "Father, if we are God's poetry, I'm only a limerick."

God's shaping hands are the fashioning liturgy of the Church, by which, to be sure, we worship him, but by which, also, he molds us to the likeness of his Son, the archetype of our holiness. Baptism, Confirmation, Orders, Marriage are not simply milestones, signifying our initiation into a new phase of our lives; they are, each of them, the beginnings of a new intimacy of God with his material, during which he labors unremittingly to achieve in us the expression of his thought. Penance, Anointing, and especially Communion provide moments of more intensive toil, when the obedient material grows by leaps and bounds toward the desired likeness. Every participation in Mass is a yielding to the divine dissatisfaction with us as replicas of Christ, a plea to be taken in hand, broken, formed again. "All those who from the first were known to him, he has destined from the first to be molded into the image of his Son" (Rom 8:29). There is something of the sculptor's repeated hammer-blows in the verbs that follow: "So predestined, he called them; so called, he justified them; so justified, he glorified them." And there is something of the artist's anguish, shaping and re-shaping, nearer and nearer to the perfect articulation, in the prayer we used to say at the Offertory. In Ronald Knox's translation it reads: "Wonderfully, O God, thou didst go to work in creating the excellent nature of man, and yet more wonderfully in re-fashioning it." The handiwork that finally emerges will vary in proportion as the material was malleable and responsive, and inasmuch as it resembles, at the last, him who was "the radiance of his Father's splendor and the full expression of his being" (Heb 1:3).

Of course what strikes us at once about this "handiwork" is that it is living. It is not like, let us say, a chalice, or a tourelle, or a lyric. It is more akin to the character in a play who seems to us more real than many we have actually met, and who reveals his nature by his words and actions: Hamlet, Falstaff, Desdemona. The difference, obviously, is that the dramatic personality, however vivid, lives only in human imagination, whereas God's handiwork enjoys substantial being. We are struck, too, by the fact that its life is not its own, but a communicated life. God's handiwork is created "in Christ Jesus"; it lives with the life of the Son of God, and "makes" handiwork in its turn, the most startling of which is its own holiness, shaped from the clay of human perceptions and aspirations by faith, hope, and love. Every Christian, then, is both artifact and artist; God, the Artist, makes the Christian, and the Christian is an artist who, collaborating with God, makes himself.

This is, I suppose, a long way round to what I intended to say, that our sanctification is, radically, God's work. How or when do we encounter God and submit to his shaping of us? In prayer, notably; in recognition and patient acceptance of trials; but most powerfully and effectively in those sacred signs—baptism and eucharist in particular—which in his love he uses to work upon us. It goes without saying, as Karl Rahner insisted, that we must give him a free hand, so to speak; the more ardently we desire and lay ourselves open to his artistry the more perfect will his sculpturing be. There is a brief prayer after communion which, in the terse, classically restrained style of the Roman rite summed up this disposition and might once have helped our people to appreciate both God's working in them and the need of their own eager concurrence with him: "*Quod ore sumpsimus pura mente capiamus, et de munere temporali fiat novis remedium sempiternum.*" This has been translated in the present vernacular missal to read, "Lord, may I receive these gifts in purity of heart. May they bring me healing and strength, now and for ever"—a translation which is fine except that it is not faithful to the original, it sacrifices rhetorical impact by abandoning an artful balance of phrases, and it substitutes the individualistic first person singular for the comprehensive first person plural. The rubric accompanying the prayer, furthermore, directs that the priest is to recite the prayer "quietly." Not much enlightenment or stimulation for the congregation in such a prayer.

However, the sign language of the liturgy is in general so clear, so direct, that he who runs may read. Think of what it would mean to the average Christian, beset with temptations, painfully aware of his frailty, his tepidity, his sad infidelities (often repented but too often repeated)—what hope, incentive, even joy there would be in the realization that God still loves him, still works in him, is still carving in his soul an ultimately recognizable likeness of the Christ. Paul writes to the Corinthians, seemingly no shining examples of virtue, "And we, with our unveiled faces reflecting like mirrors the brightness of the Lord, all grow brighter and brighter as we are turned into the image that we reflect; this is the work of the Lord who is Spirit" (2 Cor 3:18). So if, echoing Our Lady's question, we ask "how shall this be done?" we have the angel's answer: "The Holy Spirit will come upon you, and the power of the Most High will overshadow you." And the signs of his presence will be bread and wine, water, oil, fire, incense, candles, time and place, light and darkness, song, gesture and vesture, color and space.

We sing, in Advent, "our earth shall yield its fruit" (Ps 85:13), and the quotation is applied to our Blessed Lady, through whose human collaboration the Son of God, "the true likeness of the God we cannot see" (Col 1:15), was put before our eyes. Her high privilege is likewise ours, in that our cooperation with the craftsmanship of God is sought and may be consciously given. It is true, then, to say that the Christian is an artist, and that his best handiwork is himself. His work-plan is outlined for him by St. Paul: "Have this mind in you which was also in Christ Jesus, who, though he was by nature God, did not consider being equal to God a thing to be clung to, but emptied himself, taking the nature of a slave and being made like men and women" (Phil 2:5-7). The mind of Christ must become familiar to the human artist through prayerful study of the Gospels, especially in that "kerygmatic" preaching of them which the liturgy supplies. And the emptying of self, in order more completely to adhere to the infinite Good, must go on persistently and ruthlessly, that there may be a fitting conformity between what we do at Mass and what we are. Père Plus wrote long ago: "The perfect prayer of the Church is the offering of the consecrated bread in the Mass. Now in the Host, in place of the bread there is our Lord Jesus Christ; the substance of the bread is there no longer. In the same way, my life will be a perfect prayer if there is no mingling of self-interest; if, instead of self there is Christ, and I am entirely submissive to the will of God."[8] From Gethsemane ("not my will but yours") to the Christian daily life ("accept, Lord, all my liberty") runs a straight line. At Mass the line mounts upward, toward that "altar in heaven" of which the first Eucharistic Prayer speaks. The Christian artist, his intelligence tempered and attuned to truth, his will hammered ("not without a piercing cry, not without tears"—Heb 5:7) into capacity for good, achieves a handiwork that, if it does him honor, speaks with much more eloquence of the Artist who shaped and sustained him. "You have crowned him with glory and honor; you have given him power over the works of your hands" (Ps 8: 6-7).

Reflections on all this run a curious gamut. Could the vague aspiration in every soul to "make something of oneself" be as-

---

8.   Plus, *How to Pray Always*, New York, 1926, p. 24.

cribed to a primitive revelation? An injunction, not recorded in so many words, to do something better than "dress and keep the paradise of pleasure" (Gen 2:15)? Or, again, one remembers the complexity of human motivation and the terribly tangled skeins of human lives. Is there "a workman who does not need to be ashamed of his work?" (2 Tim 2:15). We must make our own the prayer of the prophet: "And yet, Lord, you are our Father; we the clay, you the potter, we are all the work of your hand. Do not let your anger go too far, Lord, or go on thinking of our sins for ever. See, see, we are all your people" (Is 64:8-9).

We who once were not of the people of God keep not only Christmas but our Gentiles' Christmas, too. We drive "dromedaries from Madian and Epha" into Jerusalem; we are among the "men of Saba with their gifts of gold and incense, their cry of praise to the Lord" (Is 60:6). But before we go there is our Advent, the image of our stay in this world, the time of waiting and working in preparation for the journey. We must unlearn the prose of failure and stir up in our hearts the enthusiasm that produces poetry (*poiema*). We must yield ourselves to the pressure of creative fingers; we ourselves must shape and mold and fashion, so that the children of adoption may begin to resemble the Only-begotten. "And may the gracious care of the Lord our God be ours; prosper the work of our hands for us, prosper the work of our hands!" (Ps 90:17).

CHAPTER 14

Prime Movers

"LET THE GREAT WORLD SPIN FOREVER DOWN THE RINGING grooves of change." Tennyson, I suspect, derived that image from the railroads that were just being built when he wrote. A hundred years later we were traveling on planes instead of trains, and the image may not have been so striking, but the "great world" itself was still spinning through change, and getting itself knocked about considerably in the process. We Americans, for instance, were fighting an inconclusive war in Korea. Spain had torn itself apart in civil war, and those among us who did not sympathize with Franco were dubbed "*Commonweal* Catholics." The tense confrontation at Selma in Alabama, where priests and nuns were prominent among the protesters, signaled a new day for civil rights, and incidentally a new role for clerics and religious. Senator McCarthy and Father Coughlin had stormed and ranted, and were at last silenced. Pius XII died after nineteen years on the papal throne; his record as a teacher in many difficult areas of Christian thought and conduct gave him a right, people said, to the title "*Doctor Ecclesiae*," but his failure to condemn the Holocaust in explicit terms brought Jewish censure on his memory. Perhaps he was timid—though timidity does not seem to have been characteristic of him. He may have been ill-advised, or simply mistaken as to the course he should take. At the time he declared, "We ought to speak words of fire against such things, and the only thing that dissuades us from doing so is the knowledge that if we should speak we would be making the condition of these unfortunate ones more difficult."[1] An old man had been elected as a "caretaker pope" to

---

1. *Actes et Documents du Saint-Siège relatifs a la seconde guerre mondiale,* Libreria Editrice Vaticana, 1970, vol. 1, p. 435.

succeed him, and no one, not even he, foresaw at that moment the enormous changes his Council would introduce.

Closer to home, Boston's Catholics, up to now a pretty solid phalanx, had been rocked by the "Boston Heresy Case." Father Leonard Feeney, a Jesuit previously known only for a few graceful lyrics, some whimsical essays, and a gentle, genial manner, became a chaplain at St. Benedict's Center in Cambridge, where Catholic students at Harvard and Radcliffe frequently came together, and began to proclaim that "outside the Church there is no salvation." He understood this in the most literal sense, and brooked no dissenting voices. Eloquent ridicule was poured on any who raised questions, and they were shown the door, the parting shot being his notification that they were surely going to hell. His contemporaries were baffled by this transformation of his personality, and their concern for him became profound anxiety as numbers of young people were converted to his views. Then he began preaching on Boston Common every Sunday afternoon, and Monday's papers were full of his diatribes against Protestants and Jews.

At Boston College we had good reason for distress: we were meeting his doctrine in the confessional. (One "penitent" told me how utterly wrong were my solutions for certain moral problems, and threatened me with hell-fire unless I changed them.) Some of our most fervent students had become his disciples, and three of our lay faculty were spending most of their class hours propagating his teaching instead of lecturing on their own proper course material. Things came to a head when these professors, having been consulted, warned, and found defiant, were dismissed. Our Provincial Superior, then, tried to defuse the situation by removing Father Feeney from St. Benedict's Center. But Father Feeney refused to leave, and finally was expelled from the Society of Jesus for disobedience. All this was very painful for the then-Archbishop Cushing, who loved the Society and had been extraordinarily generous to our schools and missions. He had, moreover, known Father Feeney personally, and was at a loss to understand this new development. Matters were taken out of his hands when Rome stepped in. Father Feeney was excommunicated. Shortly thereafter he and his most dedicated followers, whom he formed into separate religious communities of men and women and called "the Slaves of the Immaculate Heart of Mary," moved to the little town of Still River, near Worcester. It would be twenty-five years before they were reconciled to the Church, through the patience and kindness of Bishop Flanagan and Cardinal Medeiros. And no one could ever properly assess the anguish, the heartbreak, the lifelong scars sustained by those who were involved.

In the summer of 1960 I was invited to lecture on liturgy to the Jesuit students of theology at Alma College in California. The journey there in early June was a happy one; I took the train—a more leisurely and civilized mode of travel than anything the airlines could offer—and stayed for a few days in Cleveland, Chicago, and Denver to lecture and greet old friends. There was a great curiosity about liturgy in those days; few people knew much about it, but it was in the air, so to speak, and it had all the charm of novelty. Later, after the Council had described it as "a sacred action surpassing all others . . . the summit of all the Church's activity and the fountain from which all her power flows," curiosity gave way to real interest, and for some years lecturers on the subject were in great demand. I wonder now whether we failed to do an effective job of teaching, or whether there were simply not enough teachers to go around, because it seems to me that the basic theology of worship has still to be learned by most of our people. For twenty-five years after the Council, of course, we have been preoccupied with the externals of liturgy. We have had to devise a new ritual, a new music, a new architecture, a new language (the vernacular). Such explanations of these innovations as were offered—and very often they were introduced without any explanation—did not touch the heart of the matter. So the shining opportunity passed; people's attention turned to other things. And today, while liturgical celebrations have certainly improved over what they were, they are unrelated to such new emphases as individual spiritual direction, private prayer, spiritual "growth," etc. Perhaps with time the sheer power of the liturgy, "an action of Christ the priest and of his body the Church," as the Council pointed out, will by a sort of divine osmosis penetrate, irradiate, and transfigure all Christian prayer and conduct. After all, as the Council went on to say, "no other action can match its claim to efficacy."

California was, as always, lovely to look at and warmly hospitable to visitors. I keep grateful memories of the Alma faculty and of the theologians, now, as priests, working in the Far West or across the globe from Taiwan to Alaska. And I had the privilege of conducting a series of four lectures at each of the four large "motherhouses" of Sisters located in the area, as well as at the Jesuit novitiate in Los Gatos. Meanwhile there was great excitement; the Democratic National Convention was meeting in Los Angeles, and on July 13th it nominated for the presidency of the United States "John F. Kennedy of Massachusetts"! Could he possibly be elected? Only one other Catholic had ever been nominated, and he had been soundly defeated in 1928 by a coalition of Prohibitionists and anti-Catholic bigots. We were not optimistic; in fact, when I was making my retreat at Loyola University in August, I saw in the parking lot an old wreck of a car with Massachusetts plates. Two of its tires were flat and it had evidently been abandoned. On its rear fender was a banner: "Kennedy for President." Was this an omen? I was afraid it was.

My return home was circuitous and studded with stop-overs. As a small boy I used to pore over the railroad time-tables my father brought me from the South Station in Boston, and I was enchanted by the dactyls in the name of one of the railroads, "The Atchison, Topeka and Santa Fe." Now the Santa Fe "Chief" took me through the lovely orchards east of Los Angeles and the red rock country of Arizona to Kansas, where I shared happily in the very active (for those days) celebration of the Sunday Mass at Fr. Joe Nolan's parish in Wichita and went on to a joyous reunion with Fr. Gerry Ellard at St. Mary's. Then—flying because the time was getting short—Gerry and I went to Pittsburgh and the 1960 Liturgical Week. Bishop Wright was our host there, as he had been in his previous diocese of Worcester in 1955. He had worked hard to prepare for the Week, and his eloquence at the opening and closing sessions held everyone spellbound. And the attendance was the largest in our history—3600.

Philadelphia was my next stop, for a lecture at Rosemont College; then there was a workshop at Newport, and four lectures for the community at Shadowbrook in Lenox, and five for the tertians at Auriesville. The long summer's barnstorming ended when I arrived home—again, just as classes were beginning. When we were novices and were not keeping the rule of silence as carefully as we might, Father Fisher reproved us. "Some day," he said, smiling and wagging his finger at us, "You will be tired of talking." I didn't believe him then, but I came to agree wholeheartedly later.

So the sixties arrived. It seemed to me, and this is not simply hindsight, that they brought to the campus a perceptible change, not unlike the first chill of autumn. Hitherto, in twenty-odd years of teaching, I had had an uncomplicated, effortless relationship with students. I liked them and I enjoyed teaching, and they responded in many cases with an affection that continues to this day, and makes Alumni Night the happiest of the year for me. But a new generation came on the scene now: cool, not positively hostile but wary, questioning. It was the beginning of the challenge to elders, authorities, and all who in any way represented what the young people called the "institution." Later there would come the rebellions and riots that rocked campuses across the country; we had a strike at Boston College that closed the school for weeks, called into question for a while the commencement of 1970, and hastened the departure of the beleaguered president.

But that would be later. For now we had what Father Andy Greeley called "strangers in the house." A certain lack of understanding has always existed between the generations. Perhaps it's healthy, inasmuch as it indicates a disposition to clear the air, toss out stale ideas, and start afresh. Elders have to be reminded that

> There are more things in heaven and earth
> Than are dreamt of in your philosophy.

The elders will always be perplexed—yes, and a bit resentful. "Who are these unlicked cubs? What do they know? Did they fight the war?" And it's unsettling, at the least, to hear one's accumulated experience dismissed with the blithe retort: "That's history." Even the use of such catch-phrases can be irritating; they seem to point to a new and arrogantly triumphant culture from which elders are excluded. I remember how distasteful my father found the "roaring twenties"—the insouciance, the rollicking abandonment of social niceties, the use of words never heard in polite conversation. As a Bostonian, he had, of course, a developed sense of propriety, but in this respect his attitudes were not different from those of his generation. Every year, at the beginning of Lent, the pastor would read to us the diocesan regulations for the penitential season. Certain groups were exempt from fasting and abstinence: young children, the sick, the very old, and "women in delicate health and condition." It was a long time before I understood that euphemism, and an even longer time before I could bring myself to use the currently innocuous "pregnant."

Gentility has suffered in more substantial ways. On campus now, who raises his hat to a lady? (Since the JFK era, who wears a hat?) Who holds a door for the next comer? Who apologizes if he/she interrupts another? I have seen professors lecturing in T-shirts. Well, you say, would I go back to Victorian prissiness? No, but I keep remembering that Marshal Foch, the commander of

198 / *The Letter Carrier*

the Allied armies in World War I, visited the United States after the war, and someone teased him about his French *politesse.* He said, gently, "Ah, but it is the lu-bri-ca-tion that reduces the fric-ti-on."

On March 5, 1961, a group of us celebrated Father H. A. Reinhold's "emancipation" with a party in Father Tom Carroll's apartment. Father Reinhold was a richly gifted German priest who had barely made it to safety across the Dutch border, one jump ahead of Hitler's SS bully-boys. Some of his ideas, preached with a candor and vigor that we came to know as characteristic, had not squared with the dogmas of the Third Reich. He came to America expecting a cordial welcome and hoping for incardination in the Archdiocese of New York, but authorities there, reasoning with impressive logic that if he were not a fascist he must be a communist, gave him a very frosty reception. After considerable time and anxiety, he was at last given a rural parish in the State of Washington. Here again his forthright advocacy of unfamiliar ideas, especially in the area of liturgical reform, got him into hot water with his bishop. Eventually he resigned the parish, but the bishop would not release him to apply for incardination elsewhere. Dr. Tom Caulfield, a genial and persuasive psychiatrist, went at Father Carroll's instance to see the bishop and explain that Father Reinhold's painful experiences in Europe and America were responsible for his seeming insubordination, but to no avail. By this time he was suffering from the onset of Parkinson's Disease and becoming pathologically sensitive. He was invited to attend one of the high-level consultations of liturgical scholars sponsored by Rome in the fifties, but when the Board of Directors of the Liturgical Conference decided to send an official delegate of its own to the consultation, and elected Father Mathis of Notre Dame, he turned on us and accused us of wanting to spy on him. This unhappy business ended at last when his compassionate and resourceful friend, Father Carroll, devised a diplomatic approach that won him the "emancipation" we were celebrating that evening. Then Bishop Wright put the crowning touch to the maneuver by inviting him to join the community of the Oratory in Pittsburgh, where, in 1968, he died in peace.

Father Reinhold's personal ordeal did not prevent him from becoming one of the most articulate champions of liturgical renewal. He spoke and wrote idiomatic English as if he had been born to it, and his sparkling monthly column in *Worship* was the first item readers turned to. Probably he did as much as anyone

could in those days to make the idea of a vernacular liturgy acceptable. There was an old black janitor in my father's office who
used to sigh over life's inequities and then mournfully amend
Scripture by proclaiming, "The way of the transgressor—ain't
gettin' no better." I often thought that "pioneer" could be substituted for "transgressor." He who has ideas in advance of his contemporaries will pay a price for his temerity.

In 1947 Father Reinhold published a superb anthology of the
writings of Christian mystics like St. Teresa, St. John of the Cross,
Leon Bloy, Meister Eckhart and others, grouping them under titles
like "Thou Art a Hidden God," "Knowing in Part, Darkly," "A
Broken Heart Thou Wilt Not Despise," "Conformable unto His
Death." He came by personal experience to know what these holy
ones had gone through and written about. But so, in greater or
less degree, did the other pioneers of those days, who endured mis-
understanding, semi-jocular teasing, admonitions, warnings, cen-
sures, and kept on trying. At the end of one summer I said to
Father Ellard, "What are you going to do this year?" "Oh," he
said, mixing his metaphors, "I'll go on beating the drum. If you
throw enough mud some of it's bound to stick." My own hero was
the quiet, personable Father Wilmes, of St. Louis. For many years,
as Secretary, he had conducted from a little office in the basement
of his rectory all the business of the Liturgical Conference—the
correspondence, the printing and mailing of the annual *Proceed-
ings,* the multifarious negotiations for the Liturgical Week with
chanceries and cathedrals and hotels and auditoriums. In 1959 the
presidency of the Conference was open, and he seemed to many of
us to be the obvious choice. But—for the first time in the history
of this group, hitherto remarkable for its disinterested selfless-
ness—some new members of the Board executed a neat political
ploy, and he was not elected. Afterward I went to his hotel room
to express my regret. "Thanks," he said, "But it doesn't matter.
The cause is bigger than any of us." And he never slackened his
interest.

Sometimes, I admit, I wearied of singing outside the choir.
And sometimes I even wondered how worthwhile any cause could
be when so few were attracted to it. It was in such seasons of
temptation that I came to lean heavily on the group. Most of them
were diocesan priests, of extraordinary quality, zealous, highly intelligent, selfless, utterly dedicated to the Kingdom—not, however,
humorless fanatics, but quite able to roar with laughter at a situa-

tion or at themselves. I argued that the cause must indeed have merit if such men were devoted to it. To speak only of those who have gone before us (and not all of them), there were the energetic Chicagoans, Hillenbrand—full of repressed fire, as his name might indicate—and Morrison, and the indefatigable giant, John O'Connell. There was the patriarch, Martin Hellriegel, and his staunch disciples, Al Wilmes and Al Westhoff, from St. Louis. There was Syrianey from Denver, and Tobin from Oregon, and the gentle, scholarly Busch from St. Paul. Among the religious there were, of course, the Benedictines who had originally founded the Conference. Virgil Michel, the ardent apostle who had burned himself out with his writing, lecturing, and organizing at St. John's Abbey in Minnesota, was dead, but there were confreres who carried on in his spirit: Godfrey Diekmann, Michael Ducey, Maur Burbach, Bernard Sause, Bede Scholz. There was the Jesuit, Ellard, with his prairie twang and his elfin humor and his immense dedication. There was the Passionist, Mulcahy, and Mathis, of the Holy Cross Fathers, the thoroughly delightful little man who inaugurated the brilliant lectures given later at Notre Dame by such European scholars as Jungmann and Bouyer. I can never think of him without chuckling over one memory. We were at Dubuque for the Liturgical Week; I was to give the address at the morning session, and Mike was the chairman.

"Well," he began in that high-pitched sing-song of his, "I see we have a Jesuit on the platform this morning. And that reminds me: I was helping out in a black parish in Washington many years ago, and I was in charge of the Sunday School. I listened to one of the young ladies as she told her class the story of the man who went down from Jerusalem and fell among thieves. 'And they beat him and robbed him and left him lyin' in his blood. And a priest came along, and he saw the pore man, but he passed by. And a Levite came along, and he saw the pore man, and he passed by. Then a Samaritan came along, and he . . .' But one of the children interrupted: 'Miss Fanny, that priest who passed by and left the pore man lyin' in his blood, was he—was he like one of our priests?' And Miss Fanny said, 'No, no. He was like one of them Jesuits up at Georgetown.'"

The audience—there were some fifteen hundred present that morning—roared. So did I, but at the same time I was ransacking my scanty repertoire of stories. How does one respond to such an introduction? I could think of only one faintly appropriate story, and I told it. "There were four priests once who happened to be in the same room together, a Benedictine, a Dominican, a Franciscan, and a Jesuit. They were silently reading their breviaries when without warning the lights went out. And they all reacted in characteristic fashion: the Benedictine went on with his prayer because he knew it by heart. The Franciscan knelt down and asked God to let the light of Brother Sun or Sister Moon shine on his breviary so that he could read it. The Dominican started an inquiry into the four causes of light. But no one could locate the Jesuit because he had gone out to change the fuse."

Tom Carroll was in many ways the most unusual character in the group. He had grown up as the only boy among six sisters, and became in the process an inveterate tease. Long before his untimely death, for instance, he bought—through or from Ade Bethune, as I remember—a pine box, and installed it in his living room. When guests came in they would often sit on it, and after a while he would say, "That's my coffin you're sitting on, by the way," and watch them jump. It was in fact his coffin; he had bought it for $25 because he thought a priest should be poor in death as well as in life, and when he died he was laid out in it, clothed in the simple habit of a Benedictine oblate. Father Collins and I looked down at him. "He's still preaching," said Joe.

Tom was one of the most insistent among us on the need to teach that liturgy—considered as rubrics at the time by most people, or at least as something limited to the sanctuary—liturgy embraces everything in the Christian life. There is no activity, however seemingly secular, that does not derive its inspiration and sanctity from the altar. There is no activity that may not be brought back to the altar and offered as worship of the Most High. It is correct, therefore, to think of all life, long or short, enjoyable or painful, as a gift—a gift munificently given, gratefully received, generously returned. Tom saw, very early, that from this perspective life is quite simple; for the Christian it is all woven into what Cardinal Bernardin would later call "the seamless garment." So he went to Selma and marched in the demonstration for civil rights. He hired as his secretaries a roomful of black women. For years he drove to Connecticut every week to encourage and offer practical help to the blinded veterans of the war. He took over Boston's Catholic Guild for the Blind, changed its name to "The Catholic Guild for *All* the Blind," and made it a first-rate, professionally respected agency that continues—it is now named for him—to this day. He would not have permitted it to be named for him during his life-time. He wanted no honors or distinctions, and he had twice declined vigorously the rank of "monsignor" when it was offered to him. That dignity for him was meaningless, and his teasing of those who held it was constant. I still have a copy of a program he drew up—it was printed, of course, in purple ink—for the installation of a new monsignor. The opening hymn was "Oh, What Could My Jesus Do More?" and the recessional was "Red Sails in the Sunset." Not all the local monsignori were amused.

It was Cardinal Cushing's practice to invite to his residence for lunch the priests celebrating the twenty-fifth anniversary of their ordination, and when Tom's anniversary came up the Cardinal began asking questions around the table.

"What are you going to do for your Jubilee, Jim?"

"I'm having a Solemn Mass at eleven o'clock, Your Eminence, and a reception afterward at the Vendome."

"And what are you going to do, Bob?"

"I'm having a Solemn Mass, too, Your Eminence, and then a big party for everyone in the parish hall."

"How about you, Tom?"

"I'll be saying Mass as usual for the Sisters and the old blind people in the home, Your Eminence."

"Hmmm. What time is that Mass?"

"Seven o'clock, Your Eminence."

On the day of the anniversary, while Tom was vesting for Mass, the door bell at St. Raphael's Home rang, and there stood the Cardinal. "Thought I'd come over and help you celebrate," he said. He presided, and after the Gospel he said some very gracious things about Tom's work. Then he said,

"And in appreciation for all his labors I'm making Father Carroll a monsignor!" The Sisters, who knew Tom's mind on this subject, shuddered, but Tom himself showed no reaction and went on with the Mass. In those days we had a second reading, called the "Last Gospel," just before Mass ended. Tom read it, turned around to face the small congregation, and said, "It isn't customary to have a homily after this reading, but I just want to thank His Eminence for the very great kindness of his presence this morning, and for his generous words. But I have one favor I hope he will grant me on this happy day. Will he please *not* make me a monsignor!" In the sacristy a moment later the Cardinal grumbled, "I knew you were going to ask me that."

I've been not a little perplexed as to why the name of Gerald Ellard has faded so swiftly since his death in 1963. It gets little more than passing mention even in the histories of modern liturgical reform which are now beginning to appear. Maybe events and the persons involved in them are so thoroughly reported in our headlines and on our television screens that, as Andy Warhol said, in the future everyone will be famous for fifteen minutes. Maybe Father Ellard's decision—taken deliberately, as he once told me, on the ship that brought him home from his doctoral studies in Germany—to work rather in the field of popular liturgy than in pure scholarship, has erased his reputation now that the tide of renewal has risen so high beyond where it was when he began his work. Every so often he would write a scholarly piece, like his book on Alcuin, both to satisfy his academic tastes and, I suspect, to vindicate his right to speak with authority about the direction liturgical change should take today. As he said in the foreword to *The Mass of the Future,* "In the Catholic Church nothing can be said to have a future save in so far as it has a past and is deeply rooted in tradition," and he had read widely in that past, that tradition.

His bibliography of published books and articles, exclusive of simple book reviews, runs through eleven tightly printed pages. It begins in 1923, with a piece in *America* called prophetically "And the Light Shineth in Darkness," and ends in 1962, the summer before his death. It includes eleven books. *Christian Life and Worship* ran through seven revised editions and was a standard text in Catholic colleges for thirty years. *The Mass in Transition,* later called *The Mass of the Future* because the bishop who had originally approved its publication changed his mind after the book appeared and withdrew his *imprimatur,* was translated into French and Italian and earned approval from the Holy See itself. But the list includes also hundreds of articles, pamphlets, program materials, editions of papal or hierarchical documents with his own commentary, a version of the ritual in English, a missal for children, etc., etc.

If he had done nothing more than this, his contribution, one thinks, would be recognized today. But there was so much more: he taught for thirty years at St. Mary's College in Kansas, which was then the theology house of the Jesuit Province of Missouri. That meant that a whole generation of seminarians passed through his classes on their way to the altar—men who became pastors, university presidents, missionaries, professors, journalists, retreat directors, sponsors and supervisors of a thousand projects for the glory of God. It's not hard to imagine the extent of his influence. But there was still more: he taught summer courses at Boston College, Marquette University, the University of San Francisco, and many other institutions. He lectured at "institutes," "liturgical days," and "liturgical weeks" in almost every state in the union. One day I was showing him the sights along Massachusetts' "stern and rockbound coast," and we passed on through New Hampshire and came to the border of Maine. "Would you drive on a little further and then stop the car?" he asked. "Sure," I said, mystified. He opened the door and put one foot on the ground. "Now I can say that I have been in Maine," he said. "Only one more state to go."

He conducted retreats for priests, religious, seminarians, lay people. From the time of its organization in 1940 he was a member of the Board of Directors of the Liturgical Conference, and for many years, as chairman of the program committee, he suggested the theme and the program of the annual "Week." Perhaps his supreme achievement, so far as popular education was concerned, was the twelve years he spent on the faculty of Father Dan Lord's "Summer School of Catholic Action," a peripatetic institution that moved from city to city during the twelve weeks of summer. More than a hundred thousand people attended the sessions during those years, to take part in "the six days you'll never forget" and to bring home with them the SSCA *Blue Book* which was read by thousands of others.

But it was not as a word-processor or a tireless machine that I came to appreciate Gerry Ellard. He was essentially the good companion—*agréable,* as the French say, and my dictionary insists that the word does not mean what it often means in English, "compliant," or "submissive." but "pleasant," "graceful," "comfortable." He seemed to have no rough edges, no flashpoints of irritability. He could dream prodigious dreams without incessant talk about them. He surmounted obstacles, even contradictions, by ignoring them and pressing on. What a blessing it was that, though the Council's decree reforming the liturgy was not promulgated until December of 1963, and he had died in April, the decisive votes were cast at the end of the first session, in 1962, and he knew that his life-work had been crowned.

When he arrived in Boston on his last journey he was wearing a curious hat that made him look more elfin than ever. I think he quietly enjoyed the curious glances it provoked in those days of sober-suited black. But when I asked about his health he admitted to bouts of breathlessness that gave me concern. He had been invited to participate in an ecumenical colloqium on theology at Harvard—the first such event, I believe, that took place in the United States—but when he wrote that he was coming I urged him to come early; we were celebrating Boston College's centennial that year, the Jesuit Cardinal Bea would be receiving an honorary degree, and Father Hans Küng, newly famous for his book of prescriptions for the Council, would be giving the Candlemas Lecture. The latter event was stupendous; I could never have imagined an audience of three thousand for a lecture on theology, but they crowded somehow into the old Roberts Center. In the front row sat Cardinal Cushing and several of his auxiliaries, but also the Orthodox Archbishop Athenagoras and the Episcopal Bishops Peabody and Burgess. There was a solid black block of seminarians from Brighton and Weston, and another of Sisters from all over New England. Priests and ministers, especially from local faculties of theology, mingled with our own students and people whose affiliations I could not guess. In my introduction I said that the Candlemas Lectures had been founded to discuss relationships between theology and literature, but that in this instance the opportunity of hearing the eminent theologian, who was making his first visit to these shores, had led us to forego literature for once. "Nice customs," I said (I suppose it was a shameful pun), "curtsey to great Küngs." Well, the lecture touched on so many exciting themes, so many possible lines that the great Council might take, that the audience was left buzzing for an hour afterward. We sensed—and of course could have no idea then of their magnitude—that startling changes were in the making. There was curiosity, naturally, and wonder, with euphoria for some and anxiety for others. Gerry said the experience was worth the whole trip from Kansas.

We went to the colloquium, where Gerry, who was chairing the discussions on the sacraments, worked very hard for three days, setting out the Catholic positions but listening with courteous attention to the Protestant scholars present, and doing his utmost to discover possible areas of agreement under the old disputed formulations. Father Shawn Sheehan said to me that night, "Wasn't old Gerry great this morning!" He was very tired when everything ended on Saturday night, so we loafed on Sunday. When I passed his door on Monday morning there was a handkerchief on the doorknob—a "please do not disturb" sign in Jesuit communities. It bothered me because it was so unlike him, but I had a class at nine, a class at ten, and Mass at eleven. It was almost noon when I got back to find our Father Minister and the Brother Infirmarian with him. The house doctor had been summoned but had not arrived. I anointed him, and then, because he was having such difficulty breathing, had him sit up and supported him with my arm around his shoulders. "Let's pray," I said, and he nodded. His breviary was on a chair next to the bed. I opened it and found the eighth psalm. "Gerry," I said, "This is thanks for all our liturgical days together . . . *Domine, Dominus noster, quam admirabile est nomen tuum in universa terra.*" He raised his hand and gasped, "Slowly!" It was his last word.

I accompanied the body back to Kansas, and, at the funeral, told his family and the shocked community of the good work he had done at Harvard and of how he had literally worn himself out. Father Godfrey Diekmann was there from Collegeville, and Monsignor Al Westhoff and Monsignor Al Wilmes from St. Louis. We laid him to rest in the cemetery near St. Mary's, close to the old Santa Fe Trail, and there, with all the Jesuits of the previous hundred years, his body lies still, although the seminary to which he gave his talents and energies for so long has been sold and the community has been dispersed. A thoughtful friend who visited the grave later sent me a picture of the stone; on it is the legend that says so little and so much:

IHS

Geraldus Ellard

Sacerdos S.J.

Natus Oct. 8, 1894

Ingressus Jul. 27, 1912

Obiit Apr. 1, 1963

R.I.P.

One of the most lastingly profitable investments we made in the preconciliar days was the series of lectures we began for the Sisters of the Archdiocese. I chaired them for seven years, and Father Joe Collins took over for three more years after I went on sabbatical. We met monthly at Fontbonne Academy on Sunday afternoons. Attendance was never less than five hundred—almost all from the host congregation of the Sisters of St. Joseph. During my tenure we had sixty-two lecturers; most were local theologians from Weston College, Boston College, St. John's Seminary, but some were active laity—the sociologist John Donovan, Mary Perkins Ryan, Dorothy Dohen from Fordham, the Protestant ecumenists Paul Chapman and John Harmon, Mary McNiff, two brothers from Taizè. Some came from a considerable distance: Bishop (now Cardinal) Carter from Ontario, Fr. Al Longley from Minnesota, Fr. Gerry Sloyan from Washington, Fr. Vince Novak from New York.

The programs were so popular at Fontbonne that we started another for the Sisters in the northern area of the Archdiocese, and still another for those in the west. It would be difficult to exaggerate either the enthusiasm these religious women showed for the lectures or the impact—most of them were teachers—on the content of their own classes. We had speakers who addressed "liturgy" not only in the sense of formal worship but also in the the areas of concern that radiate from worship: education, for instance, or poverty, or Christian unity. They achieved a great deal in preparing minds for the magnificent document of the Council, "The Church in the Modern World," which would be given us a few years later. But they would never have occurred if it had not been for the Sisters themselves, avid for anything that would enhance their own holiness, thirsting for anything that would help them in their apostolic labors.

The Sisters' enthusiasm was not exactly paralleled in other quarters of my life. When I asked permission to make my retreat during Holy Week, and mentioned casually that I expected to preside at the liturgy during the Week at a neighboring convent, I was told that this was a conflict that only the provincial could decide. So I wrote to the provincial, and he answered that, since the purpose of Holy Week and the purpose of a retreat were quite different, I would have to make a choice. This I found quite mystifying, but I postponed the retreat. Again, I had written three articles which, in accordance with the rule, I had submitted for province censorship. The provincial turned down all three, and sent me the criticisms—unsigned, of course—of the censors he had asked to read the articles. These, too, were for the most part mystifying. Too often, they made it clear that the censor was altogether out of sympathy with liturgical renewal. One wanted to know, for instance, by what right I used capital letters in referring to "the Liturgical Movement." Another rather caustically pointed out what were obviously typographical errors in a hastily copied manuscript. A third complained of "a certain artificiality and pretentiousness of style which tends to obscurity of thought in subject matter where clarity is essential." As late as 1956 comes this criticism: "The author is answering the question why certain changes have been made in the rites of Holy Week. The reasons he gives seem to be somewhat weak, and one might question the statement that 'we Catholics have changed in our outlook, our needs.' Such a statement would seem to need clarification since the essential needs of Catholics are always the same in every century." Later he says: "It does not seem to be a fair statement that people today want to understand their worship more perfectly than their grandparents. This seems to place our ancestors in a somewhat dimmer light."

Captiousness of this sort seems petty, even amusing, now, but it wasn't at the time. The provincial came around for his annual visitation of the community, and said, with a cheeriness I thought a little out of place in view of what had happened, "Well, how's the writing going?" "Oh," I answered, "I gave that up." "Ha, ha," he laughed, "No humility, eh?" I snorted. "Why should I knock myself out over a typewriter on a hot summer afternoon only to have you give my piece to some old mossback who hasn't read a book for fifty years?" "Now, come, come," he protested. "Well, the last censor objected to my suggestion that the *Dies Irae* be dropped from the funeral rite on the 'authority' of a book published in 1908. That's just fifty years ago."

So we moved into the sixties, and everything looked serene. At Bethany, the "motherhouse" of the Sisters of St. Joseph of Boston, sixty young women were professed in 1959. At Shadowbrook, the novitiate of the Province of New England, forty candidates arrived to begin their Jesuit lives in the brand-new, spacious building that replaced the one destroyed in the tragic fire of 1956—the building we had grown up in. Forty-seven priests were ordained for the Archdiocese of Boston. There were six thousand American priests, sisters, and brothers in the missions overseas. Of all Catholic institutions, Boston College was sixth in the country so far as full-time students went, behind Marquette, Notre Dame, St. Louis University, Fordham, and the University of Detroit. Our peak enrollment before World War II had been 2,597; now it was 5,358. Our Province opened new high schools in Portland, Fall River, and Concord; new retreat houses in Connecticut and Massachusetts.

Prosperity was not "just around the corner," as Mr. Coolidge and Mr. Hoover told us in the thirties, but upon us, and things could not have looked more rosy.

CHAPTER 15

Behind the Curtain

IN A DESK CALENDAR I USED IN 1963 THERE IS MY FINAL ASSESS-ment of that eventful year: "The year the hair went white, the eyes couldn't read the phone book any more without glasses, and the walking legs gave out. Also, however, the year of the sabbatical, of the month behind the Curtain, and of the Council. *Te Deum laudamus.*"

Father Mike Walsh, one of the presidents to whom Boston College owes so much, called me aside one day in May. "I want you to apply for a sabbatical," he said. I was flabbergasted. Jesuit professors in those days taught day and night classes, summer and winter, and there was no retirement short of complete disability. "A sabbatical? What would I do?" "Whatever you like," he said, "stay here, go abroad, study, write . . . take a year off." "Egad," I said.

After some inquiry I learned that Fordham University was sponsoring a tour of cathedrals and monasteries in Europe—including Eastern Europe—that were associated with liturgical history, and I signed on. In the event, the tour was under-subscribed and cancelled, but then I was hooked by the prospect of going behind the Curtain, and joined a tour that had a similar itinerary. First, however, I would go back to Ireland with my life-long friend, Father John McCarthy. We drove around the ancestral island for two weeks, identifying by easy affinity with the soft voices, the rich vocabularies, the trick of changing meaning by shifting the po-sition of a phrase. (Thus, "Is it going down the street you are?" is different from "Is it down the street you're going?" and decidedly different from "Is it you that's going down the street?") What I remember most vividly and poignantly, however, is our standing on a street in Cork, waiting for the President of the United States to drive by on that joyous tour of Ireland he made in 1963, only six months before Dallas. When he came we waved and cheered madly, and the President saw us and shouted, "Hi, Father!" "See," said John exultantly, "He knew we were Americans!"

John stayed in Ireland to visit relatives, and I went off to Spain, wanting to see the parts of that country which I had missed in 1956. But traveling alone, even if it gives one an independence of choice, hasn't the zest provided by a good companion. I saw Madrid, and the Escorial, and the Valley of the Fallen, and was suddenly beset with a temptation to chuck it all and go home, especially when an American National Guard outfit, over there on some sort of summer training program, offered me a free flight to Delaware. Instead I boarded a train for Seville, chatted with boys from New York and girls from California, admired the vineyards and olive groves along the way. And Seville, with its history and its Moorish architecture, was interesting. It was also hot and noisy—he who finds noise oppressive should not visit Spain. Driven, in any case, by the twin devils of loneliness and restlessness, I moved on. The journey to Lisbon, by bus and train and ferry, took twelve hours. I really regretted that I had not a syllable of Portuguese; the people on the train were most courteous and eager to talk. I noted, too, with sorrow, the young soldiers on their way to Angola. At last, parched and weary, we arrived, and never shall I forget the clean, cool breeze that blew in from the Atlantic—my native ocean, so to speak, though I was on the wrong side of it, and that reflection did not assuage my loneliness.

Lisbon the next morning, however, put a new face on things. I met a young American who was likewise solitary, and with him toured the attractive city and its environs. We saw the tomb of Vasco da Gama in the Jeronimo Monastery and the monument to Prince Henry the Navigator. We also saw a monument to Pombal, the Prime Minister known to his contemporaries as "the butcher with the axe," who in the 18th century expelled the Jesuits from Portugal. This fascist dictator eventually fell from power and died in poverty and disgrace, and his body lay unburied for fifty years. When at last the rites of Christian burial were carried out, it was a Jesuit who sang the funeral Mass. I, lacking a like spirit of forgiveness, was not moved to lay any flowers at his feet.

There were three great places of pilgrimage in the Middle Ages. I had visited Canterbury, and knelt at the shrine of Thomas à Becket where the knees of praying pilgrims had worn cavities in the marble. Jerusalem, with all its sacred memories, would have to wait for a privileged visit fifteen years later. But Santiago de

Compostela, though it meant a twelve-hour train ride to the middle of nowhere, was within reach. The great Romanesque cathedral there rose up like a beckoning finger in the midst of a great plain, and I thought of the suppliant thousands who had preceded me and had welcomed that sight with joy.

In the cathedral is a handsome carving of the Jesse Tree, whose design is based on the descent of Christ from the royal line of David and takes the form of a tree springing from Jesse, the father of David, and ending with our Lord and his Mother. I was admiring it when a distraught young man rushed up to me. "I cannot work today," he cried. "I have seen my princess!" He rushed off again, and I stared after him in complete bewilderment, but a kindly English lady who was nearby explained that he was a young Dutchman employed as a guide to the cathedral, and that indeed the Dutch princess had been in Santiago that morning. My democratic American sensibilities were at first offended by this glorification of monarchy; then I remembered that I had cheered "my" President in Ireland a week before, and the more lustily because I was in a foreign country. If I had been there for some time and he had come through I'd have taken a week off!

There were ten more days before I would rendezvous with the tour. I spent them in desultory fashion, traveling by train to Brussels and then making sorties to Amsterdam, Antwerp, Louvain, Bruges. Of course I admired these picturesque towns, the flowers, windmills, canals (and the bicycles!). It was refreshing to chat with other liturgical types at Lumen Vitae and the library at Louvain and the Abbey of Mont-César. And a very gracious Benedictine, Father Peter Damien, took me in hand at the Abbaye St.-André (I had cherished a "St. Andrew Missal" for many years) and showed me every kindness. But it was with great relief that I joined my tour at the airport in Brussels and met my fellow-pilgrims. I had had a genteel sufficiency of solitude—even though my solitary wandering took me to exotic places.

Most of my friends, when they learned that I intended to visit Russia and the satellites, were either frightened for my safety or astounded that I should want to see such unrewarding places, and now I sometimes wonder why I myself did not feel more of these emotions. For all I knew, the Communist countries were still violently anti-religious and particularly anti-Roman; I might be denied entrance at the border, or worse, be quietly and permanently interred in some frozen Siberian concentration camp. Again, though

I read before leaving all the Russian history I had time for, my knowledge of the country was really limited to vague impressions picked up from Dostoievski and Tolstoy of sleighs running through forests deep in snow, samovars, Cossacks, caviar and vodka in prodigious quantities, emotional outbursts, fire and sword, unpronounceable names of unlikely people and places. Even some reading of other Russian literature, from Pushkin to Pasternak, did little to change my subconscious but strong impression of an unreal, half-lit landscape peopled by creatures whose everyday lives in no way resembled mine. Images picked up during the War and since had not helped: pictures of unsmiling men on the other side of the conference table saying "nyet" interminably, tales of Russian soldiers who took our enormous supplies of war matériel at Murmansk or Basra without thanks and without relaxing suspicion, stories of a frightening espionage system that seduced Americans and penetrated our most classified secrets: Hiss and Chambers, the Rosenbergs, Colonel Abel, Judy Coplon.

So I think we were all a bit jumpy as the Czech plane took off for Prague. We were leaving, after all, the security of the West. Who knew what awaited us on the other side of that Curtain? We were old enough to remember vividly such horrors as the Lubiyanka Prison, Katyn Forest, the Prague Spring. We could recall the Kruschkev brag, "We will bury you." We had been exposed for forty years to dire warnings from popes, bishops, and pastors about the ominous threat of "atheistic Communism." And here we were putting our stupid heads in the lion's mouth—or the bear's.

Well, our visas, obtained in Brussels after long delays, got us through the border formalities. We found our hotel, and Monsignor Pat Hannon and I began our walking about the city. There was an air of decayed gentility about Prague. Once magnificent buildings were now grimy and shabby. The people were dressed in ill-assorted and ersatz clothes. Shop windows displayed very little, even of necessities, while luxury items did not appear at all. The trolleys were ancient, clanking vehicles like the ones I rode to high school in the twenties. Trains ran on soft coal, and such automobiles as there were, small cars made in Poland, used a cheap grade of gasoline whose reek hung in the air after they had passed. The churches we visited were uniformly counter-reformation baroque, and reinforced the impression of a tired, static civilization, a people without inspiration or drive.

At dinner the restaurant was crowded with young people, singing and jitterbugging—many of the boys were leaving next day for the Army—but the merriment broke off sharply at eight o'clock. Was there a curfew, we wondered? We talked with a mysterious American from New Jersey who had been in Prague for six months, "studying the social experiment," said he. All of us put him down as a suspicious character. And we met a lawyer, a man in his mid-thirties, who spoke some English, and who asked us if we could give him any papers or magazines from England or the States. He was definitely unhappy under the regime; he could not look forward to promotion of any sort, he could not travel outside the Curtain. One of the ladies in our group asked if he were married, and he groaned; what was the use, he said, of marrying and bringing children into a world like his?

A similar combat fatigue seemed to have affected the priests we met. The churches were open and liturgies were being celebrated, but congregations were small and chiefly elderly. We talked to a Dominican pastor from outside the city; he had 15,000 parishioners, he told us, but only 600 were practising. There were about 150 weddings in the parish each year, but only fifteen were celebrated in church. I asked him if there were any Jesuits in the country, and he threw back his head and laughed. Well, I thought, if there are any, and they are incognito, their secret is safe with him. The Jesuit university was now some sort of state institution. We tried St. Ignatius Church; it was baroque, of course, the seal of the Society was still over the main altar, and the side altars were dedicated to St. Aloysius and other Jesuit saints. Devotions in honor of St. Ignatius were scheduled for his feast. But apparently I was the only Jesuit in the country.

In Old Town Square there was a church with an astronomical clock, and in the tower were statues of the twelve apostles. A skeleton pulled a bell as the hours passed and the apostles swung up to a door, bowed, and disappeared. There were also figures representing vanity (a woman admiring herself in a mirror), worldly pleasure (a young man plucking on a guitar), and greed (an old man clutching his money bags); all of them were being mocked by the skeleton. A grim reminder, indeed, and it seemed to suit the mood of the country.

Evidence of the sad and scandalous wars of religion was abundant. A statue of John Huss, burned at the stake for heresy, stood in Old Town Square. Nearby, on the pavement, were crosses commemorating the twenty-seven Protestant nobles who were beheaded there when the Catholics conquered the country in the battle of White Mountain. We visited a new Jewish synagogue where, in the apse, we read the names of the infamous Nazi concentration camps, and on the walls the names of the Czech Jews who had died in them—77,000 from Prague alone.

No one shed a tear as our train crossed the border into Austria, where we had to go to get visas for Hungary and Russia. At the last station before the border there was a depressing wait while all papers were checked and a painfully careful search was made by soldiers of every place, even under the cars, where stowaways might hide. As we went through the very high barbed-wire fence (charged electrically, no doubt) we felt like underwater swimmers coming to the surface for a gulp of air before plunging again to the depths. It was exhilarating, though we could not forget what we had seen. Few Russians, I think, have any idea of real freedom. They had none under the Czars and very little since. But the satellites remembered better days and either chafed in their bonds (Hungary, Poland) or seemed to have had their spirits killed (Czechoslovakia, East Germany). Certainly, if Czechoslovakia was the model of satellite Communism, as the Russians asserted, it bore silent witness to the brutality and spiritual bankruptcy of the system.

Vienna was a startling contrast. Gay, even hilarious, crammed with tourists, colorful, full of life and good things to eat, to wear, to use, it gave us a transfusion of its own élan. We wondered at the same time whether all that gaiety was in keeping with what the Viennese had experienced so recently, and, with the Russian bear growling at the gates, could easily experience again. Was the *heurigen* (new wine) out at Grinsing the only wisdom distilled from their experience? Father Harth, a Vienna diocesan, told us that only ten to fifteen percent of his people went to Mass with any regularity.

The train to Budapest was jam-packed, and we tourists had a difficult time getting aboard, especially with the ladies' out-size luggage, which kept getting lost. Jim Kenney and Father Pat were the heroes in this department. They found it and saw that it went with us, though not without much blood, sweat, and female squeals. It was very hot, and choking coal-dust kept pouring through the open windows; fortunately, there were two bottles of champagne to pass from hand to hand and keep us from complete dehydration during the six-hour trip. But dinner was good, and the cheery waitress planted an American flag on our table at the hotel. And next morning we gathered for Mass in a nearby church—a tiny chapel, really, where we talked to the pastor in Latin. He was allowed, he told us, to preach, to dispense the sacraments, to conduct devotions, but not to give instructions, and certainly not to have a school. There were between two and three thousand children in the parish, but only sixty made their First Communion and were confirmed. "Why are the children not trained in the faith by their parents?" we asked. "The parents think only of the children's material welfare," he replied. The worshipers were for the most part old women—but this had been true also in Spain, Belgium, Portugal. Only in Ireland did I see men in church on week-days. We noted that the Mass at the main altar was celebrated in black vestments even though it was a feast day. Communion was distributed before the Mass, which was celebrated in complete silence. The congregation participated only in the shouted prayers after Mass was over. It was just like home.

Incidentally, though I had worked and prayed for many years that we might use English in the Mass and the sacraments, I was glad that the language used at these celebrations was Latin. If it had been Czech or Hungarian I wouldn't have understood a word. But let not the conservatives whoop with joy over this seeming vindication of the old "*argumentum ex tourismo*," which one hears occasionally even now, thirty years after Vatican II. I understand Latin. I began studying it in 1921, and have read and spoken it ever since. I was happy to be able to talk in Latin to the priests I met in Europe. But relatively few Catholics travel abroad, they don't stay long when they do, and Latin would be just as unintelligible abroad as it would be at home. More so, since it would be spoken with unfamiliar accents. Our need is to speak to God and to listen to him in a language we readily understand.

We told one another that there was more drive and energy in Budapest than we had seen in Prague. Was it owing to the fact that the Hungarians had successfully defied the glowering Russians on at least one occasion? Our tour of the city was conducted by a government-appointed guide, a woman who gave us an excellent summary of Hungary's history and very frank answers to our questions. We went to the soccer stadium, which seats one hundred thousand spectators, and to the gardens at Margaret Island, and to Heroes' Square, with its magnificent statuary. We were entranced by the Fishermen's Bastion and the view it afforded of the Parliament buildings and the river, and by the splendid Church of St. Matthias; in fact, we went back to see both again that evening.

Next day we offered Mass in a nearby church that had been badly damaged by war both in 1945 and in 1956. We tried to get more information about religious freedom, but this pastor evidently believed in caution, and politely evaded our questions.

There was just one more thing to do. We called a cab and drove by the American Embassy to see where Cardinal Mindzenty, who was a great hero at home, was holding stubbornly to a self-imposed incarceration. Pat and I threw a blessing at his sanctuary.

Now came the moment of truth. We flew into Moscow—*O caro nome!*—that evening. There was a little flurry at the customs desk: some of our party, rashly apostolic, had brought with them a supply of "holy cards," intending to distribute them on the quiet to Russians who supposedly had been for fifty years denied such reminders of the faith. This might have been enough to prevent our entry, but after a protracted discussion among the officials the cards were confiscated and with black looks and much finger-shaking we were admitted. Then there was a forty-minute bus ride to the Ostankino Hotel, actually a huge complex of hotels in the outskirts, intended eventually to house all tourists. The rooms were comfortable enough, but the plumbing was primitive—the showers were several floors below, in the basement. And, on this night in early August, it was cold. We passed around a warming tot of Scotch and slid under blankets, wondering what January would be like in these latitudes.

Dina dominated our lives during the next two days. She was our guide, a youngish woman who sternly marshaled us in and out of our bus and lectured us interminably on the magnificence of what we saw and the glorious achievements of the U.S.S.R. It was like listening to a Texan or a Marine. The first stop was Red Square and Lenin's tomb. Here was a genuine shrine, visited daily, Dina said, by ten to fifteen thousand pilgrims. A soldier stood at the head and another at the foot of a tiny, waxen figure just visible under glass. "Don't genuflect," said Pat to me in a whisper. I read years later a newspaper article which asserted that it really is a wax figure there, that Lenin's body is buried secretly elsewhere, but the truth will not be known, I'm sure, until we have many more years of *glasnost.*

So this was the dreamer, the plotter, the persuasive orator, the organizer and executor who had overturned the imperial Romanovs and set up the dictatorship of the proletariat. Was he in truth the complete villain pictured by anti-Communist propaganda? Or did God use him (as he once used Nabuchodonosor) to punish his selfish people? They had perpetuated a dubiously holy union of Church and State that had refused for centuries to hear the cry of the poor and the oppressed. Would the ultimate judgment of history rank him, perhaps, with Lincoln, Daniel O'Connell, Pearse, and the other Emancipators? Or would he be considered a scourge, himself morally reprehensible, who nevertheless broke the *ancien régime* in the only way it could be broken, in blood and violence? There were those who said in 1963 that only in this way would a new order be introduced in Latin America.

The main streets were broad and the squares enormous. Apartment buildings were going up everywhere, but we saw log cabins in the side streets. The Metro was swift, clean, beautifully decorated, its platforms as free from litter as a cathedral sanctuary; unhappily, the trains roared with the same deafening racket as the trains in the subway in New York or Boston. I was reminded of a remark I made to my class once when a low-flying jet overhead forced me to suspend my lecture: "Look, my generation invented those things. I hope yours will put silencers on them." The people were not well-dressed, but seemed contented and pleasant. I wished I could talk to them.

That night two of our young people stayed in town for dinner, and later asked a woman clerk where they might find a place to dance. "It's ten-thirty," she said severely. "Go home and go to bed!" Which was not a simple procedure, but at 11:45 they did persuade a reluctant cab-driver to take them to the Ostankino. Moscow's night life was not exactly lively, and maybe that was why a young man, an attaché in the Russian embassy whom I met in Dublin, had asked me why on earth I wanted to go there. And actually there was little in Moscow except the Kremlin. We wondered why the seat of government had been shifted there from Leningrad. Was Moscow more central? Less exposed to attack? Less identified in the popular mind with the Czars? More distinctively Russian than a part of the country which had been wrested from Finland only after long centuries and then made by Peter the Great into a Paris-on-the-Baltic?

For the Russian trip our original small party of eight was joined to a larger, chiefly American group of about twenty-five. People asked me repeatedly when I came home, "Did you have to go with a party?" The answer was no; individual travel was permitted, but it was much more expensive. And since most of us knew no Russian, a guide was a real asset. Whenever we arrived in a new city our passports were collected and kept until we were about to leave, so that we could not stray very far. At no time, however, were any of us aware of being watched or followed, and when requests to go here or there were denied it seemed that the refusal was prompted rather by unwillingness to change the set itinerary than by any wish to conceal things from us. Perhaps the Russian people had taken orders for so long, from the Czars and their present rulers, that they were just not able to understand any deviational tendencies. When we were told that our tour of the Kremlin was over, for instance, we asked, "But aren't we going to see the Palace of Congresses?" "No," came the answer. And when, like normal Americans, we asked "Why not?" we received only an uncompromising stare. "What I have written I have written," as Pilate said.

On the other hand, our guide had her difficulties with us. A more motley group has scarcely been assembled since Chaucer's pilgrims. We ranged in age from the late teens to the high seventies. There was a laconic, good-natured Scotsman from Glasgow, a widowed engineer. There was a retired Jewish decorator of churches from Santa Monica, who had left Russia when he was a young man and was so delighted by the material advances he was now seeing that he kept telling the Russians, "We have nothing like this in America." We protested this, of course, and the poor old man succeeded finally in alienating most of the party. When, at the end of the tour, he was denied a visa to visit the Caucasus, he was crushed altogether, and lapsed into gloomy silence.

Hilda and Nora were middle-aged teachers from England, very jolly and good sports. Young Ann was an intense and idealistic poet who sought the good in everyone and was terribly pained by dissension. Mr. and Mrs. M., from New Zealand, puzzled us at first by their anti-American jibes; later we learned that they had been refused an American visa, and then that he was president of an organization at home called the "Friends of the Soviet Union," or some such title, and finally that they were returning to New Zealand by way of the trans-Siberian railway and Peking! There was the college student who argued with me repeatedly about the proper understanding of the Trinity, and the young Jewish doctor who was planning a residency in psychiatry, a professed agnostic who, during a two-hour trip up the River Dnieper from Kiev, discussed calmly and reasonably the cosmological argument for the existence of God and situation ethics. There was the couple from San Francisco, almost eighty, who had emigrated from Russia when they were very young. The husband's brother, who stayed at home, had kept in touch during all the years until recently, when correspondence suddenly ceased. The husband had come back to discover what had happened to his brother, and was deeply hurt and disappointed when he was refused permission to go to his native town in Siberia. Siberia, apparently, was off-limits to tourists. And of course there were the two priests. We heard that word had gone round in the party that we were "very liberal" in our views. I'm afraid that we may indeed have shocked several of the more militant and intransigent Catholics in the group, but I hope our opinions were not objectively heretical. "Liberality," after all, is a quality of mind praised by Aristotle and presumably the net result of a "liberal education." The adjective has become an epithet—the nasty word in several recent presidential campaigns—but it would seem a pity if priests could not ambition liberality—if, while hewing steadfastly to truth as known by reason and revelation, they could not grow in hospitality to new ideas, or fresh realizations of old ones, or if, at the very least, they could not listen patiently and with charity to the views of others.

Well, we set off, ill-assorted as we were, on a cool, bright morning to visit what I'm sure a young friend of mine would describe as "the heart of downtown Communism." Our first stop was the Armory Museum, which held a collection of chain mail, swords, pikes, muskets, and similar grisly reminders of man's inhumanity to man. But there was also a striking display of precious things that had once belonged to the Czars: clocks, goblets, dishes, vestments, chalices, ornaments of silver, gold, ivory, wood. The gilded domes of the cathedrals were very pretty; inside, however, they were only museums; no liturgies were celebrated there. We were told that the State was restoring the frescoes and in general maintaining churches all over Russia in order to retain for the people a reminder of their cultural heritage. With the same purpose, we learned, the State was subsidizing the training of choirs and cantors for the Orthodox liturgy, lest the great Russian liturgical music be lost. When we were told we might not visit the other buildings in the Kremlin, I returned to the bus and found the old gentleman from San Francisco waiting. "Didn't you visit the churches?" I asked. "I was here in 1912," he answered. "The soul has gone out of them now. In those days it was something to come here on Easter. Even if you were not a believer that music would make you believe."

Our lunch at the Peking Restaurant was, like most of our meals, quite heavy—rubber chicken and potatoes. In the afternoon I went with Pat to the Tretyakov Art Gallery, several blocks out of Red Square. He found a fascinating collection, going back to the 12th century, of the icons he loved, and there was also a highly interesting display of pictures showing Russian country life in the 18th and 19th centuries. They would make a pleasant complement to a deluxe edition of Tolstoy or Dostoievsky. Back at the hotel there was more chicken and potatoes, and no dessert, but I found in my raincoat pocket a candy bar (from Brussels) that I had forgotten, and it served. "The best candy on earth," the ad said, "comes from Mars."

On the bus to the airport a young black man from Cameroon struck up a conversation. He had been, he told us, a seminarian at home, but when the Russians offered him a scholarship at Patrice Lumumba University he came to Moscow, and now he was an ardent champion of socialism over the capitalist way of life. He was living with a Russian woman and had a son by her, and had given up the faith. We listened unhappily, making only perfunctory answers; he had the ardor of a recent convert, and it was clear that nothing we could say would shake him.

Our first impressions of Leningrad were unfavorable. The people were poorly dressed, the shops were nearly empty. Women were working on heavy construction jobs and driving buses and trolleys. (We were told that in all of Russia they outnumbered men by as much as twenty million.)

Father Pat and I went for a walk on the Nevsky Prospect, which was crowded with strollers. We passed one apparently Latin church—"*Domus mea domus orationis*" was the inscription over the door—but it was boarded up. Another building, in the style of the Italian Renaissance, might have been a church at one time, but there was no cross on the steeple, and obviously it was not a church now. We asked an Intourist official at the October Hotel where we might find a Catholic church, but he shrugged: "I don't know much about churches." We kept up the pressure, however, and at last were given a slip of paper with an address on it. This we showed to people in the street, and so found our objective at last, though the address was not quite correct, and at one point in our search, after climbing five flights of stairs, we interrupted the supper of a man in pajamas, and withdrew with eloquent apologetic gestures. What a handicap not to speak the local language!

The church served a colony of Lithuanians. Their priest was young, blond, very pleasant. He told us he was free to celebrate Mass, visit the sick, give the sacraments. He had had a hundred baptisms in the previous year. Children might be instructed only by their parents, but he was allowed to go to their homes and examine them. We would be most welcome, he said cordially, to celebrate the Sunday liturgy next morning. So we arrived at 7:30, and found the little church already crowded with worshipers—all of them women well into middle age. A few men came in later. Led by an organ and a choir, they were singing their morning prayers. We felt that we had come home, and proceeded gratefully to offer Mass.

On closer inspection Leningrad was very lovely. We admired the palaces, the heroic statues, the museums—especially the Hermitage, which with its two million objects of art was overwhelming—too much too fast. But it seemed to us that a somber cloud hung over Peter's city. One could say of it, perhaps, what the physician said of Lady Macbeth, that she had known what she should not. There was the Palace Square, for instance, where some two hundred desperate workingmen were slaughtered in 1905, and where the revolution that would shake the world—and shed blood over much of it—was proclaimed in 1917. And there was the unforgettable, awful cemetery where there lay in mass graves 637,000 victims of starvation and bombing during Leningrad's "nine hundred days." The Nazi armies surrounded the city on three sides, but could not close the approach from the sea, and in winter, when the sea froze, the defenders were able to bring in enough provisions to sustain them—after a fashion—during the rest of the year. The merciless hammering went on for three years; the defenders never gave in to the barbarians. But the cost was frightful. We decided that there were many monuments to the Germans in Europe, and none of them was pretty, but this was the most horrifying we had seen. And at that time we had not seen Dachau or Auschwitz.

What was once the Kazansky Cathedral had been made a "Museum of the History of Religions." The exhibits on the main floor were designed to illustrate and substantiate the rationalism of the 19th century—i.e., Christian beliefs and rites were only extensions of pagan superstition—and to glorify the contrasting achievements of science. The displays in the crypt, however, were more embarrassing. They pictured instances of religious hypocrisy, fakery, inhumanity, oppression—the burning of Joan of Arc, instruments of torture used by the Inquisition, copies of the Index of Forbidden Books, Cardinal Spellman blessing a tank. It was a painful indictment, and I found myself striking my breast and repeating Patmore's line: "How weakly understood thy great commanded good."

Kiev, the next stop on our tour, was a homey, livable city. There were trees on the streets. Even the apartment blocks had a little style, and their balconies were covered with flowers or ivy. The people were more colorfully dressed than the sober-suited citizens of Moscow and Leningrad. But our sense of alienation grew. Between songs at an open-air concert given by an Esthonian chorus, one of the ladies in our group underwent a hostile grilling by a man who spoke English quite well. What were the salaries of American workers? How much vacation did they have? I was sitting nearby, and in some context Polly happened to say that I was a priest. "A priest?" he said, "Jesus Christus? Maria?" But later, after I had left, he said I had probably gone looking for a woman. All priests, he said, had at least three women.

We had a new guide in Kiev, a domineering woman named Allah whom we immediately nicknamed "the top sergeant." Her propaganda for the superiority of the Communist system went on and on, the tourists growing more and more restive. Finally, when she told us that the Church of the Holy Wisdom, Sancta Sophia Cathedral (now a museum), was so called in tribute to the wisdom of the city's builders, she was roundly booed. It was a tiresome trip.

In the afternoon Allah took us to the "Wedding Palace." We saw two couples joined in marriage by a woman magistrate, who gave them a stern homily (summarized for us by Allah) on their patriotic duties to the nation. There were flowers and canned music (Lohengrin) and a reception line for each couple. Only one per cent of the population had a church wedding, we learned; this was the secular substitute, intended to provide a little solemnity for the rite. We thought it an improvement over the quick-fix ceremony in a dusty City Hall office at home, but still dreadfully cold.

We visited a factory on the other side of the Dnieper River that was turning out on an assembly line pre-fab sections of new housing. Women were operating huge cranes, stirring and applying cement. Then we went to the construction site, where 470 units (75 one-room, the rest two and three-room apartments) were being erected. This was only one of twenty such developments in the Kiev area to be constructed by the end of the year. There were no closets in the rooms, and we wondered what ingenuities would have to be devised to insure living space. We wondered, too, whether there were restrictions on the number of children a couple might have. Contraceptives were on sale everywhere, and perhaps one of the patriotic duties urged by the wedding magistrate was to limit severely the size of the family. At any rate, these apartments were better than the serfs' hovels of pre-Revolution days, and better than what many people had now. Allah had some reason for her enthusiasm, and the construction workers for their pride in their accomplishment.

We went looking for a Catholic church, as we had done in Leningrad, hoping to end our enforced Eucharistic fast. At the address we were given we found only a chess club, but nearby was a Gothic building, once a Latin church. It was now a radio station. The experience was chilling; we felt as the early Christians must have felt, coming perhaps into Ephesus or Corinth and trying to locate other Christians in a world of unbelievers. Maybe it was true, as Matthew Arnold said,

> The Sea of Faith
> Was once, too, at the full, and round earth's shore
> Lay like the folds of a bright girdle furl'd.
> But now I only hear
> Its melancholy, long, withdrawing roar,
> Retreating, to the breath
> Of the night-wind, down the vast edges drear
> And naked shingles of the world.

Our last experiences in Kiev are happier. We are taken to a "Young Pioneers' Camp" where about 450 children, aged seven to sixteen, are drawn up in companies to welcome us. Their brass band and cheers and radiant faces certainly do that, and everyone feels wonderful driving away. Kids are irresistible.

In the lounge that night Father Pat and I are joined by three mining engineers, who introduce themselves (they speak a mélange of English and German) as Yuri, Alexei, and Vladimir. We drink toasts to friendship, freedom, and peace, and the conversation, thus lubricated, becomes cordial. Are we married? We shake our heads. Why not? "Nobody loves me," says Pat. I point to my gray hair and say, "Too old." What do we do for a living? We are teachers. Oh, what do we teach? Theology. Um, theology. Well, theology isn't relevant in Russia just now. Russians must work, work, work to insure the future. Some day there may be time for theology, when they are rich like the Americans. I try to make the point that God, as a part of reality, should not be ignored, even for a time.

They talk about the War, and how they detest the Nazis, who slaughtered thousands and burned hundreds of villages in the Ukraine. "No more war," says Vladimir. Yuri is doubtful. "It may be needed to fight the Chinese," he says, but Vladimir and I agree that war is no solution. All men are "bruzzers," he insists; it is better to sit down and talk as we are doing. They invite us to continue the discussion in their room, but we have been warned against too much fraternizing lest we bring official suspicion on our hosts. So we break up, with real regret, shaking hands and clapping one another on the back, and Vladimir says to me, "You nicely man. You like God you teach." Which just happens to be the nicest thing anyone has ever said to me.

Yalta, on the Black Sea, was our last stop. As a summer resort, crowded with thousands of vacationers, it was intended by our hosts, no doubt, as an agreeable valedictory. We were growing restless by this time, however, and very eager to be on the other side of the Curtain. At the airport the customs officer went through all my books, papers, and letters page by page, while I fumed impotently. Was he looking, as someone guessed, for Russian currency, or, as someone else suggested darkly, is suspicion native to the Russian character? I gave a pocketful of small change to some incoming Americans, who laughed and said they would put it into the collection. They had seen me reading the breviary.

As we flew into Vienna Pat said, "None of that nonsense of kissing the ground, now." I didn't kiss the ground, but I almost kissed the pretty Austrian stewardess standing at the ramp; she seemed a personification of the freedom and cheerfulness we had seen so little of during the previous month.

CHAPTER 16

In Spirit and in Truth

IF ANYONE HAD ASKED IN 1963 WHETHER PUBLIC WORSHIP could ever be for American Catholics what it was for earlier Christians, the answer might well have been the one given so often by St. Thomas Aquinas in beginning a discussion: *"Videtur quod non."* "Apparently not."

It seemed unlikely then that our worship could ever regain the vitality it had once had. Our American way of life was too noisy, too filled with strain and hurry and glitter. Holidays were spent rocketing over the nation's roads, or recovering from the stress of activity that preceded the holiday and left us limp with weariness. Again, we lived in a pluralistic society, where many of our most sacred beliefs and practices were not shared or even understood by our neighbors. We went to Mass on certain days which had once been high solemnities, but then we had to rush off to our jobs as usual. We fasted or abstained from meat on other days, only to be invited by our neighbors to join them in a community barbecue. We lived in two worlds: the world indicated by our missals (alleluias for the feasts, ashes for the fasts) and the real world of the forty-hour week and the summer vacation, with the trip over Labor Day and the repairs to the cottage on Memorial Day as the significant highlights of the year. What to us the triumphant paeans of the Ascension, the June glories of Peter and Paul? We were sobered for a bit by Good Friday; Easter made us think of spring and long days and the end of Lent, but Easter had been replaced, really, by Christmas as the great day of the year, religiously speaking.

The suggestion was made, only half-seriously to be sure, that we should cry quits altogether in the struggle to make something meaningful of the American Christmas. Our observance tended toward a kind of schizophrenia. In church, Advent came in with December and would lead our hearts through the dark days to the Light that breaks upon them at the end, but everywhere else the

226

celebration of Christmas began in mid-November. The shops gleamed with Christmas cheer. The department store carillons proclaimed above the laurel and the spruce that Christ was born. Even Catholic schools staged Christmas plays and concerts in the middle of Advent. And people who did not believe in Christ ran Christmas parties in the office on the day before the holiday, having bestowed incredibly lavish gifts on everyone from their children to the elevator girl and the mailman. After all, we don't really know where our Lord was born, and maybe the best thing would have been to accept the twenty-fifth of December as a moderate *Saturnalia,* a mid-winter festival, devoid of religious meaning, while we selected some other date and made a fresh start with that.

Even the terminology of our calendar was outmoded and obscure. *"Septuagesima"* is the example that always comes first to mind. Even when the sonorous but unintelligible Latin name had been explained, people asked why this Sunday should be called the seventieth day before Easter when, in point of fact, it wasn't. A reasonable question. Again, no one knew for certain what the term "Ember Day" meant or how it originated—except that it had nothing whatever to do with fires or ashes. Examples could be multiplied, but the fact remains that only in a monastery or in monastic institutions like our seminaries could one hope to avoid the aforesaid schizophrenia. There the rhythm of life was altogether in keeping with the liturgical year. The struggles to achieve the same unity of outlook in the average Catholic home were brave but pathetically unsuccessful. What chance had the Advent Wreath against Santa Claus, on his throne at Macy's, and due at our house between the dark and the daylight? So much of our symbolism belonged to a lost world; as someone said, the liturgy, which used to interpret to us, now needed an interpreter.

The function of a calendar in any society is to keep green the memory of the great people and the great events in that society's history, in the hope that the new generations will be inspired to live according to the principles of their ancestors. But, as Pius XII taught (*Mediator Dei,* #165), the Christian calendar "is not a cold and lifeless representation of the events of the past, or a simple and bare record of a former age. It is rather Christ himself who is ever living in his Church. Here he continues that journey of immense mercy which he lovingly began in his mortal life, going about doing good, with the design of bringing us to know his mysteries and in a way to live by them."

"To know his mysteries and to live by them . . ." It might be said, then, that the first function of the Christian calendar is to instruct and to form worshipers, the second to give them scope for their worship. But in 1963 the word "worship" was not in the Catholic's active vocabulary. Its use might have reminded us that our prayer and sacrifice should be directed not only to our own advantage, not only to receiving gifts from God, but more urgently to the praise of God for his good gifts and above all because he is what he is.

A first requisite for the formation of worshipers would have been a crash course in the doctrine of the Mystical Body. This doctrine, so prominent in the teaching of St. Paul, had taken on new life in the writing of some influential theologians during the late nineteenth and early twentieth centuries, and it was taught consistently by liturgists before the Second Vatican Council, but it had not reached the generality of our people. Yet until we see ourselves as identified with Christ, the Worshiper par excellence, the Head who has united to himself a body of members made like himself, we fail to understand our dignity and our supreme privilege—that of declaring the excellence of him who made us and then remade us in the image of his Son. We fail to understand that our worship is no longer the private and limited effort of a single individual, however well-intentioned. It is instead the offering of a community—a community, moreover, into which one has been brought by God, and in concert with which one should naturally expect and aspire to acknowledge God.

It was clear in 1963 that the spirituality of American Catholics was not, by and large, a community spirituality. Sociologists have of late been giving us all the factors that produced the native outlook—individualistic, subjective, highly personal—and we were aware of some of them at the time. The point is that this was not the traditional Christian mentality, and that the man or woman who has it will always find social worship enigmatic, uninspiring, even repellent. Such people will want to know, for instance, why they cannot be let alone to say their own prayers, undistracted by their neighbors.

It did not seem, however, that this isolationism of the spirit could continue much longer. Every influence in the American Catholics' world was pushing them toward awareness of their brothers and sisters. Not only had they encyclicals and instructions from the supreme authority of the Church, not only did they find their parish adopting practices (like community recitation of the Mass) which were strange and at first upsetting, not only did they listen increasingly to sermons on social justice. The secular world, too, hammered away at their rugged individualism. Headlines made them aware of nations they never knew existed. The novels they read and the movies they went to see dealt not only with the tender boy-and-girl relationship but with a profounder passion, the love of the human family as a whole. Words like "community" and "dialogue" were on everyone's lips. No doubt, we felt, all this would run too far, as human tendencies have a way of doing, and the balance would have to be redressed in favor of the individual, but for the average American Catholic there seemed small likelihood of excess; the pendulum had swung long ago as far as it could in the direction of individualism, and was not likely to swing in the other direction until it had hung for a while at the center. Or so we believed and hoped, remembering that the official worship of the Church had been composed (except for some nineteenth-century Masses, easily detectible) by Christians who had a community outlook, not at all sentimental, but based squarely on Scripture and theology, and who prayed in terms of that outlook. We would not be able to use their worship unless we were converted to their outlook.

I don't think we realized fully at the time how many would find such a conversion distressing and full of questioning. It is not easy to give up the piety one has been reared in, to which one is attached not merely by tender memories but as to the firm anchor of all faith and morality. Let that anchor slip, people feel, and everything goes. Only when they come to see at last that in adopting the new outlook they are really losing nothing of what they held dear, but instead entering upon the possession of vast riches, can they take the step. And since it is unlikely that those whose spiritual formation is at an end will bring themselves to such a conversion, some of us urged that all indoctrination be directed to the young. This would have been, no doubt, the most fertile field, but it seemed then that the grace of God in our day was bent before all else on healing the wounds of human division, and we were surprised to discover how many, no longer young, found in the spirituality of the community what they had long been groping for. All those frequent communions made possible by St. Pius X in the previous fifty years were yielding their fruit.

Patience would be indispensable, we told one another, in looking for a growth that, unless it was to be cancerous, would have to be slow. Genuinely apostolic care for the flock of Christ demanded consideration for all, for those who could not relinquish the old ways as well for those who had been formed in the new. The imperative need was for instruction, repeated over and over to the point of tedium. Good people should not be shocked by sudden exposure to unfamiliar ideas. Practices that are legitimate but strange should be explained again and again. Mockery, of course, would not be only unfair and unkind but fatal to progress; it closes minds forever.

To this end, we were convinced that it would be practical to begin our treatment of the sacraments with the sign rather than with the thing signified. Our people, who could readily understand the sign-language in other matters, had lost the art of translating it where religion was concerned. They knew what tokens meant in the subway, they knew that flowers signified congratulations or condolences, they understood symbols readily enough when they saw them in advertising. They had to be told, however, that water signifies not only washing but life, that salt is a preservative but also an appetizer for a better food to come, that oil means healing and light and warmth and perfume—yes, and lithe spiritual muscles for the wrestling we must do with principalities and powers. They must be impressed with the solemnity and rich meaning not only of the essential rite but also of the sacramentals which surround it.

We had found that a particularly effective way of developing the community sense was through the various forms of the dialogue Mass and the congregationally sung Mass that were permitted then and were being introduced—sporadically, to be sure, but with growing frequency, especially on college campuses. Not only does the blending of voices make us aware of our neighbor, that we are not isolated individual worshipers in the midst of a silent crowd of strangers, but the distribution of roles teaches us that our community is an ordered, hierarchical organism, very like the body to which St. Paul compares it. Thus there are times when the presider alone speaks, or a reader proclaims the divine message. Sometimes only the choir sings, but again it will be the entire massed congregation that offers praise or petition.

The sense of community is indispensable to the formation of the Christian worshiper, but so is the sense of election. Awareness of God's predilection will give to worship a quality of enthusiasm that will make it worship "in spirit and in truth," for love begets love. Worship will not be merely the routine devoir of a half-hour on Sunday morning, the hurried recitation of an Our Father and Hail Mary at night. Enthusiasm will make it a matter of total living, of enrichment and growth.

It was odd, we thought, that we American Catholics shied away from manifestations of religious enthusiasm. Could we blame it on a lingering taint of Jansenism still in our blood, the heritage of French and Irish forbears? Was it rather an Anglo-Saxon distaste for Latin ardor? There is—or was, in the era of so-called American Innocence—a childlike quality in our national character which, one thinks, should have permitted the free expression of religious enthusiasm as well as any other kind. Perhaps our very childlikeness imposes on us a certain hyper-solemnity when our thoughts turn to religion. Perhaps it's just that we had no experience of enthusiasm in church. Low Masses (need they have always been that low?) in dim basement churches, heavy, dark wood panelings reaching to the ceiling, a vested figure reading Latin *sotto voce* in the distant sanctuary, the muffled stir as the congregation rose and knelt and at last made gratefully for the exits, satisfied that duty was done for another week—this is what one remembers from boyhood. No wonder some of our senior citizens rebelled against what seemed to them only indecent "noise" in church.

These attitudes were the prevailing ones, by and large, in 1963. But there was evidence that not everyone accepted them as natural or desirable. The word "enthusiasm" meant, when it was coined, the emotion of one who believed himself to be "in God." And if it is objected that the word "enthusiast" now connotes frenzy, or fickle instability, one can only mourn the deterioration of a good word. It need not refer to the religious seizures of a Holy Roller, or to the orgies of a Dionysiac. Only Puritans (and Cathari, and Albigenses, and Janenists—Malvolio *redivivus* in all ages) hold for the stern repression of legitimate feeling. There is a splendid passage, the fiftieth chapter of *Sirach*, which describes the religious enthusiasm of the Jews. Who can forget David's dancing before the Ark, or the singing of the pilgrims who went up annually to sacrifice in the Temple? How can we daily read the Psalms, with their talk of trumpets and psalteries and flutes in the divine service, or St. Paul, urging us to praise God in "hymns and spiritual canticles" (Col 3:16), and still think enthusiasm an invariably dangerous thing to be kept always under very tight rein?

Granted, emotion should spring from a profound conviction, from a fresh realization of unalterable truth. But isn't that exactly what we hope for when we assemble in church? It may be the sacred place itself, it may be the Word of God, piercing hearts like a two-edged sword, that is read there, it may be the homily or simply the adventitious grace of the moment, but something, we hope, will move us to know vividly again how long and how tirelessly God has loved us, and then we shall be moved to tears or remorse or to heart-warming peace or exultant joy. Indeed, using the words that express strong feeling, in concert with others, whether we speak them or (preferably) sing them, helps us actually to experience the emotion.

Mass for the Eighth Sunday after Pentecost, in the old missal, used to begin with a verse from one of the psalms (48:10): "O God, we ponder your kindness within your temple." If we had in fact done this pondering of God's love consistently, and thought of Christianity not simply as a compilation of doctrines, and surely not just a code of moral precepts, but as what it really is, a history, we should have found it much easier to know ourselves as the people of election, a people, St. Peter tells us, "whom God means to have for himself" (1 Pet 2:10). Our history is a record of God's incredible love for our race, an account of how he has personally intervened in our affairs for our good. It begins with the history of our creation and of our gross failure to love God in return; it continues with the story of the centuries of waiting for the promised Redeemer who was to right that prodigious wrong. These were the ages of preparation and purification that ran until the fullness of time, when at last he came to do for us mighty deeds of dying and rising so that in him we might die to our sins and rise to everlasting life. Now we are in the last age of the world, when through his Church the Redeemer is gathering many to himself. This age will be followed by eternity, when we shall be presented by our Lord to his Father as those who have loved him, and the Father will therefore love us. We cannot, then, accept the belief of ancient philosophers (and some modern ones) that time is meaningless, presenting us only with a weary round of the same old pattern: birth and death, rise and fall. Time *has* a meaning and a purpose. God's ends will be achieved—are in fact being achieved, despite our human fumbling. This conviction is the strengthening and heartening effect of our listening on Sunday to the words of Holy Scripture: we ponder God's mercies to us in the past that we may be sacramentally joined with them now and look forward eagerly to their fulfillment, our eternal union with him, in the future.

The ancient Jews delighted in meditating the prodigies God had worked for their race, the delicate attentions he had paid them. They composed songs (see Psalms 78, 105-107) about them, and taught the songs to their children, so that what they had learned from their fathers might be handed on to the rising generation. They knew that without their deserving it God had deigned to enter into a contract with them, and they said: "He has not treated us as he has treated other peoples" (Ps 147:20). Moses was the mediator of this contract, and the whole nation had accepted it and sealed it with the blood of a lamb. Keeping the contract's terms was their most serious obligation but also their supreme privilege: the stone tablets of the Covenant would be their proud badge forever. It was good to be a Jew. It excited them. They were grateful for their intimacy with God. They were zealous for the honor of his name. They were dedicated to the lifelong fulfillment of his law. In a word, they were enthusiastic.

Now this history had a sequel. Everything that God had accomplished for the Jews was done with us in mind, too, for we are those in whom that history reached its fulfillment. The vocation of Abraham, in whose seed we are blessed; the contract at Sinai, consecrating a people to publish the holy Name and to brood over the "immense presentiment" of its own destiny; the mission of the prophets to make straight the way of him who would come—all this led directly to us. For we Gentiles were to be given, in God's generosity, the salvation which is, radically, "of the Jews." We were not of that Chosen People; we could not claim Abraham as our father in the flesh. We were strangers, outside the pale, who had somehow to be brought in by means of a new contract. God for this enormous task sent no other than his Son, who would be the mediator of a new and everlasting covenant, and seal it with his blood, the blood of the Lamb of God. At our baptism we accepted this covenant, vowing to keep our part of its provisions while we lived, and knowing that the God of truth would keep his. The cross on which our mediator sealed the covenant with his blood is our proud badge now and forever. Isn't this exciting? Doesn't it make us feel that it is good to be a Christian? Isn't enthusiasm justified? God help our weak minds or our stubborn hearts if we cannot experience gratitude on pondering such things, if we cannot want to sing and shout our praise of such a Father, such a Redeemer-Brother.

There had been twenty-three annual Liturgical Weeks by 1963, and their mood and tempo had been markedly enthusiastic. But they taught consistently the grounds for enthusiasm. Worshipers should hear again and yet again, in sacred reading and in sermons and by every device of teaching, the history of the magnificent things God has done for them. No sterile moralizing would do, no mere committing to memory of capsulized doctrine. They should be shown that the Christ who was their mediator is not dead, like Moses, but risen and living and acting still for them. That the sacraments are personal encounters with Christ, not transactions by which they can pile up, like some supernatural miser, heaps of grace to exult over. They should be brought to see that morality is simply a matter of what befits a son or daughter of God. There are some things that "aren't done" by a member of this family—even more important, there are some things that are done. Worship, then, is an abiding attitude as well as a particular act; it is carried out every day of the week, and it extends to the whole Christian life. No mere "Sunday Catholics," then. None of that double-dealing which gives such scandal to one's brethren as well as to unbelievers. No trying to make the best of both worlds, but an all-embracing commitment made in faith and gladness, and because nothing less is worthy of God.

So the enthusiasm of the worshiper should be encouraged to express itself, both in formal religious rites and in all the areas of parish, diocesan, and civic life. Even before 1963 it had become absorbing to watch the development of lay participation in public worship, on the one hand, and the emergence of lay "witnesses" in every sphere of American life on the other. Surely, we thought, this betokened a clearer understanding of the Church as a body with many members, each with its own function and its own contribution to make to the welfare of the whole. Little by little laypeople were recovering a voice they had lost long ago, a voice given them, certainly, for use in both the praise of God and the service of their fellows, to be raised in the Christian assembly when it was their role to speak and in the assembly of their peers on such topics as social justice, racial equality, a just wage, decent housing, and the like. For God is the Lord of all life, and nothing human is alien to our worship of him.

To make comprehensible our public worship, which is steadily oriented to another world, the Liturgical Weeks had emphasized the theology of history and a complete eschatology—not just terror of the Last Judgment. A first priority was given to teaching the full meaning of our Lord's resurrection, not only for himself but for us as well. Too long had we seen that glory only as an apologetic miracle. The Weeks emphasized as well the resurrection of the human body as the complete achievement of our redemption and the full restoration of our dignity. The return of Christ to the world in his Second Coming was presented as the means by which we would be inseparably united with him, but also as a triumphant vindication of the wisdom of God, now bringing all things to their full achievement and giving meaning to each. The Second Coming was something every real Christian has yearned for (*"maranatha Jesu,"* said the early followers of Christ). In the age of Sartre and The Bomb it took on more significance than ever. So far as the formation of the worshiper is concerned, it is a governing idea. One's outlook is transfigured by it—indeed, the world itself is transfigured by it, and this sudden establishment of the relative values of all things is most useful to us Americans, who possess so much—and are in danger of being possessed.

Worship is a response to God's merciful initative. It is our word in reply to God's. The worshiper, then, should be carefully and profoundly formed in Scripture, which not only records God's part in the dialogue but provides examples of how men and women have responded in the past, and even offers an inspired text for our use. It would be difficult to exaggerate either the riches that were available to us in Scripture or our poverty in those years without them. Many of us were, indeed, like the desperately poor in some parts of Asia, who do not know how destitute they are because they have never seen the things that make people wealthy. The Old Testament, despite a most promising beginning after World War II of biblical studies on the college and high school level, was still unknown country for most Catholics, and even the New Testament, aside from the fragments of it that formed the readings for Sundays, was a closed book, too.

Which of our young intellectuals, until recently, knew enough biblical history to listen with appreciation to Handel's *Messiah*? Of course it was difficult for us to establish our distinctive culture here; there can be no Christian culture apart from Scripture. But there can be no Christian worship, either. The Easter Vigil, for example, revised in 1955, was thronged at first because of its novelty, but then largely deserted. People were not familiar even with the story of *Exodus*. They could not see their own history typified in the majestic yet pathetic history of Israel, the People of Election who gave now a full-throated, now only a dusty answer to God. That history, St. Paul says, was "written for our instruction," (1 Cor. 10:1). Similarly, our lack of acquaintance with bible history and biblical habits of mind prevented our ready use of the Psalms, which had been the inspired prayer-book of Christians for centuries. We found even chants and acclamations taken from the Psalms alien and a little quaint, and for most priests the Breviary was what it was called, an "office," a duty, a burden.

Here, parenthetically, it might be noted that the skies were brightening somewhat; under the inspiration of the Holy Spirit the threads were drawing together. It seemed, for instance, that the liturgical movement and the biblical revival had had no common human ancestry, but scholars in both fields had begun to labor side by side, and the harvest promised to be extraordinarily fruitful. And the ecumenical trend of those days seemed to have sprung—humanly, again—from quite other roots, but we were already aware of what an impulse it gave to biblical and liturgical studies, and of how well these had prepared us for thinking in ecumenical terms.

When the Program Committee of the Liturgical Conference, for instance, sat down to prepare the program for the 1960 Liturgical Week in Pittsburgh, they found themselves at a loss. The theme of the Week, designated by Bishop Wright, was to be "the Liturgy and Christian Unity." Should the program consist of a series of studies of Oriental liturgies as contrasted with our own? Should it, instead, strive to point out the doctrines and attitudes held by Catholics, Orthodox, and Protestants alike, so that we might recognize our common heritage and the "bridges" across which we might go to find one another? Ultimately it was decided that before all else we Catholics should ponder our duty to pray and to be ourselves better witnesses to Christian unity. The program was then developed along these lines, and the papers presented at the Week studied the vocation of all men and women to worship God, the interventions of God in human affairs at different stages in the history of salvation, the sacraments as personal encounters with Christ present and active in the Church, the Christian response of faith in worship and daily living, the Eucharist as the celebration of unity, and the radiant charity, drawn from the liturgy as its primary source, that should distinguish the Christian at work in today's world. It is easy to see in such a program the blending of liturgical, biblical, and ecumenical themes.

The relation between social worship and Christian social action was becoming clearer, too. Those working in the field of interracial justice seemed to have grasped it best, but sociologists, economists, journalists, and people in similar fields had begun to see that humanitarianism was not good enough, and that human beings must be loved for the image of God that is in them, or, in other words, as an act of worship. "Liturgists" had also seen that worship which stopped at the church door was not enough, either, for anyone who proclaims love for God and will not help a brother is—not to put more fine a point upon it than St. John does (1 Jn 4:20)—a liar. Strange how long it took us to see that John Q. Citizen, who goes to Mass on Sunday morning and goes home to live—he hopes—peaceably with his family, and then goes to work on Monday morning, is one and the same individual. He is not three different people, though we split him three ways for a long time.

It had not been hard, of course, to see how liturgy was related to the arts. Music, architecture, and the decorative arts had been perennially the handmaids of worship, and the needs of worship had purified the arts of such eccentricities as operatic Masses, churches more like salons or theatres than houses of prayer, and statues or paintings which expressed the idiosyncrasies of their creators rather then any idea that might assist reverence.

Even the last redoubt, that of the canonists and moralists, had begun to show signs of crumbling. True, your typical lawyer still looked sidewise on "all these changes," and muttered about the "liberalism" in the air, but he was a man better acquainted than most, perhaps, with the vagaries of human beings, and could be indulged a little for his caution. There was one remark that a moralist made in my hearing, however, which should be preserved if our children are to know how hardly won was the integral outlook they themselves might take for granted. "I have nothing against the liturgy," said this generous soul. "I just prescind from it." Which would seem, in view of everything that has been said, to demonstrate a remarkable ingenuity.

Worshipers—to attempt a summary—must be, as St. Paul said, "in Christ." But Christ was the worshiper par excellence, the priest apart from whom there is no priesthood. He gave the definitive reply in the human dialogue with God, and we have only to join our voice with his in order to be heard. Since Arianism we had got further and further away from thinking of our Lord as our leader in the worship we are privileged to offer our Father, but twentieth-century currents of theology and spirituality were sweeping us back to it, carrying us out of any private bywater of our own into this main stream of worship. Of course our struggles for virtue, our sorrow for sin, our whole interior life were rightfully ours; only we could have them. It would be our joy to praise God with the gifts and talents he had given us personally, and we would avail ourselves of whatever school of spirituality we had found helpful. The Spirit breathes where he will. But before all else we had been baptized into Christ, and it would be in Christ that we would go to the Father. The work of our personal redemption, in other words, would go forward to our last breath, with God's grace shaping us closer still to the perfection he wants of each of us, but the world's redemption would go on to the end of time, and we would be fitted into that vast beauty, so that the one Priest might offer it "without spot or wrinkle or any stain" (Eph 5:27) in one sublime and eternal gesture of worship.

Every parish church, then, every Catholic school, every religious order and pious society, every instruction in the faith would have for its ultimate object the formation of worshipers. This was the object of the liturgical year, according to Pius XII. By means of the liturgical year we were to come to know Christ's mysteries—those events of his earthly life by which he enlightens us, corrects our vision, patiently persuades us to make our full commitment to him, atones for our malice, unites us permanently with himself in adoration. What we don't know we cannot love or embrace. But knowledge, in a proverb we don't hear quoted much any more, "maketh a bloody entrance." And so the lesson would have to be repeated over and over as the earth turned and our years mounted up. Sometimes one thinks that the Lord himself is amused when, late in life, the full, blinding truth of some oft-heard principle at last comes home to us, and we say, "O! I see!" as if we had heard it for the first time. Well, a certain amount of this is inevitable; we haven't the angels' intuition, and even our human equipment was damaged in the Fall. But perhaps the fault is not always traceable to our indifference, distractions, or muddle-headedness. Perhaps, as in an old movie on television, the pictures are not made sharp, and so our attention flags, in spite of our good will. Perhaps people keep crossing between us and the screen, people who don't belong in the room. Or maybe the dialogue is in a foreign language, without enough sub-titles. Or the film may be run off at such speed that we just can't follow it. Odd how many of us would die for the philosophical principle that nothing enters the mind except through the senses, and yet cannot see the need of impressing the senses in order that the truth about Christ may penetrate.

It was becoming clear in 1963 that if we wanted American Catholics to understand public worship, the first hurdle we would have to get over was our esoteric language. Thurston Davis, S.J, wrote an amusing article in *America* (March 4, 1961) in which he reproached ecclesiastics with "laziness or stultifying routine" for not translating Latin or Greek terms into acceptable English equivalents, even though they must have sensed that popular mystification could be the only result of using them. He cites "Septuagesima," too, and "Epiphany," but he might have mentioned many more. The feasts ending in "shun," for instance: Ascension, Assumption, Immaculate Conception—all of them simply transliterations of the Latin. One of them had a very simple and lovely name among the Greeks; it was known as "the Falling Asleep of Our Lady." I have wondered if another could not be known as "Our Lady's Privilege." The early English Catholics showed a spirit of sturdy independence and a respect for their own language by coining their own names for the feasts: Christmas, Michaelmas, Whitsun, Candlemas, All Hallows. My own favorite in these matters was the term "Extreme Unction." Couldn't we have called it "Last Anointing," even though the sacrament was not in fact intended exclusively for the final moments of life? We thought it was, and as we pronounced the name it seemed that we received several "munctions" during life, and asked for an "extra munction" at death.

Clinging to an unintelligible, foreign, and clumsy vocabulary is like clinging to a bygone style of architecture, such as Gothic, without even the compensation of getting something quaint or pretty. You give the impression that the modern world has passed you by, that you have nothing to say to your contemporaries or you would try to put your thought into comprehensible language. Theologians protested that their science requires a language of utmost precision, that certain terms are irreplaceable, but even they were beginning to realize that they were talking only to themselves, and that they must labor to discover ways of phrasing their ideas that would make ready sense to educated contemporaries. And anyway, our concern here is not with the precisions of theology so much as with the faith and devotion of the multitudes, who know no Latin and less Greek, and who have really better things to do than to memorize esoteric nomenclature or struggle to adjust themselves to the customs and folkways (however holy) of an age long dead, or of a part of the world thousands of miles away from them.

The frustrations of missionaries had been rehearsed vividly in papers presented at Assisi in 1956 and at Nijmegen in Holland in 1959, and many changes would of necessity come about in such places as Asia and Africa. But the Church in America had long since come of age, and we did not need to continue indefinitely dependent on the lexicon or the devotional habits of Europe. It was a fact that our people (and there were forty millions of them) did not understand or share in the public worship of the Church. The effects of this deprivation were evident enough: ignorance of doctrine, poverty of prayer, joylessness, a merely juridical mentality where the service of God was concerned. It was also a fact, stressed emphatically by St. Pius X sixty years before, that intelligent sharing in the worship of the Church was the primary and indispensable source of the true Christian spirit. So we needed a Moses to strike the rock and liberate the life-giving waters for us.

Words were meant to be heard, pondered, savored; as Al Smith used to say with his East Side accent, "the poipose of woids is to convey a meaning." Words mean little if they are gabbled or murmured inaudibly, just as signs mean little if they cannot be clearly perceived by our senses. Bread should be tasted (and therefore should taste like bread), water should flow, incense should be smelled. And to shrug off signs as "frills" is not only evidence that a man has forgotten his psychology; it is scarcely courteous to the Lord who in his wisdom and mercy used them and gave them to his Church.

The Church's worship evolved in an agrarian culture, when people were close to the soil and lived out their lives in the rhythm of the seasons. Nowadays our city dwellers see little of growing crops; they don't really know what darkness is. Many liturgical images form no part of their personal experience. The ritual of "Rogation Days," for example, could not be very significant to a housewife whose nearest approach to a spring sowing or a harvest was her visit to a supermarket.

On the other hand, the imagery and language of the liturgy are basically biblical, so it could be hoped that increasing familiarity with Scripture would make the liturgy more understandable. In 1963 most of our people were not only unacquainted with the great figures of the Bible—Moses, Elijah, David, Saul, Jeremiah—and with the great events of redemptive history—the story of Joseph, the Exodus, the Babylonian captivity and the return—but they did not think in biblical language, they did not pray in biblical imagery. What Catholic, for instance, asked God to be his "rock," as the Psalms so often do? Who among us, offering himself or herself to God's purposes or making a great renunciation, thought of the act as a "sweet-smelling sacrifice"? When we thought of a lamb, we were likely to have in mind an innocent, playful little animal, gamboling on the White House lawn at Easter; in the eyes of a Jew in biblical times a lamb was essentially an animal whose wool could provide clothing, whose flesh could be eaten, and which was often slaughtered as a gesture of adoration. So we were faced with the choice of either discarding Scripture or learning it. Obviously, the first alternative was unthinkable; we would have to learn it. And we believed that as we learned it, meditated it, savored it, we would come to love and prefer it. At the same time our missal and breviary would begin to make sense and to be our normal and favorite way of praying. Incidentally, we believed that our thinking about God would probably be more correct, too.

For all these reasons it was felt that there should be a more generous citation of Scripture in the liturgy. Ours is a faith that "comes from hearing" (Rom 10:17); it is an act of humble response to God who deigns to reveal himself to us in a Word which shall not pass away. But if we were to have more Scripture we would need more explanation of it. The Scripture scholars of the country had done splendid work in making their studies available to priests and educated laypeople; there were excellent books, articles, courses, summer "institutes" and the like. But this enriching and stimulating material would have to be carried to *all* the people. Perhaps it would be done, at first, largely through college classes, but it should be extended through Sunday sermons, missions, retreats, novenas, occasional instructions, and whatever means might be open.

Our ritual needed to be explained carefully, but even more necessary was a steady presentation of the doctrines that underlie the ritual and justify it. The Jewish Quahal or Assembly and its vocation to worship. Its coming together through faith in the Lord Jesus. Its initiation by baptism into his dying and rising and by the Eucharist into his life and glory. Its prayer as the "loud cry" offered jointly with his, and heard "because of his reverent submission" (Heb 5:7). Its destiny as the Elect of God to praise and rejoice in him forever, with full possession of human dignity in soul and body.

So that was the state of things in 1963. The "good Pope John" had summoned the Second Vatican Council, and the Council, after a hot preliminary scrimmage that determined whether it would do its own business or simply rubber-stamp the Roman Curia's blueprint, spent almost the entire two-month session debating—of all things—a program for the reform of the liturgy. There were some rather sour remarks to the effect that Nero was again fiddling while Rome burned. With all the aching problems facing our poor old world, here were 3300 bishops fussing interminably over rubrics. It would be part of the Council's function, and a large part of the Council's aftermath, to demonstrate that something was at stake that was weightier and more decisive than rubrics for the Christian enterprise.

CHAPTER 17

The Great Council

THE FLIGHT FROM CHICAGO WAS SMOOTH. TWA HAD MADE arrangements for me to offer Mass in the chapel at Orly Airport in Paris, and Bishop Franz of Peoria, who was the only other clerical passenger, kindly served the Mass. I enjoyed especially the flight over the Alps—the Matterhorn was pointed out to us—and the flight down the "boot" of Italy in the clear Italian air. The Fiumicino Airport was crowded with clerics arriving and other clerics meeting them. I was happy to encounter Cardinal Cushing and his party—Msgr. Walter Furlong, former chancellor, Msgr. Robert Sennott, chancellor at that time, and Fr. Charlie von Euw, professor at St. John's Seminary and a former student of mine at Boston College.

Rome, as I rode into the city on a bus, looked very different from the Rome I remembered from my three months' stay there in 1946. At that time the city was still in a state of shock from the war: no buses or trolleys, little business except military business. Now things were humming; advertisements shouted their wares from every billboard, traffic was dense and dangerous to life and limb, people were gay and busy. I began to recognize landmarks like the Coliseum, the "ice cream monument," as the G.I.'s called it, of Victor Emmanuel, the Forum, the *Termini* or railroad station, the *Lungotevere* or Road-along-the-Tiber, the Castel San Angelo, and—yes, there it was in all its tingling magnificence—St. Peter's and the piazza with its clasping colonnades. By this time I was excited as only Rome can excite one. A cab took me to the *pensione* operated by the Franciscan Sisters of the Atonement, high on a hill overlooking St. Peter's on one side and a pleasant countryside, rapidly being filled with new apartment buildings, on the other. The Sisters welcomed me cordially; I discovered that two of them had been stationed at Assisi when I visited there with Father Joachim Daleiden in '46, and found them almost starving. (We left behind a case of C-rations to help that situation.) My room was small but bright and pleasant, and very quiet at night, though the school children kept the welkin ringing all day in the playground outside my window.

It was September of 1963, and the Second Vatican Council was meeting for its second session. One great change had occurred since the close of the first session: Pope John XXIII had died. There was some speculation about the new Pope. Would he continue the Council? Would he give it the same direction John had given it? Doubts and rumors were banished by the magnificent address of Paul VI at the Mass opening the Second Session.

Since it was the second session, people settled quickly into the accomodations and the routines they had become familiar with the year before, and work began without preliminaries. Nor was there any of the jockeying for strategic advantage that had delayed matters in the first session, when the Roman Curia tried in its muscular fashion to impose on the Council both its own selection of members on the various commissions and its own documents to be automatically ratified. Which is not to say that the Curialists (the *"Immobilisti,"* as the Italians called them) had abandoned their determination to keep the *status quo ante*. They would dispute every inch of the ground before surrendering it.

I had not been at the first session, so it took me a little longer to get established. Every corner of every Jesuit house had been spoken for and occupied, and lodging of a modest sort elsewhere was hard to come by, but I managed at last to find a room at the Franciscan *pensione*. Several American and Canadian bishops and priests were there already, and made me welcome. It proved to be a congenial group, though one of the bishops regularly took the head of the table and the dominant role in the conversation. He hadn't yet succumbed to the democratization of the bishops which came about almost inevitably because there were twenty-five hundred of them in the city, and the usual compliments and devoirs had to be abridged. He was given somewhat to pronouncements which for the most part went undisputed, but one day, when he was telling us how ungrateful American liturgists had shown themselves for the support they had been given by their hierarchy, my resolve to keep a discreet silence crumbled. "Bishop," I said, "I don't like to contradict you, but on that subject I'm quite knowledgeable. And I would say, saving your reverence, that with a very, very few exceptions, the American hierarchy, so far from giving support to the liturgical movement, put every possible obstacle in its way. And I can cite for you, if you like, chapter and verse." It was well known that the two hundred American bishops, at the beginning of the Council, had grouped themselves behind Cardinal Spellman in opposing any changes in the liturgy. By the end of the second session, when the text of the decree on the liturgy was solemnly approved, there were only twenty negative votes—two of them, it was said, by Americans. The bishops had been educated by the wonderful experience of dialogue, with one another and with the *periti*—the theologians they had invited to assist them.

Father Frank Rodimer—now happily reigning as Bishop of Paterson—had a ticket for the solemn opening of the second session, but I had none. However, we drove the bishops to the basilica, waited a few strategic moments, then, on the strength of that single ticket, calmly walked by three sets of frowning Swiss Guards. It was the most barefaced gate-crashing I had ever done; I began to wonder if I had become the Invisible Man, or whether the Guards' eyes were being held. (Who says they were not?)

We looked down the long nave, its bleacher-type seats filling up with mitred bishops in white copes; we noted the Orthodox and Protestant "observers" seated within twenty feet of the altar, the helmeted Swiss Guards leaning on their pikes, the diplomatic corps and chamberlains in their formal dress, the incredible variety of habits among the religious men and women. At last a thousand lights went on, the Cardinals entered in procession, and the Holy Father *walked* (no *sedia gestatoria*, thank God) down to his throne on the platform of the high altar while everyone applauded. The Mass, offered by Cardinal Tisserant after the Holy Father had intoned the *Veni Creator*, was celebrated on a temporary altar facing the people. The Vatican choir, I noticed, fell silent in order to allow all present to sing the Ordinary of the Mass; this was a practice begun at the previous session of the Council at the express request of the bishops.

Like everyone else, I felt the spirit of Pope John present. He had launched all this against tremendous opposition, and now, it seemed, he was there with his characteristic smile and his patient, cordial love for all the world. After Mass and after the Cardinals had greeted him, the new Pope read a profession of faith, kneeling, and then sat down to read the address which would formally open this session of the Council. It was very long (a little over an hour), but I thought it absolutely magnificent. The Holy Father read it deliberately, his voice rising and his pace slowing as he sought to emphasize his points, and once, while he was speaking of reunion with the Orthodox and the Protestants, his voice broke and he seemed close to tears. I don't suppose anything similar had been said in all the centuries of dissension. He asked forgiveness of non-Catholics for our lack of charity toward them, and freely forgave for all we had suffered. What a grace, I said to myself, to be alive in a day when such things could be said, and to be given a Father who would say them.

But before that he had referred with evident reverence and affection to Pope John, "the first Father of this Council," and had gone on to insist on John's program of *aggiornamento* as the primary task of the assembled Fathers. He even inserted John's phrase, *Mater et Magistra,* into his text as a name for the Church, indicating thereby that he was approving and aligning himself with all that John taught.

His principal topics, after he had insisted that Christ our Lord must be our beginning and end, our life and our guide and our hope, were these: the Church must devotedly ponder herself and come to know herself better. She must reform herself interiorly, sanctifying herself by making courageously those changes which are necessary today. She must seek to be united with all other Christians. She must maintain a constant intercourse with the contemporary world, seeking to make religion and theology relevant in our time. The Holy Father ended with a few words of salutation to the Orientals in both Greek and (I think) Russian or Slavonic. Before his address the Holy Scriptures were solemnly enthroned on a lectern facing the altar; this is, I believe, the customary practice at every Council, but it had special interest now in view of the contemporary revival of Scripture studies in the Church and the effort toward unity with the Protestants, to whom the Scriptures mean so much.

One of the great sights during the Council was to see the cardinals and bishops crossing the piazza at the beginning and end of each day's labors. Crowds gathered at the barricades to feast their eyes on that riot of color: crimson and purple robes, pectoral crosses, grays and black-and-whites among the prelates who were religious, any color one liked among the Orientals. And of course there was color, too, in the complexions one saw—white, yellow, brown, gleaming ebony. I was disappointed that I never saw Archbishop Sison of Vigan, in the Philippines, who was parish priest of the town (San Fabian) we were billeted in after the invasion of Luzon in '45.

That evening Father Rodimer and I drove out to Tivoli and wandered for an hour among the gardens and the fountains of the Villa d'Este, lighted romantically by both the full moon and the hidden spotlights and floods that had been installed since my last visit there. Like Robert Browning, I lost my heart to Italy the first time I saw it, and the Villa d'Este is only one of a thousand reasons why.

Father Rodimer and I were not as successful next day when we tried to slip by the Swiss Guard. We were not official *periti* of the Council but only theologians accompanying a bishop, and that wasn't good enough to get us a seat even in the balcony of St. Peter's. By way of compensation, we did get passes for the daily press panel which was introduced this year as a welcome departure from the standard Roman practice of secrecy about even trivial matters. Pope Paul, who didn't suffer from this hang-up, called a special meeting of journalists and spoke most cordially, almost sighing as he looked pleadingly at us and asked for *vérité* (he spoke in French) in reporting the Council's activities. About 250 representatives of the press were on hand, plus some people who, I suspect, were connected with the press only because they read the newspapers regularly. For example, the group I was with derived special amusement from watching two tiny nuns thread their way through the crowd as we ascended the stairs. They were like termites boring through soft wood, and when we last saw them they were thirty feet ahead of us and must have wound up at the very feet of the Holy Father. Romans generally, as is well known, use elbows and knees and hips to wriggle their way ahead in any crowd, and that age-old habit expresses itself today in the frightfully congested Roman traffic. I once thought we Americans were mad drivers, but, after sharing in the insane races and tangles of Madrid, Brussels, Lisbon, Paris, and Rome, I began to think we are relatively sane. Crossing a Roman street is like plunging into a torrent or running a broken field in football. Driving is a game of "chicken"—will your nerve give out before his does? Riding a bus or a cab, I read my breviary or studied the floor; watching the near-misses could bring on a heart-attack.

My impression of the press people, after some observation, was that they really tried to get the truth; they went to briefings and press conferences and lectures, they asked good questions, and, by and large, they wrote sober, non-sensational dispatches. Of course the information available to them in this session was much more abundant than in the last, and they were aware, I thought, that the kind of grinding work going on in the Council did not lend itself to scare headlines or human interest stories.

It was not too difficult to get a pretty accurate idea of what had been said in the Council chamber. Every afternoon, for each of the language groups, there was a briefing of the press by a selected panel of *periti*. The Americans started this practice in the first session when the official communiqués were wretched and the press people were stymied and befuddled; other language groups followed suit. This year's communiqués were a little better, and although it was forbidden to link the names of any prelates who spoke in the morning sessions with what they had said, the American communiqué listed the speakers by numbers—which numbers miraculously corresponded with the numbers of the paragraphs below containing the substance of what had been said. In any case, one would only have to wait until the next morning to read a very complete account of everything in the French Catholic paper, *La Croix*, which read like a stenographer's record. *Le Monde*, also of Paris, was excellent, too, and the *Corriere della Serra* of Milan. The Roman papers, except for *Il Messagero*, printed only what had been officially released.

The briefing of the press was the most interesting and valuable event of the day. Present were reporters from the Associated Press, the Religious News Service, *Time, Newsweek,* Irish Television, the New York *Times*, the Kansas City *Star, America, Our Sunday Visitor,* the diocesan papers of Baltimore, Philadelphia, and other American sees. The rest of the group made me think that I was at a Liturgical Week: Msgr. John Oesterreicher of Seton Hall University, Colonel Ross-Duggan, Father Placid (Max) Jordan, Carol Jackson of *Integrity,* Father Bob Quinn of the Paulist Center in Boston. The panel of *periti* who undertook to answer the reporters' questions was chaired by Father John Sheerin of *The Catholic World* and made up of Fathers Fred McManus, Tavard, Gregory Baum, O.S.A., Gus Weigel, S.J., Frank McCool, S.J., Francis Connell, C.SS.R., and Robert Trisco of Catholic University.

At the initial press conference the Holy Father was vigorous but composed—on top of his job, so to speak. He gave us his blessing, chatted briefly with several cardinals and bishops present, and, pleasantly but skillfully evading a rush of importunates, escaped with a smile. Poor man; everyone, from the waiters in the restaurants to the bishops, compared him with Pope John—"*il santo*," the people called John. Well, as an American Jesuit put it, "Pope John was everyone's grandfather," and Pope Paul had to be himself. There were old hands in Rome who were saying that he would be a combination of Pius XII and John, which I thought would be a marvelous combination indeed. Incidentally, it was nice to hear someone say, this week, that Pope John could never have done all he did if Pius had not prepared the way, especially by his writing and speaking. I myself was persuaded that the Council could never have taken the turn it did in the first session—or might never been called at all—if it had not been for *Mystici Corporis, Mediator Dei*, and *Divino Afflante Spiritu*, those mighty encyclicals of the forties, not to mention such things as the Congresses of the Lay Apostolate, the Assisi Congress on Pastoral Liturgy in 1956, the constant teaching on every subject from the age of mankind to the role of psychiatry, from the holiness of the family to the danger of atheism. And as for Pius' being "aristocratic," "aloof," "cold,"—well, I could never forget a private audience in 1946, when he gave me the impression that he had been waiting for years for me to come to Rome, and why hadn't I come much sooner? And at that time he was receiving Americans, from the top brass to the lowliest G.I.'s, by the hundreds.

An interesting insight into the Roman legal mind, active and passive, was afforded the press one afternoon when Dale Francis, of *Our Sunday Visitor*, told us that he had asked Cardinal Ottaviani about the decree banning the sale in the Roman Vicariate of the books of Hans Küng, Xavier Rynne, Robert Kaiser, and Teilhard de Chardin. The Cardinal said the decree had not come from his office, though he acknowledged that he had known about it, and that it concerned only Rynne's and Kaiser's books, and that it prohibited not the sale of these, but only their prominent display. Shortly after that Mr. Francis visited a well-known bookshop on the Via della Conciliazione and saw a display of Rynne's book; when he asked about it the Brother in charge replied that it wasn't, after all, a *big* display.

On that same Via della Conciliazione one afternoon I had a happy encounter with Father Barnabas Mary Ahern, the Passionist Scripture scholar, who at my invitation had been Candlemas Lecturer at Boston College several years before. Over coffee and pie à la mode at the American snack bar Father Barnabas insisted that the division of the Council into "conservatives" and "liberals" was altogether too facile, that most of the bishops did not fit into either category, and that those he had worked with were astonishingly humble, zealous men who eagerly wanted and worked for the welfare of the whole Church. It made good listening for me. And maybe, I thought, it might have its effect even on Paul Blanshard, author of a scathing attack on the Church a few years before. He was in Rome for six months to write a sequel, and he sat in, looking very pleasant and very much at home, at the press conferences every afternoon. I confess that, as I sat behind him one day, I tried to catch a glimpse over his shoulder at the notes he was making, but couldn't read them.

As the weeks went by it became obvious that the Council would have to go on to at least one, perhaps two or three more sessions. The schema on the Church was having a protracted but very fruitful debate, and, it was clear, would have to be re-written. I attended a meeting of American bishops and theologians that was devoted to the subject of the collegiality of the bishops. Father Owens, a Redemptorist teaching in Rome, pointed out that the term "collegiality" was of quite recent origin, and could have a variety of meanings ranging from a jurisdictional corporateness to a simple fraternal communion of mutual solicitude. Since the nature of the Church depends altogether on what our Lord intended when he established it, there must be an inquiry into what his will was. How could the infallibility of the Pope, defined in the First Vatican Council, be reconciled with the corporate magisterium? The ghost of Gallicanism was still in the wings and aroused fear in some quarters.

Then Father Gene Maly, of Cincinnati, explained the Old Testament background of the concept, showing the corporateness of the Twelve Tribes of Israel. These tribes were wrenched apart after the death of Solomon, but the prophets predicted that one of the fruits of the messianic reign would be the reunion of the Twelve in "the perfect Israel." Then Father Barnabas complemented Father Maly beautifully and cogently, showing how there was nothing fortuitous in our Lord's choice of "the Twelve" who would "judge the Twelve Tribes of Israel"; in his mind the unity of the Church was intimately connected with the Old Testament dream of the perfect Israel. He communicated the fullness of his power to these Twelve: "All power is given to me . . . go and baptize . . . I am with you all days even till the consummation." And the Twelve's successors now share this power with the whole Church for its service and joy. Father Barnabas made a great point of the fact that we cannot look in the New Testament for our technical

theological language, since the New Testament is not written in polemical terms, but that the needs of our day oblige us to approach
non-Catholic Christians with this New Testament picture of the
Church rather than the one we usually presented, with its stern
façade of authority.

Evenings like that—and there were very many of them—were
surely educational, but the Council Fathers were beginning to manifest impatience with the interminable debates and the slow progress. At the rate things were moving they would be in Rome
forever. It was said that six plans for accelerating matters were cir-
culating among the various groups. Cardinal Frings was for reduc-
ing everything to five schemata. Archbishop Hurley of South Africa
was for doing only what could be done in one more session, limit-
ing discussion of each topic to three days only. Finally the suggestion of Cardinal Suenens to put five propositions to the vote was
acted on, and the Theological Commission (which certainly seemed
to be dragging its feet) was given, if not a mandate, at least a clear
directive from the Council as to how the schema on the Church
should be rewritten. One or more of the bishops seemed to have
diverted drowsiness or boredom by composing limericks:

> We are two thousand Fathers in session,
> Who grow weary of endless succession
>   Of Cardinals talking
>   And lesser lights squawking;
> Thank God the bar's so refreshin'.

And again:

> There's Rahner and Murray and Küng,
> Whose praises have loudly been süng,
>   But some fine *domani*
>   A bold 'taviani
> Will have them conveniently hüng.

And yet again:

> Coadjutors are very intent
> Lest their bishops, whose lives are far spent,
>   In a moment neurotic
>   Take an antibiotic
> Without their advice and consent.

Father Clifford Howell, the English Jesuit liturgist, called me
and proposed a week-end excursion. So on Saturday morning we
hired a tiny Fiat and set off out the Via Flaminia: Father Howell,

Monsignor Buckley, who was a pastor in Liverpool, a French bishop of a diocese in China near Tibet, and myself. The bishop's name was *formidable*, and I never did get it straight. At any rate, he had been a prisoner of the Communists for fourteen months and was finally exiled; now he was helping in Liverpool as an auxiliary bishop. His English was broken, but his lovely, simple personality bubbled through it and won us completely. We drifted along past Mount Soracte (no snow—Father Vincent McCormick told me that in all his years in Rome he saw it snow-covered only once, so old Horace must have been reporting a freak of weather). We stopped for an outdoor lunch at a roadside *trattoria*, and reached Orvieto at sundown. But along the way we decided to leave the highway and see one of the mountain hamlets that perched on crags high above us at every turn. The one we chose is called Montecchio—unknown to fame, as far as I am aware. We went up at precarious angles on a twisting road and passed through incredibly narrow streets into a tiny piazza. There we alighted and, seeing through an open door some men pressing grapes on an ancient hand-press, asked if we might watch the operation. They were delighted with our interest, and soon most of the townspeople were with us in the dim, vaulted cellar, crowing with pleasure over the visitors. Such faces! A portrait-painter could work there for years. They offered us glasses of delicious Orvieto wine, and so many clusters of grapes that we should have been sick if we had eaten half of them, and even—when they heard I was an American—handfuls of peanuts. Then the pastor arrived and insisted that we see his church and stop for a bit in his rectory. We went away, at last, in a fine glow of good feeling that was induced not so much by the wine as by the warm humanity of the village. I have remembered Montecchio.

At Orvieto we admired the lovely façade of the cathedral and its spacious interior. Here, they told us, one of the anti-Popes was elected at the time of the Great Western Schism, and not far off was the house where St. Thomas Aquinas and St. Albert the Great lived, as well as the church where, it was piously believed, St. Thomas heard the crucifix say to him, "You have written well of me, Thomas." In the morning, in those pre-concelebration days, we offered Mass individually. I was assigned to a side altar in the chapel at the same time that our bishop was celebrating at the main altar; an old nun read the lessons in Italian and led the people's responses in Latin, and the archpriest made the announcements and preached, so I was hard put to it to achieve any concentration.

Why they didn't use the high altar of the cathedral itself (all the parish Masses were in this chapel, with a small overflow listening to loud-speakers outside) was as mysterious as the fact that, in a parish of some thousands of souls, only a few hundred appeared for Sunday Mass.

Perhaps the answer might have been found in the tremendous emphasis given to quite peripheral matters. After the bishop's Mass, for instance, the archpriest gave us a treat. High above the altar in the chapel, in a panel much more securely locked than the tabernacle, was kept the "holy corporal." According to the legend, there was a priest whose faith in the Eucharist was crumbling— back in the 13th century, this was—and one morning the Lord took pity on him. When he broke the host it bled, and the corporal was stained with the blood. Well, the archpriest pressed a button, a hidden motor groaned and began to hum, and suddenly, out of the floor just behind the altar, a huge platform erected itself. We watched open-mouthed as the girders rose and stiffened into posi- tion, providing a flight of about twelve steps leading to a platform to which the archpriest mounted, clad in surplice and stole and car- rying smoking incense. He unlocked at least six locks and swung open the double doors, then descended and incensed the corporal, which was visible, yellowed but bearing unmistakable dark stains, behind plate glass. "I say," breathed Father Howell into my ear, "What an incredible religion!" But we had to go up, at risk of life and limb, and venerate the relic, though I was thinking of how we pile mystery on mystery and get further and further away from the simplicity of a certain Supper long ago, when the Lord took com- monplace things, good bread and table wine, and gave them to those he loved, to feed them with his body and blood.

After breakfast we strolled through the pretty town, stopping at a ceramics shop to admire the goods and wish that we could bring any number of them home. While we were there, the clerk suddenly laid her finger on her lips and quickly closed the doors of the shop and lowered the curtain—"*un funerale*," she said. A mo- ment later the cortege went by. There was a single car bearing the body; the mourners walked. Groups of men carried floral tributes, then came the priest, leading the rosary, then the mourners. We noticed that only the women in the procession recited the rosary; the men marched in silence. When we asked the owner about this, he said that there was too much human respect among Italian men; they could not bear to be thought devout. This was confirmed by the pastor at Todi, whom we met later in the day. He told us also that only six hundred of his fifteen hundred parishioners were practising—at his Mass that morning there had been only twelve Holy Communions—but that even these six hundred voted Communist regularly. We might have brushed this off as one of the mystifying inconsistencies of the Italian character, but, taken together with other data we had picked up, it was troubling—as, for example, the fact that there was only one seminarian to be ordained that year for the Diocese of Rome, and only one Jesuit scholastic for the Roman Province.

We drove off about noon across the hills in the soft Umbrian sunshine, and came to Todi. (Jacopone lived here and may have written the *Dies Irae* here, though I wished he hadn't. At least I wished that we wouldn't sing it at funerals.) Todi was another captivating town with a gorgeous view of the surrounding valley. The piazza, decorated as it was for the town *festa,* would have made a stunning set for an opera or for *Romeo and Juliet.* Father Howell wanted to take a different road home but succeeded only in going in a long circle ("a little vicious," the bishop observed with a sly chuckle), so as night drew on we took to the new *autostrada* and spun along into the outskirts of Rome, where we got ourselves properly lost and only by dint of many, many *"dove's"* found our way to the Jesuit Curia and dropped Father Howell. I, who had been the only driver, was drooping by this time, but revived when the bishop and the monsignor invited me to dinner at the house where they were living, and I had not only a generous meal but a delightful conversation with many bishops from France and North Africa—Algeria, Oran, Carthage.

Cardinal Cushing went home midway through the second session. He joked that because of his absence the collections for his charities were suffering—"I'm losing $20 thousand every day," he said. No doubt this was true; he had an inimitable and irreplaceable genius for fund-raising. But I think that his activist temperament simply could not endure the endless debates, most of which, as he ruefully acknowledged, he could not follow because they were in Latin, and in Latin spoken with European accents. He had offered twice to pay for a system of simultaneous translation. It was painful to see him in the council chamber, his craggy face frozen, holding himelf rigidly immobile.

Several of us Bostonians went over to the North American College to say goodbye, and someone complimented him on his address the previous day on the Jewish question. "You know who came up and complimented me on that yesterday?" he said. "Cardinal Ottaviani!" Then, with a wink, "But I know what was on his mind. His sister runs an orphanage, and she has been after me for a contribution!" A moment later, "How many are you? Wait a minute." He went into his bedroom and emerged shortly with six relics of St. Pius X, handsomely mounted in tiny reliquaries. "Give this to your mother," he said to each of us. Rome was colder and darker after he left.

I think often what a grace I have enjoyed in living during the time of popes like Pius XII, John XXIII, and Paul VI, and, in Boston, during the time of Richard Cushing. Possibly some facets of his personality might be evident in an address he gave at a dinner he sponsored annually for his charities. This one was in 1954, and there were almost a thousand people in attendance.

> Last year when you and I met together I talked to you about the wolf at the door. I told you that he was my favorite beast, that he kept me on the go, and that if I ever got to heaven I'd have the wolf at the door to thank for it. Such show of virtue as I manage to develop is due to the work I have had to do to keep the wolf away from the door!

> Well, since that happy evening a year ago, I came within a glimpse of heaven! I didn't get in, so I came home. I might as well tell you, here and now, that in spite of any rumors to the contrary, I came home to stay, to stay as long as God lets me, and that, please God, will be a long time indeed!

> While I was loitering around the gates of heaven I saw the birds of St. Francis flying about, high above the walls. There was also the eagle of St. John. I heard the dog of St. Roch barking to his heart's content, and I thought I heard a growl or two from the lion of St. Mark. There was a pretty lake nearby, and in it I saw the fishes of St. Anthony. But when I got home, there at the door was the wolf of Poor Richard!

> To tell you the truth, I think he was glad to see me. However, he snarled a bit, all the same, by way of reminding me to get back to work. And so I am glad to see so many of you and I am grateful to you for bringing to this banquet so many bones that I can throw at Poor Richard's mascot—the famous old wolf at the door!

> While I was sick I decided a number of things. One was that, even at the longest, life is too short for tears. I de-

cided that everything in this life should be a joy to the convinced Christian. I wish you the joy of hard work and prosperity in the year ahead—and, by the way, I plan to be here a year from tonight to take some of your prosperity away from you and add to your joy.

The critical decision of the Council to include the schema on Our Lady in the schema on the Church, instead of treating it separately, was preceded by some very sharp debate and was watched with considerable interest. When the vote was reported in the American press (at least in the international editions we saw in Rome), some language was used that could have caused perplexity at home. "Vatican Council Votes Smaller Role for Mary," was the *Herald-Tribune's* headline. "Council Votes De-Emphasis of Mary," said the Rome *Daily American.* The *Times* was more precise: "Schema on Mary Barred in Rome." (In general, the *Times* man, Mr. Milton Bracker, though Jewish, manifested a clear and comprehensive acquaintance with Catholic thought and won us all by his courtesy and humor.)

A few days before the Council's vote was taken, a panel of American theologians presented its views on the subject to the American hierarchy. Two bishops publicly credited the panel with having convinced enough of the Fathers of the soundness of their views to swing the conciliar decision; the vote was very close. But, as the panel's argument made clear, the vote did not in any way "let Our Lady down."

Father Barnabas Ahern, C.P., introduced the discussion by giving reasons against a separate schema. (a) Practical reasons: the Council was not writing a theological textbook to include all the Church's teachings; moreover, there was no separate schema on Christ our Lord, and should not be one on his mother. (b) Pastoral reasons: in many countries devotion to Our Lady runs to all manner of excesses; a Chilean bishop was quoted as saying that in some places there were two Catholic religions, one of Jesus and one of Mary. Giving Our Lady a place in the schema on the Church would put her in proper perspective. (c) Ecumenical reasons: there was no question of diluting Catholic teaching on Our Lady, or withdrawing from dogmatic positions already taken; the Orthodox would not accept this, nor would educated Protestants. We were trying to know Our Lady in relation to the Church, and if we should succeed she might come to be understood and loved by non-Catholics. (d) Critical reasons: the existing schema on Our

Lady was poor and incomplete. It omitted altogether, for example, all that modern scriptural studies had discovered in St. Luke's history of the Infancy. And the writings of the Greek Fathers were poorly represented.

Father Gene Maly gave a thorough exegesis of the Mariological *loci* in the Gospels (Luke's accounts of the Infancy and the Crucifixion and chapter 12 of Revelation) and drew two conclusions as to the question at issue: (1) the schema should begin with what Scripture tells us about Our Lady, and (2) she is important only in the context of salvation history, which is to say only in the context of the Church. Godfrey Diekmann, O.S.B., reviewed patristic teaching on Our Lady: the earliest of the Fathers, he said, spoke of her only in connection with Christ, but later she was described as "the second Eve" ("mother of all the living") and the prototype of the Church; the titles by which we salute her in the Litany of Loreto were applied also to the Church.

The last speaker, Father William Coyle, C.SS.R., reviewed recent theology on Mary, pointing out several difficulties in the existing schema. It stated, for instance, that Our Lady died, but this opinion could not be traced back any further than the seventh century, and Pius XII, feeling that it was not clear enough to include it in the definition of her Assumption in 1950, prescinded from it. The more common opinion today was that she did die, but there was still controversy on the point, and a definite assertion of it should not be included in a conciliar document. The schema also stated that Mary was conscious at the time of the Incarnation of the messiahship and divinity of her Son and accepted her role as his mother. This was at one time, indeed, the common belief, but it was now questioned by several Mariologists, who felt that Our Lady had had a progressive revelation on these points. They cited "his parents did not understand what he said to them" and thought that she began to grasp the situation at Cana. Again, on the topic of her mediation, all theologians agreed that Mary was a collaborator in the redemption, since she gave her Son the body he offered on the cross, but some questioned whether her resignation at the foot of the cross actually contributed anything to the price of human salvation. All theologians agreed, too, that she dispenses some of the fruits of the redemption, as the apostles were dispensers of the mysteries of God, and as all Christians dispense them, but many asked whether she were the cause of all grace—how did she cause grace in the saints of the Old Law, or how does she cause it in souls living today? The nature of the causality is far from clear. According to Pius XII, there was much in this problem that was still theologically immature; therefore he withdrew the feast of Our Lady Mediatrix of All Graces from the calendar and substituted for it a feast of the Queenship of Mary. Father Coyle concluded by saying that it would be better to have Our Lady included in the schema on the Church. Like all Christians she received the gifts of God, and we should not make her into a "fourth person of the Trinity." She was a prototype of the Church in that she practised all the virtues Christians are asked to practise—faith, humility, conformity to the divine will. Like the Church, she is "virgin of virgins," not only as to sexual purity but in her complete dedication to God. Like the Church, too, and by the usual divine paradox, she, though remaining a virgin, was made a mother.

When the Feast of All Saints fell on a Friday and an Italian national holiday on the following Monday, there was a short vacation for the Fathers of the Council. Bishop John McEleney, S.J., Bishop Vincent Kennally, S.J., Bishop Leverman of New Brunswick and I went off on a tour of Siena, Perugia, and Assisi. We tried to cover too much, actually, and it rained steadily almost all the time, so that the excursion was somewhat disappointing. I myself would have preferred to spend the whole time in Siena, which is an almost completely preserved medieval town. However, it was good to see again the town of St. Francis, which still holds so much of his enchanting personality and holiness, and to pray at his tomb and at the tomb of St. Clare. Her incorrupt body is still to be seen there, and not far away is San Damiano, her convent, with its tiny chapel and refectory—the inroads of termites on its tables have been halted—and the porch where, by holding up the Blessed Sacrament, she repelled the invading Saracens. Altogether, the story of Assisi is a fairy story, but with this immense difference, that it is true, and has every bit as much relevance today as it had in the 13th century. I have often envied the Franciscans their heritage and admired the wonderful way they keep it alive by their simplicity, joyfulness, and prodigal hospitality.

On the ecumenical front, so to speak, it seemed that there was some indisputable foot-dragging, but people hoped that before the end of this session a statement on religious liberty might reach the floor of the Council. Protestants in particular were watching this development, and felt that unless something strong on this subject came out of the Council the ecumenical movement would be seriously retarded. I attended a meeting of American theologians which was chaired by Father Stransky, the Paulist assistant to Cardinal Bea in the Secretariate for Unity, and addressed by Dr. Robert McAfee Brown, of Stanford, and Dr. Lukas Vischer, of the Faith and Order Commission of the World Council of Churches. Dr. Brown told us what he and many Protestants hoped would be included in the statement: (1) that faith is a gift of God, and cannot therefore be coerced, and that any effort to coerce it is sinful on this account. Dr. Brown felt that the statement should be theologically grounded in this way, i.e., on the nature of the act of faith rather than on expediency. He said (2) that the statement should make it clear that any faith may be proclaimed, since a person must bear witness to the faith of which he or she has become convinced. And (3) there must be accorded a right of association, because people so convinced should be able to join with others to express their faith corporately. And finally (4) that the Church should oppose and try to have removed civic penalties for the practice of any religion. Dr. Brown said that Protestants were agreed that there must be limitations on the expression of religious freedom, so that there would be no utter and absolute license, nothing against the common good. But he acknowledged that it is not easy to say what the limitations should be or who should impose them.

Dr. Vischer, a Swiss with a very gentle manner and a most winning smile, told us that even in the World Council it took forty years to get a common statement on religious liberty. It was finally adopted (at New Delhi) because, he thought, of an increase of fellowship among the churches of the Council, and this fellowship in turn derived not so much from a desire just to get along together as from an increasing awareness of Christian responsibility to bear a common witness to the world. The Council's statement distinguished proselytism (defined as the use of human means to impose belief) from witness, and condemned it.

In the discussion that followed, Father John Courtney Murray, S.J., said that the West must return to a sound and liberal political philosophy, which was lost, he said, at the rise of the classical French monarchy. Dr. Vischer shied away, it seemed to me, from any reliance on philosophy, as being merely human reasoning. He admitted that the religious heritage of a country is a good to be protected, but said that it is less and less possible today to have a completely closed society, owing to increased migration and to the growing awareness among all peoples of ecumenical problems and of the possibilities of mutual enrichment; nations were becoming more and more pluralistic.

Father Francis Connell, C.SS.R., made a careful distinction between the physical and moral freedom to believe, and the subjective and objective right to preach, that effectively terminated the discussion; no one could shed any light on the problems he raised. But Father James Finucan, of LaCrosse, made what seemed to me a very telling point when he said that the difficulties involved in making and applying such distinctions are clear evidence that religious freedom is essentially a question for theologians to settle, not the state. I myself shrank, however, from the idea that theologians might be employed by the state, or even might make their decisions and call in the secular arm to enforce them. No more Inquisitions, thank you.

Father Howell and I took advantage of an invitation to speak to the Holy Name Society of the American military in Naples and spent five days touring that city and its fabulous neighborhood. We climbed to the very top of Vesuvius' crater (the last stretch in a chair-lift), felt the live steam issuing from the rock, and shivered a bit when the guide said that the volcano erupts every twenty years. The last time was in 1944; what if the old monster should anticipate a little and suddenly shrug his massive shoulders now, under our feet? A day in Pompeii made us realize that here was nothing to trifle with. Of course that was not at all the only reflection we took away from Pompeii. There, as in the Roman Forum, half-forgotten classical lore returned to life. What a pity we could not have been transported here when we were reading classics long ago! We wandered all day through that eloquent, miraculously preserved city, its sophisticated culture evident on all sides. A verse of Swinburne's kept running through my mind as I thought of all those men and women whose "eyes went seaward a hundred"—no, two thousand!—"years ago."

The following day was unabashed luxury. We took a half-hour ride in a hydrofoil across the Bay to Capri, and found that, like Lake Louise in Canada, this was a tourist's attraction that really lived up to its advance notices. We dickered with an aging guide to take us to the Blue Grotto in his rowboat, beat him down a thousand lire on his asking price, and were so thoroughly delighted by the excursion that we gave him all he had originally asked and something more. Along the cliffs on the way to the Grotto the water is deep blue. You seem to be floating in a bowl of ink—it's that dark and viscous. But inside the Grotto some trick of light makes it water again—water, however, of such an un-earthly blue that you cry out with delight. The guide splashed it with his oar and sent up a shower of liquid amethyst.

Back at Marina Grande, the harbor, we went up by funicular railway to the town of Capri itself, and then by bus to Anacapri, a hamlet near the summit. Father Howell had to leave then, but I wandered for several hours through the streets and shops, looking at Axel Munthe's villa (San Michele), visiting Marina Piccola, and returning late in the afternoon to Capri for a cup of coffee and the privilege of sitting in the sun with the sea at my feet.

Colonel Leo Holly, of Worcester, took me to dinner that night at the NATO Officers' Club in Naples, and we met there Lieuten-ant Fred Howard, of Scarsdale, who generously offered to drive me next day along the Amalfi coast. So we set out in the morning in his Austin-Healy sports car, and were soon doing 85 and 90 miles an hour down the new *autostrada* to Salerno—a little too much ve-locity for my taste in any sort of car on any sort of road; it was like riding a projectile. Our first stop was Ravello, where there was a breath-taking view and a very interesting 11th-century cathe-dral. We had lunch at a restaurant in one of the towers along the road which looked Norman to me, but this one was called "*Il Saraceno.*" The scenery, as everyone knows, is incomparable, and deserves a much longer visit than I could give it, but perhaps one cannot live by scenery alone. The waiter at the restaurant evidently thought so. I overheard him asking Lieutenant Howard what my nationality was, so I turned and said, "*Sono Americano.*" "*Beato lei,*" he retorted. When we Americans celebrated our bicen-tennial in 1976 it was this incident that came back to me, and I kept saying gratefully to myself, "*Beato lei.*"

I loved Amalfi, with its cathedral and cloister, its sprawling homes and shops up and down the side of the cliff, its serene cove, but the town which took my eye forever and ever was Positano—here I could have remained forever, "the world forgetting, by the world forgot." We arrived at Sant' Agata, the very summit of the hills, at sunset, and looked down into the "*due golfi*" on either side, then coasted into Sorrento just at dusk, going on to Castellamare and plunging into the mad Naples traffic by way of a rude awakening to reality. My last morning I spent looking at the fabled Bay of Naples (my room afforded a 180-degree view of it), walking in the shadowed garden of the seminary, and strolling to the top of the Posilipo hill, about which my friends Fathers George

Smith and Bob Dyson, who had studied here years before, used to tell me so much. The train back to Rome was fast and smooth, and I was glad that it was to that perennially magical city I was returning after such a feast of color, beauty, and history. It would have been hard to return to a place distinguished by nothing save the drab, prosaic light of everyday.

November 22nd was the feast of St. Cecilia, a day for remembering a heroic girl and for relishing once more the lovely legends woven around her name. It was a significant anniversary for liturgists, too; on St. Cecilia's Day in 1903, sixty years before, Pope Pius X had published a *motu proprio* in which he asserted that "the primary and indispensable source of the true Christian spirit is active participation in the public and solemn prayer of the Church." We used to quote that flat, all-inclusive pronouncement several times a day during Liturgical Weeks. (Until *Mediator Dei* in 1947 it was about the only official utterance we could quote.) "Primary," we used to say, "that is, nothing is to be preferred to it. And indispensable: nothing can be substituted for it." On that anniversary—I'm sure it was more than a coincidence—the final approval of the schema on the liturgy was voted. During the first session of the Council the document had been endlessly debated— 329 bishops had made speeches supporting or opposing its every phrase—and it had been rewritten again and again. Now, at last, it was overwhelmingly approved and would be solemnly promulgated by the Pope and the Council on the last day of this session.

There are some events that demand celebration. Accordingly, a group of us who had been working for liturgical reform—Fathers Godfrey Diekmann, Fred McManus, Colman Barry, Vincent Yzermans—joined Bishop Leonard Haggerty of Nassau at the Rome Hilton for a jubilant dinner. We were having a merry time indeed when I noticed that the waiter was plucking at my sleeve, trying to get my attention. "Your *Presidente*," he said, "he have been shot." I pushed back my chair. "My President has been WHAT?" An American couple at a nearby table nodded confirmation; it was true. With a common impulse we left our dinners half-eaten and walked out. I turned up my coat collar, hoping I would not be identified, ashamed for the first time in my life of being an American.

CHAPTER 18

A New Day?

I'M SURE THERE MUST BE A SOUND BUSINESS REASON WHY ALMOST
every flight from the United States to Europe leaves in the evening. No doubt the canny travel agents persuade tourists that this
will give them an extra day for sightseeing. So they race at seven
hundred miles an hour to meet the sun, doing their best to snatch
uneasy catnaps. And since the last few days before leaving are
usually hectic, they are not in the most receptive mood for enjoying the beauties of the Old World when they arrive. In 1964 the
plane ride was the blow that killed Father, following as it did on a
busy summer and two weeks on the road. So on arrival in Dublin
I went to the Intercontinental Hotel, locked my door, and laid out
the body until the following morning, when there occurred a resurrection of sorts, and I developed an interest in bacon and eggs.

Let it be known that on one Saturday in September, 1964 no
rain fell on Dublin. I suspect that this was a thing scarcely heard
of since Patrick's time; certainly it had not occurred during any of
my previous visits, and on the next day, Sunday, the downpour
more than made up for it. It's easy to see why the Irish have such
warm hearts; they have to have them to withstand the cold and
damp of their native air. But there's no doubt about the warm
hearts. Sean and Kathleen O'Siochain, who are cousins of Father
Shawn Sheehan of Boston, had me in for supper and then took me
to the Abbey Tavern for the evening. This was a shed of the sim-
plest imaginable construction, roofed with a sheet of galvanized
iron. About a hundred and fifty people crowded in to sit at rude
tables and listen to the music and singing of a group of young people who played pipes, an accordion, and a fiddle, and sang genuine
Irish songs—not the synthetic type composed on Broadway like
"Galway Bay" or "Ireland Must Be Heaven." Some of the songs
were lovely and some were merry; the audience joined in on many
choruses, and I enjoyed watching the animated, glowing faces.

These were not the Angry Young Men (or Women) I had left behind me; they sang their patriotic songs without self-consciousness
and their ballads with verve and zest. I was impressed, also, with
the fact that although the performers had been singing together for
more than a year, they listened attentively to each of their own so-
loists as if they were hearing them for the first time—a rare and
delightful courtesy.

Next day was too short, but I did manage reunions with my
friends Hamilton Delargy, director of the Irish Folklore Commission, and Michael Hayes, former Speaker of the Lower House of
the Dail and now Senator. I had met them in the course of an unforgettable trip to Clonmel in 1946, when I was hunting for relatives and they were gathering folk tales in the vicinity of
Slievenamon. (For any unfortunates who may not know of
Slievenamon, let me tell them swiftly that it is the home of King
Brian Connors and the Good People, and recommend earnestly that
they read a charming book on the subject called *Darby O'Gill and
the Good People*, by Hermione Kavanagh.[1]) My grandfather was
born in the shadow of that mountain, but it has other claims to
fame, and Professors Delargy and Hayes did more than most to
vindicate them. Delargy started in the twenties of this century to
gather materials for a social history of Ireland, and now there is an
archive containing a million and a quarter pages of manuscript,
plus records, tapes, drawings, paintings, and artifacts. His work in
preserving the tradition of the Irish people was recognized by honorary degrees from the Universities of Edinburgh, Belfast, Wales,
Iceland, Dublin, and several others; he had a decoration from the
King of Norway and another from the President of Iceland, and he
was largely instrumental in setting up the School of Scottish Studies at the University of Edinburgh and the Manx Museum on the
Isle of Man. For many years he dreamed that the Church might
establish an archive of folklore of the peoples in the mission fields.
It would not only educate prospective missionaries in the culture of
the people they hoped to evangelize, but also provide a collection
of primary materials for scholars in linguistic, ethnological, and an-
thropological sciences by the one agency most able to bring it together. His efforts to interest the Congregation for the Propagation
of the Faith in the project having failed, he turned at my sugges-

---

1.   New York, 1903.

tion to Cardinal Cushing, but for some reason I never fathomed the Cardinal, who was usually very interested in the missions, did not warm to the idea. We do now have several programs, like the one at Maryknoll, for those going to the missions and for the renewal of veterans in the field, but nothing, so far as I know, on the scale Delargy envisioned.

It would be difficult to summarize the following week, during which I saw at first hand so many boyhood *pietates.* Any week that would include Glastonbury and Stratford-on-Avon would be uniquely wonderful, but there was much more. I took the little Anglia (an English Ford) into the choked stream of the traffic outside London Airport with fear and trembling; I was feeling for an unfamiliar shift with an awkward hand, my left, and I was driving on the wrong side of the road. There were then no speed limits between towns in England, and Her Majesty's subjects whipped along those narrow roads at sixty and seventy. So I was content to call it a day when I reached Winchester. A leisurely exploration of the cathedral (Jane Austen's grave is there, by the way) took up the late afternoon, and, after supper in the "Buttery" of the Wessex Hotel, I was glad to think of knitting up the raveled sleave. Next morning I had a delightful stroll along the serene banks of the local stream and through the grounds of Winchester College, founded by Henry VI and in reputation second only to Eton among English "public" schools. I liked very much a Latin inscription I found in the college chapel: "Fifty years ago a benefactor gave these glass windows so that you who look on their man-made beauty might conclude what that Beauty might be that lasts forever. The same benefactor gave this bell, whose voice admonishes you to think on what you owe to God and what, according to God's wishes, you should want to render to your neighbor. Depart, then, determined that today you will prove yourself neither blind nor deaf."

Out on the road again, in a lashing rain, I was struck by the politeness of the signs. There were no billboards (when shall we outlaw the hideous things?); directions were small but visible. We are accustomed to curt orders and demands: "No Passing," "Keep Out," "Strictly Private," and so on. The English post courteous signs reading "Please do not obstruct," or even "The directors kindly request . . ." Nothing could surpass the neatness and orderliness of the countryside and the towns, or the cordiality shown to visitors, or the even temper and good humor of shopkeepers and landlords and civil servants. One got the impression, too, that the whole island had been made into a garden. Late summer flowers—asters, salvia, marigold—clustered in every dooryard and made one want to stop and gladden his eye at leisure. "A garden *is* a lovesome thing, God wot!"

At Salisbury the sun was shining and the cathedral, dedicated to Our Lady of the Assumption, stood, gray and weathered, in its close of green lawn. On the high street just back of it was St. Osmund's Roman Catholic Church, so tiny in relation to the cathedral that it looked like a dory tethered to an ocean liner. As I came out from a visit there I met the parish priest and his assistant and chatted with them. Their views on the present use of the cathedral were not, I'm afraid, altogether ecumenical; it was from them that I heard for the first time the mocking phrase "mixed bathing" to describe ecumenical activities.

Touring one of these great cathedrals is like reviewing one's history of England. The knights of the Crusades lie, sculptured in marble on their tombs, silent these seven hundred years. One notes that the dates of a bishop's reign are inscribed on his tomb, and that they coincide with the reign of Henry VIII, or Mary, or James I. What account of his stewardship was the poor man able to give? The regimental colors that flew bravely with Clive in India or in the Crimea or when Mafeking was relieved are falling to tatters on the walls. And then there are the terribly frequent and pathetic memorials to Second Lieutenant So-and so, who fell at Ypres in 1916, or to Colonel Sir John Such-and-such, who died of wounds suffered in the withdrawal from Dunkirk in 1940. It should not be concluded, however, that the cathedrals are only historical museums; they retain a genuine atmosphere of prayer, and several times I sat and listened with devotion and gratitude to Evensong.

Having been brought up in Dorchester and spent much of my boyhood in Milton, I moved into Dorset with interest. This was Thomas Hardy's country, too, and it was easy to see poor Tess, all Hardy's dice loaded against her, moving across the rather desolate fields to the black flag that marked her unhappy end. When I saw a sign marked "Milton Abbas" I decided that I couldn't pass this up. The English Milton has a long and interesting history. It started in the ninth century with a Saxon chapel, still standing. In the tenth century it became an abbey, so that when I was there it was celebrating its thousandth anniversary. Major Harrison, repre-

sentative of a fund-raising firm that had been retained by the
Church of England to collect money for the restoration of the
place, showed me around. There was a very lovely Jesse window
and a hanging tabernacle (empty, of course) which is the only one
of its kind left in England. After the dissolution of the monasteries
under Henry VIII, the Abbey became a private home, but the
owner was so offended by the odors that kept coming between the
wind and his nobility that he tore down all the neighboring cot-
tages and built new ones some distance away, thus creating the
first model homes. These, too, were still standing, and very
charming they were. The Abbey was now a boys' school, and the
boys used the chapel daily. The Major and I had dinner together
(most of the tourists had gone home, and he was at leisure), and
went back then to see the church floodlighted. He told me that a
stone from the church had been sent to Milton, Massachusetts, and
incorporated into the First Parish Church there, in the village not
far from the Five Corners and the Library where Wil and I had
spent so many happy hours forty years before; this was an item
that gave me great pleasure. I became a "Friend of Milton Abbey"
and resolved to send some of the literature about it to George
Ryan, was was writing in the *Pilot* about the relations between
places in Old and New England. That night I was snugly bedded
down in the "Milton Arms," and so spent my first night in an authentic English inn.

It was interesting to see so many Italians as porters in the hotels and waiters in the restaurants; I had not suspected that they
had immigrated in such numbers. Their soft, slurred English contrasted strangely with the clipped, precise speech of the natives. I
wondered how they got their tongues around some of the English
place-names, which are by turns utterly lovely, like Saffron Walden
and Burnt Fen and Walgrave St. Peter's, or banal, like Six Mile
Bottom and Staple Bumpstead and Upton Snodsbury, or incomprehensible, like Chew Magna and Nether Wallop. There are Norman
echoes, I suppose, in Hetton-le-Hole, Poulton-le-Fylde, and Strat-
ton-on-the-Fosse. I should like to live in a place so romantically
named as Waltham-on-the Wolds or Weston super Mare or Cradley
Heath, but imagine giving as your birthplace the village of Seaton
Sluice or Toller Porcorum or Hartburn!

Next day I went through Dorchester in pouring rain, but the
skies were clearing as I turned off to see Lyme Regis, a popular
seaside resort where the Channel was lashing the breakwater, and

hundreds of small craft, the season being over, were waiting to be stored away for the winter. It wasn't a very attractive place, and it decided me not to go on down through Cornwall, though I had always associated Cornwall with King Arthur and Dickens' *Great Expectations* and had wanted to see a place as well named as Land's End. Instead, after seeing the very pretty cathedral in Exeter (Richard Blackmore, author of *Lorna Doone*, is buried there), I swung northwest through the congested towns of Bridwater and Taunton and arrived in Glastonbury, a much belated pilgrim, at dusk. There was literally no room in the inn, but Father Sean McNamara, the pastor, generously shared his presbytery with me. He had a Legion of Mary meeting during the evening, but that gave me time to read his copy of Hugh Williamson's *The Flowering Thorn* and so to brush up on the history and legends of Glastonbury. He came in then and we talked popular liturgy and allied topics until the small hours. When I apologized for keeping him up so late he said, "Ah, but the crack was good," and I recalled that Michael Hayes had used that phrase, too; what they meant was that the conversation had been worthwhile.

Everyone, I imagine, has some knowledge of the Arthurian legends, at least in Tennyson's version, and so the name of Glastonbury calls up dancing visions of the Holy Grail, and the Table Round, and Launcelot and Galahad and Mordred's treachery and Bedivere's throwing of Excalibur into the mere, where a hand "clothed in white samite, mystic, wonderful" reached up and drew it under. What seems not to be so familiar is the legend that our Lord visited Glastonbury before his public life. You don't believe this, eh? Well, read Williamson and maybe you will be "not incredulous but believing." The immense Abbey and Church of Our Lady at Glastonbury is only a ruined shell now; "the proud high sanctuaries are dust," as Wilfred Childe wrote sadly, and the grave of King Arthur is only conjectural. But I was awed and happy to offer Mass in Father McNamara's little church of St. Mary across the street from such dead splendors, dating back perhaps to "St." Joseph of Arimathea. Who knows? Maybe "a greater than he was here."

This story is getting too long and I should follow Quiller-Couch's advice to writers about "murdering their darlings." The little Anglia and I pushed on to Bath, where I saw the imposing palaces of the Restoration and the warm baths of the Romans, and then through the Cotswolds to Cheltenham, Evesham, and Stratford.

Although this was Shakespeare's quadricentennial, the town was not as crawling with tourists as I had feared it might be, and I had a perfectly lovely morning to stroll along the Avon's beautiful banks to Trinity Church and Shakespeare's grave, admiring the graceful swans in the river as I walked. Ronald Gower's statue had made me think of someone's characterization of Shakespeare as "the first modern," and so the prayer that came spontaneously as I leaned over the grave was Hamlet's line to his father's ghost, "Rest, rest, perturbed spirit." How immense a debt of inspiration and pleasure I owed to this man! It would be consoling to think that he had indeed attained, after the merriment of *Twelfth Night*, the torments of *Lear*, and the sour disillusionment of *Timon* and *Troilus*, to the serene harmonies of *The Tempest*. That night I reveled in a production by the superb Royal Shakespeare Company of *Edward IV*, a telescoping of the three parts of *Henry VI*, magnificently staged and acted, an intoxicating piece of pageantry that sent me to bed light-headed.

My last day on the road took me to Coventry, where I saw the ruins of the cathedral bombed by the Nazis in 1940, and next to it the really glorious new cathedral opened only two years before. Anyone aspiring to build a new church should go to Coventry. The use of contemporary materials, especially of glass, is striking evidence that the Gospel can be expressed in an idiom comprehensible to modern men and women, and that we need not go on copying the styles of the dead past. I was taken particularly with the glowing baptistry window, the Chapel of Unity, the mosaic of the Agony, and the Chapel of Christ the Servant—the latter idea a grateful change from the "triumphalism" so evident in Rome, and one that kept coming up in the deliberations of the Council. Incidentally, I saw at this time pictures of the model of the cathedral being planned then by Archbishop McGucken for San Francisco, and thought how good it was that he, too, was building for our own age. My English tour ended at what was then our scholasticate, Heythrop College, in Chipping Norton not far from Oxford.

And so to Rome, where, alas, my first and all-pervading impression after England was of dirt and noise, especially of noise. The number of Italians now in a position to buy cars, I reflected, must be much larger than when I first saw Rome immediately after the war. By day and by night the streets were torrents of traffic, the cars being augmented by scooters, motorcycles, buses, trucks, and nondescript vehicles on three wheels, all going at full throttle, many without benefit of mufflers. The cacophony had to be heard to be believed. The Italian Tourist Bureau posted signs all over the city, asking *libertà dal rumore* (freedom from noise), but they had no effect. It scared me to think that with the multiplication of cars at home we might be in for some such perpetual tumult as this, destructive of sleep, concentration, and peace of mind.

The third session of the Council moved more resolutely and swiftly than either of its predecessors. Epoch-making decisions on collegiality, religious liberty, relations with non-Christian religions made it clear that the *aggiornamento* of Pope John was becoming an achieved fact. It seemed certain that the era of absolutism was over, that there would be much more free inquiry and opinion; in fact, one of the Protestant observers said that we had opened a Pandora's box, and hoped we could deal with what came out of it. Things were moving so fast that the Council was half-way through the schema on divine revelation and the inspiration of Scripture— the issue which had divided the progressives and the conservatives so dramatically two years before. Speeches were now being prepared on the lay apostolate and the all-important statement on the Church in the modern world, which would, we hoped, take strong positions on such problems as human dignity, the community of nations, hunger, peace, the population explosion, the economic order, the family, and so on. Could the Council finish all this before the end of the session? There was an obvious effort being made by the General Secretariat to do so, and the "Immovables" like Cardinal Ruffini, though they still insisted on presenting their negative views, seemed to have lost hope of winning the battle, while Cardinal McIntyre, who was of course old and weak, had gone home.

We speculated a great deal on how collegiality would be worked out in the concrete. Would the Pope appoint a "senate" of bishops to govern the Church with him? Would the regional conferences of bishops elect such a senate? What would be the authority of these regional conferences? Since it would be incongruous for bishops to be giving orders to Roman congregations headed by cardinals, did this mean that there would be no more cardinals? If so, how would the Popes of the future be chosen? By this senate? Our mystification might have been tartly summed up by an unknown wit some years after the Council ended:

> Vatican One, for good or ill,
> Declared the Pope infallible.
> Vatican Two, the recent sequel,

Made Pope and bishops more co-equal.
And that is why ('twixt you and me)
The Pope isn't calling Vatican Three.[2]

My sadly missed friend Father John Ryan once recited a coda for that rhyme (he never told me whether it was original with him, but he obviously relished it):

But should there be a Vatican Three,
Each bishop with his wife will be.
And if there were a Vatican Four,
Each bishop would have one husband or more.

It was heartening to see in this session the active participation of the American hierarchy, which up till now had been diffident and generally silent as the two European wings of opinion collided. In fact, the speakers on religious liberty were so exclusively American that the steering committee was looking for bishops of other nationalities to speak and make the interest in the problem seem more universal. Cardinal Cushing's two addresses attracted the interest of everyone in the Council chamber, and he himself was delighted by the experience. He left before the session ended; "If I stay I'll be bankrupt," he told us. There had been a constant stream of cardinals, bishops, priests, and sisters visiting him at the North American College—all looking for help on some good project, and most of them getting it generously. But he left an indelible mark behind him when he spoke to the Council "not only in my own name but also in the name of almost all the bishops of the United States," and insisted that the declaration on religious liberty should be approved. "If I may quote words famous in our American history," he said in his last intervention, "Such a declaration would manifest 'a decent respect for the opinions of mankind.'"

When Pope John convoked the Council, he asked us all to pray earnestly for its success. And, across the Christian world (and perhaps outside it), we did. The result? It does not seem too much to say, thirty years later, that we were given a new Pentecost. From Pope John's opening address, the thrust of the Council was pastoral, i.e., solicitous, caring, compassionate. John called for "the medicine of mercy rather than the weapon of severity." He

2. Quoted in a speech by Bishop James Malone of Youngstown and reported in *Origins,* 27 June 1974.

said that the "prophets of doom," who, "though burning with zeal, are not overly endowed with a sense of discretion or judgment," and "say constantly that our era, in comparison with the past, is growing steadily worse," were to be ignored, and they were. He wanted this Council to "persuade men and women to welcome the good news of salvation more favorably," and certainly the suasive approach taken by the Council was more conducive to this end than anathemas and excommunications.

Young people today can only imagine what the Catholic world was like before they came on the scene. Father Yves Congar, O.P., himself one of the most influential theologians at the Council, tries to picture it:

> I would like to begin by saying something about the re-sponsibility of the Council for what people call the crisis. In my view, the Council does indeed bear some responsi-bility, but that is inseparable from the grace and benefits which it has brought to the Church and even, one might say, to the world. This benefit has mainly taken the form of a departure from Tridentism. By that I do not mean the Council of Trent itself but Tridentism as it was defined by Giuseppe Alberigo, in particular in his three lectures at the Collège de France. This Tridentism is a system developed *after* the Council of Trent under the influence of three very conservative Popes—Paul IV, Pius V, and Sixtus Quintus —who were followed by others. It was a system which took in absolutely everything: theology, ethics, Christian behavior, religious practices, liturgy, organiza-tion, Roman centralization, the perpetual intervention of Roman congregations in the life of the Church, and so on."[3]

Father Congar cites a French sociologist, who says, "The Counter-Reformation was essentially concerned to bring the faithful into line on the basis of an effort at doctrinal clarification and the development of a totalitarian catechesis which divided the world into the thinkable and the unthinkable, the prescribed and the forbidden" (p. 4). But "people have gone on thinking since Trent and Vatican I, and the world has changed," Father Congar notes, and so a Swiss Jesuit, Father Mario von Galli, points to three dom-

---

3.   *Fifty Years of Catholic Theology*, Philadelphia, 1988 p. 3.

inant trends of Vatican II: "from a law-centered to a life-centered Church, from defensiveness to dialogue, from fixed ideas to historical change."[4]

I was especially privileged during this third session of the Council to live in a *pensione* operated by German nuns. (You could eat off the gleaming floors). It was known as "the house of the rebels," and some uncomplimentary remarks were passed among the conservatives about its proximity to the Roman zoo. Monsignor John Quinn of Chicago was the moving spirit of the house; he had assembled most of the residents and he regularly invited guests who, he shrewdly foresaw, would stimulate lively discussion. So, at dinner and often far into the night, we listened to and argued with people like Father Yves Congar, O.P., Father Hans Küng, Father John Courtney Murray, S.J., Father George Higgins, Father (later Bishop) William McManus, Monsignor Luigi Ligutti, Monsignor (now Cardinal) William Baum, Bishops Ernest Primeau and Charles Helmsing, and many—very many—others. John Cogley, covering the Council for the Kansas City *Reporter* (now the *National Catholic Reporter*),[5] described this community of laughter and good talk: it was "a group of bishops and priests, almost all Americans, who for the duration of the Council have formed a kind of loose-knit community in a large *pensione* open only to the clergy. This house is a beehive of activity, discussion, and clerical camaraderie. It is visited by eminent non-American Fathers, who enjoy participating in the discussions held there, and has become not only a center of intellectual power and influence but the most 'in' place for the American clergy in Rome to live. A room in the *pensione* Villa Nova is now roughly the clerical equivalent of a listing in the Social Register."

Our mood at the time, and certainly mine as I came home, was decidedly euphoric. To see so much being realized that one had dreamed of and in one's own small way striven for—a revitalized worship of God in our own language, a new awareness of the Church as (Congar again, p. 43) "a spiritual communion, a communion on the basis of the Word of God received in faith and grace," a progressive deliverance from form and legalism and authoritarianism, a leading out of the People of God free—this was joy indeed.

4.　*The Council and the Future*, New York, 1966, p. 63.
5.　24 October 1964

There would be obstacles, confusion, even ferment, no doubt, and the reactionaries would dispute every last issue. Still, it would seem churlish and mistrustful of our generous Lord, who had given so much so swiftly, not to be serene and optimistic about the future. One felt this even with the headlines about Vietnam and the Congo before him, even though the horror of President Kennedy's assassination still haunted and depressed the mind, even though the blacks were still second-class citizens and millions still suffered from hunger and disease. We had been shown with new clarity what a Christian is, and where his witness must be given in the twentieth-century world. There seemed, moreover, a wonderful resolution on the part of many—priests, religious, laity—to respond generously to the graces of the time. I could not help feeling that the future would be strenuous, but it would be better, purer.

Thirty years later, the euphoria has evaporated. One begins to see that the profound psychological changes called for by the Council simply could not have come about overnight. A whole generation—maybe two generations—would have to pass from the scene. Cardinal Hume observed recently that "Vatican II has not yet got into our bloodstream." So far as liturgical renewal is concerned, there has been progress, unquestionably, but most of it seems to have been related to externals—nice externals, even indispensable externals, but externals none the less. We had, after all, to devise a new liturgical language, a new music, a new architecture, a new art. And this has been so engrossing that we have spent our energies on how to do it, neglecting to say, clearly and with great emphasis and unwearying repetition, what it is that we do, and why we do it. In other words, we have not taught a sound and comprehensible theology of worship. It was available, in the Council's decrees, in the writings of the pioneers. But so far liturgy has not generally been presented as "the primary and indispensable source of the true Christian spirit," "an action of Christ the priest and of his body the Church, a sacred action surpassing all others," "the summit toward which the activity of the Church is directed, and at the same time the fountain from which all her power flows"—which was the language of the Council. So, much as we divided our liturgical celebrations from our devotional practices in the old days before the Council, we have kept rigidly separate our participation in the liturgy from our private, highly individualistic piety, from our efforts to attain social justice, from the

Christian witness we are expected to bear before the world. We have yet to see that "it all goes together," that all life is worship.

Bishop Aloysius Wycislo, late of Green Bay, published recently his recollections of the Council: *Vatican II Revisited: Reflections by One who Was There.*[6] He worries (p. 173) that future Catholics may be estranged from the Church because of our slack implementation of the conciliar documents. "As I look back," he says, "more than two decades after Vatican II, I must re-emphasize that most of its documents had little or no follow-up. We have reached a point in Church history at which it needs to be said that the Council created many expectations which have yet to be fulfilled. There's been a progressive clouding of the significance of Vatican II. The 'heresy' of the traditionalists who confuse restoration with renewal perdures. Although there was hope that the 1985 Extraordinary Synod of Bishops called by Pope John Paul II to assess the impact of the Council provided some clearing of the air, the fact remains that this Synod did not generate formidable plans to bring the Council documents into life again" (p. 174).

The Bishop sees a new source of inspiration and dedication, however. "In recent years we have witnessed a vibrant growth of lay ministry alongside the ordained ministry. This has been one of the blessings of the post-conciliar Church. The laity in the United States, especially, have come forward in increasing numbers to be of service in the pastoral life of the Church."

Which takes us back to Father Congar again: "We (the clergy) are the repository of the message of salvation, but sometimes it is others (the laity) who liberate."[7] And one speculates: were not Benedict, Francis, Ignatius, who spearheaded renewal in their day, all laypeople, at least when they began their work?

Bishop Byrne of Wichita, whose Liturgical Commission published the booklet, "New Horizons in Catholic Worship" that I wrote in 1964, told me that it had sold at that time some 76,000 copies. This was most gratifying, of course, but it served as a reminder that I should be producing more of the same instead of traipsing around Europe. I would have to pay court to Duty, "stern daughter of the voice of God." But there was time for one last fling. Four of us—Father Joe Grant, editor of Boston's diocesan

---

6.   New York, 1987.
7.   Id., p.20.

paper, the *Pilot*, Father Bob Quinn of the Paulist Information Center in Boston, Father Jack Joyce, editor of the Oklahoma Catholic paper, the *Courier*, and myself—drove down the *autostrada* toward Naples, but swung off after some forty miles and took a country road across the hills toward the sea. We were fortunate in coming upon a small town where a *festa*—a combined celebration of the Feast of the Holy Rosary and of St. Francis, Patron of Italy—was being celebrated. The main street was lined with booths in which all manner of goods were offered for sale, and as we looked them over a rather ragged procession, led by a band and brought up by the parish priest carrying a relic—presumably of St. Francis and not of Our Lady, though one cannot always be sure in Italy— marched past us. We were all struck, I think, by the cleavage between this world and the world we had been living in. How would one go about explaining collegiality to these peasants? On the other hand, we noticed that the "peasants" were quite well dressed, and that among the things offered for their purchase were record players, television sets, automobile accessories, etc. In one breath we could sympathize a little with the conservative Italian bishops who wanted to retain the "simple faith" of their people. But it was evident that the era of such simplicity was over and gone, and that the Church, if she were not to lose touch altogether with her children, must see them as they really are, must answer their questionings and incarnate herself in the life they are living today.

We drove away and came at last to Terracina, where we ate *pasta* and chicken in the warm afternoon with the waves lapping gently at our feet. It was almost dusk by the time we reached Anzio and found the American cemetery there. We could be proud of it; it was a lovely place. At the same time it was infinitely pathetic: 7500 graves of young Americans, and almost an equal number of names of the missing inscribed on the monument. Fragments of the Gettysburg Address kept running through my mind, and I thought of the other American cemeteries I had seen, in Normandy and Cambridge and Manila and Maastricht, and of the 3500 young men I had myself buried at Santa Barbara in Luzon. Somehow, we thought, with God's grace we must not let this happen again, ever, ever. We got back to Rome at the height of the Sunday evening traffic, and the incredible tumult and turmoil made me think of the movie that had been showing in the States that summer, "It's a Mad, Mad, Mad, Mad World." The movie was then being shown in Italy, and the Italian name seemed somehow more expressive: *"Questo Pazzo, Pazzo, Pazzo, Pazzo Mondo."* But in spite of its madness, God continues to love our world, and the Council provided one of the best proofs of this. *Gloria in excelsis.*

I heard that a chartered plane was going to carry priests and bishops back to Montreal and Chicago when this session of the Council ended, and I went to see Monsignor (now Archbishop) Marcinkus, who was arranging the journey. With cordial kindness he put me aboard the flight. There were 96 bishops and three priests beside myself, and as we took off I said to the Canadian bishop who sat beside me, "This plane would make quite a splash if it landed in the Atlantic." "Might be the best thing that ever happened to the Church," he growled.

CHAPTER 19

Revolution in Progress

IN A MORE LEISURELY AGE, THE FAMILIAR ESSAY WAS A POPULAR literary form. Hazlitt and Lamb, at least in one man's opinion, practised it most delightfully and gave its characteristic gentility and gloss, though others came later, like Leigh Hunt, Stevenson, Christopher Morley. The tone of the familiar essay indicated that conversation was in order. No controversy was intended; often it was clear that nothing of any major moment would be brought up. The author—who evidently could hold his own, if he chose, in a serious discussion—preferred for the moment to tread softly, to introduce topics without examining them in full detail or offering any solutions for problems. It was playful, if you like, but it was civilized. It recognized that one cannot always live, think, or talk at fever pitch. It acknowledged, as a wise man must, that there are things about which it is possible to have two opinions, and neither the last. It allowed for humor, for large-mindedness, for tolerance. It permitted things to be seen against the background of the total human experience and to assume their proper dimensions.

Very often the tone of the familiar essay was set by its title: "On Going a Journey," "Poor Relations," "A Dissertation upon Roast Pig," "An Apology for Idlers," "A Gossip on Romance," "On Running after One's Hat." Very often, in fact, one could detect the mood the writer intended by the presence in the title of the preposition "on." Hilaire Belloc used to collect at intervals the essays he wrote for the daily press and publish them in book form, but he avowed, after naming successive volumes "On Everything," "On Anything," "On Nothing and Kindred Subjects," that he had run out of generic titles and would call his latest collection simply "On."

The present writer knows sadly that he cannot boast the wit, the charm, or the acuteness of the great tradition. Even if he had all these he would not attract many readers, probably, in the present age, which reads "articles" instead of essays, and looks for information rather than for discussion, for argument rather than conversation. In wartime the gentler arts suffer, and our world has been at war since 1914. Television and the jet plane, moreover, are at once too noisy, too headlong, to encourage urbane thinking out loud. They destroy the atmosphere which might invite a man to put on view the intellectual curios he has acquired in a lifetime of reflection. It is unpatriotic, or frivolous in the light of the Present Situation, or anyhow inopportune, to be playful.

I once wrote a piece called "On Being Caught in a Revolution." The title, probably, was enough to condemn it. (It was rejected, actually, by several magazines, and never published.) Clearly, the author of such a piece could not be Wholly Serious. Revolutions, even palace revolutions, are grave matters in these days when a coup in Managua or Jakarta can bring the Security Council together in Washington. And as for being caught in one, has the writer ever waked up to the chatter of machine guns and the rumble of tanks outside his quiet hotel? Has he ever been pleasantly entertained by a mob screaming "American go home"? Does he think he would have enjoyed the amenities of life in St. Petersburg under Lenin or in Havana after Castro had marched in?

Well, no. One may be brave in the face of physical danger, and even stoical in enduring pain. One cannot be said to enjoy the experience. But you see how the modern reader reacts instantaneously, with taut nerves, to a suggestion of this kind, as one who has seen too much evil at close range. As the Doctor said of Lady Macbeth, "She hath known what she should not."

Let's suppose, however, that the revolution has been bloodless, and, though no one has been hurt in the process, a government diametrically opposed to the previous one is now in the saddle. New faces in the Capitol, new voices in the Chamber, new ideologies in the press, new laws on the books, new forms to fill out, new and odious routines to follow. Let's suppose, too, that even among our friends we discover enthusiastic converts to the change, and suddenly realize that we are considered old-fashioned, out-of-step, reactionary, even in the way. We are asked questions we cannot answer because they touch on matters we never thought about before, and which, indeed, we would have regarded as beyond question. Our teachers had never mentioned such things. When we were young (and that was not so long ago, either, by George), people observed the decencies a little better. We'd see what all these bright ideas would come to, and whether they'd do any more than we had to bring about a brave new world. Meanwhile we'd continue to call the shots as we saw them. We might have to conform outwardly to the new regulations, because the government was really putting on the pressure—and getting help from people we would have trusted to stand on their own two feet—but that didn't mean we had to agree with them.

One wonders what happened to all such champions of the Ancien Régime in the revolutions of the past. Did they go their increasingly solitary way until the grave closed over their protest? Did they lend their prayers and energies to Bonnie Prince Charlie, the "Young Pretender," to Don Carlos or the Archduke Otto, in a romantic but hopeless effort to recover a lost world? Were some—the younger among them, anyway—able to readjust, to re-educate themselves, to see how the world had changed and that they had to change with it, and that this involved no compromise of principle, really, but a broadening of horizons and a seeing of things as they were? Not very likely, one supposes. The mold is set early, and is not easily broken. Nor does one lay aside easily the sentiments, prejudices, habits developed during one's middle years. Bewilderment hardens as a rule into resentment.

Of course it is not pleasant to be swamped by the Wave of the Future, especially if it catches you when you are not looking. But one wonders a little why the Wave does take so many unawares. Nowadays we have warnings of imminent hurricanes, blizzards, stock market slumps, icy roads, and other threats to our well-being. Could some genius not invent a barometer for public opinion, or a radar device that would broadcast a Distant Early Warning about human needs smoldering and smoking away and getting dangerously close to explosion? How good is our education if it does not equip us to read the signs of the times? Or is it that, for too many, education ends with the diploma and the degree, the college textbook is the last serious book one reads, the commencement address is the last lecture one attends? No wonder, then, if one flunks out ingloriously thirty years later. The world has a way of coming up with new material for examinations.

Writers like Alvin Toffler have attempted to chronicle the changes that have come over the world since, say, the beginning of the present century; more, they have tried to show that the speed of change has increased year by year. It's been like a ride on a roller-coaster, a snail's pace at first, but then such a jerking acceleration as pins the patrons against their seats in panic. Tennyson, though he lived in the last century, saw as poets do what the future would bring: "Let the great world spin forever down the ringing grooves of change." One can only hope that the car will somehow stay on the rails.

So things are different. Are they better? That might be answered, Irish fashion, by asking another question: would you go back to where we were?

Well, now. In religious matters that would mean, wouldn't it, going back to legalism, authoritarianism, the siege mentality, bickering among the sects, Father Knows Best, petty tyranny in the name of God. It would mean going back to an imposed obscurantism in Scripture and Theology. To a moral code that seriously infringed on the freedom wherewith Christ has set us free. To a liturgy frozen solid since 1570, in which baptized Christians had no role except that of spectators. I think the only possible answer to the question would be a soft but ever-so-firm one: no. Not ever.

What we have now is not, God knows, a well-ordered Paradise. We must still grope toward the light, resigned to never having all of it, but striving to keep what we have and get as much more as we can. We have had a bruising ride, and not a few have tumbled out of the car; on the other hand, it has been a rich experience to have come across eighty years from There to Here, and to sense profoundly, almost with a shudder, how enormous that distance was. On that score, at least, a good time to have lived in. Many prophets and kings would have given a lot to see it.

We seem in this chapter to have come a long way, too, from the mood of the familiar essay. Wasn't argument about serious matters prohibited? Yes, but, as Chesterton said, "Only the serious man can be truly hilarious." And one would like, as the thread winds down, to be hilarious.

I settled in gratefully with the very congenial community at Evanston and tried to establish a daily schedule for writing. But the invitations to lecture on the Council, especially on its program for liturgical renewal, were many and difficult to refuse. At the end of 1965 I counted 198 lectures, sermons, retreat conferences, and the like, which I had given that year, with an estimated audience of 26,250. Sean O'Faolain, in his autobiography, *Vive Moi!*, tells us that he found he could support himself and his family by writing 500 words a day. That seemed to me when I first thought about it a ridiculously small output. But of course he meant 500 words corrected, revised, ready for the printer. He also meant 500 words as an average, so that if he took a holiday, or was interrupted in his work, or the muse refused to smile on him (she is a *very* fickle jade), he had to double his output next day. I came to understand, by keeping tally on my own production, that on these terms 500 words make up a quite decent total. And the only way to achieve it is to follow the best piece of advice ever given to aspiring writers: "Attach the seat of the pants to the seat of the chair and remain stationary." But the effort to do that, and simultaneously to flit around the country, talking on a variety of platforms, was not healthy, then or later. I note a terse little entry in my desk calendar for November 19, 1965: "Ulcer redivivus." And I am reminded of Porky's remark in "Pogo," my favorite comic strip: "Two minutes of silence prolly don't make that big a deferments to the *outside* world, but it sure makes a world of differmints to my *insides*."

Then, one lovely spring day, there arrived a summons. My Rector, Father Mike Walsh, who had suggested my sabbatical in the first place and then agreed to its extension a year later, wrote one of his unfailingly kind and gracious letters. He knew, he said, how rewarding I was finding my life and work in Evanston, and he regretted his having to interrupt it, but, he said, he needed a chairman for the Theology Department, and so he was calling me home. It was one of the very few times in my life when the vow of obedience really hurt. I had had no experience in administration, didn't care for it, didn't think I had whatever talents it required. Moreover, I was quite aware of the special problems I would face at this point in time and with this particular department. The upheaval that the Second Vatican Council would bring about had scarcely been felt yet, but one could sense the tremors and guess what was to come. And the members of the department, all Jesuits, many of them elderly, all trained in rigidly scholastic theology and committed to passing it on as a precious and unalterable heritage, would not take kindly to changes in content or style of presentation.

For many years the program in theology had not varied; sixteen credits, two each semester, were required for graduation. There were no electives. Father William Casey, a previous chairman, had substituted courses in biblical studies for the outworn "Apologetics," but these were offered only to the "Honors" students. In the course on the sacraments, room had been made for an extensive treatment of marriage. Otherwise the program was pretty much a watered-down version of what we ourselves had had at the seminary, and even at that a frequently heard complaint was that there wasn't enough time to do the subject justice.

On the way to my first department meeting I dropped in to see the Rector. "Mike," I said, "What would you think of electives in theology?" Mike leaned back in his chair, waited a moment, and then, without saying a word, made a large sign of the cross over my head. The blessing was silent but eloquent. Armed with it, I began the meeting with a few preliminaries. Then I said, "I was just talking to Father Rector. He wants us to introduce electives." Well, I had expected some opposition, but not the hubbub of protest that ensued. At last Father Maurice Dullea, a senior and much respected professor, got the floor.

"Bill," he said, "Was this Father Rector's irrevocable wish?"

"Well," I answered, "He didn't qualify it."

"Then could we represent our views to him?"

"Of course," I answered.

"In that case," said Maurice, "I think we should get a sense of the department's attitude on the matter."

So the question was put to a vote. Twenty-four of the members were opposed, three (Father Fred Moriarty, Father Frank Devine, and myself) were in favor. There was an obvious air of satisfaction in the room; that proposal had been clearly defeated. We had another meeting a week later, and I presented a "white paper" defending the idea. It did not change anyone's opinion. Then, knowing that electives had been introduced at Holy Cross, I invited Father Jack Brooks, chairman of the theology department there, to tell us about the innovation on his campus, hoping that the experience of our sister college might encourage us to a similar venture. But Jack's presentation elicited only skeptical looks and much shaking of heads. As far as the department was concerned, the proposal was dead.

This conclusion, however, was premature. By dint of a great deal of off-stage plotting (of which more later), and with the very active collaboration of Father Joe Flanagan and Dr. Tom Owens of the Philosophy Department, a schedule of courses was put together that was academically very respectable and that students might elect for credit toward their degree. In December the campus newspaper proclaimed the option in banner headlines. Then, of course, having flouted the wishes of the department, I was nothing but a Nazi. But the students gave their Man of the Year Award for 1965-66 to Joe Flanagan and myself, *ex aequo,* and I thought I could afford to shrug off the slur. The episode did give me to understand very clearly that in attempting to bring about any other changes I would be pretty much in the situation of the Lone Ranger.

I did not like this situation, then or during the next four years. After all, I not only worked with these colleagues; I lived with them, respected their dedication, cherished their good opinion. It was anything but pleasant to be regarded as subversive of their values and destructive of their life's work. By and large, we were not a happy community during that time. People were identified as either progressives (a.k.a. "radicals") or conservatives (a.k.a. "reactionaries"). When we talked at lunch or dinner—and we did carefully maintain civilities—we skirted dangerous topics. We discussed the vagaries of the New England weather, or the fortunes of the football team. And if these conversational wells ran dry we could always fall back on memories of the dear dead days when we were novices. But it was a strain, all the more painful because our earlier association had been so genial, so relaxing, so supportive.

Every day, it seemed, brought challenges to our way of life, to the customs we had lived by for years, and not seldom to the convictions which underlay these practices and which we had thought unassailable. Bells stopped ringing. Birettas and cassocks disappeared, and were replaced by casual dress, but the ultimate *trahison,* in the eyes of the conservatives, was to make one's appearance in a necktie. Such hallowed community devotions as benediction, litanies, "graces" at table were dropped, and efforts to find substitutes were rarely successful. When Father Provincial came for his annual visitation, for instance, and it was announced that all were invited to join with him in the "new" way of concelebrating the Eucharist, only eighteen of the one hundred priests in the community appeared. "Bible Vigils" were tried and found wanting. Communal recitation of the Hours, a practice regarded as absolutely alien to Jesuit observance, was never even suggested.

It was a time of aching transition on all fronts. Our students, hitherto compliant and tractable, suddenly became, like their peers across the country, rebels against anything they saw as "the institution." The Jesuit faculty in particular, who had enjoyed a happy, affectionate, fatherly relationship with their students, found them sullen, antagonistic, mutinous. They dropped the correct dress formerly required for class and appeared (when it pleased them—mandatory attendance went by the board at this time, too) in deliberately provocative jeans, sweaters, T-shirts. Luxuriant beards and mustaches flowered on what had been clean-shaven chins. The campus newspaper became the organ of the rebellion, editorializing stridently against restrictions of any sort, hoarsely demanding the concession of "rights," running advertisements for contraceptive counseling and abortion clinics. There were mass demonstrations, threats to take over university buildings and paralyze operations. Inasmuch as "the institution" was the archenemy, the Jesuits, who more or less personified the institution, were obvious targets, and hostility focused especially on the Theology Department, which was staffed exclusively by Jesuits and symbolized all that the students saw as repression and reaction. As chairman of that department, I sometimes wondered whether I should not begin wearing a bullet-proof vest.

The first item on my agenda, after lining up the new elective courses, was to find teachers who were professionally qualified and who were not temperamentally opposed to new directions. This was far from easy. Not many Jesuits—except those destined to teach in our houses of study—had been assigned to pursue advanced degrees in theology, and those who had were often shifted early out of the classroom into administrative posts. There would have to be another departure from tradition: lay people would have to be called on. Not that there were many of them available, either. Theology had been for so long a clerical preserve that the laity, seeing small prospect of employment, had steered clear of it. The very few Catholics who had ventured into the field had been trained in Protestant or secular universities, since there were virtually no graduate programs in Catholic schools, and consequently they were eyed with suspicion. Finally, it was never said out loud, it was simply taken for granted that no woman could ever teach theology. These considerations meant that the pool of candidates for employment in our department was practically dry.

Today, twenty-five years later, the department has grown from a membership of twenty-seven, all Jesuits, to forty-seven. Nine of these teachers are Jesuits, but only six are full-time. There are five other priests, diocesan or from other religious orders. There are two members of the Jewish clergy. All the others (thirty-one) are laypeople, and ten of these are women. Here is a vast change indeed, brought about largely through the vision and cheerful persistence of two chairmen, Father Thomas O'Malley and Father Robert Daly. But a beginning had to be made in the sixties, and it was not welcomed, either by the Jesuit community in general or by some on the higher echelons of administration. One likely candidate for appointment was objected to because he was Dutch, and Dutch Catholics at that time were leading the field in "dangerous" experimentation with new forms of liturgy. Another was approved and a contract was signed, but then the candidate announced that he was leaving the priesthood. There was consternation; lawyers were consulted. The upshot was that the new teacher was not permitted to teach or to identify himself with the University in any way; his salary was paid for the year, and he was not re-hired.

The euphoria of Vatican II, the sense of being released to create new things, persisted in spite of such difficulties. There was an immense amount of plotting, some of it in open session, some of the "smoke-filled room" variety. A committee made up of representatives of Boston College, Boston University, Andover Newton Theological School, Harvard, and Weston College met to discuss an institute "on theology and the university." The institute never materialized, but it was a remote ancestor of the Boston Theological Institute, which came into being two years later. There was a meeting at St. John's Seminary on inter-seminary cooperation. I visited the deans and the chairmen of the sociology, history, economics, and English departments to propose joint efforts on electives. Faculty from our department and from Andover Newton lunched together to explore possibilities for a joint graduate program—the beginning of a collaboration which continues happily to this day. Three Jesuits and three lay professors who had been close friends for years began unpublicized meetings which proposed new ventures and alternated between seriousness and hilarity. Another unofficial and somewhat clandestine group which met monthly at Boston College was made up of priests from our faculty and theological students ("scholastics") from Weston College, the Jesuit seminary which at that time was experiencing unheard-of modifications in its monastic way of life—the very fact, for example, that the scholastics were permitted to leave for an evening their sequestered enclosure in the country, and on one occasion were even joined by their Rector. It was a time of exhilarating ferment, of fresh proposals and possibilities—a doctoral program, an "institute" on the philosophy of religion or on Christian community or on theology and literature or on liturgical music, a summer program with distinguished lecturers from Europe. Almost all of these suggestions were, as a matter of fact, implemented and carried out. And the chairman was discovering that, while he himself was not very good at originating projects, he could recognize a good idea when it was proposed and see that it got a local habitation and a name.

A procession of stimulating lecturers came to campus at the department's invitation: the historian Robert McNally, the literary critic William Lynch, the theologian (afterward Cardinal) Henri de Lubac, the philosopher Thomas Corbishley, from London, the theologian Hans Küng, from Tübingen, the ecumenist Robert Nelson, the biblical scholar Barnabas Ahern, the liturgist Gerald Ellard, the patristics scholar Walter Burghardt. Europeans came to conduct summer courses: Ladislaus Örsy and John Witte from the Gregorian University, Juan Mateos and Max Zerwick from the Biblical Institute in Rome.

According to unauthenticated legend, the Boston Theological Institute had its beginnings in a chance conversation aboard a Chicago-to-Boston plane in the fall or winter of 1965. Father Frank Shea, S.J., of Boston College, and Dean (later Bishop) John Coburn of the Episcopal Divinity School in Cambridge, not previously acquainted, happened to sit together and floated the possibility of a consortium of theology faculties in the Boston area. The idea germinated for a bit and at last, on the sixth of April, delegates from five schools—Boston University, the Episcopal Divinity School, Andover Newton Theological School, Harvard University, and Boston College—met to see what could be done. Weston College and St. John's Seminary sent delegates shortly after. The group, known to its members as "the Cabal," came together for twelve lengthy discussions in the following year and a half. A constitution and by-laws that would be agreeable to seven boards of trustees had to be formulated—a fairly delicate business that was adroitly managed by Dean Walter Muelder of Boston University, acting as chairman. I was struck not only with the Dean's skill and patience but by the way our Protestant colleagues in general negotiated and brought difficult issues to consensus. We Catholics, by contrast, accustomed all our lives to following orders from on high, had never developed a like proficiency. We didn't know how to go over, through, or under an apparent impasse.

I was learning a lot about and from these new Protestant friends. They were as eager—perhaps more eager than we were— to find a way out of the four hundred-year-old feuding, and I sometimes thought we were like lovers after a quarrel, hoping for and groping toward a reconciliation. In the Army, twenty years before, I had got along pleasantly with the Protestant chaplains, and had enjoyed a more intimate friendship with two Presbyterian ministers, Bob McCaslin at the Chaplain School and Marty Hardin in the Philippines. But on the Catholic side in those days there was no thought given to union except on our terms, i.e., return and complete submission. Protestants were heretics who had fallen away from the faith; there was no recognition of them as distinct churches or even as "ecclesial communities." But the Council brought new light and new hope. Dialogue had already begun, looking toward new formulations of doctrine that would be mutually acceptable. We Catholics had abandoned the defensive crouch we had adopted and maintained for so long, but we were not sure how to overcome our awkwardness in the new relationship. The breach dividing us had been so wide that we really did not know the Protestants. Perhaps because he sensed that, Dr. William Morrison, Secretary for Education in the American Presbyterian Church, invited me to a dinner of his fellow-clergy and would not take no for an answer. After the dinner we attended an ecumenical worship service at which the Anglican Archbishop of York was the preacher. Then Bill simply whisked me off to his hotel room, where a number of his associates joined us and generously made me feel that I was one of the group. So much kindness is irresistible, and I resolved that in future encounters I would imitate it by trying to overcome initial awkwardness.

The B.T.I., as everyone now calls it, was organized on a "share the wealth" basis. Resources were to be mutually available: faculty, library, instruction, students. Dr. Henry Van Dusen, former president of Union Theological School in New York, was brought in as consultant, and the Rev. Walter Waggoner, affable and energetic, shepherded the young organization through its first years.

The press conference announcing the formation of the B.T.I. was scheduled for December 8, 1967. But it seemed only proper, before the public announcement was made, to convoke the faculties of the several schools, acquaint them with all the details of the project, and celebrate an ecumenical collaboration absolutely without precedent in Boston. Boston College hosted a genial dinner, and, one by one, the deans of the member schools described the new consortium and its prospects. By way of conclusion, and to emphasize the singular character of the gathering, I told a story I had heard from Father Dan Ryan of our department, who had it from a friend of his, a primary school teacher in New York. This teacher, Father Dan said, had had in her class the previous year a little girl who from the first day of class maintained an absolute silence. September went on into October, and October into November, and November into December, and still this little party hadn't said a word. Just before Christmas there was a heavy snowfall in New York, and the schools closed. On the following day the going was still bad, and not many of the children appeared, so the teacher gathered those who had come into a small circle and sat down in the midst. Whereupon, without prompting, the hitherto shy and silent little girl became vocal. "I went to see my guppies this morning," she announced. "I always go to see my guppies when I get up in the morning. I have two guppies in a tank. But when I went to see my guppies this morning I found that the tank was full of little guppies. And I said to myself, I said, "What the hell goes on here?"

When the laughter subsided I continued. "Please look," I said, "at that picture over the door. That's Father Edward Welch, for whom this dining hall is named. In the middle of the last century he was born into a Boston Brahmin family, strongly opposed to the beliefs and practices of the Church of Rome. But in his youth he fell victim to sinister influences and became a Catholic. He even went so far as to become a Jesuit, and one of the pioneer professors at Boston College. And I'm sure that as he looks down on this unprecedented assembly, he is saying, in the eloquent words of the little girl, 'What the hell goes on here?' "

CHAPTER 20

Combat Zone

PROBABLY WE SHALL HAVE TO PUT MORE DISTANCE BETWEEN ourselves and the sixties before we can assign rhyme or reason to that turbulent period. And I wonder if we who were then of an elder generation could ever understand it. We had with pain and persistence survived the Great Depresssion. We had beaten Hitler and Tojo and out-faced Stalin. We had handed the world to young Americans on a platter; never had a crop of youngsters been born into an age of greater prosperity. We hadn't solved all the problems, of course; we hoped that they would take care of some we had missed. Then we watched as they, the self-styled "Flower Children," lounged on the grass at Woodstock, smoking pot and damning as "the institution" all that we had built up. We listened until our heads ached to the yawping and squawking that was their music. We thought about 1776; now *there* was a revolution that had some point to it. We thought of 1861, when the Union was preserved and slavery ended forever. We remembered the Winning of the West, and the emancipation of Labor, and the hard-won triumph of the suffragettes. What were these youngsters after? What program did they come up with to replace what they didn't like about ours? One of the graffiti on the walls of Paris in 1968 read: "I have something to say but I don't know what."[1] The same author goes on: "By what society should the society they seek to destroy be replaced? The 'movement' does not know, and it contests the question. Let us first destroy, and the creative outburst will be set free which will invent a society quite different from those which can be imagined at the moment."[2]

---

1.   Eugen Weber, *The Western Tradition*, Boston, 1970. p. 1007.
2.   Id., p. 1032.

Many of us found Vietnam revolting, as they did; we were outraged, as they were, by Kent State and the Democratic Convention in Chicago. But we didn't think those tragedies gave us a license to throw in the towel and quit, much less to limit our contribution to shouting slogans and writing obscene graffiti on the walls of venerable buildings.

At Boston College the "campus unrest," as the media called it, was moderate in comparison with what went on elsewhere. There were "sit-downs" in faculty offices and demonstrations and a strike that closed down the campus for six weeks and almost prevented the commencement exercises of 1970. But for the most part our students did not go beyond hostility to regulation of any kind, expressed in editorials in the campus newspaper and a sullen demeanor toward even sympathetic deans and faculty. It was a strange time, indeed. We bachelors were given a glimpse of what for many parents is a common, highly unpleasant experience.

Someone—was it a reputable historian?—has said that about every five hundred years there occurs a real cultural explosion. If that is so, then, counting from the beginning of the Christian era, ours was right on schedule, and Vatican II, two years before it happened, had tried to prepare us for it:

> Today, the human race is involved in a new stage of history. Profound and rapid changes are spreading by degrees around the whole world. Triggered by human intelligence and creative energies, these changes recoil upon us, upon our decisions and desires, both individual and collective, and upon our manner of thinking and acting with respect to things and to people. Hence we can already speak of a true cultural and social transformation, one which has repercussions on our religious life as well.
>
> As happens in any crisis of growth, this transformation has brought serious difficulties in its wake. Thus, while we extend our power in every direction, we do not always succeed in subjecting it to our own welfare. Striving to probe more profoundly into the deeper recesses of our own mind, we frequently appear more unsure of ourselves. Gradually and more precisely we lay bare the laws of society, only to be paralyzed by uncertainty about the direction to give it. . . . A change in attitudes and in human structures frequently calls accepted values into question, especially among young people, who have grown impatient on more than one occasion, and indeed become rebels in their distress. Aware of their own influence in the life

of society, they want a part of it sooner. This frequently causes parents and educators to experience greater difficulties day by day in discharging their tasks. The institutions, laws, and modes of thinking and feeling as handed down from previous generations do not always seem to be well adapted to the contemporary state of affairs; hence arises an upheaval in the manner and even the norms of behavior.[3]

The upheaval was visible enough in our lives as Catholics, as priests, and, specifically, as Jesuits. For example, the immutable (as we thought) law of abstinence from meat on Fridays came to a sudden end on November 18, 1966, bringing intimations of financial disaster to the Gloucester fishermen and giving many of us reason to fear that we might choke on that succulent and hitherto forbidden sirloin. Celebrants and congregations found themselves embarassed when the altar was turned around and they began facing each other. The hallowed Latin of the liturgy, in use since the early Middle Ages, was replaced by a vernacular which was understandable but which many felt was sacrilegious. Unauthorized experimentation with the ritual in some places ran afoul not only of the law but of any standard of good taste. I remember that a friend, pastor of the cathedral in his diocese, went away to study at a summer "institute." During his absence the curate who was in charge presided at some rather "far-out" liturgies, and climaxed the summer's bizarre offerings with what he called a "Circus Mass": the procession was led by a trained dog, and he, dressed as a clown, brought up the rear, eating fire (an accomplishment of his). When the pastor returned, he found a letter from the bishop, asking with some concern what was going on. The pastor replied, "We seem to have made a mistake here. I guarantee that we shan't make that mistake again. However, I can't guarantee that we shall not make others." The first "folk-song Mass" was celebrated on campus in April of 1966, and the first "guitar Mass" in May; these innovations, dramatic enough in themselves, were made more spectacular by the fact that the Masses were concelebrated by a number of priests.

Obviously, "the changes," as they were called, were not received with equal enthusiasm on all sides. "Conservatives" and

---

3.   "The Church in the Modern World," #4, 7.

"progressives" condemned or defended them with considerable asperity. One of the latter group asserted that two attitudes had dominated preconciliar piety. The first he called "rain-dance theology," and said it resulted in prayers and devotions that were largely magical in their expectation. The other he called "ambush theology;" this, he said, was exemplified by the Rector of the seminary in his time, who warned the seminarians, "If you are not faithful to the rule now, some day you are going to need a special grace to overcome temptation and God is not going to give it to you." Now, he went on, there was "nausea theology," a favorite with his conservative classmates, who rejected "the changes" wholesale by shouting "That makes me sick!"

Much more substantial, and much more painful and troubling, was the resignation of so many priests and religious. Explanations were offered, but none really satisfied. Was it simply the chaos of the times, when people lost touch with the values that had sustained them till now? Had there been unsuspected flaws in the process of their formation, so that they had never arrived at a full maturity? Or had we been from the beginning too eager to accept all comers, without looking hard at their psychological qualifications? The parable of the sower and the seed was cited, as well as the old scholastic axiom, "Whatever is received is received according to the capacity of the receiver." But the phenomenon gave rise to misgivings, not often expressed, about the whole enterprise. The young people were saying to us, "What we learn from you does not help us as persons." Did that mean that celibacy, for example, could only result in malformed, or at least grossly immature personalities? Would "blind obedience" take away, inevitably, one's ability to make morally significant choices, and in the end undermine one's God-given dignity as a person?

Some of those who departed had, perhaps, been nursing resentments for a considerable time. We had all smarted periodically under capricious, even despotic superiors. Others foresaw that the reforms mandated by the Council would come about very slowly, and they did not want, as one man put it, to go on for a life-time knocking their heads against the wall.

I myself was spared, mercifully, the racking anguish that must have accompanied such decisions. I was never tempted, even mildly, to leave. For one thing, I was not convinced that the alleged malformations of character did not exist outside the priestly or religious life. Pastoral experience had provided abundant evidence that marriage could and did often produce gnarled and twisted personalities, or at least was no cure for them. Nor did I see that people "in the world" had that much independence of choice. Their lives were circumscribed with all manner of limitations, financial, familial, cultural. And they had no option except to submit when the autocrat (or the bully) in the boss's chair told them what was good for them.

Moreover, as Father Andy Greeley was to say later, I liked being a priest. I was glad when I could be a counselor or an advocate. I thought (and still think) it's a privilege to be asked to hear a confession, or to witness a marriage, or to preach. I believed (and still most firmly believe) that when I went to the altar for Mass, or recited through the day the prayer of the Church, the Lord Jesus most completely identified me with himself in his office as mediator, intercessor, reconciler. How had I ever deserved this? How could I ever relinquish it?

I find it more than a little mysterious that we Catholics—and, so far as I know, most Protestants—seldom advert to the fact that our Lord was preeminently a priest. The Letter to the Hebrews is a glorious exposition of the doctrine as, evidently, it was cherished in the apostolic Church. Pope Pius XII, twenty centuries later, wrote an encyclical on the subject. Nonetheless, it seems to have small place in our theology and in our devotions. We think of Jesus as Master, Teacher, Redeemer, Shepherd, Son of God, Son of Mary. But it was as a priest that he fulfilled his mission most perfectly, since it is the function of a priest to be a mediator, a go-between, a bridge, and he was surely that—a bridge spanning an infinite abyss, across which God comes to his creatures and they go to him. Our commonest prayers, if we reflect on it, acknowledge the priesthood of Jesus. We pray with assurance because we invariably conclude our prayer "through Christ our Lord." We sum up our vocation as worshipers when we unite our prayer with his, for "through him, and with him, and in him, in the unity of the Holy Spirit, all glory and honor is yours, almighty Father, for ever and ever."

Parenthetically, one thinks that all our efforts to renew liturgical participation during the last twenty-five years have not had their full effect because we have not emphasized this fundamental doctrine. We have not emphasized sufficiently the fact that our spirituality, long before it is Ignatian, or Carmelite, or whatever, is a Trinitarian spirituality. The Council's document on the liturgy—before it discusses changes at all—makes this abundantly clear.

Perhaps (to continue the parenthesis for a bit) perhaps some genius among us will hit upon a "devotion" that will embody this idea. I once suggested to the Religious of the Sacred Heart that their favorite devotion, now that it seems to have lost the immense popularity it once enjoyed, might be revived if it were oriented to Christ the Priest. The idea of reparation, so prominent in the devotion as we practiced it, could with a little twist be seen as intercession, merged with the "Father, forgive them" of the cross and offered by Christians for the entire human family. We could be "the salt of the earth" and "the yeast in the flour" not only in our conduct but also in our generous prayer for others. And the theme of God's overwhelming, personal love for us all, which characterized the devotion from its beginning, and to which people turned with relief and enthusiasm after listening to the fearful rigidities of Jansenism, is surely dominant in such passages as this:

> Since, then, we have a great high priest who has passed through the heavens, Jesus, the Son of God, let us hold fast to our profession of faith. For we do not have a high priest who is unable to sympathize with our weakness, but one who was tempted in every way that we are, yet never sinned. So let us confidently approach the throne of grace to receive mercy and favor and to find help in time of need (Heb 4:14-16).

End of parenthesis. I was saying that I liked being a priest. There was always more for me to do than I had so far accomplished. My classmates had always teased me about being a "hyper-achiever," and perhaps I would have been in any walk of life, but in this one there never seemed to be a point where I could call a halt. Annually at least I repeated that meditation of St. Ignatius on the "Two Standards," ingeniously devised to set disciples of Christ ablaze with zeal for his glory. I had never been able to get it out of my mind, actually, since that October night long ago when Father Fisher set it before us. I resonated, as they say these days, to words of the Lord that I found poignant and inspiring: "I must walk today and tomorrow and the day following" (Lk 13:33), and "I have come to light a fire on the earth. How I wish the blaze were ignited!" (Lk 12:49). Ideas like these were uppermost in my mind on Ordination Day when I felt Bishop Emmet's commissioning hands on my head, because I had chosen another Lucan text for the memorial card I would give my friends: "You shall be called the prophet of the Most High, for you will go before the

Lord to prepare his way, to give his people knowledge of salvation by forgiving them their sins. In the tender compassion of our God the dawn from on high shall break upon us, to shine on those who dwell in darkness and the shadow of death, and to guide our feet on the road to peace" (Lk 1:76). And finally, I had come upon a sonnet of Edna St. Vincent Millay's, little anthologized or quoted because, perhaps, we know of no experience in the poet's life which might have inspired it. It did seem to add up to an *apologia pro vita mea:*

> My earnestness, which might at first offend,
> Forgive me, for the duty it implies;
> I am the convoy to the cloudy end
> Of a most bright and regal enterprise,
> Which, under angry constellations, ill-
> Mounted and under-rationed and unspurred,
> Set forth to find if any country still
> Might do obeisance to an honest word.

> Duped and delivered up to rascals, bound
> And bleeding, and his mouth stuffed, on his knees,
> Robbed and imprisoned, and adjudged unsound,
> I have beheld my master, if you please.
> Forgive my earnestness, who at his side
> Received his swift instructions, till he died.

Change a detail here and there and you have a reasonable approximation of the urgency a priest might feel after meditating on the Last Supper discourse in St. John and the accounts of the Passion. "Burn-out"? Unthinkable.

But what about loneliness? What about the absence of a confidante, a patient and staunch support, who would "double one's joys and halve one's sorrows"? What about the fulfillment a man must know when he has fathered a child? I remember the first time I realized that I would never have that experience. I was visiting my brother, and because my visits at that time were very few (I was still in the seminary), my little niece, who was ill, was permitted to come downstairs and join the family. After some time, however, my brother said, "Time for bed, Mary Lou." He picked her up and started upstairs, but the phone rang and he turned to me. "Hold her for a minute," he said. She stretched out her arms to me, and it was as if a knife went through my heart. Someone like her could have been mine. And no one ever would be.

In the long run it dawns on us that there is no complete human cure for loneliness. Augustine said it all: "Thou hast made us for thyself, O Lord, and our hearts are restless until they rest in thee." On the other hand, God himself said, "It is not good for man to be alone" (Gen 2:18), and provided a companion who might assuage the ache at least to some extent. The question then arises whether a priest should be required to abjure marriage as a condition of ordination. The discipline of celibacy in the Roman Church—and it is a discipline, not an article of faith—has been questioned seriously, especially at and since the Second Vatican Council, on the grounds that celibacy should be a free choice, but both Pope Paul VI and Pope John Paul II have reaffirmed it. Meanwhile the steady drain of departures from the active ministry and the falling-off of candidates have brought about a crisis. Parishes, especially in poorer countries, but increasingly at home, are being deprived of the Eucharist. "The hungry sheep look up and are not fed." It is clear that this situation cannot be tolerated indefinitely.

The Pauline argument that celibacy enables a priest to give undivided attention to his ministry never struck me as compelling. My friends among the Orthodox and Protestant clergy have seemed as zealous and as free from distractions as the average Catholic priest. I remember one meeting at my office of the delegates who were working on the constitution of the BTI. For some reason I was the only Catholic representative present that day, and I happened to notice that I was the only man in the room not wearing a wedding ring. Yet these married men were every bit as eager for the success of the project and as hard-working as I was, and they seemed able to devote just as much attention to it.

For myself, as a member of a religious order with a vow of permanent chastity, celibacy was not an issue. I had made that choice ten years before I was ordained. But I suppose that, with the new emphasis on personalism and the new awareness of sexuality as a dimension of the human personality, even friendly critics of Church practice might raise questions about such a commitment. Would it not be likely to damage one's integrity and maturity? Would it not alienate a man from others not so committed, make him think himself a cut above them, render him incapable of genuine understanding and sympathy? Is a life like his not a refusal of one of the Creator's precious gifts?

One might respond that there have been many men (and women) who have deliberately elected a celibate life so that they might pursue unhampered a preferred objective. Perhaps they

wanted to concentrate all their forces on some exalted purpose—
the liberation, let us say, of their people from oppression. Perhaps
they were intent on discovering a medical remedy for a disease,
and did not want to divide their energies. Perhaps they had undertaken the care of children left orphans by the death of a brother or
sister, fully aware that by so doing they were minimizing the
chances of marriage for themselves. We honor such people, and
feel that in some way their selfless generosity prevents their becoming introverted or neurotic. Or at least that there is ample
compensation for the sacrifice.

But celibacy chosen for religious reasons seems not so intelli-
gible. And it may be that those who elect it on those grounds must
resign themselves to being considered peculiar, even fanatic. One
day our master of novices, Father Fisher, must have been feeling a
bit low. "You know," he said in what I think was a quite ex-
tempore burst of confidence, "Ours is a very unnatural way of life.
To choose it and persevere in it means that one has to be infatuated with Christ." . . . "Infatuated." I didn't like the word. It implied that one had abandoned reason. When we said that a boy or
girl was infatuated we meant that he or she did stupid, silly things,
things they would never do in their right minds. And when we
who looked on tried to account for them we could say only that
they were in love—"head-over-heels," as we put it, in love. They
gave gifts they couldn't afford, for example. Nothing that they
could give was too much. They cast about for extravagant ways to
prove their love. It didn't matter that they were impoverished by
the gesture. It didn't bother them if people thought they were ridiculous. The more precious the gift the more they wanted to lay
it at the feet of the beloved.

Or again (still trying to get over that unsavory word, "infatuated"), it was noticeable that people in love strove to be like the
beloved. There was a novice in my time who idolized Father
Fisher. He imitated Father's ways of speech, his mannerisms. He
even tried for a while to imitate his walk. He persisted even when
he knew we were laughing at him.

Well, then, for two years, before we made any commitment to
this "unnatural" life, we looked at the picture of the Lord Jesus in
the Gospels. Here was one who had "emptied himself," in St.
Paul's phrase (Ph 2:7), that he might convince us of his love for
us. "He who was rich became poor for our sake" (2 Cor 8:9).
And during his life he did unreasonable things, things that could be

explained only if he were, well, "infatuated" (that word again) with us. Peter took him aside and tried to "talk sense" to him. His family came to bring him home because he was clearly a little daft, needed a rest. He continued on his reckless path even though he knew very well what his enemies had in store for him. And when they had done their worst he prayed that they might be forgiven. In St. John's comprehensive phrase, "Having loved his own who were in the world, he loved them to the end" (Jn 13:1)—not just to the end of his life, but to the end even of the possibilities of loving, of giving.

If we wanted to requite such a spendthrift love we could not in decency be stingy. What good thing did we have that we could offer him in return? Was there some asset or possession of ours that we could make over to him, whose surrender would at the same time help us to be like him? Because by this time we had come to admire him enough to want to imitate him in all his ways. He was wonderfully gentle, perceptive, compassionate, but he could be resolute and uncompromising, even demanding. He wept with the mourners (Martha and Mary when their brother died); he rejoiced with the merry-makers (at the wedding feast at Cana). He silenced his critics with the rapier-thrusts of his debate, he poured corrosive acid on the heads of hypocrites (as in that terrible twenty-third chapter of Matthew), he stood in silent dignity, refusing to defend himself, in the presence of that old lecher, Herod, and of Pilate, the politician who was caught between Caesar, the mob, and his conscience. But he was gentle even to tenderness when he reproached his blundering disciples, when he woke to new life the dead youth and "gave him to his mother" (Lk 7:15), when all he said to Judas was "Is it with a kiss that you betray the Son of Man?" (Lk 22:48). St. Paul tried to sum it up: "There has appeared to us the goodness and kindness of God our Savior" (Ti 3:4)—winsome, magnetic, enthralling. We loved him, and we wanted desperately to be like him.

But he never married. So—it was not an impulsive decision; we had plenty of time to think it over—we would not, either. It was a costly gift when we made it, and the struggle not to reach up and take it back from the altar would be lifelong. But we hoped it would be incontrovertible evidence of our love for him. Extravagant? Not more so than what he had done for us. Unnatural, absurd? But his own life was knit together in the paradoxes he proposed to his disciples. The seed in the ground had to die before it could produce fruit (Jn 12:24). "Anyone who wants to save his life will lose it, but anyone who loses his life for my sake will save it" (Mt 16:25). Fanatical? So be it, we said; "they" would never understand, but he who loved "to the end" would understand, and it was he who would be our judge.

Padraic Pearse was an Irish patriot who organized the rebellion against British tyranny and died in the hopeless but gallant uprising of Easter, 1916. He was also a poet, and I (perhaps comparing great things with small) always thought one of his lyrics could be an apologia for religious celibacy as we undertook it in 1927:

> Since the wise men have not spoken, I speak
>   that am only a fool;
> A fool that hath loved his folly,
> Yea, more than the wise men their books or
>   their counting houses, or their quiet
>   homes,
> Or their fame in men's mouths;
> A fool that in all his days hath never done a
>   prudent thing,
> Never hath counted the cost, nor recked if
>   another reaped
> The fruit of his mighty sowing, content to
>   scatter the seed;
> A fool that is unrepentant, and that soon at
>   the end of all
> Shall laugh in his lonely heart as the ripe
>   ears fall to the reaping-hooks
> And the poor are filled that were empty,
> Tho' he go hungry.
>
> I have squandered the splendid years that the
>   Lord God gave to my youth
> In attempting impossible things, deeming them
>   alone worth the toil.
> Was it folly or grace? Not men shall judge
>   me, but God.
>
> I have squandered the splendid years:
> Lord, if I had the years I would squander
>   them over again,
> Aye, fling them from me!
> For this I have heard in my heart, that a man
>   shall scatter, not hoard,
> Shall do the deed of today, nor take thought
>   of tomorrow's teen,
> Shall not bargain or huxter with God; or was

it a jest of Christ's
And is this my sin before men, to have taken
him at his word?

The lawyers have sat in council, the men with
the long, keen faces,
And said, "This man is a fool," and others
have said, "He blasphemeth;"
And the wise have pitied the fool that hath
striven to give a life
In the world of time and space among the
bulks of actual things
To a dream that was dreamed in the heart, and
that only the heart could hold.
O wise men, riddle me this: what if the dream
come true?
What if the dream come true? and if millions
unborn shall dwell
In the house that I shaped in my heart, the
noble house of my thought?
Lord, I have staked my soul, I have staked
the lives of my kin
On the truth of thy dreadful word. Do not
remember my failures,
But remember my faith.

And so I speak,
Yea, ere my hot youth pass, I speak to my
people and say:
Ye shall be foolish as I; ye shall scatter,
not save;
Ye shall venture your all, lest ye lose what
is more than all;
Ye shall call for a miracle, taking Christ at
his word.

And for this I will answer, O people, answer
here and hereafter.
O people that I have loved, shall we not
answer together?

So we headed into the world of Vatican II. Gerard Philips, in
his *Achieving Christian Maturity*,[4] listed the problems the Christian
community faced then: the immaturity of the laity, a realization of

---

4.   Chicago, 1966

the dignity of the laity, Christian presence in the world, Christians in a divided world, inner struggles, criticism in the Church, virile holiness, adaptation. Here was a future that might daunt the bravest. Personally, I found the prospect of "inner struggles" distasteful. People with the loftiest motives and the deepest convictions were certain to line up for combat on both sides of any issue, and diplomatic compromises would satisfy neither. Feeling was already running so high that there was small likelihood even of temperate discussion. Gilbert Highet, the classicist, had a story about an unnamed scholar who was once asked what he judged to be the greatest contribution of the Greeks to the world's life. He replied that the greatest contribution of the Greeks consisted of the two words *men* and *de*, for *men* means "on the one hand" and *de* means "on the other hand," and without these two balances we cannot think truly.[5] But among Catholics of the postconciliar period there was little room for *men* and *de*. See the "letters to the editor" section of Catholic newspapers and magazines during these years, *passim*, for examples of unlovely contention and even of invective.

Back at the ranch, so to speak, activity was intense, even if on a much smaller scale. I often thought of my brother Fran's question as he came to his office in the morning: "What's the number one crisis today?" Paging through my appointment calendars now, I note emergencies, due dates, reminders and exhortations to myself: "seven sections still uncovered," "lecture tonight," "call Dean," "appoint *ad hoc* committee," "grades due Monday." Off campus, I gave 480 lectures, homilies, conferences, retreats, etc., from 1965 to the end of 1967 (I have misplaced the calendars for '68 and '69), to an estimated total audience of almost 60,000, from Boston to Chicago to California and after that out of all whooping. They were for the most part efforts to familiarize people with the liturgical renewal and the theology of worship. I was interviewed by *Newsweek*, photographed by *Time*—a sort of apotheosis in our time. As "the changes" multiplied on campus and in the worldwide Church, however, and as many good people felt the solid ground slipping away under their feet, any eminence on the "radical" side became precarious and decidedly uncomfortable. One of the faculty, already identified as "far-out," proposed that the depart-

---

5. Quoted by Paul W. Hoon, *The Integrity of Worship,* Nashville, 1972, from Gordon Rupp, *The Old Reformation and the New,* Philadelphia, 1967.

ment sponsor a conference on the "Underground Church," which was a loose coalition of dissenting and clamorous Catholics bent, apparently, on ousting authority in all its forms. In view of the publicity they had engendered, I thought it might be a good idea to sit down and listen to them. Maybe they had not only legitimate gripes—we all had a few of those—but some constructive suggestions as well. Of course there was a row; we shouldn't encourage such people by giving them house-room. Well, they came to town and had their say; the audience was small and made up chiefly of like-minded people. As far as I could tell, those who attended with open minds were not converted; they were put off by endless, shrill denunciations of "the institution." But perhaps we learned something; at least we listened to people in pain. It seemed a civilized, Christian way of dealing with dissent, and in any case the phenomenon of the "Underground Church" as a kind of rival organization melted away soon enough, although individual dissenters of course remained. These, I believe, do not get a hearing often enough; we are hard on our prophets. After their deaths, naturally, we rehabilitate many of them. Some of them we even canonize.

In the turmoil of those years the figure of Father Mike Walsh stands out, a tower of strength and kindness. I could never be grateful enough for the encouragement and support he gave me. He always had time to talk, to listen. In those days, before the Jesuit Community was separately incorporated, he was both Rector and President—a heavy assignment at any time, but a virtually impossible one in the late sixties. Under his guidance Boston College became a university; in fact, he tried hard to find a name for the school which would convey its new character without alienating thousands of alumni. "Boston College" was always being confused with "Boston University," our neighbor at the other end of Commonwealth Avenue. Legend has it that when that small Methodist foundation migrated from the hills of New Hampshire and sought a charter in Massachusetts, the Jesuits at Boston College were asked if they had any objection to the Methodists' taking the name "Boston University." "No," they are supposed to have replied, "We shall always be a small liberal arts college." Alas for the clouded crystal ball of those days. A more substantive story was told by Mike himself. Over lunch one day with Dr. Daniel Marsh, President of Boston University, the conversation turned to the confusion of names. Dr. Marsh suggested that "Boston College" change its name to "Boston Catholic University." Mike replied that he would make the change the day after Dr. Marsh announced that his school would be called "Boston Methodist University." And so the confusion continues—not locally, where natives make a clear and sharp distinction, but nationally. And since both schools now have a large national enrollment and constituency, that's matter for regret.

Mike's tenancy of the President's office, 1958-1968, was remarkable on many scores. He added building after building to the campus, he strengthened the several schools and recruited distinguished faculty, he presided—he was a master politician—over the mutinies threatened by the students (and an occasional professor) and kept them within bounds. He had a wonderful personal charm and a sense of humor that disarmed most antagonists, even those alumni who thought the college of their youth was abandoning its heritage and riding to disaster. He conducted what we called his "fireside chats" for the Jesuits in our common room, keeping us, with a trustful candor very rare among superiors in those days, up to date with his plans and hopes for the school. Alas, he never won over a small but influential faction (known as the "fourth floor reactionaries" because they gathered in that quarter of St. Mary's Hall) who were alarmed by what they considered his "liberal" tendencies and persuaded the Father Provincial to replace him. Fordham University was in serious administrative and financial difficulties at the time, and requested his services as president there. In three years he put the situation to rights and, his health failing, entered into a semi-retirement; he was, however, always occupied with committee memberships, trusteeships, and advisory boards. When he left Boston College he was given a public testimonial, and the program for that event carried an appropriate tribute: "He was full of valor as of kindness, princely in both."

The "unrest" on campus, fed by the lamentable war in Vietnam, continued. The students were looking for a cause, and found one in the Mary Daly case. Dr. Daly, the first woman to teach theology at Boston College, had come with unusual credentials three years before; she was the holder of three doctor's degrees and had excellent recommendations from her previous employments. But, she told me, she did not want to teach Scripture, or soteriology, or the sacraments, or moral. It became evident as time went on that what she wanted to teach, and did teach passionately, was feminism, and this seemed to me—allowing for some tangential relations with theology—to belong rather in the sociology than in the theology department. She refused to talk to other professors, since they were male. She would not permit male students in her class. She was rarely in her office for counseling. She came late to department meetings and sat silent, contributing nothing. When, therefore, she told me after three years that she wanted to apply for promotion and tenure, I was surprised, but said that of course she was free to do so. In the event, her application was turned down successively by the department, the college, and the university committees. Whereupon she resorted to the press and the media, asserting that she was discriminated against because of her feminism. She made her students missionaries for her cause, and in no time they had the campus ablaze with protest. Undergraduates who had never heard of her and knew nothing about her except that she was against the administration signed a petition supporting her. A thousand students marched with the petition to the president's office. At last Father Seavey Joyce, who had succeeded Father Walsh as president, appointed a special committee to review the case and bring in a recommendation. When I learned who was on the committee I knew what its recommendation would be; all three members were professors known to be anti-administration. Whether Father Joyce was previously aware of their attitudes I never found out. They recommended unanimously that Dr. Daly be promoted and given tenure, and then, of course, the president had no option, even though it meant overturning the verdicts of three regularly constituted academic committees. Interestingly, when some years later Dr. Daly applied for full professorship, was denied it, and tried the same tactics to win support, the atmosphere on campus had changed. The students were apathetic, or, to give them credit, at least dubious about the alleged injustice, and the press had nothing sensational to report. The issue died a-borning.

Father Frank Shea, the executive vice-president, had been interviewed while the controversy was at its height. He was quoted in a highly partisan article in the *National Catholic Reporter* as saying, "We've had problems in the theology department for a long time now." When he was asked about rumors that I would be dismissed as chairman, he said that they were "probably true." The awkward feature of the whole affair was that I felt myself bound by confidentiality not to discuss it; "no comment" was my standard answer. But that, taken together with Father Shea's remark, made some people conclude that I was on Dr. Daly's side. All in all, I was beginning to weary of the incessant wrangling; no one, during the War, had spent four uninterrupted years in a combat zone. It

was time, perhaps, for someone with more talent for conciliation—
or a larger appetite for brawling—to take over. And if the sorry
issue of the business was to be nothing better than a curt dismissal,
I could forestall that. I could resign.

I found a message on my desk one afternoon from my secretary:
"Your brother Fran asked me to write you a note and say the following: He doesn't want to bother you on the phone but wants you to
know that he is totally behind you during all the confusion reported in
the newspapers. This 'vote of confidence' includes the names of Cath
and Eleanor (our sisters), Mary Lou, Jack, and Kathy (his children)."
That was a wonderfully comforting and touching gesture, quite in
keeping with Fran's generous nature. Equally generous was a letter
from my Provincial, Father Bill Guindon: "If I am not rushing in to
open old wounds, may I express a word of sympathy for you in these
troubled times at the Heights. Everything seems to have zeroed in on
you at once. I am fully confident that no storms like this can really
damage your priestly and Jesuit fiber. We all have to put our trust in
the Lord sometimes, despite the big waves." George Peck, Dean at
Andover Newton Theological School, with whom I had worked in the
"cabal" that organized the BTI and the committee that laid the
groundwork for the joint Andover Newton-Boston College graduate
program, wrote: "Dear Bill: I am disturbed by things I am hearing
about your situation at B.C., and would like in some way to offer my
personal support and reenforcement. Is it possible for us to have a
quiet lunch or supper somewhere soon? Sincerely, George."

I was deeply moved by letters from former students. Dr.
Harry McKone wrote from Hartford:

Dear Father Leonard,

I just read in the *NCR* about your problems at B.C., and
decided to do my bit to help. I'm enclosing a copy of a
letter that I just mailed to Father Joyce. I hope that this
will hit him where it hurts. In any case, this is just to let
you know that you have hundreds of persons like myself
on whom you can rely. If I can be of any help (although
I don't know how), please let me know. Thanks for what
you did for us as seniors. Best of luck in the future.

Jack Hollohan, down in Maryland, wrote to Father Shea, who,
to my surprise, sent me a copy of the letter.

Recent newspaper reports tell of the Mary Daly "incident"
and you are mentioned as the College spokesman. I do
hope you'll be able to do something to help keep Bill

Leonard at Boston College. If he is "released," my confidence in Boston College's rise as an academic Christian university is badly shaken. The idea that the words JESUIT and CATHOLIC should be writ large at Chestnut Hill is a fine one, providing that CHRISTIAN stands at the head of the page. I'm sure that there are many pro's and con's re Mary Daly, but are our memories so short that we have forgotten all that Bill Leonard has done to put B.C. on the college theology map? It isn't so many years ago that I as a freshman there was memorizing my apologetics. In the wings was Bill Leonard, doing all his liturgical/biblical homework so that when Vatican II came he was ready to lead us to ever-new insights. To replace him as part of this incident will be quite a black mark on B.C.'s post-Vatican II slate. *Aien aristeuein* (ever to excel) is still the school's motto, isn't it? He stands for that all the way.

Dr. Herbert Richardson, whom I had known when he was at Harvard, and who was then at the University of Toronto, wrote a very long letter which I hope to keep while I live. It closes this way:

Sorry, here I am rambling on when I intended simply to tell you how much my heart has been with you. Look, Bill. Just remember in these days who is the true judge of men. You will not think, I know, that it is your administration or that it is those who protest against it and perhaps even against you. You will not think that it is any other man. But I half suspect—and so write to you—that you may, in such difficult days, treat yourself as if you were rightly your own judge. You may allow yourself to be broken and wearied by the contradictions and pressures of life—and agree with the harsh judgments of men. And you may think that you have the right to despair and feel that you should not have tried to do as you have done with your life. You are not to judge yourself. I think Jesuits especially need to be told this. At least Jesuits like you and Calvinists like me! You are to let yourself be. You are to try to feel within exactly what you know you should try to feel, that God calls every man to do the best he can do and then leave the outcome and the judgment to him. You have done what you have done and you have done all you could. You have been brave and kind and wise—but you have not been able to do everything you wanted to do. Even God himself cannot; no, he has bestowed freedom on men and cannot compel them to act as he would have them act. So just relax. If I have ever known a good man, it is you. I believe it—and I hope you do, too. With the deepest affection.

Herb.

I replied a month later:

Dear Herb:

Your generous letter deserved an earlier reply, but I have been exhausted and couldn't bring my thoughts together. Incredible how these emotional strains deplete one, so that the eyes, the brain, the will refuse to function. When I was summoned to take this job I knew how little taste I had for it, how small is my store of patience and resourcefulness for political maneuvering, and how wide was the chasm over which I would be required to throw some kind of bridge. But I told the Lord that if any department could be considered his, this was it, and that if I were to accomplish anything it would have to be his doing. It's consoling (in my calmer moments) to remember that I did this, especially since things have ended so dismally. It gives point to your exhortation, "You are not to judge yourself." Incidentally, I shall keep by me for help on other occasions your perceptive remark about the tendency of Jesuits and Calvinists to judge themselves. Especially if they have had a dram of Black Irish melancholy instilled into their ancestry.

I shouldn't even say that things have ended dismally. I shall be happy to be relieved of administration, which is simply not my cup of tea, and to begin knowing people again. And the department can never be again what it was in 1965. In fact, the confusions of this year have already issued into the first concrete evidences of renewal, or a real desire for renewal, on the part of the higher echelons. Proving for the umpteenth time the truth of that bit from *Hebrews*: "*Nulla redemptio sine sanguine.*" ("There is no redemption without the shedding of blood." Heb 9:22)

I think it was just before Holy Week that—while I was grousing over the situation and feeling sorry for myself—I suddenly remembered the Passion, and how many times, making the *Spiritual Exercises*, I had even asked to taste a little of the bitterness of that awful Thursday-Friday, so that (as Ignatius suggests) I might identify more nearly with the Beloved. Now it had come, and I was spewing it out with disgust and protest. A fine disciple, to be sure.

And at this very late stage in my "imitation." Here was matter I might justly judge myself on—the missed chance to be like him who "opened not his mouth" (Is 53:7).

Do pray for me sometimes. I'm not yet sure what I'll be doing next year, or where. I might stay here, but there remain only four more years before mandatory retirement, and perhaps this is the time to start that "second career" the gerontologists talk about. I don't readily find words to thank you for your letter, which so obviously came from a big and warm heart, and which I shall keep for the dark moments. But thanks, and God bless you.

Affectionately,
Bill

CHAPTER 21

Recording the Earthquake

FOR THE FIRST TIME SINCE HIGH SCHOOL SUMMERS I FOUND myself job-hunting. I had resigned the department chair, and the resignation had been accepted without protest, so giving substance to the intimations I had picked up about my forthcoming replacement. But now what? A radical shift at my age to some other primary occupation than teaching did not strike me as advisable or attractive. Furthermore, I had prepared to teach, I had—except for my stint as a war-time chaplain in the Army—done it consistently since ordination, I enjoyed it mightily, and I thought I had done it reasonably well. To go into parish work and do that effectively would require, I thought, re-tooling for at least a semester. Hospitals were requiring specialized training for their chaplaincies. I was too old to go back into the Army. Another Jesuit university invited me to teach, but stipulated that I would also be department chairman, and I had had a genteel sufficiency of that. At this critical point a letter arrived from Father Dick McBrien, then Dean at Pope John XXIII Seminary, inviting me to join the faculty there.

Cardinal Cushing, some years before, had tried to persuade the American bishops to establish a seminary for older men. He was convinced that there were many potential candidates, and that their age and experience would be better served if they had their own seminary, apart from young men just out of college. When the hierarchy took no action on his proposal he decided, characteristically, to go ahead on his own. It meant that his Archdiocese would have to carry the financial burden and provide the staff, but it was likewise characteristic of the Cardinal that the priests who would be educated at this seminary would not serve only in Boston but would be shared with other American and Canadian dioceses and even with countries as far away as Australia. The first class of graduates had been ordained only in the previous year, so the project still had the zest of a new venture. Father McBrien's cordial letter pointed out some of its attractions:

Dear Bill:

Frank Devine has told me of the unsettled situation in the Theology Department at B.C. He thought, in fact, that you might be a "free agent" by next fall. If that is the case, I am sure you will have several good offers to consider. At Frank's suggestion, I am writing at this time to ask you to consider Pope John Seminary as one of those options. For reasons which I cannot explain now, our faculty will be in need of replenishment in the next academic year. Needless to say, we could take full advantage of your expertise in sacramental theology and in pastoral theology. You would also be an extraordinary asset in a seminary such as this, where we have men of experience and diversified backgrounds. As you know, we have a relatively young faculty, and although the gap has been narrowed in recent years, we have not completely established a balanced situation.

A major personal advantage to you would be the opportunity to remain in the Boston area, removed from the turmoil at B.C., with almost ideal conditions for reading, study, reflection, and writing. I realize that Pope John Seminary cannot compete as yet on an academic level with the colleges and universities that would certainly be interested in your services. However, you may want to consider the specific assets which we have to offer here against the academic strengths of these other institutions.

In any case, Bill, I want you to know that Pope John Seminary would be proud to have you on its faculty. Please keep this in mind as you consider your more prestigious invitations.

My reply was written a week later:

Dear Dick:

Your very kind letter came at a time when, for reasons that I think you could appreciate, it did a good deal for my morale. I'm grateful for your invitation, which I'm sure was seconded by your Rector, to join the faculty of Pope John Seminary.

At the moment my resignation as Chairman has just been accepted and I am still in the process of making up my mind exactly where I should go from here, if indeed I should go from here. I have some six or seven options at the moment, but feel that I am not able to select the proper one yet. When the situation simmers down and I gain some needed clarity, I'm sure I can give you an answer.

I fully appreciate all the advantages you mention, and I may say that your invitation is very nearly the most attractive that has come to me so far. Please be patient and let me think about matters. I promise not to keep you waiting too long.

Letting go may be a part of wisdom, but it is seldom easy. I had come to Boston College just thirty years before, and seen it grow not only in student enrollment, not only in the quality of its faculty, but in—how shall I describe it?—in awareness of its identity. It had been for many years a small denominational school, intended to educate the sons of unlettered immigrants, and above all to save their faith. You might say that it had no identity of its own, but was simply another useful instrument of the Church. Now, like a child who grows up and is recognized as more than so-and-so's son or daughter, it had begun, while remaining staunchly loyal to the family's values and principles, to have its own distinctive personality. We noticed that we were now educating the grandchildren, even the great-grandchildren of our alumni. They were vastly different in outlook from their forebears, more sophisticated, shaped by events and influences altogether new. Their college, grateful as it was to have these dynasties of graduates, could not treat them as it had their predecessors. And in adapting to their needs the college itself was manifesting the features, the tone, the cachet, if you will, that would distinguish it eventually not only from what it had been but from other institutions, Catholic or even Jesuit in inspiration.

So it was not easy to leave in the midst of this fascinating maturation. I reflected at the same time that with mandatory retirement only four years away, even if I did not leave the college the college would be leaving me—high and dry. In the end I compromised. I moved out to Pope John and taught a full program there, but I kept one course at Boston College.

The Seminary was all that Father McBrien had promised. It afforded even more attractions—the challenge, for instance, of teaching men who would one day be priests, community leaders, heralds and exemplars of the Good News. Their words, spoken privately or in public, might set up echoes generations later. They would preside at events crucially important for the good order of society—at weddings, at christenings, at funerals. They would fortify the dying, console the bereaved, give new hope to the despairing. Day in and day out, they would go to the altar and lead their people in praise, in thanksgiving, in intercession for the needs of a weary world. Teaching them would surely be a responsibility. I preferred to think of it as a privilege.

They were certainly a diversified group. There were widowers as well as men who had never married; there were even grandfathers. There were men who had been religious brothers, but now felt called to the priesthood. There were former engineers, teachers, insurance agents, sales managers, lawyers—there was a Navy commander and an Air Force colonel, a pharmacist, a detective. Some had college and even advanced degrees, some had only high school diplomas but could point to specialized training in a variety of fields and a wealth of experience. Before their admission they had been carefully screened by psychologists for maturity and for motivation. We noted that many of them tended to be rigid in religious matters, tenacious of what they considered "tradition." This was to be expected; they had had to take a firm stand for many years against the world, the flesh, and the devil, and the struggle had made them wary. They found the "changes" introduced only a year or so before by Vatican II especially unsettling. Where now was the "firm foundation" on which they had manfully built their faith and their virtue? Four years of reassurance and re-education would not be too long for some of them to adjust. And if they showed no signs of doing so they were gently but firmly encouraged not to continue. Our people were having enough trouble accepting unfamiliar attitudes and practices; they didn't need priests who would be wedded inexorably to a vanished past.

Discipline at Pope John was nothing like what seminaries had imposed in the preconciliar days. A totalitarian regime of that kind would have been manifestly unsuited to older men. (It was unsuited to younger men, too, but some seminaries took their time about relaxing it.) There was a horarium, of course, affecting such mass movements as class, meals, daily Mass. Otherwise the men were largely free to select their own best times for study and recreation. This had the effect of creating a healthy autonomy for individuals and an air of relaxation for the community. Relations between faculty and students were, in general, informal and easy, though the students knew that we would be the ones who would pass judgment on their academic and spiritual qualifications for the priesthood, so there was no temptation to back-slapping familiarity. Within such limits I made many very happy friendships— friendships that, alas, I have not been able in most cases to keep fresh; once ordained, my friends scattered to dioceses from Montreal to Miami, from Altoona to Anchorage.

It was at the faculty table and in the faculty common room that I found the genial companionship, never divorced from a sense of serious purpose, that had vanished from life at Boston College. I laughed more in the first month than I had in the previous four years. Three of us were religious: Frank Devine and I were Jesuits, Steve Doyle was a Franciscan. The others were diocesans. All of them were a good twenty-five years younger than I, but they gave me such a welcome and such support that I keep them in my affection and my prayers to this day. We met each night in the common room; the pretext was the news, but unless that was something extraordinary we listened to one another rather than to the broadcast. Frank Reagan was a most accomplished mimic. He would give us Cardinal Cushing's stentorian pronouncements with the exact nasal quality and the unique gestures of the original; then he would shift suddenly to Bishop Wright's curious falsetto. The Bishop (who was really eloquent) could not for some reason pronounce the letter "r"; he had moreover a trick of smacking his lips after delivering an especially pungent remark. Frank had him down to the life.

When I remember now all these assets and advantages, I wonder why, after three years, I left. Perhaps there was a "passage" involved here, from middle to old age. If so, I was certainly not conscious of it. I think, rather, that I could not adjust to the inevitably small world of the seminary after the excitement, the sense of being on the threshold of immense possibilities, that I had experienced in the chairmanship. My pulses refused to slow down. There must, I told myself, be something bigger to do while the energies lasted and before the enthusiasm engendered by the Council died away. I had always thought Tennyson's "Ulysses" his best lyric, and now it seemed almost prophetic:

> Old age hath yet his honour and his toil.
> Death closes all, but something ere the end,
> Some work of noble note, may yet be done,
> Not unbecoming men that strove with gods.

So I resigned at Pope John, with abiding gratitude and affection for the students and especially the faculty there, and returned to Boston College. There, to be sure, I had a full program with the undergraduates—for one year. Then I watched incredulously as the classroom doors closed forever. At sixty-five in those days one was retired—period. No possibility of staying on as a part-time teacher. There was a little party in the President's office; nice things were said, and the retirees were awarded easy chairs—a gift whose symbolism was altogether too clear. We had become, as the Army used to say during World War II, superfluous to the war effort.

Some of my fellow-retirees were delighted. They told me how eagerly they looked forward to a life of freedom and relaxation. I wished them well, but inwardly I was raging. Who said I was finished? Who was the genius who decided that everyone was ready for the scrap-heap at sixty-five? Wasn't this arrant discrimination on the single issue of age—just as outrageous as discrimination on the grounds of color or race or gender? Other cultures put a high value on the contribution of older people; in fact, the really outstanding figures of our time had been older men: Churchill, de Gasperi, Pope John, Roosevelt. This was a cheap maneuver: two instructors could be hired for what a full professor was paid. If a teacher were hired by committee and promoted by committee, why couldn't a committee decide whether retirement was in order? *Et cetera, et cetera*, and far into the night.

It was, of course, totally unavailing, and I was adrift again. What to do?

I wasn't idle. I directed retreats, counseled people in endless interviews, took over parishes in the summer, sat on liturgical committees, directed three discussion groups, assisted in the office of the Province Director of Formation, presided at weddings and baptisms, helped to edit a short-lived magazine and a homiletic service. But my anger and depression grew deeper and deeper. I participated in the new "sensitivity sessions," but found them distasteful and unhelpful. Six months with a psychiatric counselor helped to identify the problems, but not to cope with them. I went off to live alone for a month and try to put things together, but friends got worried and persuaded me to give it up. That way, as Lear said, madness lies.

It was a long three years. For the first time I understood how deadening, how damaging mental depression can be. The surgeries and other physical illnesses I had had were trifles in comparison. I remembered and felt a new sympathy for men like my brother Fran who, in the thirties, were qualified and eager to work but could not find employment. The worst feature was my own perplexity: there was plenty to do, but I could find satisfaction in none of it. The one job I enjoyed and believed myself still quite able to do well had been taken from me. And the implication was clear: you have nothing more to offer. Go away somewhere and be quiet.

Actually, I was down in Key West, taking the place of the pastor who was on vacation, when my Provincial, Father Dick Cleary, phoned from Boston. How would I like to go to New York? To New York? Yes, the Jesuit community that published the weekly magazine *America* was looking for a superior. It made no difference that I had never been a superior, never thought I had the gifts such an office called for. What mattered was that Dick thought I could handle it, that I could still make a contribution.

Some weeks later a terse cable came from Rome: "Leonard approved." I packed up and went to New York. There the community gave me an unfeigned welcome and helped me to begin the *vita nuova.* It was clear that I was to have nothing to say or do with the editorial policies of the magazine; those were in the capable hands of Father Joe O'Hare and his staff. I did contribute a book review now and then, but my assignment lay with the religious life, the health, the material necessities of the community. If it should become necessary, I gathered that I was to mediate between the editor and any members of the staff. It never did become necessary.

The community was an extraordinarily varied and richly talented group. They came from all over the United States—except for Father Michael Chu, who had managed to escape from mainland China, where two of his brothers, both Jesuits also, had been imprisoned by the Communists, were released, and then again clapped into jail by the Gang of Four. They were at the time still languishing in durance vile. I once asked Michael how long his family had been Christian. He knew precisely how long—it was more than three hundred years. None of us, I reflected, could have produced such an exact record of our family's conversion.

There was a preponderance in the community of New Yorkers born and bred, or of people who had taken New York to their hearts. One grey, cheerless February morning, for the fun of it I proposed at breakfast that we move the whole operation of the magazine to the sunnier climes of Fort Lauderdale. There was immediate consternation. Leave New York? Sure, I said; think of the advantages—no oil bills, no overcoats, no ice or slush, no grime or crime, an invigorating swim after a hard day's work . . . But what about libraries, museums, people to consult or interview? Well, I said, some of those resources just might be available outside of Manhattan, and in any case we would have a handy modern device called the telephone . . . There ensued much grave shaking of heads, and for a time I was under suspicion as a quisling who could wreck a prospering enterprise.

Meeting a weekly deadline is hard work. And humanly unrewarding work, lacking the stimulation of a responsive audience such as one might have in a church or a classroom. Almost the only response one could look for was a letter—frequently, in those days, an abusively angry letter—dissenting from a previously published article or editorial. The staff ploughed through reams of manuscripts, recommended them for acceptance or rejection, suggested deletions or clarifications or other improvements. Comment had to be made on current events within hours, sometimes, after those events were reported in the hot headlines of the daily press, and before their significance could be clearly discerned. Feature articles and special issues had to be planned, and each member of the staff had to keep up untiringly with developments in his area of competence. It was grueling work, and its price was hours, days, of lonely concentration.

My own contribution to all this was minimal. I had to make sure that food was on the table, that the elevator was working, that the laundry arrived on time. Next door, contractors were dynamiting for a new building—skyscraper apartments were built to the left of us in my first year, a sports complex to the right of us in my second year, and a hotel across the street in my third year, so giving point to the remark that New York would be a lovely city if they ever finished it—and, after seeing with concern the cracks that were appearing in our foundations, we installed a Geiger Counter in the basement to record the shocks and thus provide evidence for the lawsuits that almost certainly would ensue. A bag lady took up residence on the grating in the sidewalk outside our door and angrily refused all offers of assistance. Two young men appeared in our lobby; one engaged the receptionist in conversation while the other slipped up the stairs and appropriated five hundred dollars which the superior had thoughtlessly neglected to conceal. Central

Park, only three blocks away, offered a sylvan refuge for gentle exercise so long as one went there in broad daylight, kept to the more frequented paths, and glanced regularly over one's shoulder to be sure one was not being followed. New York was aggressive: "Get out of my way!" seemed to be the watchword on the teeming, jostling sidewalks, and indeed might have been a slogan for the entire hurrying, headlong city. But the place could be amusing, too. One day, out for a walk, I came upon a large number of police at the corner of our street. No one seemed to know what they were there for, and they weren't telling. At last one woman spoke to a pleasant-looking cop: "Is there somebody here?" she asked. "Well, lady," he said, "You're here. I'm here. We're somebody, ain't we?" (Later I learned that they were there to control a threatened demonstration against a magazine that had published fifty jokes about Puerto Ricans.) On another walk I encountered a group of Con Ed workmen about to call it a day. One of them climbed into their truck and, blowing the horn furiously, scattered pedestrians, including me, and backed up ten yards or more against oncoming traffic so that the others could come aboard. One of the men looked him over and said, "Now we know you can blow the horn. What else can you do?"

Restlessness, a pernicious demon, was at my door again. To be sure, I was not as desperate as a former superior of the community had been. He, the story went, disliked his job, and held in special abomination the pigeons which nested in the alley outside his window. He would save burned-out light bulbs and throw them so that they would explode against the brick walls, causing a mad whirring of wings that served to appease what our resident psychologist called his Impotent Rage Factor.

I went back to Boston regularly for meetings of my discussion groups, but did not succeed in efforts to organize anything similar in New York. Then Phil McNiff, director of the Boston Public Library and a close friend of many years, came up with what seemed to me a brilliant idea. "Look," he said, "It's almost twenty years since Vatican II. The changes in our liturgy have been enormous. Older people are throwing away the very things—books, pamphlets, devotional artifacts, mementoes—that historians will need to document and illustrate the transition. You should begin to collect those things before they all disappear!"

I liked the idea, but thought it should be expanded. Liturgy wasn't the only feature of Catholic experience that had changed.

Some pretty basic attitudes were different now. Theology had changed, and catechetics, and pastoral practice, and religious life, and creative writing, and about everything else. Moreover, the Council had insisted that the activities and concerns of Christians should take their inspiration and support from the liturgy and be brought back to the liturgy to be blended with the worship of the one great Priest. In other words, "liturgy" was not limited to sacred ceremony or to the hour spent in church on Sunday. It was a comprehensive term that included all our faith, hope, and charity and whatever these involved us in. So my collection, if it were to be a truly "liturgical" collection, would have to range far beyond missals, breviaries, rituals, and the like. It would have to be what I decided to call it: "Liturgy and Life."

But first I had to assure myself that no one else had undertaken such a project. I went to the likely places—Collegeville, Notre Dame, Catholic University. They had collections, of course, but none that specifically addressed the transition from the preconciliar to the conciliar period. So I could go ahead without fear of duplicating someone else's effort. Dr. Tom O'Connell, the affable and imaginative University Librarian at Boston College, was enthusiastic when I proposed the idea, and the President, Father Don Monan, hired me as a sort of curator by remote control.

When Pope John XXIII called the Second Vatican Council, he said he was only opening the windows to let in a little fresh air. What he let in was more like a tornado. Or, as the Father General of the Jesuits said fifteen years later, what the Pope produced was an earthquake. And the rubble lay all about us. To be sure, the rubble consisted of customs, observances, habits of thought and piety that were at best only peripheral to the faith. But they pervaded all our Catholic life; to many they seemed so identified with it that when they vanished swiftly and utterly it was as if that life itself had become extinct.

At no time in church history, perhaps, had so vast a cultural change come about in so short a time. And probably none of us who survived the earthquake will ever be able to explain what happened. We were too close to it. We can't properly evaluate the forces that came to a boil beneath the surface, were rigidly repressed, and at last exploded. This will be the task of historians who will have the advantage and the perspective of time.

What we could and should do is to provide the historians with the raw material for their work: primary sources like records, letters, clippings from the press. But also those irreplaceable things that are so often thoughtlessly discarded: photographs, tape recordings, pamphlets, well-thumbed prayer books once in daily use, devotional pictures, medals, badges—even curiosities like holy water fountain pens or clicking confession counters. Carefully sorted and annotated, a collection of such materials could help to explain the religious attitudes of an era and illustrate the shift from one religious culture to another. We are aware, to take an example, that at Rome, some time before the fourth century, Greek was abandoned as the liturgical language and Latin was adopted. But we don't know exactly when or how. Was it primarily the result of a directive from authorities or a response to popular demand? If more had been known on this point twenty-five years ago, when we abandoned Latin and began to pray in our own language, the shock many experienced on shifting to the vernacular might not have been so great. I remember the good lady who—sincerely if a bit dramatically—explained to me why she no longer went to Mass. "I'm one of the broken-hearted Catholics, Father," she said.

It was clear to me that the collection could not be limited to materials related to the theology and practice of public worship. I remembered that the first American Liturgical Weeks, which began in 1940, had attracted only people interested in that area. In later years, though, people with other primary interests came to see that progress in their fields was intimately bound up with the renewal of the liturgy. So, throughout the forties and fifties, we began to see them at the annual Weeks—first, as one would expect, the Scripture scholars, then the artists, architects, and musicians, then the racial justice and the social action workers, then the systematic theologians, and at last even the moralists and the canon lawyers. "It all goes together," as the pioneer liturgists used to say, and the great Council of 1962-65 backed them up by publishing decrees that affected not only the liturgy but all those other disciplines and activities, and precisely in their relation to the worship of God and the coming of his Kingdom.

So if the collection were to mirror the times accurately and comprehensively, it would have to show, to some extent at least, the changed attitudes that began to be noticed in all areas of Catholic life. Furthermore, it would have to show the transition that took place—the *terminus a quo* as well as the *terminus ad quem*—where we came from, as the psychologists like to say, and where we had arrived. This is not to say that the reform has been completed; it never can be. But perhaps the most dramatic and traumatic changes are behind us—or maybe we have simply become accustomed to change. At any rate, the capacities even of a university library are limited, and so it was decided, for the sake of round numbers, to work on the period between 1925 and 1975.

Those fifty years embrace the earthquake, but leave a margin on both sides to let us see what built up to it and what came after. An unprecedented cultural transformation such as we have experienced does not occur spontaneously, without cause. Neither do the waves it makes subside and return to their former channel. Our young adults have no awareness of what Catholic life was like before the Council, or even how the transition came about, while those who were involved longest are passing from the scene, seldom leaving any memories behind them. An archive of primary source materials, catalogued and accessible under one roof, could fuel many penetrating studies and preserve the memory of what the American Church experienced during those fifty years of radical transformation.

We would need, to be concrete, books, magazines, pamphlets, leaflets that would indicate where we were or where we were going spiritually, theologically, devotionally, liturgically, socially, ecumenically. We should have a collection of Father Daniel Lord's pamphlets, of Father John O'Brien's apologetics, of the books of Archbishop Fulton Sheen, Thomas Merton, Abbot Marmion, H.A. Reinhold, Sigrid Undset, Father Finn. We would need files or at least samples of periodicals like *America, Commonweal,* the *Messenger of the Sacred Heart,* the *American Ecclesiastical Review,* the *Homiletic and Pastoral Review, Integrity,* the *Catholic Worker, Jubilee, Cecilia,* the *Catholic Biblical Quarterly, Ave Maria, Thought, Theological Studies, Columbia,* the *Magnificat,* the *Liturgical Arts Quarterly,* the *Critic, Today, Worship.* The many publications of the Liturgical Press, Sheed & Ward, Helicon, Bruce, Newman, P.J. Kenedy, Benziger Brothers, Herder and Herder would be valuable. We should have missals, breviaries, rituals, catechisms, seminary and college textbooks, hymnals, novena booklets, prayer books, even "holy cards." Records of associations, local or national, like the Sodality of Our Lady, the Confraternity of Christian Doctrine, the Holy Name Society, the Knights of Columbus, the Liturgical Conference would be useful. Correspondence, especially of bishops or leaders of movements, would be especially important. We would welcome the programs of conventions or other meetings held by liturgical, scriptural, social action and similar groups, or papers read at such conventions. Pastoral letters, diocesan directives, and the legislation of religious congregations—constitutions old or updated, rules, custom books—should be in the collection. Especially welcome would be photographs or recordings of individuals or groups who influenced Catholic life during those fifty years.

Dom Gregory Dix, whose erudite and stimulating book, *The Shape of the Liturgy*[1] appeared just before his lamented death fifty years ago, provided a fitting rationale for such a collection:

> No subject can have a greater appeal for its own sake to Christians than the record of what has always been the essential life not only of the Church corporately, but of all the individual saints and sinners who have gone to God before us in the Body of Christ—the tradition of Christian worship, unbroken since the Upper Room. . . . The study of liturgy is not rightly to be regarded as a branch of canon law or Christian administrative history; it cannot be treated as the mere study of a series of "regulations" about Christian worship. We have forgotten that the study of liturgy is above all a study of life, that Christian worship has always been done by real men and women, whose contemporary circumstances have all the time a profound effect upon the ideas and aspiration with which they come to worship. . . . Thus arises the ever-shifting emphasis of Christian devotion and "devotions," which play around the liturgy, interpreting it afresh to every generation and to every race. This is a psychological study of the utmost fascination, which requires insight and human sympathy as well as wide knowledge. . . .
>
> To those who know a little of Christian history probably the most moving of all the reflections it brings is not the thought of the great events and the well-remembered saints, but of those innumerable millions of entirely obscure faithful men and women, every one with his or her individual hopes and fears and joys and sorrows and loves—and sins and temptations and prayers—once every whit as vivid and alive as mine are now. They have left no slightest trace in this world, not even a name, but have passed to God utterly forgotten by men. Yet each one of

---

1.   London, 1945, pp. 741-745.

them once believed and prayed as I believe and pray, and found it hard and grew slack and sinned and repented and fell again. Each of them worshiped at the Eucharist, and found their thoughts wandering and tried again, and felt heavy and unresponsive and yet knew—just as really and pathetically as I do these things. The sheer stupendous quantity of the love of God which this ever repeated action has drawn from the obscure Christian multitudes through the centuries is itself an overwhelming thought. (All that going with one to the altar every morning!)

The first step was to get the word out. I wrote a release that was carried by more than fifty diocesan newspapers, and another that appeared in the more professional journals. I wrote personal letters to deans and chairmen of theology departments in Catholic universities across the country, and to all members of the Boston College departments of theology, history, and sociology, together with suggestions as to how the collection might be used (specifically, a list of a hundred topics that might be treated in term papers, dissertations, research), and a cordial invitation to visit the collection personally or to bring students to see it.

Gifts of books and other materials poured in from all over the country, and I wrote more than a thousand personal letters in grateful acknowledgment. Most packages came from older people; they were accompanied, often, with touching notes, saying that they hated to part with things that had been in the family for many years, but were glad that they would have a "good home." One lady wrote that she was sending some things that had belonged to her uncle, a priest—his stole, his ritual, and his suspenders. When I opened the package, there they all were. And I suppose that her uncle could not have functioned adequately as a priest if any one of them had been missing.

So there it was, a jumble of books, sacred music, candlesticks, rosaries, statues that glowed in the dark, sick call sets, birettas, vestments and altar appurtenances, a "clacker" that substituted for bells during Holy Week, pictures of little girls in First Communion dress, habits of religious women, and "holy cards"—a perfect blizzard of these. I had been shoveling them aside as of little value, but one day, impelled by curiosity, I took about a thousand of them to my room for closer examination. I wondered if I could discover in them any pattern of spirituality—a mirror, so to speak, of the American Catholic piety of our time. I was particularly interested, since the Second Vatican Council had directed (SCL., #13) that popular devotions should harmonize with the liturgy, in learning whether in fact there had been any accord between the two, and how much. And I wrote a piece for *America* (September 12, 1981) in which I listed my impressions. (See Appendix III.)

In our time we have seen a tremendous emphasis on prayer. In religious circles no topic has been discussed so earnestly; books, lectures, courses on prayer abound. But most of the attention has seemed to be given to private prayer, as if this were in no way related to the public prayer one engages in regularly with one's fellows. Even if one has heard nothing of the papal teachings of the last sixty years, and nothing of the conciliar decree on the liturgy, one should, it seems, be beginning to sense that something is wrong with a prayer life that would be lived in two incommunicable compartments, neither influencing the other in any way. How could a Christian actively participate in the Mass, for instance, without feeling some reverberations of that experience in the prayer he or she might offer afterward, alone? It would be like expecting a married man to plan and act without reference to his wife and children. And how could a Christian take an honest part in the Mass who never lifted his heart to God privately, never made a holy resolution to serve God better, never praised God or asked pardon for his sins or prayed for what he needed? We cannot thus divide ourselves, nor do we attempt it in any other department of life; a man who is, let us say, a physician or a business executive is not because of that profession less a husband or a father.

There should, then, be an intimate relation between our public and our private prayer. One should feed the other; for example, a young man who has just been ordained is surely prompted to thank God during his chapel visit that evening, or (the other way round) a young husband whose first child has just been safely born would surely be moved to dedicate his fatherhood to God the next time he participates in the Mass. If I meditate on the Passion of our Lord and my own sins, as I do, let us say, during a retreat, then my next confession is likely to be more fruitful. And (the other way round again) I may linger in the church after Mass to ponder prayerfully and privately the grace that has been mine in Holy Communion. Human beings are like coins, which have two faces—heads and tails, as we say. We are members by baptism of a community, and should therefore join that community in public worship; we retain, however, our own highly individual, incommunicable personalities, and should pray as such, personally. To say that the two sides of our nature should never assist each other is absurd; it would be to advocate a kind of schizophrenia.

Historians like Jungmann and Dix could throw light on the interesting question as to how a separation between the two ever came to be a possibility in our religious lives. There are fashions in piety—or it might be better to say that there are deep, soundless tides in cultures and civilizations which carry us unwittingly this way and that and make us the creatures we are in a particular historical epoch. It is a fact that our private prayer became detached in large measure from our public worship and from Holy Scripture as well. Now, however, we are being officially encouraged—even if so far many of us have not notably been influenced by the encouragement—to establish a reunion of the two aspects of our Christian personalities, so that we may become whole once more, in prayer as well as in action.

It is not difficult to see how private prayer helps us to share more completely and more meaningfully in public worship. We don't seem to be aware, however, of how public worship can nourish our private prayer, and it might be worthwhile to linger on this point for a moment, since public worship, as Popes and Council have insisted, has the greater dignity and efficacy, and should shape and govern private prayer.

The Second Vatican Council (SCL, #10-12) emphasizes the commitment we make when we engage in public worship. This is obvious in regard to baptism, in which we undertake to shun evil and to follow Christ; it is this commitment we mean when we speak of "renewing our baptismal vows." But it is true also of other liturgical acts; when we marry, for instance, we solemnly pledge to create a union which will be with God's help a miniature replica of the Church, Christ's body. When we receive Holy Communion we commit ourselves to work for that unity in society which the sacrament of the Eucharist proclaims and consolidates. Our participation in the act of public worship overflows, as it were, into our private life, giving it direction and vitality. This should be the case with our prayer, too, but in neither case will it happen unless there is a profound involvement in public worship. Our act of public worship will have to be more than formalism, more than routine, more than an obligation to be discharged and so checked off.

I remember reading some years ago Daniel-Rops' meditation, in his *Sacred History*,[2] on that strange event in the life of the patriarch Jacob (Genesis 32) when Jacob wrestled with the angel. Up to this time Jacob had been a shrewd and restless schemer who stole his brother's blessing and his uncle's flocks, a selfish opportunist who cared for little except his own prosperity. But something happened that night when he struggled with the invisible power and would not let him go until he forced the power to bless him. "All that in Jacob was of doubtful worth," Daniel-Rops says, "his attachment to riches, all the turmoil of passions and failings of character, seem to have been abolished forever by the breath of the spirit. From this time he followed in the steps of his fathers, and became a Patriarch, like Isaac, like Abraham, and his sense of his mission was apparent in all his actions." Our participation in public worship will have to be something like this, a wrestling (and perhaps in the darkness, too) with the invisible, a constraining of God, a pleading to be taken in hand, broken, and shaped nearer to the divine plan. When it is this living thing, it will most certainly provide subject-matter for our private prayer; it will give focus and energy to all our meditation.

Let me suggest, then, without implying that I am doing more than scratching the surface, five themes that are basic to liturgical worship and which could supply us with the material for endless meditation and prayer when we are alone.

The first is the Exodus theme. We see it graphically dramatized in the Easter Nightwatch, but it underlies the sacrament of baptism and indeed provides the basic motivation we Christians have for giving thanks to God. As the hopeless slaves in Egypt were, against all their expectations, snatched from misery and rescued from extermination by their pursuing enemies, so we without any deserving on our part were rescued from damnation and, incredibly, made sons and daughters of God. Once not a people at all, as St. Peter says (1 Pet 2:10), we are now God's people—free, beloved, fed and supported as we march steadily toward our Promised Land. On Cardinal Newman's tomb, before his death, he had had engraved words which he believed summed up all God's goodness to him, a convert: "*ex umbris et imaginibus in veritatem*"—he had been led out of darkness and illusion into truth. This is so-

---

2.   New York, 1949.

berly true of each one of us. We acknowledge it when we begin the Eucharistic Prayer of every Mass: "Let us give thanks to the Lord our God." And, as St. Ambrose said, there is no duty more urgent than that of giving thanks, publicly or privately, or both. Perhaps the early Christians had a more vivid idea than we of what they had been rescued from and what they had been given; at least there seems to be a more frequent expression of thanks in the New Testament than in contemporary Christian writing. But we have every bit as much reason to be grateful, and should say so.

Another theme that is basic to our liturgy and at the same time a fruitful source of private meditation is the theme of the Covenant. This was (and is still) the dominant idea in Jewish piety. The proudest boast of the Jew is that God deigned to enter into a contract with his people. At Sinai, with Moses as mediator, God offered the terms of this contract and promised to abide by them so long as the tribe of Israel would do the same. If they would keep his commandments he would prosper them and preserve them from their enemies. They were to be holy because, as he said, he was holy. The people, with gratitude and enthusiasm, accepted this covenant. It was a solemn commitment on both sides, and it was ratified, as we remember, with blood, the blood of sacrificial animals. But then in his providence and mercy God wished to extend the Covenant to the Gentiles. He sent his Son into the world as a new Moses, a mediator who would shed his own blood to inaugurate and ratify a new and everlasting Covenant, as the prophet had predicted (Ez 36). Christians by accepting baptism solemnly engage to live the new commandment, the commandment of love, and God for his part engages to protect them and to give them heaven and himself.

Here we have indeed a "mystery of faith"—or, as that phrase may also be translated, a "pledge of faithfulness," on both sides. We are forcibly reminded of it when we renew our baptismal vows at Easter, but every Mass is a similar exchange of vows between the faithful God and ourselves. Every time we receive a sacrament we affirm once more the abiding contract. In our meditation on this shall we select God's astounding condescension in binding himself to creatures? Shall we ponder instead the consecration that has, so to speak, descended on and enveloped us, setting us aside for divine worship? When shall we have enough time to appreciate the dignity that the least of us has acquired by becoming party to an agreement with the most high God? There is no lack of material here for our private prayer!

A third idea that we can draw from our public worship is that of fellowship. God has brought us, in St. Paul's phrase (1 Cor 1:9), into the fellowship of his Son. Rugged individualism, in the selfish sense at least, has no place in the Christian scheme of things. We are most definitely our brothers' (and sisters') keepers. Were they not created by the same God who made us, and redeemed by the same precious blood? Do they not raise their voices with us at Mass in praise and petition? Do they not approach, hungry as we are hungry, the same table, and are they not fed with the same lavish generosity? Of course we must carry one another's burdens.

But our sharing in the common offering of public worship teaches us also that we must strive to improve our personal offering so that the total worship of the community will be more worthy of God. We must think of how we can make during our lifetime a contribution to the common good instead of a purely personal and selfish achievement. The development of our talents and opportunities, the fostering of our knowledge, love, holiness, human perfection of all kinds will be our gift, gladly given to augment the holdings of the community and to enhance the community's offering of love and gratitude to God. Here, surely, our joining in public worship instructs us in Christian living and gives direction and focus to our private aspirations.

Still another theme of the liturgy will be endlessly helpful to us as we pray privately, and that is the victory theme. We might call it the Easter psychology, since it is most evident in the season of our Lord's resurrection, but it is never out of our thoughts, really, even during Lent, even during times of sorrow and seeming abandonment. It is the conviction that God's plan will be achieved; he is not mocked, he will not be withstood. Christ rose as he predicted that he would, in spite of the jeers of the Pharisees at the foot of the cross, in spite of the stone rolled against the mouth of the tomb. This conviction, the very essence of the good news, is announced most impressively at Easter, but every Sunday is a little Easter proclaiming the same stupendous fact. In every sacrament we encounter the risen, the living Christ. God is faithful to his word; he said he would do it and he did. In the Church at large and in me personally his love will have its way, no matter what obstacles it must surmount. Such a psychology creates joy, of course; we listen to it in the *"Exultet"* of Easter, in the Alleluias of the whole year, but (and particularly in these days when hope seems to have died out of so many hearts) it should irradiate our personal lives, assuage our private sorrows, give meaning to our possibly drab occupations, lift up our hearts in gratitude to the all-powerful and victorious God we serve.

A last theme drawn from the liturgy to feed our private prayer might be the priestly or mediatorial theme. We have all been given a share in Christ, so we share also in his priesthood. But a priest's office is to worship and to intercede for his brethren, and for this we are uniquely consecrated and deputed by baptism and confirmation. We exercise our priesthood supremely at Mass, where we are privileged to offer with Christ our Head the peerless worship of the only Son, and to say with him the prayer of the Mediator: "Father, forgive." But we go out from Mass to carry on this mediation through him and with him and in him, asking forgiveness for sin wherever it occurs, deflecting, as it were, the wrathful vengeance of God from our brothers and sisters, offering to the eternal Majesty not only the homage of one of his creatures but the grateful adoration of them all. Who will venture to estimate the good accomplished by such priestly intercession?

To sum up: none of us has a double nature; we are not two men, two women, though we do look both inward and outward. The way we pray when we come together as the Christian assembly can and should help us after we leave the assembly. By the same token, our private prayer can prepare us for whole-hearted sharing in the community prayer. Traffic flows in both directions on this two-way street.

CHAPTER 22

Let Us Bless the Lord

THE "LITURGY AND LIFE" COLLECTION HAS GROWN AND PROSPERED. Fifteen years after its inauguration it holds 27,000 volumes and any quantity of materials illustrative of Catholic life and piety before and after the Second Vatican Council. Gathering all this has given purpose and vibrancy to a life that seemed at a dead end before I started the project, and I owe a great debt of thanks to Phil McNiff who suggested it. But managing it from a distance became increasingly difficult. Life with the congenial community in New York was decidedly pleasant, but what I was doing there did not accord with my temperament or talents. After three years I applied for relief, and came back to Boston College.

One of the first things I noticed on my return was that the altar my soldiers had built for me in New Guinea had disappeared. I had had it shipped home from the South Pacific because I thought it would be a unique souvenir of the war and a memorial to our faculty and students who had served. But for reasons that I never quite understood it had not attracted much attention or been considered especially worth preserving, and it was moved from one inconspicuous corner of the campus to another. Now I discovered it in the cellar of one of our residences, and realized that its next stop would probably be the dump. Happily, I learned about this time that the Army had a museum to house and display items related to the history of its Corps of Chaplains. I called and asked the curator if he would be interested in the altar and its appurtenances, and within a week a truck appeared and took it all away. My heart smote me as the truck vanished down the Avenue. It was carrying my last and best souvenirs of the vivid years—the faraway, reeking jungle, the unnatural life we led amid the strains and anxieties of war, and also the comfort and courage we Christian men found in our assemblies around that altar. But now it stands in the Chaplains' Museum at Fort Monmouth in New Jersey, the centerpiece of the World War II exhibit, looking just as it did fifty years ago in New Guinea. I was asked to write and record a brief account of its history and an explanation of its symbolism, so now visitors at the museum may push a button and listen as they look.

I was a Jesuit for ten years before anyone in the communities I lived in celebrated a Golden Jubilee. In those days people—in religious life or out of it—did not live as long as they do now, when fifty-year anniversaries are fairly common. In my own case, the physicians and surgeons who cared for me repeatedly with skill and devotion deserve most of the credit for a long life. I keep them in my grateful prayers.

When one can look back on half a century in any walk of life, however, the occasion does not go unnoticed. Long thoughts are in order; ineradicable memories of sad and happy events, regret over the evanescence of youthful energies and aspirations, gratitude for the graces that sustained the original commitment and made perseverance possible—in the nick of time, perhaps, and when all one's inclinations ran the other way. What will it be like to look back in the clear light of eternity and know, as the old man Jacob knew, that "God has been my shepherd from my birth to this day" (Gen 48:15)? Eternity will not be long enough to sing grateful alleluias for such shepherding.

One of my happiest recollections is that of my parents' Golden Wedding. We had a Mass of Thanksgiving, of course, and my father and mother came to the altar and renewed their marriage vows, amid smiles and, yes, not a few tears in the congregation. We all knew or could surmise pretty accurately the joys and sorrows of those fifty years together. What struck me most forcibly was the attitude of relatives, neighbors, old friends at the reception after Mass. They approached my parents almost, it seemed to me, as if they were approaching a shrine, and in their manner was as much awe and reverence as there was glad greeting. Here— this seemed to be their feeling—were two people who had entered into a covenant of love half a century ago and had been faithful to it. What an achievement for frail human nature! How much giving and forgiving had gone into it, how much sharing of pain and pleasure, how much forbearance and selfless concern for the other. Was this not beautiful, and was there not something holy and sacred about it? And was it not fitting that such fidelity should be celebrated with joy and thanksgiving, and renewed publicly before God's people as it had been entered into years before?

"I have loved you," God said to his people, "with an everlasting love" (Jer 31:3). It is not easy for us to realize that we are deeply loved even by another human being, and less easy to realize that God loves us—has even solemnly bound himself to love us. But every page of revelation testifies to the fact, and the Jews of old, in the Psalms, cried out their praise of God for his faithful love. "He said he would do it," they shouted, "and he did!"

A covenant—to return for a moment to that immensely supportive and stimulating idea—creates a lasting bond and an intimate union between the two parties that contract it. Moses had been the mediator of the old covenant between God and man; it was sealed with the blood of animals. The new and everlasting covenant was mediated by Jesus Christ and sealed with his blood, so that, as St. Peter said (1 Pet 2: 10), God made us a chosen race, a royal priesthood, a consecrated nation—his people, in short. This affected us individually at baptism, when we were received into that people, when the covenant was extended to include us. "Age after age you gather a people to yourself," as the third Eucharistic Prayer has it. We became his sons and daughters, the brothers and sisters of Christ, heirs with the beloved Son of the Kingdom he would inherit. Since most of us were infants at the time, the pledges required of us as partners in the covenant were made for us by others. We came only slowly to understand what was expected of us. Maybe some of us have never taken in what God bound himself to do. In other words, we have never learned to savor and to lean confidently on his changeless love for us. And our Christian life is dreadfully impoverished as a result. We walk in fear; we should, as St. John urges us (1 Jn 2:10), walk in love.

Our renewed familiarity with the Bible, the revitalized retreat movement, the charismatic movement, Marriage Encounter and other contemporary developments have been awakening us to the power of love in our spirituality, and may prove to be among the fruits of the Spirit for which we prayed so ardently when Vatican II was in session. But we need to relate these good things to the weekly celebration of the Mass among us, so as to preserve the primacy of the Eucharist in our spirituality and to make sure that our piety avoids easy sentiment and retains the corporate, social dimension our Lord gave it.

How shall we go about this? By talking about the covenant a great deal, in the first place. The word, which now has an archaic ring, is not adequately translated into more current terms like contract, alliance, treaty, agreement, pact. But it need not be discarded. It can be made familiar again, as words like liturgy, eucharist, reconciliation have been made familiar. Dramatic, colorful narratives from the Old Testament, of the events at Sinai (Ex 24; 34) or the renewals of the covenant at Shechem (Jos 24) or under Josiah (2 Chr 34; 35) or Ezra (Neh 8-10), even when they do not constitute the readings appointed for the Sunday, could be woven into our homilies. These episodes initiated or reinvigorated the covenant of the Old Law and formed peaks in the uninterrupted dialogue of the Jewish people with God. Above all, the supreme moment of the Last Supper, when our Lord lifted the cup and said, "This is my blood of the new covenant," might be explained as the fulfillment of the earlier types and the beautiful promise of Jeremiah 31:

> The days are coming, says the Lord, when I will make a new covenant with the house of Israel and the house of Judah. It will not be like the covenant I made with their fathers the day I took them by the hand to lead them forth from the land of Egypt, for they broke my covenant, and I had to show myself their master, says the Lord. But this is the covenant which I will make with the house of Israel after those days, says the Lord. I will place my law within them, and write it upon their hearts; I will be their God, and they shall be my people.

But perhaps, after all, our people may not grasp the fact that the covenant is bilateral, that they as well as God have pledged themselves to its terms—that, indeed, their whole practice of the Christian life is a response in love to God's unwavering love of them. So this must be emphasized. However, we learn more readily by doing than by instruction. Once we learn that our "Amen" at the end of the Eucharistic Prayer is not a mere conclusion but a solemn ratification and commitment, we shall shout it with enthusiasm. It is our "yes" to God and his generosity, our willing surrender to his love, our cheerful taking up of the cross once more on the strength of his promises.

At Sinai and in the annual celebrations of the covenant carried on by the Passover meals through hundreds of years, the people of the covenant sat down to feast with God. Their eating and drinking together was a powerful sign of the communion now established, the intimacy with the Most High brought about by their mutual acceptance of each other. But in our piety the long separation of Holy Communion from the covenant sacrifice still shapes our attitudes. How can we make Communion such a sign at our Sunday Masses? By insisting once again that recognizable bread, not wafers, be employed? By distributing the Eucharist from this Mass, not from the tabernacle? By multiplying extraordinary ministers of the Eucharist and sharing the cup more often than we do? By taking a few silent minutes, after the last communicant has retired from the altar, to "taste and see how good is the Lord"?

Fidelity to one's commitments is not, they say, a virtue highly prized in our time. Nevertheless, as Golden Weddings and Jubilees prove, we cannot withhold our admiration of those who, like God, say they will do a good thing and steadfastly do it.

I had been thinking for a long time how good it would be to assemble all the surviving "pioneers" of the liturgical movement in this country and gather their recollections of what the liturgical situation was forty years before, what they hoped then to do about it, what obstacles they encountered, and so on. Many who might have contributed to that history—Michel, Hellriegel, Busch, Ellard, Hillenbrand, Mathis, Reinhold, Carroll, Howell, Morrison, Ross-Duggan, Sherry, O'Connell, Ducey—had already gone to the rich rewards their vision and their labors merited, leaving behind, in most cases, all too little in the way of materials that a historian might find useful. The survivors, I thought, could prod one another's memories and come up with recollections, grave or gay or grim, that would let posterity know what worship was like *in diebus illis*, and what it cost to bring about a *novus ordo saeculorum*. Since those days there had been a tremendous turnabout in Catholic life and piety; a whole sub-culture had vanished, at a speed unprecedented, perhaps, in the history of the Church. Young people now had simply no idea of what it was like to be a Catholic in 1940—or even in 1960. Would the pioneers endorse all that had happened? Were the present situation and prospect fulfillments of their lonely dreaming? What directions, in their opinion, should the renewal take now?

But then it struck me that it would be an even better idea if a number of younger scholars and leaders were invited to join the pioneers and with them to hold a consultation on the present state of renewal. I remembered that it was in 1943 that the Liturgical Conference had been established. Twenty years later, in 1963, Vatican II had published its Constitution on the Sacred Liturgy. Since then twenty more years had slipped away; it was 1983, and time for a really close look at where we were and where we'd like to be in, say, 2003—another twenty years down the road. Wouldn't it be great if the veterans of the forties could study again, this time with the insights of younger, more vigorous and highly trained allies, the great charter of the Council? I knew them well enough to predict that they would enjoy the opportunity to talk again about a cause they had loved and labored for. And recommendations from such a cluster of *periti* would undoubtedly be well received in pastoral and academic centers, and even by the American bishops.

It remains true that when you want something done you ask a busy person to do it. The committees I asked to plan the Consultation were made up of gifted, productive, very busy people, yet generous enough to come together for seventeen long-ish sessions. The tentative plan we worked out at first called for a presentation from the pioneers which might be called "Where We Were And Where We Hoped To Go." This would be followed by a statement by the contemporaries under the heading "Where We Came From And Where We Think We Are." It would be a case of "Early Vision" and "Present Vision," pointing toward "The Shape of Things Undone." Both parties, in other words, looking forward. The tone could be gentle, paying a mutual tribute, including a bit of raillery, perhaps, but no caricatures. We should try to point out the good in each period, even, it was implied, in the somewhat frenetic exuberance of the sixties.

We wanted to spend some time on questions touching the theology of worship. In our teaching, how could we get beyond—or under—the "noise of solemn assemblies," the "how to do it"? Theologians were using new language, asking new questions in the area of symbolism. There seemed to be a "transitional" language about the Eucharist in particular. Then there were pastoral issues—what Mary Ryan used to call the "liturgy and" questions, which were taken up in many of the old Liturgical Weeks, but which called for renewed emphasis now. For example, Latin had been a problem for liturgy in 1943; it was solved by Vatican II's concession of the vernacular. The role of women in liturgy was a problem in 1983; we did not know how it would be solved. Topics therefore for this pastoral session should include whatever seemed to be emerging or developing. How, for instance, could we recover some variety in our prayer-forms, instead of our present exclusive reliance on the Mass? Was it likely that the sacramentals would come into use again? What about Sunday communion services in parishes without priests? There seemed at the moment no future for bible vigils or for the liturgy of the hours, but communal penance rites were popular; how should these be shaped and encouraged? Then there were the cultural and ethnic aspects of liturgy in the United States. How do we meet the needs of diverse populations, especially of Afro-Americans and Hispanics? What can the base communities and the advocates of liberation theology teach us? There were sociological questions, too; for instance, the more people share worship the more homogeneous the congregation becomes. What does this say about our present parish structures? About the appropriateness of our present rituals? We would certainly have to find room for discussion of the environment of worship: art, architecture, music, dance. It was clear that there would be no lack of materials for discussion; in fact, a semester— if it had been practicable—might have been a better time-span than three days.

The short-term or long-range benefits of such gatherings must be left to the computers in the hands of recording angels. In any case, this one was for me a last hurrah. As one's vital energies wane, the thought of the endless practical arrangements that must be made for such events is enough to make one quail. At the same time, as somebody put it, "I shouldn't see myself as ashes where once I had been fire." I was no Ulysses, but *mutatis mutandis*, and eliminating bravado as far as I could, I wanted to say with him,

> Though much is taken, much abides; and though
> We are not now that strength which in old days
> Moved earth and heaven, that which we are, we are—
> One equal temper of heroic hearts,
> Made weak by time and fate, but strong in will
> To strive, to seek, to find, and not to yield.

In the meantime, to fend off any grim thoughts, the transcriptions of tapes made during the meeting of the "pioneers" arrived. Our secretary, it was evident, had been born after Vatican II, and the vocabulary of the preconciliar Church was an unknown tongue to her. She reported that we had talked about a "solid high Mass," celebrated with a "Roman Missile," and had referred to a magazine called "O'Reilly Fratres" and a document of Pope Pius X named a "mode approprio." One of us, too, had been a chaplain of "the

Senical" and had often had business at the "Chancy Office." She must have wondered why we spoke so often of the "Christian Mysteries," which she heard and recorded as the "Christian miseries." (See Appendix IV.)

The teaching of Vatican II reached the general Catholic consciousness much more swiftly than did the decrees of previous councils. Hundreds of avid journalists crowded into Rome during the years 1962-65 and filed elaborate reports with newspapers and magazines across the world. Radio brought the names (and the characteristic outlooks) of popes and bishops into every living room, and television supplied faces to go with them. Within a year of the Council's close Father Walter Abbott managed somehow to publish every conciliar document, translated, annotated, and supplemented with ecumenical commentary. All this sudden, massive publicity was like a cold shower on a generation brought up to believe in a changeless Church, and to glory in it. Church history had had no place in any college curriculum, much less in any catechism, so the struggles and crises and changes of earlier times were unknown. Good people, for instance, knowing nothing of the history of the Mass, seemed to believe that Christ our Lord celebrated it in the Supper chamber exactly as Father did last Sunday in the parish church, and they were horrified and profoundly scandalized when the rite was changed. Conciliar ideas like religious liberty, ecumenical collaboration, Christian service to the world were shocking, too, for people who inherited the attitudes of a Church which had stood intransigently aside from the currents of political, scientific, and religious thought of four centuries.

The historian whose name I can't remember but who proposed the "500-year convulsion theory" pointed out how the barbarians, savage, primitive hordes, swept down from the north about the year 500 on the Roman Empire and put the lights out all over Europe. It then took five hundred years for them to be Christianized; they had to be civilized first. There followed the synthesis of the high Middle Ages, with Dante and the cathedrals and the theological "summas" of Aquinas. But this synthesis broke down, as human constructs have a way of doing, five hundred years later, with the Renaissance, the Reformation, the discovery of America, and commercialism. And *that* synthesis—if it deserves the name—has broken down in our time, so the convulsion we are witnessing—and are caught up in—is punctually on schedule. Some distressed

Catholics seem to have overlooked the fact that it has affected not just the Church but all of society.

How could an age which brought in the automobile and the airplane, electric light and power, radio, television, the computer, x-ray, space travel, and a thousand technological mini-miracles *not* be different from its predecessors? Could events like the Great Depression, two World Wars, the rise and fall of Communism (dramatized by the breaching of the Berlin Wall and the razing of Lenin's statues), our sudden awareness of a populous Third World aspiring to its long-denied place in the sun—could such seismic events leave our way of life untouched? Could a missionary Church, commissioned to carry the Good News to a lacerated and bewildered humanity, not try with all its strength to up-date its language and its methods, and above all to manifest its sympathy, its compassion?

In great part the euphoria, the optimism that for a short while suffused the Catholic world in the sixties derived from the new attitude of the official Church toward human concerns as voiced by the Second Vatican Council. Pope John, who convoked the Council, had asked it to refrain from condemnations, and to explore new ways of talking and listening to the men and women of a new generation. Accordingly, the Council declared its disinterested wish to learn and to serve:

> This sacred Synod proclaims the highest destiny of humanity and champions the godlike seed which has been sown in it. It offers to men and women the honest assistance of the Church in fostering that relationship of all which corresponds to this destiny of theirs. Inspired by no earthly ambition, the Church seeks but a solitary goal: to carry forward the work of Christ himself under the lead of the befriending Spirit. And Christ entered this world to give witness to the truth, to rescue and not to sit in judgment, to serve and not to be served.[1]

> Just as it is in the world's interest to acknowledge the Church as a historical reality, and to recognize its good influence, so the Church itself knows how richly it has profited by the history and development of humanity. Thanks to the experience of past ages, the progress of the

1.   Documents of Vatican II, Abbott and Gallagher, "The Pastoral Constitution on the Church in the Modern World," New York, 1966, p. 201, #3.

sciences, and the treasures hidden in the various forms of human culture, human nature is more clearly revealed and new roads to truth are opened. These benefits profit the Church, too. For, from the beginning of its history, the Church has learned to express the message of Christ with the help of the ideas and terminology of various peoples, and has tried to clarify it with the wisdom of philosophers, too. Its purpose has been to adapt the gospel to the grasp of all as well as to the needs of the learned, insofar as such was appropriate. Indeed, this accommodated preaching of the revealed Word ought to remain the law of all evangelization. For thus each nation develops the ability to express Christ's message in its own way. At the same time, a living exchange is fostered between the Church and the diverse cultures of people. To promote such an exchange, the Church requires special help, particularly in our day, when things are changing very rapidly and the ways of thinking are exceedingly various. It must rely on those who live in the world, are versed in different institutions and specialties, and grasp their innermost significance in the eyes of both believers and unbelievers. With the help of the Holy Spirit, it is the task of the entire People of God, especially pastors and theologians, to hear, distinguish, and interpret the many voices of our age, and to judge them in the light of the divine Word. In this way, revealed truth can always be more deeply penetrated, better understood, and set forth to greater advantage.[2]

Let it be recognized that all the faithful, clerical and lay, possess a lawful freedom of inquiry and thought, and the freedom to express their minds humbly and courageously about those matters in which they enjoy competence.[3]

To make matters more painful, very shortly after the Council anarchy and bedlam broke out, especially on college campuses, and climaxed in the tragedy at Kent State. This unrest spread like a contagion to the Church. Authority was flouted. Priests, nuns, even bishops doffed their religious garb, then resigned and, in many cases, married. Bizarre liturgies were celebrated. It should have been no surprise that people took sides, or that there swiftly developed a conservative wing (known to its opponents as "those

2. Id., p. 245, #44.
3. Id., p. 270, #62.

reactionaries") and a progressive wing (called by its opponents "those liberals") in the hitherto monolithic American Church. Controversy, fueled by frustration, fear, and anger, boiled up, especially in the correspondence columns of Catholic papers and magazines. Now, only thirty years after Pope Paul solemnly closed the Council, the euphoria it generated has steadily drained away as a centralized authority has striven to reassert itself, publishing stern warnings and threats, repressing free speech, making appointments exclusively from the conservative wing.

How long the convulsion of our times will last, in the Church and in society generally, is anyone's guess. It shows no sign of abating nor, as perplexities multiply, has any new synthesis emerged. We seem, in fact, unable to discover or create a consensus on any issue or value of importance. And meanwhile, as Homer said of the stalemate before Troy, the funeral pyres of the dead burn ever higher and higher.

The problems that confront our world as the century wears down are so enormous, so bewildering, that we Christians should— for a time at least—suspend any strictly internal wrangling and bring all the compassion and wisdom we can call on to help find solutions. The poor of the world cry to heaven for justice. One race oppresses, enslaves, and, often enough, slaughters another. Women still look for equity in the family, in the workplace, in the Church. Drugs, frightening new diseases, and street violence afflict our young people. Illiteracy is widespread abroad and growing at home. The likelihood of total, utterly devastating war is never remote, and we have yet to learn whether the damage we have done to our environment is irreparable.

The intramural problems we Catholics face are likewise multiplex and boggling. I hope, however, that I don't minimize or oversimplify them if I say that the great Council, the Pentecost of our time, holds the keys to their solution, and therefore that we must return over and over to those enlightening and refreshing documents. The advocates of ever-increasing centralization, repression, clericalization are still with us; so are Pope John's "prophets of doom," who lament the present state of the Church as "confusion," "chaos," "anarchy." How much more acquaintance with history, how much more readiness to examine new ideas—especially if they are not new but quite ancient, really—one finds in the assessment of our present situation offered by the canonist and historian Ladislas Örsy, S.J. Father Örsy writes:

The Roman Catholic Church entered into an intense movement of conversion at Vatican II. The conciliar conversion, however, has taken place mainly on the level of insights and proclamations. After the council, the time came for the transformation of structures. Then the movement of conversion slowed down considerably. We should not be surprised. New insights into long-held truths can arise and even cascade with breathtaking swiftness (especially with the assistance of the Spirit), but the transformation of centuries-old structures by which the community has lived and operated as far as living memory goes (and beyond) is a slow, often painful, always cumbersome task. Our church is in the midst of a process. It is moved by fresh perceptions, and it is hampered by old institutions. That is where we are at present.[4]

In the hubbub of voices talking currently about "spirituality" and private prayer on the one hand and social involvement on the other, no unanimous agreement is yet detectible that we derive *all* Christian activity from the central, indispensable action of our assembly and return it there as the supreme gesture of adoration. St. Paul laid down the principle long ago: "Therefore, my brothers and sisters, I implore you by God's mercy to offer your very selves to him: a living sacrifice, dedicated and fit for his acceptance, the worship offered by mind and heart" (Rom 12:1). Vatican II reiterated that unifying principle for the Christians of our time: "The liturgy is the outstanding means whereby the faithful may express in their lives and manifest to others the mystery of Christ and the real nature of the true Church. . . . It is the summit toward which the activity of the Church is directed; at the same time it is the fount from which all its power flows."[5]

The divisions among Christians must be a scandal to those who do not believe as we do; they must surely be an obstacle to evangelization. And they are a standing, stinging rebuke to us who read so often the prayer of our Lord at the Last Supper, "that all may be one," and do so little about it. Here again, no doubt, patience is required. One does not undo in thirty years, even with the best intentions, the damage done in four or six hundred. We

4.   *America,* 30 May 1992, p. 482.
5.   *Constitution on the Sacred Liturgy,* #2, 10.5.

have stopped calling one another names; we can meet now with some mutual respect and trust, and even undertake jointly projects that benefit us all. But I think few of us have understood yet that each Christian church must look within, at ourselves, and in honesty determine what changes *we* must make in attitudes and policies to bring about a more perfect resemblance to the Church envisioned and founded by Jesus Christ. As we draw nearer to that ideal we shall draw nearer to one another. For us Catholics, perhaps, the outstanding difficulty will be to acknowledge, tolerate, even welcome the differences that will emerge as infinitely diverse human beings strive to reproduce in their own time and culture the fellowship of Christ. Father Örsy puts it eloquently:

> The See of Peter is and remains the principle of unity in the sense that our Tradition teaches and as the two Vatican councils articulated it. The question for our times is how it can also be an effective promoter, and respectful supporter, of diversity. If the gift of unity is ever granted by our gracious Lord (as we trust it will be), it will not be given to install a monotonous uniformity, but to bring about a much greater variety than we enjoy now. Everything in the creation and all events in the history of our salvation indicate that God delights in diversity. Indeed, a diversity arose right from the beginning; the churches of Jerusalem, Antioch, Rome, Alexandria and later Constantinople, all had developed specific characteristics, to the point of each having a collective personality that manifested itself in language, liturgy, discipline, and theological speculations. Thus we can complete the conciliar expression that the See of Peter is a principle of unity with the statement that it is called also to be a promoter of diversity, precisely because the one church of Christ cannot but be diverse in the member churches. Such a development would also be strong protection against an excessive centralization that the council certainly wanted to avoid in the future. The church of Christ, to be true to itself, must contain and represent the incarnation of the Gospel in so many diverse cultures.[6]

Someone has said that for Chaucer, in the 14th century, the world was a pilgrimage. For Shakespeare it was a stage. In the

---

6.   Id., p. 486.

18th century it was a formal garden, but in the 19th it became a machine. Eliot thought the first half of the 20th century was a wasteland, but after Auschwitz and Chernobyl and AIDS it begins to resemble a nightmare. Some day we shall know why the Lord Jesus, who said to his followers, "You shall be witnesses to me," selected us to witness to him today, to be light in a dark hour for humanity and salt for an otherwise tasteless world. We cannot know now, but perhaps, with his grace and a certain winner-take-all mentality, we can respond. And perhaps we can be instructed in how to do that by the effort we are called upon to make at Mass. Consider:

It's obvious that we cannot always be thinking of God. Many other things legitimately ask for our attention. But at Mass there comes a moment when, so far as we can, we should resolutely seek to fix our thoughts on the Lord alone. After we have listened to the Word of God, after we have prayed together for the "intentions" we are most concerned about at the moment, after we have placed on the altar our earthly tokens of surrender to God's love, we are bidden to relax, to forget for a while our worries and sorrow, to ascend, as it were, where the angels cluster around the throne of God and to join them in pure adoration.

The celebrant calls out, "Lift up your hearts," and emphasizes this directive by lifting his arms toward heaven. His gesture should be deliberate: appealing, encouraging, almost imperious. The president of any assembly must direct attention to what is of supreme importance, and now we are beginning the Great Prayer of the Church.

The Great Prayer . . . here are gathered those who must be considered God's beloved, chosen for baptism and so living the life of Christ. Their prayer is one with his, as truly as if they had been standing on Good Friday at the foot of the cross. It is a prayer of exalted praise ("all honor and glory"), of effectual petition ("remember, Lord"), of impetration ("see the Victim whose death has reconciled us to yourself"), and preeminently of thanksgiving ("we offer you in thanksgiving this holy and living sacrifice"). Here "we celebrate the memory of Christ your Son," that ineffably precious memory which refuses to die out no matter how long the centuries roll. Here God gathers, age after age, a people to himself, "so that from east to west a perfect offering may be made to the glory of his name."

A prayer like that demands the best effort we can give it. Of course it isn't easy to divorce oneself from the world that envelops us so totally. But think how swiftly that world changes. We don't know what terrors will come from the rising tide of violence in our cities, or what, if anything, will stop the dizzying spirals of inflation and unemployment. Shall we have gas for our cars? Will our pension be adequate to cover the cost of living? What's this rumor about the company's closing down, or moving out of town? Should I check with the doctor about that funny pain in my chest? Can we afford orthodontia for the youngest child?

"Lift up your hearts!" There is space and time now to do for a while what we were created to do, to rehearse what we shall be doing for all eternity. Our omnipotent Lord, Jesus Christ, has pledged solemnly that we shall see God, and in that vision we shall be caught up, enraptured, and cry out in ecstasy. Lionel Johnson tried to express what that moment—that indivisible "now" of an eternal moment—will mean to us:

> My window opens to the autumn night;
> In vain I watch for sleep to visit me.
> How should sleep dull mine ears, and dim my sight,
> Who saw the stars, and listened to the sea?
>
> Ah, how the City of God is fair!
> If without sea, and starless though it be,
> For joy of the majestic beauty there,
> We shall not miss the stars, nor mourn the sea.

"Lift up your hearts!" What will it be to be caught up to the breast of God, to know that loneliness is forever banished, to feel that all our shackles are off and we can expand, stretch, be totally ourselves, to the delight of the Father who imagined what we might be and then brought us into being? Shall we not dance for him? Shall we not pirouette and let him see the graces which mirror, ever so slightly yet authentically, his own?

They are loved, these hearts we are bidden to lift up to him. Scarred they may be, and more than a little weary of the long road and the dark, but the road will make a last turn and end in glory, the dark will blaze into brilliance, the scars will be smoothed by infinitely tender fingers. We should lift up our hearts oftener in tiptoe anticipation of that day.

Toward the close of the third Eucharistic Prayer we say to God, "We hope to enjoy for ever the vision of your glory." This seems to me a very pallid, limp translation of the Latin, "*Fore speramus ut simul gloria tua perenniter satiemur*," but I'm not sure I could provide a better one. "Satiety" in English usage connotes a rather disgusting repletion, a glut. Shelley speaks mournfully of "love's sad satiety." Could we use "satisfaction"? No, this word fails for the opposite reason. It doesn't, precisely, "satisfy"; it isn't strong enough. We want to be more than merely filled-up-to-here. We hope to revel in abundance, to be carried out of ourselves, to be intoxicated with God.

In the Bible, especially in the Old Testament, God's glory is represented as a luminous brilliance, a great light. What is meant is God's presence, all-pervasive, blotting out everything save itself, storming and overwhelming the capacities of the creature. We are asking for this. In the concrete, what we want is the resurrection of the body and its restoration to harmonious union with the soul; we want eternal life, unclouded by any threat of termination; we want unhampered freedom; we want nothing less than the indwelling of the Blessed Trinity. These are the so-called eschatalogical gifts, and they sum up what we mean when we talk about "salvation."

That pathetic pessimist, A.E. Housman, who could turn a phrase so deftly, retold in one of his lyrics the legend of Mithridates, king of Pontus. Mithridates, like all rulers, had to fear assassination. In order to make himself immune to poison, he took a few grains of it every day, and in this way frustrated his enemies. Housman says, "Mithridates, he died old," and in like manner we should immunize ourselves against despair by reflecting consistently on the emptiness of any human hopes. A dreary counsel, but it suggests another idea. We Christians spend our lives trying, as St. Paul urges us, to "put on Christ," to think and act as he did, and so to grow steadily into his likeness. To that end we take each day a few drops of his blood, a specific for healing and growth. Is this grossly realistic? Not if we read John 6:51-58: "I tell you most solemnly, if you do not eat the flesh of the Son of Man and drink his blood, you will not have life in you. . . . As I, who am sent by the living Father, myself draw life from the Father, so whoever eats me will draw life from me." It was Father Martindale, years ago when Jansenism was rampant and people feared that if they received communion too often they might not have the proper reverence, who reassured them: "If you said nothing to the Lord at Communion except 'Do what you came for: feed me,' you would have made an excellent Communion." The frailties, the vacillations, the compromises we lament in our conduct, the inconstancy of our love, *can* be healed. Our resemblance to the Son of God can grow, even if we ourselves will be the last to see it. And the gift we bring each day to our worship will be purer, holier. So is vindicated the paradox of the old "*Quid retribuam*" prayer: the only return I can make is to take more.

But not without appreciation. Not without gratitude. In a phrase so familiar that we are likely to let it become perfunctory, we continue the Eucharistic Prayer with a mutual exhortation: "Let us give thanks to the Lord our God." To lift ourselves out of the rut of routine, it might be helpful to recall what we are thanking God for. As created beings, we must give thanks for the gift of life, to be sure, but as distinct, unique personalities, freshly minted, so to speak, by God's creative power and never repeated, we must give thanks for life as we and only we have received it. Then there is the gift of the new life, by which, as branches on the vine, we are grafted on the Lord and begin to live with his life. There is, too, the gift of faith, by means of which, as St. Peter says, we are drawn out of darkness into his marvelous light. And there is our particular vocation, through which as his disciples we "bring forth fruit, fruit that will last" (cf. Jn 15:16). And we must give thanks for all those who surround us, some easily loved and some in need of love.

I have always liked a litany of thanksgiving used by the Religious of the Cenacle:

> For all you have given, thanks be to God.
> For all you have withheld, thanks be to God.
> For all you have withdrawn, thanks be to God.
> For all you have permitted, thanks be to God.
> For all you have prevented, thanks be to God.
> For all you have forgiven me, thanks be to God.
> For all you have prepared for me, thanks be to God.
> For the death you have chosen for me, thanks be to God.
> For the place you are keeping for me in heaven,
>   thanks be to God.
> For having created me to love you for eternity,
>   thanks be to God,
>   thanks be to God, thanks be to God.

It is worth emphasizing that when the early Christians were casting about for an appropriate name for what Jesus had done at the Last Supper, and had told them to continue in his memory, they called it "the Eucharist," "the Thanksgiving." The action of course had other meanings, and they knew them, but this one seemed pre-eminent. As Father Joseph Jungmann, S.J., notes: "In the linguistic usage of that time *eucharistein* means to consider and conduct oneself as *eucharistos*, that is, as one richly overwhelmed with gifts and graces—an attitude that found expression in words but did not exclude expression in the form of a gift."[7] That might be for many of us a novel and powerful motive for spiritual renewal—so to live that one's whole life is an utterance of thanks.

But it comes over us periodically that no thanks of ours could ever be adequate for the flood of blessings that has come our way. Like St. Therese of Lisieux, who exclaimed, "I shall sing the mercies of the Lord forever," we feel that only eternity will give us scope and space for gratitude. At such times—and also, perhaps, when we are sluggish and cannot bring things into focus—it is good to unite our intentions with those of our great priest, Jesus Christ, who offers for men and women of all ages the peerless thanksgiving of the Mass, and says with eloquence what we cannot properly articulate.

At the head of the Jesuit scriptures stands the sentence, "Human beings were created to praise." And to praise not only in words, not only in ritual, but by being what God has made us: "a chosen race, a royal priesthood, a holy nation, a people he claims for his own to proclaim the glorious works of the one who has called (us) from darkness into his marvelous light" (1 Peter 2:9). Even in an age of convulsion we can be all this—perhaps more successfully than in a time of peace, because it will be very clear that the net result will be his work, not ours.

As the thread winds down I find that Compline, the night prayer of the Church, has begun to do double duty. Not only is it an appropriate way to close out the day; it provides support and comfort as well when the limitations and hazards of age give peremptory notice that one is not immortal. Like the rest of the breviary, Compline was revised in 1970, and one or two of my favorite passages were dropped—although I slip them in now when only the Lord is listening—for instance, the plaintive "You are in our midst, O Lord, and we are called by your holy name. Don't abandon us!" (Jer 14:9). That prayer reminds God (*si sic loqui licet*) of the baptismal covenant to which he is sworn and which he is

---

7.   *The Mass,* Collegeville, Minn., 1976, p. 33.

bound by his own holiness to implement; it also reminds *me* that God is an abiding presence, strong and swift to protect, wise in counsel, resourceful and utterly dependable.

Compline opens with an examination of conscience and a plea for mercy that reach back over the day now ending but also over the years of one's life as well. I must renew my sorrow for my selfishness, my stupidities, my tepid response to God's overtures of love. May he in his mercy forget them as I myself would like to forget them.

The fact that our Lord, in his dying moments, used the aspiration from Psalm 31, "Into your hands I commend my spirit," and may have recited the entire Psalm, would be enough reason for a disciple to use it as a last confident expression of trust, whether the oncoming darkness were simply another night or the looming shadows of death. For one reared according to the mind and heart of Ignatius Loyola, it would carry a reminder of the "*Suscipe*" prayer suggested at the end of the *Spiritual Exercises*, in which one surrenders to God one's entire being, everything connoted by the word "spirit." Personally, I think of it as an echo of the special covenant a religious contracts with God. For us Jesuits, that contract is cogently summarized in the formula of our vows, where, after solemnly declaring our intention to give God our entire selves in a profession of poverty, chastity, and obedience, we call on him to sustain us in that intention: "as you have given the grace to desire and offer all this, so you will give abundant grace to carry it out."

Whether one is ending a day or a life, the prayer of Simeon, taken from St. Luke's Gospel (2:29-32), is appropriate. Like Simeon, the Christian has been accorded some knowledge of God's saving plan for humanity, and waits vigilantly for the coming of the Anointed. Maybe it's only the day's labor that is being laid down; maybe it's the burdens of a lifetime. In either case there is grateful relief, surcease, anticipation . . .

The old text of Compline had a prayer which, as a member of a caring, congenial community I could say for my brethren: "Visit, Lord, this house. Drive far from it all snares of our enemy. May your holy angels dwell here, and keep us in peace, and may your blessing be always upon us." The revised Compline has dropped this prayer, but I have always been something of a night owl, and I like, when the house has fallen silent, to say it still, and to accompany it with a huge, sweeping sign of the cross, reaching in gratitude and affection to the most remote of my sleeping brothers.

Compline ends with a filial salute to the Mother of God, whom the Lord gave us as a last precious bequest. We take our cue from the season of the year, and, in accordance with the sacred events we are thinking of especially at the time, we find new reason to bless her memory in Advent, at Christmas, at Easter, and through what we call "ordinary time"—as if any time could be ordinary in which God is actively loving us and Mary is showing us what her tender, motherly intercession can do for us.

"No duty," says St. Ambrose, "is more urgent than that of giving thanks." Thanks, then, for the beauty of this created world, and for its nourishing abundance. Thanks for my father and mother, for the love of two happily remembered brothers and two devoted sisters, and for hundreds of loyal friends. Thanks for the priesthood, and for the quickening, sustaining, forgiving, genial Company in which I have been privileged to spend almost seventy years. Thanks for the solemn pledge that when I die I shall be led, undeserving, to what a friend of mine, a diocesan priest, once called "that big Manresa in the sky."

In the play, her lady-in-waiting says to Cleopatra, who is planning suicide,

> Finish, good lady; the bright day is done,
> And we are for the dark.

Against that despairing counsel St. Paul writes to his converts in Thessalonica: "It is not as if you live in the dark, my brothers and sisters, for that Day to overtake you like a thief. No, you are all children of light and children of the day; we do not belong to the night or to darkness" (1 Th 5:4-5). For the grace to believe that I am most humbly thankful. Praised be the gracious Father of all things, who sent his Son among us so that we might learn how dearly he loves us: *apparuit nobis benignitas et humanitas Salvatoris nostri Dei* (Ti 3:4)—a sentiment which does not for me translate satisfactorily into English, but which is rather easily understood, so I shall leave it in the sonorous and wonderfully consoling Latin where I first found it.

Appendix I

ON THE QUESTION AS TO WHY MORE JESUITS, IN THE PRECONCILIAR years, were not actively involved in liturgical renewal, the English Jesuit, Clifford Howell (himself one of the most effective apostles of that renewal), sought to correct for his brethren a long-standing misconception of the attitude of the Society's founder toward the public worship of the Church. That misconception, often voiced in recreation rooms or at table, took some such form as this: "Ignatius wanted his men to be free from the obligation of choir and all that liturgical stuff, didn't he?"

He surely did, but, as Father Howell pointed out, "Few people nowadays realize what the Choral Office involved then. Religious bound to office in choir used to sing all the Hours in the form which these had before Pius V pruned them so drastically in 1568. The Office itself was of portentous length, and yet it was prolonged still further by accretions of several kinds. For instance, the entire Office of the Dead was sung in addition to the Office of the Day, excepting only on the greater feasts. This was for dead benefactors. For living benefactors the community sang all the fifteen Gradual Psalms before Matins and all the seven Penitential Psalms after Prime. As if this were not enough, they also sang the whole Little Office of our Lady every day as an act of devotion. The climax of the Choral Office was, of course, the Conventual Mass. This also, in St. Ignatius' day, was in its unreformed condition. It was of unconscionable length; its texts were padded out by tropings; the melismata of its chants were hypertrophied; it abounded in prolix sequences (over a hundred occurred in the course of a year), and the ceremonies had a complexity and duration which we of the twentieth century could hardly imagine. A Conventual Mass lasted anything up to three hours. As Father Jungmann remarks, "an Office so extensive could be carried through only by contemplative orders." But the Society was to be an active order, and could not possibly find time for this sort of thing, which occupied most of the day and half the night. So their office must be as short as possible—which meant private recitation—and their Masses must be as simple as possible—which meant Low Masses for the most part, though not always. By excluding Office in choir from Jesuit life our holy Father by no means intended to exclude liturgy. He excluded only the solemnities of the liturgy. Moreover, he did not exclude all solemnity, but only that which would be habitual and obligatory. Daily Choral Office and Conventual Mass would hinder our apostolate—that is the sole reason why he was against them. But whenever he deemed that solemn liturgical celebrations would help the apostolate, we were to use them. We have Polanco's word for it that St. Ignatius himself ordered that there should be High Mass and Sung Vespers in our churches on Sundays and holydays of obligation. All this fits in with his third rule for thinking with the Church:

> We should praise the frequent hearing of Mass, also hymns, psalms, long prayers both in and out of church, and likewise the Hours ordained at fixed times for the whole Divine Office, for every kind of prayer, and for all the canonical hours.

How anybody can think of St. Ignatius as an unliturgically-minded man just passes comprehension.

One hears it said sometimes that the foundations of the liturgical movement were laid a century ago by Abbot Prosper Guéranger of Solesmes, who rescued the liturgy from mere formalism and led many to appreciate its spiritual richness and beauty. All honour to the great Abbot for what he did, but nowadays it is generally recognized that the liturgical movement as he conceived it was primarily archeological and aesthetic. We have gone a long way past that now, and have learned to esteem and use the liturgy as the most potent pastoral instrument available. What very few people seem to have noticed is that this was the viewpoint of St. Ignatius about the liturgy, and that the roots of the modern pastoral liturgical movement could with much greater justification be traced back to him rather than to Guéranger.

For Ignatius was, in fact, a liturgical pioneer—but was never called such because he was campaigning for that which lies at the heart of the modern liturgical movement some three hundred years before anybody else saw that it had anything to do with the liturgy. The liturgical movement became pastoral only from the days of St.

Pius X; one of its roots was the Decree on Frequent Communion. But that is precisely the field in which St. Ignatius was such a bold innovator. In his day Communion was a rarity; practising Catholics received once a year, religious just a few times a year on the greater feasts. Yet, at a time when enclosed contemplative nuns received Communion perhaps ten times a year, Ignatius—still a layman—was insisting on the right of going to Communion every week! And he was persuading others to do the same. He got in trouble with the Inquisition at Alcalà on this point, but they could not shake him. He was in more trouble about it later on at Salamanca. But he maintained his position and propagated it through the *Spiritual Exercises*, where we find it in the second "Rule for Thinking with the Church." He incorporated it into the *Constitutions*, enjoining weekly Communion and recommending even daily Communion to our scholastics. Under his leadership our early Fathers campaigned for frequent Communion in the teeth of fierce opposition. With unerring instinct Ignatius saw that what the people needed more than anything else was sacramental participation in the holy sacrifice of the Mass. He sent both Favre and Araoz to preach this in Spain, Landini to preach it in Italy; he made Salmeron write a book about it; and finally he won his point through the arguments put forth by LeJay, Favre, Salmeron and (most of all) Lainez at the Council of Trent. The victory was publicly won only after his death, but it was nonetheless a victory for Ignatius when the Council declared, in 1562, that "the holy Synod would wish that at every Mass the faithful who are present should communicate not only spiritually but sacramentally by the reception of the Eucharist, that they may thereby share more abundantly in the fruit of the sacrifice."

Appendix II

AT A TIME WHEN CONGREGATIONAL PARTICIPATION IN THE LITURGY was at its lowest ebb, the Spanish Jesuit, Alfonso Rodriguez (1538-1616), advocated a method of silent meditation which could be aided by fanciful interpretation of the ritual. Well-meaning but quite divorced from the action of the Mass itself, it typified the efforts of ascetical writers of the period to make profitable the time spent by the congregation:

"From what has been already said, I feel in some degree bound to speak of the manner of hearing Mass. I shall therefore speak of three things, in particular, which are to be done during Mass, and which we ought to do with respect, since it is the Church itself that proposes them to us. First, we must suppose that Mass, as I have already said, is a representation of the death and passion of Jesus Christ, who wishes hereby to remind us of his love and sufferings, in order to excite us to love and serve him with more fervor, and to prevent us from being guilty of an ingratitude similar to that of the Hebrews, 'who forgot the God who had saved them' (Psalm 106:21).

"Now according to this, one of the wonderful things which we ought to apply ourselves to in time of Mass is to consider with attention the mysteries of the Passion, which are therein represented to us; and by this view to excite ourselves to produce acts of the love of God, and to make a firm resolution of serving him. But as to understand all the things that are said and done in Mass will extremely contribute hereunto, it is proper to explain here beforehand what they signify, that this knowledge may induce us to meditate more deeply on the holy mysteries they represent. For there is not one word said in Mass, nor even the least action or ceremony, but indicates something holy and mysterious; nay, even the ornaments which the priest wears at the altar have also a mysterious signification.

"The amice, which is a piece of linen cloth that the priest puts about his neck, and which covers his shoulders, represents the veil with which the soldiers covered the face of the Son of God when, striking him, they said to him, 'Prophesy who it is that struck thee' (Luke 22:6). The alb signifies the white robe which Herod, in mockery, caused to be put upon him, when he sent him back to Pilate. The cincture represents the cords with which he was bound when he was apprehended in the garden, and the whips with which he was torn by command of Pilate. The maniple signifies the cords with which he was bound to the pillar in the judgment hall; this he puts upon his left arm, which is next the heart, to signify that it was the excess of his love that made Christ suffer this cruel flagellation for our sins, and that we ought to correspond to this love by all the tenderness our heart is capable of. The stole represents the cord which they cast about his neck when he carried the cross. The chasuble or vestment, according to some, was the purple robe which they put upon him to scoff him; or, according to others, the tunic or coat without seam which they stripped him of to crucify him.

"The entrance of the priest into the sacristy to put on the ornaments represents the descent of the Son of God into the womb of the holy Virgin, where he clothed himself with our flesh and with our humanity to go and celebrate the sacrifice upon the cross. The choir that sings the Introit when the priest goes out of the sacristy represents the ancient patriarchs who expected the coming of the Messias, and who begged him of God in these words: 'Send, O Lord, the Lamb, governor of the earth' (Isaias 16:1); 'O that thou wouldst break through the heavens and descend' (Isaias 54:1). And they repeat the second time the Introit to mark the holy impatience they were in, and the frequent prayers they made to God upon this subject. The Confiteor, which the priest afterward says as a sinful man signifies that Jesus Christ has vouchsafed to charge himself with our sins and to satisfy for them, and that we might become just and holy. And the Kyrie Eleison, which signifies 'Lord, have mercy upon us,' represents the miserable state we were in before the coming of our Saviour.

"It would be too long to set down in particular the signification of each word and ceremony, but in fine, there is not one but indicates some mystery. For example, the many signs of the cross which the priests make upon the host and the chalice signify the many sufferings of Jesus Christ upon the cross. The elevation which is made of the host and chalice at consecration, that the people may adore the body and blood of the Son of God, is besides this made to represent what the Jews did when they elevated the cross of our Saviour, to expose him to the view of all the people. Every one according to his own choice may apply himself to consider one or two of these mysteries, according to the idea we have now given of them. But above all we must endeavor to render this meditation profitable by exciting ourselves as much as we can to correspond to the love and benefits of the Son of God, which will be far more profitable than to pass over many mysteries slightly."

Appendix III

IN MY *AMERICA* ARTICLE (SEPTEMBER 12, 1981), I CITED GREGORY Dix, who, in his *The Shape of the Liturgy* (p. 586), has some instructive things to say about the relation between liturgy and popular devotions. "The history of Western Catholicism," he says, "is littered with discarded devotions of all kinds, most of which found their representation in the missal for a while until popular interest waned and that Mass was removed. These are the inevitable effects of a living contact of the liturgy with the prayers of the Christian people in each age. The people have a certain right to be vulgar, and the liturgy, even while it must teach them, has never a right to be academic, because it is their prayer. The ease with which the Western system of variable prayers can enable it to respond to the people's special interest and devotions at any time may have its dangers. But it has given the Western rite a closer and more intimate grasp of human life than any other."

Applying this principle to "votive" Masses (of which, by the way, fifteen—not counting "Masses for Various Needs and Occasions" and Masses for the dead—still remain in the Sacramentary of Paul VI), Dom Gregory makes a point (p. 593) that might serve as an admonition to some liturgial purists:

> There had always been occasions which the Church reckoned desirable for the Eucharist which did not properly concern the whole Church, e.g., weddings and funerals. If the Eucharist is that act by which Jesus of Nazareth brought himself and all his circumstances finally under the realized Kingship (or into the Kingdom of God), then it is right that those who are his members should seek to bring themselves and the particular circumstances which affect their whole individual life (e.g., marriage, sickness) under that Kingship, by a deliberate entering into his act. Even though the whole Church is not concerned with them in this, they do so as members of his body, with and through

the authorized representative of that body. The rise of the Western variable prayers had opened to the liturgy a great opportunity of direct association with and consecration of the joys and sorrows and cares of daily life.

But Dom Gregory's basic thesis is that in the Latin Middle Ages popular devotions and the liturgy began to run on parallel but distinctly separate tracks.

> Piety and edification may take many forms, and modern eucharistic piety (he is writing in 1945, before the reforms of Vatican II and the as yet unbridged hiatus in eucharistic devotions) still feels this particular medieval form to be entirely good and natural. But it is legitimate to point out the difference between this and the piety of the primitive Church, for which the *corporate liturgy itself* formed the substance of devotion, and the *corporate action* its expression. In the Middle Ages it begins to be the *supplementary prayers* and the *private emotions* which take their place in this respect (p. 525).

This attitude became more and more the settled one. Many of us can remember a day when these supplementary prayers were put together as "methods of hearing Mass" and were in common use. The very word "hearing" is significant. "It was in the Latin Middle Ages that the Eucharist became for the first time essentially something 'said' rather than something 'done' (the East has never accepted such a change)" (p. 13).

> The old corporate worship of the Eucharist is declining into a mere focus for the subjective devotion of each separate worshipper in the isolation of his own mind. And it is the latter which is beginning to seem to him more important than the corporate act. The part of the individual layman in that corporate action had long ago been reduced from 'doing' to 'seeing' and 'hearing.' Now it is retreating within himself to 'thinking' and feeling.' He is even beginning to think that over-much 'seeing' (ceremonial) and 'hearing' (music) are detrimental to proper 'thinking' and 'feeling' (p. 599).

All of which sounds not a little familiar; we have heard much in these last few years about the "noise" in church, the difficulty one has in saying his private prayers during Mass, etc. What happened to create this introversion during a seemingly communal ritual? Dom Gregory points to a variety of causes:

1. The origin in the Latin Middle Ages of the idea that the Eucharist is something "said" rather than something "done" (p. 13).

2. The removal from the liturgy of public, corporate intercession in what we now call "the prayer of the faithful." Many of the laity came "to suppose that intercession is a function of prayer better discharged in private than by liturgical prayer of any kind." The notion of the priestly prayer of the whole Church, as the prayer of Christ, the world's mediator though his body, was lost (p. 44).

3. The excessive clericalism of the later Middle Ages— only the clergy acted or had a voice in the liturgy—produced among the laity an excessively individualistic conception of prayer (p. 45).

4. The absorption of later scholasticism in the nature of the Real Presence in eucharistic theology, together with the loss of the idea of the eucharist as the source of unity of the Church, led to individualistic and subjective devotion, concentration on the sacrament less and less as the source of the unity and corporate life of the Church (and through this of the spiritual life of the individual soul), and more and more only as a focus of purely personal adoration of the Lord therein present to the individual soul (p. 249).

5. Deprived of frequent communion and with a liturgy in Latin, all that was left to the unlettered layfolk was private adoration (p. 249).

But let me discuss the "holy cards" that came by the hundreds into my collection and emphasize that they were not selected with any preconceived theory in mind, but quite at random. Arguing from the frequency with which they appeared, the devotions in honor of the Sacred Heart, Our Lady—under a wide variety of titles—and St. Joseph are clearly favorites. After them one finds cards commemorating St. Anne, St. Dominic, St. Therese, the Saints of the Mass, St. Bernadette, St. Columban, St. John Bosco, the Holy Child Jesus, the Holy Family, St. Alphonsus, the Holy Name, the Wound in the shoulder of Jesus, St. Anthony, Jesus Christ King, St. Gerard Majella, St. Rita, the Infant of Prague, the Most Precious Blood, the Five Wounds of our Lord, St. Charles Lwanga, St. Frances Cabrini, St. Jude, St. Pancratius, St. John Neumann, St. Raphael, St. Gabriel, St. Paul of the Cross, St. Peregrine,

St. Catherine Labouré, St. Martin de Porres, St. John Vianney. There are prayers for the beatification of Pius X (1934) and of Junipero Serra. There are also leaflets with novena prayers to Our Lady of Fatima, St. Frances Cabrini, Our Lady Queen of Peace, Our Lord Jesus Christ King, St. Elizabeth Seton, St. Dymphna, the Sacred Heart, Mary Help of Christians, the Miraculous Medal, the Immaculate Conception, the Infant Jesus, the Little Flower, and St. Jude, together with a novena in preparation for Pentecost and another in preparation for Christmas (to run from November 30th to Christmas Eve—curiously, the duration of Advent rather than nine days).

There are also cards with prayers for the Pope (Pius XII, John XXIII, Paul VI), prayers for perseverance in difficulties, prayers to St. Anthony for the recovery of things lost or stolen. Way of the Cross leaflets are frequent, and leaflets published by the Apostleship of Prayer. The prayer before a crucifix, "Look down upon me, good and gentle Jesus," occurs often; so do the promises of the Sacred Heart to St. Margaret Mary. There is a poignancy in the frequent prayers in time of war, and in the prayers for the missing prisoners of war in Vietnam. Our Lady of Fatima is invoked for the conversion of Russia. There is a memento of Pope Paul VI's "Mission of Peace" to the United Nations in New York, and (very frequent indeed) a memorial card for the assassinated President, John F. Kennedy.

Some attitudes are manifested so frequently that they seem typical. For example, there are very few prayers which are not followed by a parenthesis indicating the specific indulgence that may be gained by reciting them, and it is hard after a while to avoid the impression that the prayer is not to be said so much for its intrinsic value as for a less seemly profit motive. Again, there seems to be a greater emphasis on contrition than on other possible themes for prayer. In one instance, the very first among several recommended "Prayers after Holy Communion" reads, "My Jesus, forgive us our sins; save us from the fires of Hell, and lead all souls to Heaven." In sudden contrast to this self-abasement, one encounters a "Novena in honor of Our Lady of Victory," which suggests a litany of 37 aspirations in each of which the word "triumphant" occurs prominently. This novena, by the way, emanates from "the Seat of the All-American, Coast-to-coast PRAYER CRUSADE to the Patroness of the United States." More typical, however, is a quite pervasive—well, "gloom" may be too strong a word; call it "gravity," or "soberness," or even "severity." It is probably allied to the consciousness of sin alluded to above. Those who have made the parish mission are given cards with stern reminders of their obligations as Christians, summed up in the admonition: "The only important thing in life is that you SAVE YOUR SOUL." Or there is the "Prayer for a Happy Death":

> When my feet, unable to move, shall warn me that my life's course is well-nigh run, merciful Jesus, have mercy on me. When my hands, trembling and benumbed, shall no longer be able to hold the crucifix, but against my will shall let it fall upon my bed of suffering, merciful Jesus, have mercy on me. When my eyes, dim and troubled through fear of approaching death, shall fix on Thee their languid, dying gaze . . . When my lips, cold and quivering, shall for the last time utter thy adorable name . . . When my face, pale and livid, shall inspire the beholders with pity and dismay; when my hair, bathed in the sweat of death and stiffening on my head, shall indicate that my hour has come . . . When my ears, soon to be forever closed to the discourse of man, shall be open to hear thy voice pronounce the irrevocable sentence that will decide my lot for all eternity . . ." and so on through eight equally graphic and cheerless invocations.

"Devotions in Honor of St. Joseph" include the hymn that some of us will remember:

> Dear Guardian of Mary, dear Nurse of her Child,
> Life's ways are full weary, the desert is wild;
> Bleak sands are all 'round us, no hope can we see;
> Sweet Spouse of our Lady, we call upon thee!

Memorial cards for the dead, naturally and properly, are very common. By far the most frequent prayer they carry, however—perhaps because such cards were often printed by the undertakers, who followed a set formula—is "Have mercy on the soul of thy servant. Be not severe in thy judgments, but let some drops of thy Precious Blood fall upon the devouring flames . . ." Very occasionally there will be a prayer from the missal, or a quotation of the *In Paradisum* (in English), and even more rarely a quotation from Scripture; I found Colossians 3:15-17, Psalms 23 and 107, Jeremiah 31:3. (On one card, commemorating the death of a 42-year-old man, is the legend: "Jesus has plucked this lily in its freshness to decorate the heavenly home." This *lily*?)

In keeping with the motif of severity, there are the frequent "demands" made by our Lord or our Lady, and the "threats" of impending doom in store for those who neglect them. "Our Lady demands the Family Rosary." Or, more expansively,

> Do you know there is a Secret to be opened in 1960? The last Secret of Fatima! Sister Lucy, to whom the Secret was given by our Lady of Fatima some 40 years ago, said, "When the Secret is revealed in 1960, some will be glad, but many will be sad." Will you be glad that you have fulfilled our Lady's requests? Are you doing what our Lady of Fatima asked you to do while there is still time?

Or there is the "Chaplet of Mercy" (a "Rosary of the Holy Wounds of our Lord Jesus Christ"), whose recitation "is a counterpoise to my justice; it restrains my vengeance." Or again, "The Blessed Mother can no longer restrain the hand of her divine Son from striking the world with just punishment for its many crimes."

On the other hand, prompt and well-nigh automatic answers to certain prayers or observances are guaranteed. A prayer to St. Joseph carries this note: "This prayer was found in the fiftieth year of our Lord and Savior Jesus Christ. In 1505 it was sent from the Pope to Emperor Charles when he was going into battle. Whoever shall read this prayer or hear it or keep it about themselves shall never die a sudden death or be drowned, nor shall poison take effect on them; neither shall they fall into the hands of the enemy, or shall be burned in any fire or shall be overpowered in battle. Say for nine mornings for anything you may desire. It has never been known to fail, so be sure you really want what you ask." Incidentally, I wondered often as I went through these cards who first invented the category *"Pie creditur,"* and what theological weight it might now carry. The preceding prayer (though not, possibly, the explanatory note) bears the *imprimatur* of an East Coast bishop still happily reigning. Another prayer begins, "O Divine Child, source of every good, never dost Thou refuse the request of those who implore blessings through the Merits and Perfections of Thy Blessed Infancy." Another is entitled "An Irresistible Novena," and a note tells us that "a Poor Clare, recently deceased, appeared to her abbess, who was praying for her, and said: 'I have gone straight to Heaven because by means of this prayer, recited every evening, I paid all my debts.'" There are four stanzas on another card, of which one might be a sample:

> When all other friends have failed,
>   Pray to St. Anthony,
> And your hopes are all derailed,
>   Pray to St. Anthony.
> If a sorrow fills your heart,
> Or you fail at all you start,
> When bad habit plays its part,
>   Pray to St. Anthony.

Numerology seems to exert its perennial fascination. Special graces are available to those who observe prayerfully the Five First Saturdays or the Nine First Fridays. "Heaven is opened by the practice of the three Hail Marys." A "Powerful Novena of Child-like Confidence" is "to be said at the same time every hour for Nine Consecutive hours—just One Day." Among other rich favors promised to those who will say seven Our Fathers and seven Hail Marys every day for fifteen years is that "they will receive the same reward as if they had shed their blood for the faith." Anyone who recites a certain prayer 33 times before three o'clock on Good Friday will "obtain any request." And the same infallible answer to prayer is insinuated in the many prayers that begin "O most blessed so-and-so" (Our Lady, St. Joseph, St. Anne), "Never was it known that anyone who sought thine intercession was left un-aided." Something a little less savory is introduced by the suggested letter to the Director of the Shrine: "Dear Father _____: Yes, I will join you in the two Solemn Novenas of Masses and Prayers to St. Anne. Please include my petitions as noted below, and pray for them each day. For your wonderful work I enclose my offering of $ _____." Or by the verse, "Little Lights of Love," urging the spiritual value of vigil lights, and distributed by a candle manufacturer.

But one does come on prayers that are less self-centered or convey a certain magnanimity. A prayer for peace "commemorating the visit of His Holiness Pope Paul VI to the United Nations" is the terse and dignified one from the old missal:

> O God, from whom all holy desires, right counsels, and just works proceed, give to thy servants that peace which the world cannot give, that, our hearts being devoted to the keeping of thy commandments and the fear of enemies being removed, our times by thy protection may be peaceful.

Or this anonymous "Holy Year Prayer":

Lord God and Father, in the death and resurrection of
Jesus Christ your Son you willed to reconcile all mankind
to yourself and so to reconcile men with each other in
peace. Hear the prayer of your people in this year of
grace and salvation. Let your Spirit of life and holiness
renew us in the depth of our being; unite us throughout
our life to the risen Christ, for he is our brother and savior. With all Christians we seek to follow the way of the
Gospel. Keep us faithful to the teaching of the Church
and alive to the needs of our brothers. Give us strength to
work for reconciliation, unity, and peace. May those who
seek the God they do not yet know discover in you the
source of light and hope; may those who work for others
find strength in you; may those who know you seek even
further and experience the depths of your love. . . . Father,
of your great goodness, hear in the words of your people
the prayer of the Spirit to the praise of your glory and the
salvation of men.

There are scriptural, theological, and ecumenical resonances in
this prayer which mark it as a product of recent, post-Vatican II
times. And if the sexist phrases ("men" and "brothers") indicate
that it is not altogether up to date, the use of the contemporary
idiom and the absence of pious clichés make it more acceptable to
a younger generation. The prayers on the older cards have certain
stylistic features which identify them: the use of "O" before each
name invoked; the archaic "Thou," "Thee," "didst," "deign,"
"vouchsafe," "I cast myself at thy feet;" "regard not my lack of
merit" (inversion is characteristic of this style); "O God, who by
thy unspeakable Providence," and so on.

In some cases it was not possible to assign dates to the Cards,
and so there were a few surprises. I found four prayers to the
Holy Spirit, and even a whole novena, and a handsome card with a
translation of the *Veni Sancte Spiritus*, seemingly antedating the
charismatic era. One leaflet (*not* published, as might have been expected, by the Liturgical Press) had the Stations of the Cross, with
prayers taken from the missal, and carried the exhortation, "Let us
pray with the church that we may better follow Christ." Another
Way of the Cross concluded with "Christ is risen, alleluia" and the
Good News of the Resurrection in Mark 16:14-16. There were a
few scattered Easter cards; one had a translation of the *Regina
Coeli*. Perhaps the greatest surprise was my discovery of a card

which presented "The Catholic Program." Under that simple but all-embracing title were printed the Beatitudes—nothing more.

Generally speaking, however, among the thousand cards I remarked the virtual absence of any mention of God the Father, of Trinitarian spirituality, of the paschal mystery, of the Resurrection, of the Church, of Scripture (except for a very few tags). There was a heavy emphasis on petition and contrition, a minimal suggestion of any other themes for prayer. Our Lady and the saints were so constantly invoked as to create the impression that our Lord had yielded up his office as Mediator. Except on All Souls' Day there seemed to be small awareness of a corporate union of the faithful. The Mass was the atoning sacrifice, but not the means or the expression of community, and the priest—to judge by the ordination cards—was regarded rather as an ambassador from heaven to the community than its servant. Holy Communion, at least on the older cards, was something added to the Mass on special occasions. Devotions abounded, subjective and individualistic in tone, with little reference to the liturgical year. It was clear that the common piety had never been introduced to the Psalms or even to most of the classic prayers of the Christian ages, such as one might find in the breviary.

"The people have a certain right to be vulgar," says Dom Gregory. But "the people" (a dangerous generalization at any time) are now vastly more sophisticated than they once were, even as recently as fifty years ago. And their capacity under grace for grasping the pivotal ideas of the faith, for "drinking with joy at the fountains of the Savior," should not be underestimated. Piety must, one supposes, be simple—i.e., candid, direct, unpretentious; there is no reason to think it should be impoverished. Or that it should be so divorced from the official prayer of the Church as to run for the most part on a parallel but separate track.

As far as these things can be judged, there seems at the moment to be some movement back to the popular devotions of yesterday. Last month, in my diocesan paper, the Dominicans on the West Coast advertised a "Solemn Novena" in honor of St. Jude, with "Mass, Short Sermon, Blessing with Relic of St. Jude." (Can some incredulity about the relic be permitted?) In the same issue the Franciscans on the East Coast advertised a "Solemn Novena of Masses and Prayers" to "the Saint of the Impossible." "St. Jude, the cousin of our Savior, is the patron in hopeless cases and in things almost despaired of. So many have had their desperate pleas answered by devotion to St. Jude, I am sure God will grant *whatever you ask* (italics mine) of him as patron." I have been told, but have no statistics on the subject, that the trade in religious articles (medals, holy cards, devotional literature), which had plunged almost to zero after the Council, is now brisk. One wonders: are these items any different? Has the renewed liturgy had any influence on them? Here is a good topic for a Master's thesis.

For some years now individual prayer has been extensively cultivated, often under the supervision of "spiritual directors" whose interest in liturgy seems small indeed. Will there be in these cases reverberations, mutual enrichment, between the two types of prayer such as the Council mandated?

It is clear that there must be popular devotions. The Mass should not be the only celebration we have. The "Bible Vigils" that were introduced after the Council never really caught on, probably because most people were simply not ready for a biblical spirituality. Valiant efforts have been expended in preparing editions of morning and evening prayer that have the spirit if not the precise form of the old Lauds and Vespers, those "hinges" on which the Christian's daily prayer was supposed to turn, but the number of parishes—or even of religious communities, perhaps—that have adopted them cannot be large. On the other hand, penitential rites, or services of reconciliation, scripturally based, seem to be fairly common, especially before the great feasts. Perhaps we can look only for a slow evolution of new devotional forms. In sacred music, the *Liber Usualis* was the product of a thousand years. How many chants must have been discarded as unworthy during that time! And, in the development of a new musical repertoire for the liturgy in English, how many styles have already come—and gone, mercifully, in some cases—during the last thirty years! So one may hope that out of the current vacuum there may emerge, some day, devotions which reflect the integral Christian faith, which complement the official liturgy and lead people to it. *Hoc erat in votis.*

* * * * *

Appendix IV

WE WERE GRACED AND BLESSED, NOT TO SAY DIRECTLY INSPIRED, in our choice of speakers for the "Consultation" at Boston College in 1983 (see pp. 335-37). Father Shawn Sheehan, leading off for the pioneers, reviewed the story of the American liturgical movement from its beginnings in the thirties and forties, countering a prevalent opinion that the movement began only as a response to the decrees of Vatican II. His presentation reflected the early leaders' concern for the objective aspects of the liturgy—that it is our participation in the worship offered by Christ to the Father, and that all Christian living is embraced and swept up into that worship. Father Peter Fink, who dealt with the postconciliar implementation of Vatican II (1963-1983), reminded us that current philosophies like personalism and existentialism had forced us to consider the worshiping subject as well. And the conciliar reform itself, by relaxing the fixed forms of the Tridentine liturgy and introducing flexibility and variety, had acknowledged this necessity, although, in the light of certain excesses that had cropped up here and there since the Council, it was evident that some caution and restraint were required. Nonetheless, since liturgy is after all the prayer of people, and in our case of American people, their culture, their temperament, must be reckoned with.

Father Michael Fahey asked us a provocative question: which came first, changes in the Church that then were expressed in the liturgy, or liturgical changes that brought about changes in the Church? Some of us were reminded of the question that surfaced perennially in the old Liturgical Weeks: does community make liturgy—and therefore earns the right to prior cultivation—or does liturgy make community, and therefore merits our first attention? The answer in each case, as Father Fahey put it, is "a bit of both." He went on to list changes since the council that in fact affected both: the reformulation of the Church's public image, the stress on collegiality, attempts at inculturation, sensitivity for the ministry of justice, and the acceptance of pluralism. He pointed to many excellent things that gave grounds for hope, but left us under no illusion about the vexing problems we faced.

Father Kevin Seasoltz's paper was even more bleak in its assessment of the present cultural situation. In a brilliant analysis, he identified technology, and the mentality induced by a dominant technology, as the chief obstacle not only to liturgical renewal but to religion in general, or indeed to any hypothesis that might lend meaning to human life. The liturgical experience, he said, taken together with the Christian doctrine distilled from it, provides symbols that are meaningful and that challenge the secular society we live in, and efforts were being made to adapt these to our contemporaries. But it was uncertain whether the results were entirely compatible with Christian faith and worship. He left us with fifteen questions that provided abundant material for small-group discussion. One of them seems especially pertinent in view of the current wistful search for a satisfying "spirituality": "Is the liturgy set out as normative for the development of Christian spirituality or is the liturgy simply an appendage not really integrated into the program?"

Abbot Patrick Regan's approach was historical. He described the situation in nineteenth-century Europe, where industrialization had made a new kind of serfs of the working class, and where the former united Christendom had shattered into small nations, each grimly and sometimes savagely intent on maintaining its identity. In France, Gallicans and Jansenists joined forces to create a liturgy of their own, very different from the ancient Roman. They were opposed by a succession of leaders whom the abbot saw as the pioneers of the liturgical movement: Guéranger, Pius X, Lambert Beauduin, and Virgil Michel. Vatican II, following their lead, updated the tridentine liturgy in what was more a restoration than a new creation. Owing to popular ignorance of liturgical history, it perplexed and shocked many, afflicted as they were by the heavy emphasis in modern times on the subjective and by the social turmoil, especially in the United States, of the sixties.

Monsignor John Egan, addressing the relation between the liturgy and social activism, delivered an eloquent challenge. He pointed out the astonishing silence of Vatican II on this issue. Even since the Council, he said, despite the rapidly developing social teaching of the Church, and despite fairly successful liturgical reform, very few people in either field seemed to perceive the relationship. It was necessary to go back to the pioneers for basic principles, and it would be very helpful to begin using once more their favorite image of the Church as the Mystical Body of Christ. Since awareness of the real nature of community involves a radical conversion, failure to achieve it means that liturgists turn progressively inward, while social activists lose their association with God's purposes. Both must give their attention to the whole community and its relationships to the whole world; the liturgy is the indispensable source of Christian social regeneration. Monsignor ended his forceful talk by calling for a pastoral statement, to be worked out by liturgists and social activists in earnest collaboration, on the unity of liturgy and social life, "with practical recommendations as to its implementation." As of the present moment, almost ten years after the proposal, such a statement has not appeared. Perhaps another Consultation is called for.

Father Stephen Happel spoke with grace and authority on the thorny subject of worship and art. He presented for our consideration five possible models or attitudes: 1) worship against art; 2) worship of art; 3) worship above art; 4) worship and art in paradox; 5) worship and the transformation of art. Clearly in favor of the last model, he said that worship should accept art as an indispensable collaborator. Art needs worship to say something about itself, while worship needs art if it is to be embodied. Three artists—Peter McLaughlin, an architect, Alexander Peloquin, a musician, and Carla diSola, a dancer—followed this theoretical exposition with vivid illustration from their own arts.

The last speakers had as their purpose to evaluate the Consultation and to add or emphasize ideas that might have been overlooked. The Reverend Joseph Bassett underlined the need for ecumenical collaboration and for a grounding of the liturgy's future in serious theological scholarship. Sister Jamie Phelps spoke movingly of the unhappy experience of black Catholics and pleaded for a recognition of what the black community has to offer to the life of the Church, especially in terms of the liturgy. Sister Alita Lisbeth introduced her critique by asking the pragmatic question, "If you do what they say, does it work?" Sister was director of liturgy in the Catholic parish in Anaconda, an economically depressed mining town in Montana. Her slide presentation dovetailed neatly with one given at the opening session by Father Thomas Kane, in which, with a rapid but comprehensive survey of recent liturgical history, he had outlined possibilities for our own time. It was the liturgy, Sister testified, that had infused life into the Anaconda community and kept it vigorous in spite of external pressures. This was convincing evidence from the field.

Portions of each day during the Consultation were given over to "structured conversations"—i.e., small-group discussions presided over by previously appointed leaders, who had been furnished with forty possible assertions or questions touching on the issues developed by the main speakers. Some of these were in the area of liturgical theory—for example, "The pioneers of the liturgical movement sought a change in mentality rather than in rites," or "What comes first: liturgy, urged preeminently by the well-known pastor, Monsignor Martin Hellriegel, or social action, emphasized—though not by any means exclusively—by Monsignor Reynold Hillenbrand, national chaplain of several large organizations for the laity?" "Is it better to experience and practice 'liturgical spirituality' than to know its definition? Can at least some of its features be enumerated?" "Is there any awareness today of 'Trinitarian spirituality'?"

Other topics dealt with the history and growth of a liturgical sense among our people: "To what extent have the pioneers' dreams and the directives of Vatican II been realistically implemented?" "Can liturgy be imposed from on high? Is it better to teach the theology of worship and let the forms grow? Are we overly preoccupied today with forms?" "How do we create a new view—global, planetary—for the rising generation?" "How can we recover variety in our prayer-forms? The Mass alone cannot carry the whole devotional burden." "How can we learn from cultural and ethnic minorities? From base communities, from liberation theology?" A final set of topics converged on immediate problems, the attitude, for instance, of our people toward public prayer. (A recent survey had asserted that 75% of American Catholics preferred prayer in private.) "Does scripture form our piety? Have we not run off into Bible study groups, on the one hand, and charismatic groups, on the other?" "Lay participation in the liturgy is superficial. Where do we find the good pastor?" "Should we be preparing for Sunday communion services in parishes without priests?"

These conversations—and there were many unstructured conversations, of course, in the dining room and about the campus— were taped, and the leaders submitted summaries. As I look back now, I regret that at least their substance was not published some-where. Father Virgil Funk, founder and president of the National Association of Pastoral Musicians, devoted an entire, handsome issue of his journal, *Pastoral Music* (Dec.-Jan., 1984), to the six principal papers, and *Worship* ran an extended, generous, and acutely perceptive review of the Consultation by Dr. John Barry Ryan. (Unfortunately, similar reviews, written by Father Kevin Irwin and Father Thomas Clarke and offered to other magazines, were not published.) What was lacking, as Dr. Ryan pointed out, was some mechanism—general sessions of all participants, per-haps—that would sort out all that was said and shape it into a statement of policy or recommendations for action. Our planning committee saw in rueful hindsight that we had scheduled too much for such a brief meeting.

The pioneers at the Consultation numbered about twenty-five. They had been the leaders in what was called, in the thirties and forties, the "liturgical movement." As such they had been the founding members of the Liturgical Conference, the organizers of the annual Liturgical Week, tireless lecturers and writers and artists and musicians. Often lone voices in their seminaries, their dio-ceses, their religious communities, their parishes, they had perse-vered in their vision of better things to come, when God's people would understand and actively participate in his praise. They had not only become fast friends during those years; they had drawn from one another support and encouragement. But many of them had not met since the heady days of the Council, so their reunion at Boston College was a joyful one indeed. Their special evening together was a long one, and many of its highlights (and its per-sonalities) were taped and preserved—not for the sake of history only, but also, one hopes, so that similar crusaders for good causes, tempted perhaps to doubt their convictions or to falter in their dedi-cation, might take heart from the happy outcome of these labors. Some of the most influential laborers, of course, could not be with us because they were now celebrating the eternal liturgy of thanks-giving before the throne of God and the Lamb (Rv 22:1). There were affectionate references all night long to Ellard and O'Connell, to Hellriegel and Virgil Michel, to Carroll and Ducey and Morrison and Ross-Duggan and Burbach, to Reinhold and Mathis and Hillenbrand. Some others—McManus, Diekmann, Marier, Sloyan—were prevented from joining us because they were contin-uing their labors for the cause elsewhere.

It was an evening too full of gladness to have any formal structure, but some shape was given to the reminiscences by the answers to two questions. The pioneers were asked how, at a time when few gave much attention to liturgy, they became interested in it, and what changes in their own attitudes, their own spirituality, were brought about by this interest. Their replies afford an accurate and fascinating bit of history, the history of American Catholic life and piety. They also say a good deal about the talent, the faith, the optimism and good humor—yes, and the persistence— that was invested prodigally by this group, who believed, as Father Al Wilmes said on one personally painful occasion, that "the cause is bigger than any of us."

Quite naturally, there were many stories that evening about the personalities we had known and loved. Father Wilmes told us, for instance, of Monsignor Hellriegel's last days—how, totally blind at the age of ninety, he still continued to celebrate the liturgy each day and even to preach a short homily on the day's readings. "The Mass," he used to say, "is the sunshine of my life." When he died that sun continued to shine, for there were three Masses of Christian Burial celebrated for him—in the cathedral, at Holy Cross parish which he made a model for parish liturgy long before Vatican II, and at the chapel of the Precious Blood Sisters in O'Fallon, where he had been chaplain, and where he is buried. Crowds of people came to each celebration and sang the hymn he had translated and made famous: "To Jesus Christ our Sovereign King." He asked for only two words on his tombstone: "dilexit Ecclesiam"— "he loved the Church."

I told how Father Ellard had died in my arms while I recited from his breviary the eighth psalm: "How great is your name, O Lord our God, through all the earth!" The most poignant story was told by Monsignor Jack Egan, who had been a seminarian when Monsignor Hillenbrand was rector of Mundelein Seminary in Chicago, and remained a close friend through the years when "Hilly" was pastor in Hubbard Woods. "I knew," Jack told us, "that he was in poor health, and one day I felt impelled to visit him. I found him sitting in his chair, wrapped in a bathrobe but still correctly dressed as always in his clerical suit. We talked for a long while, and at last he astonished me by breaking down in tears. 'Some people have told me,' he said, 'that I spent my energies foolishly in working for the liturgy and for the development of an articulate, zealous laity. Jack, do you think I have wasted my life by doing this?' It wasn't difficult for Jack to rehearse the names and achievements of the many people—beginning with a long list of priests—who owed their inspiration to "Hilly." "I finally had to go," Jack said. "But I hugged him, knelt down and asked for his blessing, and gave him mine. He died a few days later, and as I was leaving the church after the funeral I was stopped by a wonderful man, a deacon in the parish, who had cared for him all during his illness, and who told me that my visit had lifted his depression, and he had died at peace."

Frank and Maria Gale, a husband-and-wife team who train lectors in Philadelphia parishes (Frank had been my assistant in the Army forty years before) wrote me when they returned home after the Consultation. Frank said:

> It was a unique experience, one that will be remembered for a lifetime, and we are so thankful you asked us to be part of it. The absolute worst part of such an experience is in returning to reality, which we had to face and overcome today, Sunday. . . . I wish we could sit down with you and talk about our thoughts. We realize that there are not any more answers 'upstairs' than there are in the trenches. If we brought anything back, it is the thought that there remains a sizeable portion of Catholic people who are not yet part of the assembly, who are satisfied if the ministers up front perform for them, read well, speak well, sing well. The liturgical renewal has not yet given the average Catholic his/her ministerial role in the assembly.

Maria's reaction was similar:

> I sometimes feel that in spite of the work that has been done and the time that has elapsed since the beginnings of liturgical reform, we are still standing on the threshold. Being with the people who have been molding, with the help of the Spirit, the present liturgical and theological thinking, gave me a feeling of elation that quickly evaporated in the face of our Sunday Mass, to say nothing of our daily liturgy. The people in the pews still have no idea that they are central to the celebration. Liturgy is not something we watch; it's something we live, and I was glad to hear this thought expressed many times in our days at Boston College. But what is the solution? Perhaps, like the prophets, we can only keep ourselves open to the truth, and present it to the people as we see it, realizing that all we can hope to do is keep alive a future we

ourselves may never see. I hope that doesn't sound pessimistic. I can say one thing without hesitation: the knowledge I gained, the people I met, and the beauty I experienced will sustain me for a long time to come.

I heard echoes of these brave but wondering letters "from the trenches" some years later when I read an address given by Archbishop Rembert Weakland of Milwaukee (*NCR*, 12 October 1990):

I wish we could integrate more clearly the question of suffering and the cross into our spirituality and not see that it is in any way contradictory to Christian hope. We live in a period when few people have signs of hope for the future. So many are disillusioned with both world and church. I would like to quote a Brazilian author, Ruben Alves, in this regard:

'The two, suffering and hope, live from each other. Suffering without hope produces resentment and despair. Hope without suffering creates illusions, naiveté, and drunkenness. Let us plant dates, even though those who plant them will never eat them—we must live by the love of what we will never see.'

If the future is going to be hopeful for all of us, then we have to accept the cross right now. It means that we have to accept the fact that prophets are never truly accepted among their own. It means that often we have to speak a word that neither church nor world wants to hear. . . . The world needs to take again that attitude of Vatican II, which was one of enthusiasm and hope for the kingdom, and renew it today in a more mature and realistic way after twenty-five years of much sacrifice and stumbling. It means that we say within our hearts that it was the Holy Spirit that brought about and brought to conclusion Vatican II and gave so many new insights and so many sources of renewed inspiration. That same Holy Spirit is with us today, in our generation, in our day. That same Holy Spirit will continue to guide us in a truly creative and expansive way. A global Church that is concerned about every individual and every aspect of this planet awaits us. The Spirit pulls us on to an even greater involvement if we have the courage to say yes.

* * * * *